COMMENDATIONS

Entangled with platforms and power, the modern church stands at a crossroads. Dr. Newberg uses history and scholarship to pose the ultimate question to fivefold ministry leaders: Will we rise up into Spirit-empowered leadership or descend further into authoritarian rulership?

Jay Gary, PhD
CALP member, International Leadership Association

All of us have a leadership paradigm shaped by our inherited values. This book examines our Spirit-empowered heroes and the leadership models they perpetuate. That examination provides powerful tools to emerging leaders for self-understanding and cultural assessment that can inform their own leadership formation choices.

John Thompson, PhD
Oral Roberts University

FOREWORD

In *Paradigms of Spirit-Empowered Leadership*, Dr. Eric Newberg offers a timely and inspiring vision for leadership in the midst of the remarkable global growth of the Spirit-empowered movement. With wisdom drawn from Scripture, history, and lived experience, he calls leaders to deeper character, spiritual sensitivity, and faithful stewardship of influence. This book reminds us that true leadership is built on integrity, humility, and a life shaped by the Holy Spirit. It is a meaningful resource for those who desire to serve Christ and the church with courage and conviction across cultures and generations.

Dr. William M. Wilson
President, Oral Roberts University
Global Chair, Empowered21
Chairman, Pentecostal World Fellowship

FOREWORD

More than twenty centuries of Christian history have been recorded, usually with an emphasis on dominant theological and socio-cultural themes and with biographies of thousands of men and women who played leadership roles. Serious historians have studied these leaders, especially those who established or otherwise affected these spiritual movements. Unfortunately, Christian leaders have been identified but with little emphasis on their leadership. Until now, this deficit has been especially present in our study of the modern worldwide Pentecostal and charismatic movements.

This volume, written by the outstanding scholar and university mentor, Rev. Dr. Eric Newberg of Oral Roberts University in Tulsa, Oklahoma, has turned our attention to forces or influences that helped to create Holy Spirit-led leaders in our recent history, as well as in the biblical periods. Newberg skillfully analyzes an amazing array of both the processes that each leader employed and the products that resulted in each case.

Truly excellent history is written by high-level scholars, such as Dr. Newberg, who recognize that, in many cases, the lives of such Christian leaders have had an incredibly positive impact on the Christian world. These he classifies into apostles, prophets, healing evangelists, pastorpreneurs, and teacher-scholars. But Newberg also recognizes that not all "Christian leaders" have had an unblemished record as their quest for power and influence and their lack of integrity and morality has led to chaos, confusion, and even prison.

Finally, our author then suggests ways in which true leaders can be developed. Through it all, Newberg reminds us that leadership in renewal ministry must be fully Spirit-led.

Drs. Ruth V. and Stanley M. Burgess
October 24, 2023

PARADIGMS OF SPIRIT-EMPOWERED LEADERSHIP

Implications for Leadership Development

PARADIGMS OF SPIRIT-EMPOWERED LEADERSHIP

Implications for Leadership Development

Eric N. Newberg

ORU
PRESS

Tulsa, Oklahoma, USA
2026

Paradigms of Spirit-Empowered Leadership:
Implications for Leadership Development
Copyright ©2026 Eric N. Newberg

Published by ORU Press
7777 S. Lewis Ave., Tulsa, OK 74171 USA

https://orupress.org/

ORU Press is the book and journal publishing division of Oral Roberts University.

Cover design: Jiwon Kim
Editor: Trish Lyons
Copyeditor: Linda Gray
Photos and Indexing: Jaime L. Riddle
Interior Designer and Compositor: Sandra Kimbell

ISBN: 978-1-950971-37-4 (paperback)
ISBN: 978-1-950971-46-6 (hardback)
ISBN: 978-1-950971-40-4 (ebook)

Printed in the United States of America

Dedication

To Dr. Flaud C. Wooton, my maternal grandfather,
a brilliant scholar and storyteller, leader of teachers,
and specialist in the history of education.

ACKNOWLEDGMENTS

This book represents a collective endeavor involving many friends and fellow travelers. Colleagues in the College of Theology and Ministry at Oral Roberts University (ORU) have cheered me on as I shared budding insights and progress reports. Gestation of the method and structure of the book advanced with formative conversations with experts in the field of leadership studies, Jay Gary and John Thompson, to whom I am indebted for their astute reviews of the final draft. Most of the spadework of research took place during a year-long sabbatical leave in 2021—22 granted by Oral Roberts University, for which I am deeply grateful. For the actual writing of the book, which required many hours sequestered in my study at home, I am thankful for my partner in life, Carol Ann Lewis-Newberg, who expressed constant encouragement and support. For funding of the project, I owe a debt of gratitude to President William Wilson's Fund for Excellence in Teaching and Research. In preparing the book for publication with ORU Press, I benefited from the overall guidance of Wonsuk Ma, the expert copyediting of Dr. Linda Gray, and the adept indexing and attribution photos by Jaime Riddle. The opportunity to have the book edited by Trish Lyons fulfilled a long-standing wish, which goes back to help she provided gratis on a prior publication. Her wisdom and professional skill made this work much better than it would have been without her keen attention to form, flow, and detail. Tiffany Collier, an honors student at ORU, collected and assembled the photographs. I am grateful for the input provided by my Ph.D. students as I shared excerpts from the book in lectures and journal articles. Lastly, I want to acknowledge Dr. Stan Burgess, ORU Trustee Emeritus, and Dr. Ruth Burgess for mentoring me in the dual crafts of scholarship and pedagogy and playing a crucial role in providing me with the opportunity to serve on the faculty at Oral Roberts University.

Contents

INTRODUCTION

The explosive growth of the Spirit-empowered (Pentecostal-charismatic) movement[1] can be largely attributed to the dynamic influence of its innovative leaders.[2] This generation will build upon the accomplishments of past and present leaders, and it behooves us to equip emerging leaders with the heritage and critical analysis of leading figures in the movement. While leadership is a spiritual gift, it also requires practical skills to be developed. This book represents an applied study, informed by the author's experience of charismatic empowerment and personal exposure to Spirit-empowered leadership in various settings, including pastoral ministry, denominational meetings, the academy, international travel, and mentoring relationships. The author's previously published research is concentrated on historical and theological studies, with particular interest in the Pentecostal mission in the Middle East. In this introduction, the author, Dr. Eric Newberg, offers sketches of his charismatic experiences, exposure to charismatic leadership, and the rationale for writing this book.

Charismatic Experience

After college, I attended North Park Theological Seminary in Chicago, graduating in 1979. One day I had a remarkable experience in the seminary library. Our New Testament professor gave us the assignment of reading through the entire Acts of the Apostles without stopping. I tried but could not quite complete the assignment in one sitting because I was overcome by a remarkable spiritual

---

1. The term "Spirit-empowered movement" is a moniker referring to a constellation of movements making up global Pentecostal and charismatic Christianity. Such movements are distinguished by special identification with the Christian Pentecost in Acts 2. They share charismatic practices such as lively worship, speaking in tongues, prayers for healing, and baptism in the Spirit. Todd M. Johnson and Gina A. Zurlo, *Introducing Spirit-Empowered Christianity: The Global Pentecostal and Charismatic Movement in the 21st Century* (Tulsa: ORU Press, 2023).

2. Truls Åkerlund, *A Phenomenology of Pentecostal Leadership* (Eugene, OR: Wipf & Stock, 2018), 1; Daniel D. Isgrigg, "Toward Spirit-Empowered Leadership Distinctives: A Literature Review," *Spiritus: ORU Journal of Theology* 5, no. 2 (2020): 200.

manifestation. As I was reading Acts 2, I sensed a wind blowing in my body. It felt as if my mind was being inflated like a balloon. This was so overpowering that I had to get up and walk around to regain my composure. I returned to my seat, yet the sensation grew stronger. When I completed the assignment, I asked a classmate, Tom King, a bona fide charismatic, for his input concerning this experience. Tom smiled and said, "Man, you have been baptized in the Holy Spirit!" From that time on, I felt like something had shifted in the intensity of my prayer life and worship.

After seminary, I was called to serve as associate pastor of an interracial congregation in Minneapolis. Community Covenant Church is situated in a neighborhood surrounded by public housing on three sides. My wife and I actively participated in a ministry of feeding the community's poor. We teamed up with a local Pentecostal couple, Dave and Genie, and their interracial ministry called Love's Rainbow, named after their multiracial family consisting of eighteen children, thirteen of whom were adopted "crack babies." At this time, a neighbor and some congregants asked if I would transport them in the church van to the state penitentiary in Stillwater, Minnesota, to visit loved ones who were incarcerated. I wrongly assumed that this would be a one-time event. To my surprise, I discovered that my Pentecostal friends with Love's Rainbow were involved in a weekly Bible study at the prison, along with parents of children in the two free preschools of Community Covenant. As I sat in the church van in the parking lot that first evening, Dave rapped on the window and exclaimed. "You should come inside for the Bible study; that's where the action is!" I accepted Dave's offer and added the prison ministry to my weekly schedule.

During my first time at the prison Bible study, a participant asked for prayer, confessing that he had robbed a gas station and wanted to get back on track with the Lord. I joined others in laying hands on him. As we prayed for Joe, he jumped to his feet with arms raised, euphorically speaking in tongues, then falling backward into my arms. I physically felt the wind of the Spirit rushing through Joe's upper body. Amazed, I concluded once and for all that the charismatic gifts of the Spirit are real. Further proof of the authenticity of the gifts of the Spirit was forthcoming on a regular basis during weekly meetings of the prison Bible study. From then on, my wife observed a distinct difference in my energy level and enthusiasm for pastoral ministry.

Subsequently, during senior pastorates in California and Washington, I promoted and participated in charismatic ministries. This was during the years of the Toronto and Brownsville Revivals, and I personally witnessed instances of healing and renewal of congregants. If you were to ask me to recount highlights of my experiences of empowerment with Holy Spirit in pastoral ministry, I would point to two experiences: first, the healing conferences we attended at St. Clare's Retreat in Soquel, California, led by David Gereats, abbot of the Pecos Benedictine Monastery, and second, the Alpha Course, a twelve-week course for new believers and the unchurched, combining the apologetics of C. S. Lewis and the "stuff" of John Wimber, through which I witnessed the Holy Spirit bringing about supernatural transformation.

However, along with many joyous highlights of charismatic empowerment, I also witnessed the dark side of the charismatic movement. Worst of all, was an encounter during my pastorate in San Francisco with an imposter claiming to be John the Baptist *redivivus* (come back to life) and his sidekick who claimed to have the mantle of King David. I couldn't have made this up; it was so wildly preposterous. These two deceivers ensconced themselves in a small group and offered "therapy" to survivors of sexual abuse in a voyeuristic fashion. When two deaconesses brought these occurrences to my attention, I immediately asked for an appointment with the two. John the Baptist left town, but King David met with me. When he insisted on justifying his twisted identity based on revelations outside of the Bible, I firmly banned him from further contact with the church. As he hurried out the door, "King David" accused me of being a bad pastor. What did I learn from this encounter with the dark side? Those of us in spiritual leadership must always be on guard and ready to practice the discernment of spirits when necessary.

Charismatic Leadership

My initial close acquaintance with a charismatic leader occurred during my years at North Park Theological Seminary in Chicago. Dan Simmons, charismatic pastor of an Evangelical Covenant church in Missoula, Montana, came as a guest speaker and brought along a large group of college-age followers. The church had been in steep decline until Dan assumed leadership. A Spirit-filled businessman with no seminary training, Dan led the church through a remarkable turnaround, propelled by manifestations of charismatic spirituality. As Dan told the story of how he was baptized in the Spirit and embraced the ethos of the Jesus People movement, my spirit was stirred. Dan's radical faith seemed to ruffle the feathers of our professors, yet the students were won over, especially after one member of the Missoula group, Tom King, enrolled in the seminary. He is the same person who encouraged me in the library with the words, "Man, you have been baptized in the Holy Spirit!"

My interest in the academic study of Pentecostalism originated during my time at seminary in Chicago. I regard it as providential that Donald Dayton came to North Park as professor of theology. At that time, Don was working on his doctorate at the University of Chicago, researching the theological roots of Pentecostalism, he was actively involved in the Society for Pentecostal Studies (SPS). In fact, in 1975 Dr. Dayton invited me to attend the annual meeting of SPS in Ann Arbor, Michigan, hosted by the Catholic Charismatic Word of God community. We stayed in one of the communal houses and interacted with the leaders of the Catholic Charismatic Renewal (CCR), Steve Clark and Ralph Martin. Getting acquainted with Catholics who spoke in tongues like Pentecostals certainly broadened my horizons. At the first meeting of the SPS conference, I met Vinson Synan, a renowned scholar of Pentecostal history. Years later, Dr. Synan served as the Dean of Regent University Divinity School during my Ph.D. studies there. Recently, I served alongside Dr. Synan on the theological faculty of Oral Roberts University.

During a 2002 sabbatical at the Tantur Ecumenical Institute in Jerusalem, I crossed paths with Dan Simmons. At that time, Dan served as director of World Vision projects in Israel and surrounding countries. He invited our sabbatical cohort to tour the World Vision projects in Gaza and the West Bank, where we had firsthand exposure to life in Palestinian refugee camps. This was a life-changing experience. One weekend we attended a Palestinian Pentecostal church in Bethlehem with Dan, where we worshipped with a Spirit-filled Arabic congregation. After the service, we were invited to a barbecue at the church's outreach center in Beit Jala. The pastor and his wife, Nihad and Selwa Salman, shared their story with us, relating how they were brought together by a Pentecostal missionary, Margaret Gaines, who developed them as leaders. Little did I know that a few years later this dynamic couple and their missionary mentor would be featured in my Ph.D. dissertation on the history of the Pentecostal Mission in Palestine.

Looking back, I recognize that I was predisposed by previous charismatic experience to be receptive to the influence of three well-known charismatic leaders, John Wimber, C. Peter Wagner, and Leanne Payne. I see a crimson thread running through my life, leading to my involvement in the charismatic wing of Christianity. During my pastorate in San Francisco, I supported a Friday night charismatic prayer fellowship that was inspired by the ministry philosophy of John Wimber and the Vineyard. I strongly resonate with Wimber's notion of living in the tension of the "radical middle," simultaneously embracing the biblical moorings of evangelicalism and plunging into the ecstasy of charismatic spirituality. Wimber's mediating perspective is captured in his adage: "All Word and no Spirit, we dry up. All Spirit and no Word, we blow up. With the Spirit and the Word, we grow up."[3]

C. Peter Wagner first came to my attention as a proponent of the homogeneous unit of church growth, with which I disagreed. Later, I was drawn to Wagner's writings on spiritual warfare. Wagner served for thirty years as Professor of Church Growth at the Fuller Theological Seminary's School of World Missions until his retirement in 2001. During his tenure at Fuller, Wagner gravitated toward the charismatic movement, due to team teaching a course on signs and wonders with John Wimber. Later, Wagner popularized the New Apostolic Reformation (NAR), a movement dedicated to the restoration of the offices of apostle and prophet and the supplanting of traditional denominational structures (Orthodox, Catholic, and Protestant) with apostolic networks.[4] The movement largely consists of churches and movements that have opted for independent networks as an alternative to denominationalism. Wagner also embraced and promoted dominion theology.[5] While not numbering myself among those who were attracted to Wagner's anti-denominational network or his version of dominion theology, I found his writings on spiritual warfare to be apropos for dealing with power encounters during my pastoral ministry in San Francisco.

Leanne Payne made a significant contribution to the ministry of healing prayer through over forty years of authoring books, teaching, counseling, and conference leadership. Payne exercised a significant influence on my pastoral ministry, specifically regarding my embrace of healing prayer and promotion of healing services. Payne inspired me to train church leaders by means of her publications and attendance at her School of Pastoral Prayer. The philosopher Dallas Willard describes Payne as a "great soldier for Christ." Payne founded Pastoral Care Ministries (PCM), dedicated to teaching, healing, and pastoral

---

3. Bill Jackson, *The Quest for the Radical Middle: A History of the Vineyard* (Cape Town: Vineyard International Publishing, 1999), 136.

4. For an analysis of the rise of apostolic networks, see Brad Christerson and Richard Flory, *The Rise of Network Christianity: How Independent Leaders Are Changing the Religious Landscape* (Oxford. Oxford University Press, 2017).

5. For Wagner's version of dominion theology, see C. Peter Wagner, *Dominion! How Kingdom Action Can Change the World* (Grand Rapids: Chosen Books, 2008).

care. She wrote seven books in print in English and twelve other languages. In 1982, she incorporated PCM and provided pastoral care through prayer and counseling mainly by means of weeklong PCM schools and annual conferences conducted throughout North America, Europe, Hawaii, and Australia. Her books include *Crisis in Masculinity, The Healing Presence, Restoring the Christian Soul, Listening Prayer, and Heaven's Calling,* her spiritual autobiography. The theologian Donald Bloesch says of *Heaven's Calling,* "It poignantly shows how the author has been mightily used by the Spirit of God to spearhead a ministry of renewal and celebration."[6] In 2009, with Leanne Payne's endorsement, Ministries of Pastoral Care was founded, for the purpose of ensuring that her pastoral care schools would continue beyond her retirement.

I have had the privilege of working with distinguished Spirit-empowered leaders of academic institutions, at which I studied and was employed as a professor, including Regent University, Alphacrucis College, and Oral Roberts University. During my Ph.D. studies at Regent University's School of Divinity, I was impressed by the leadership of Pat Robertson and his vision of "Christian Leadership to Change the World." During my first full-time academic job as head of pastoral theology at Alphacrucis College in Australia, I taught and worshiped at the main campus of Hillsong Church. What impressed me most about Hillsong, other than the consummate worship led by Darlene Zschech, was Brian Houston's vision for influencing all sectors of global culture. After a one-year stint back at Regent, I was hired by Oral Roberts University in 2011 as a faculty member in the College of Theology and Ministry, serving with two presidents, Dr. Mark Rutland and Dr. William Wilson, both of whom honored God's commission to Oral Roberts: "Raise up your students to hear My voice, to go where My light is seen dim, My voice is heard small, and My healing power is not known, even to the uttermost bounds of the earth. Their work will exceed yours, and in this I am well pleased."[7] These leaders updated the ORU mission statement, focusing on the development of "Whole Leaders for the Whole World" by means of holistic education in a Spirit-empowered context. Both, along with Richard Roberts, followed the precedent set by Oral Roberts of combining entrepreneurial leadership of a global ministry with their presidential duties.

---

6. The tributes of Dallas Willard and Donald Bloesch are found on the front page of Leanne Payne, *Heaven's Calling: A Memoir of One Soul's Steep Ascent* (Grand Rapids: Baker, 2000).

7. ORU Vision, Oral Roberts University, accessed November 22, 2023, https://oru.edu/news/oru-general-info-media-kit.php#:~:text=God%20gave%20the%20following%20commission,uttermost%20bounds%20of%20the%20earth.

During the tenures of Oral Roberts and Richard Roberts, the Oral Roberts Evangelistic Association played an integral role in the infrastructure of ORU. Rutland founded Global Servants in 1977, offering leadership training. During his tenure at ORU, Rutland recruited students to participate in leadership seminars for which they received academic credit.[8] A distinguished global evangelist in his own right, Wilson has provided visionary and strategic leadership as President of ORU since 2013, implementing a shared governance model of leadership, stipulated by generous benefactors as a prerequisite for their magnanimous donations.[9] Wilson serves as the Global Chair of Empowered21 (E21), founded in 2010 as a consortium of charismatic leaders dedicated to shaping the future of the global, Spirit-empowered movement by means of international conferences, networking, and publications. The vision of E21 calls for every person on earth to have an authentic encounter with Jesus through the power of the Holy Spirit by 2033. The stated goals of E21 are to promote the empowerment of the Holy Spirit, unite the Spirit-filled movement, and address critical issues facing the Spirit-empowered church. Wilson is known for inspiring and cultivating emerging charismatic pastorpreneurs,[10] some of whom are regular chapel speakers at ORU.[11]

Rationale for Writing the Book

The impetus for this book was the prospect of a sabbatical during the 2021–2022 academic year. The goal of the sabbatical was to research styles of leadership in the Spirit-empowered movement and produce a book compiling the findings of my research. The specific objectives of the sabbatical project were as follows:

1. **To understand** the best practices of prominent Spirit-empowered leaders as observed by those that they mentored.
2. **To specify** attitudes, principles, and practices that are worthy of emulation by emerging Spirit-empowered leaders.
3. **To propose** an effective strategy for leadership development in the context of the Spirit-empowered movement.

---

8. "Our History," *GlobalServants.org*, accessed November 25, 2025, https://globalservants.org/our-history.

9. Neil Eskelin, *The New ORU: Empowered for the 21st Century* (Tulsa: ORU Press, 2018), 55, 101.

10. The term "pastorpreneur" was coined by John Jackson. It refers to entrepreneurial pastors. He writes, "My term pastorpreneur means a pastoral innovator, a creative dreamer willing to take great risks in church ministry with hope of great gain for Christ and his kingdom." John Jackson, *Pastorpreneur: Creative Ideas for Birthing Spiritual Life in Your Community* (Colorado Springs: Biblica Publishing, 2011), 2.

11. "Empowered21 Global Council," accessed February 25, 2025, https://empowered21.com/about/global-leaders/.

The intended audience for this book includes college and seminary students, pastors, scholars, and general readers interested in a Spirit-empowered approach to leadership development. The book is designed as a text for a class in ministry leadership at a university aligned with the Spirit-empowered movement. The aim of this book is to assist the reader in his or her development as a Spirit-empowered leader and trainer of leaders.

Organization of the Book

Part I: Anatomy of Spirit-Empowered Leadership

The first part utilizes Max Weber's theory of charismatic leadership as a *modus operandi* for an investigation of the defining characteristics of Spirit-empowered leadership. The opening chapter describes the essential characteristics of Spirit-empowered leadership, including definitions, methodology, thesis, patterns of charismatic leadership in the Old and New Testaments, and an exposition and analysis of the theory of charismatic leadership. The second chapter states the problem posed by three lacunas in the practice of Spirit-empowered leadership, setting the stage for the argument of the book.

Part II: Historical Sketches of Spirit-Empowered Leaders

The second part presents historical sketches of formative leaders of the Spirit-empowered movement arranged according to four periods: Precursors, Early Pentecostal Leaders, Neo-Pentecostal Leaders, and Global South Charismatic Leaders. Each sketch includes brief biographical data, the leader's accomplishments, contributions to the Spirit-empowered movement, and how each leader acts as a model for present-day leadership. These case studies serve the purpose of illustrating stages in the development of Spirit-empowered leadership, thereby providing emerging leaders with cues for understanding the tasks, tests, and challenges that are germane to the phase of leadership emergence in which they find themselves. The approach in this part of the book is diachronic or chronological, providing an account and analysis of the development of Spirit-empowered leadership. Each chapter features original research on the historical development and diffusion of Spirit-empowered leadership, showing that it is grounded in experiences of Spirit baptism, leadership calling, and empowerment by the Holy Spirit.

Part III: Paradigms of Global Spirit-Empowered Leadership

The approach of the third part of the book is typological and addresses two questions: (1) What are prevalent types of global Spirit-empowered leadership?

(2) How do these diverse types of leadership preserve or maintain continuity with the charismatic core of Spirit-empowered ministry leadership? The answers will emerge through synchronic analysis, postulating the following five paradigms of global Spirit-empowered leadership, adapted from the five-fold ministry gifts of Ephesians 4:11: apostle, prophet, healing evangelist, pastorpreneur, and teacher-scholar. The author argues that these paradigms are linked in continuity with charismatic gifting as the integrating principle of Spirit-empowered ministry leadership.

Part IV: Implications for Leadership Development

The fourth part of the book offers a proposal for Spirit-empowered leadership development. The final chapter and the epilogue provide benchmarks for developing emerging Spirit-empowered leaders and a plan with a working framework for a course in Spirit-empowered leadership development. The aim of last chapter and epilogue is to propose an approach to developing leaders in the context of Spirit-empowered Christianity, undergirded by J. Robert Clinton's theory of leadership emergence. According to Clinton, "Leadership emergence is a lifetime process in which God intervenes throughout in crucial ways to shape that leader towards his purposes for the leader."[12]

---

12. J. Robert Clinton, "The Emerging Leader: Three Umbrella Concepts," Barnabas Publishers Reprint (J. Robert Clinton, 1989), 1.

PART ONE

ANATOMY OF SPIRIT-EMPOWERED LEADERSHIP

"Spirit-empowered leadership" is a relatively new term designating a genre of leadership, associated with Pentecostal-charismatic Christianity, commonly thought to consist of three waves: (1) classical Pentecostalism, (2) charismatic renewal in the major denominations, and (3) independent charismatic movements, including neo-Pentecostals and new apostolic networks. In a recent interview, Todd M. Johnson and Gina A. Zurlo provided a concise summary of statistical data concerning Spirit-empowered Christianity:

> Today there are an estimated 664 million Spirit-Empowered Christians in the world, or about 26% of all Christians. Of these, 124 million worldwide are Pentecostals; 268 million are charismatics in mainline churches; and 252 million are independent charismatics. The growth of the Pentecostal and charismatic movement over the last 120 years has been in tandem with dramatic changes in Christianity's overall cultural and linguistic composition. In 1900, over 80% of all Christians were European or North American. Today, that percentage has fallen to less than 33%. This demographic shift has formed the basis for most major analyses of world Christianity in the past 40 years. Perhaps not surprisingly, the shift has been more pronounced among Spirit-empowered Christians. Today, fully 86% of all Spirit-empowered Christians live in the Global South (Asia, Africa, Latin America).[1]

J. Kwabena Asamoah-Gyadu captures the essence of Spirit-empowered Christianity as referring to churches, movements, and fellowships that emphasize salvation in Christ as a transformative experience wrought by the Holy Spirit in which pneumatic phenomena including speaking in tongues, prophecies, visions, healing, and miracles in general, are perceived to be standing in historic continuity with the experience of the Early Church as found in the Acts of the Apostles. In

---

1. "Spirit-Empowered Christianity: An Interview with Todd M. Johnson and Gina A. Zurlo," *Pneuma Review: Journal of Ministry Resources and Theology for Pentecostal and Charismatic Ministries & Leaders*, January 6, 2021, accessed November 18, 2023, http://pneumareview.com/spirit-empowered-christianity/. Todd M. Johnson is the Paul E. and Eva B. Toms Distinguished Professor of Mission and Global Christianity and co-Director of the Center for the Study of Global Christianity at Gordon-Conwell Theological Seminary in South Hamilton, MA. Gina A. Zurlo is co-Director of the Center for the Study of Global Christianity at Gordon-Conwell Theological Seminary, South Hamilton, MA.

11

Pentecostal-charismatic Christianity, these pneumatic phenomena or charismatic manifestations are sought, accepted, valued, and consciously encouraged among members as signifying the presence of God and experience of his Spirit.[2]

Odd as it may seem, not much of an academic nature has been published concerning patterns of leadership in this rapidly growing sector of Christianity.[3] A gap exists in the literature due to a dearth of scholarly research on Spirit-empowered leadership.[4] Consequently, the genre is not well known—much less understood—by emerging leaders and students.

In the study of Christian leadership, most scholars look to Jesus as the ideal model of a Christian leader. It goes without saying that Jesus Christ is the supreme model for Christian leadership. Åkerlund cites Virginia Christel, who holds that "Pentecostal leaders primarily look to Jesus' example of servant leadership and try to translate this ideal into an effective leadership style in leading their congregations."[5] This vision of Spirit-centered leadership is grounded in a personal and faithful relationship with Christ. Brian J. Dodd, in his book *Empowered Church Leadership*, calls Christian leaders to abandon the weak and unbiblical secular theories "from the flesh" and to pursue a new powerful leadership "from the Spirit." He pleads for a "Spirit-led and Spirit-empowered ministry through weak vessels, prayer, suffering, and the like."[6] A few years ago, Jay Gary published an article, advancing the argument that Spirit-empowered leadership is modeled after the life of Jesus, which he sees as a developmental process encompassing personal, interpersonal, and generational dimensions.[7] Gary's article does not zero in on the Holy Spirit as the driving force of leadership empowerment. Given the primal role of the Holy Spirit in giving rise to, shaping, and sustaining the genre of Spirit-empowered leadership, it seems fitting to accord a more prominent place to the Holy Spirit in our exposition of the subject at hand.

---

2. J. Kwabena Asamoah-Gyadu, "Pentecostalism and the Transformation of the African Christian Landscape," in *Pentecostalism in Africa: Presence and Impact of Pneumatic Christianity in Postcolonial Societies*, ed. Martin Lindhardt (Leiden: Brill, 2015), 101.

3. Åkerlund, *A Phenomenology of Pentecostal Leadership*, 1.

4. Isgrigg, "Toward Spirit-Empowered Leadership Distinctives, 200-201."

5. Åkerlund, *A Phenomenology of Pentecostal Leadership*, 30; Virginia A. Christel, "The Pentecostal Pastor," in *Religious Leadership: A Reference Handbook*, ed. Sharon Henderson Callahan (Thousand Oaks, CA: Sage Publications, 2013), 121.

6. Brian J. Dodd, *Empowered Church Leadership: Ministry in the Spirit according to Paul* (Downers Grove: InterVarsity Press, 2003), 13.

7. Jay Gary, "Spirit-Empowered Leadership: Exploring Three Dimensions," *Spiritus: ORU Journal of Theology* 5, no. 2 (2020): 235.

1

DEFINING CHARACTERISTICS

It is my privilege to welcome you as a reader to an amazing journey, as we traverse places near and far where the Holy Spirit has called and empowered leaders. You will see how God has raised up leaders and equipped them as servants of the Kingdom. The story of Spirit-empowered leadership begins in the Bible, carries on throughout church history, and continues today in every corner of the globe. Leaders are emerging everywhere, but you may or may not think of yourself as a leader. The way this book defines leadership draws a circle in such a way that there is a place for you. Leadership is influence. You have to be in charge of something to be a leader.

This first chapter defines terms, explains the methodology to be employed, advances a thesis, and delineates the normative touchstones that will guide our analysis—the Bible and the Spirit.

Definitions

The origins of the term "Spirit-empowered leadership" can be traced to two publications, a book by Timothy C. Geoffrion and an article by John P. Smith. Geoffrion sees the Holy Spirit as playing a transformative role in leadership. He writes, "As the Holy Spirit gains greater influence within us, we become Spirit-led people who live out our calling in life by God's leading and power." Seeking the Holy Spirit's leading for themselves and their team members as they work together, "they are Spirit-led leaders who seek to pilot Spirit-led teams and organizations."[1] Smith suggests that the model of Spirit-empowered leadership is grounded in Acts 2. He claims that the fellowship, sense of community, prayers, and miraculous signs and wonders observed in Acts 2 resulted from divine empowerment of the church by the Spirit of God. He writes, "It is important to understand that this was not something that they were doing on their own, but this empowerment was being done by the Lord through the Holy Spirit."[2]

---

1. Timothy C. Geoffrion, *The Spirit-Led Leader: Nine Leadership Practices and Soul Principles* (Herndon, VA: The Alban Institute, 2005), 40.

2. John P. Smith, "Acts 2: Spirit-Empowered Leadership," *Emerging Leadership Journeys* 1, no.

Leadership

There is no limit to the variety of definitions of leadership. According to Bennis and Nanus, "Decades of academic analysis have given more than 850 definitions of leadership."[3] Gary Yukl offers an informative array of definitions of leadership by leading researchers in leadership studies, with the proviso that there are as many definitions as there are scholars in the field.[4] Yukl's definitions of leadership are clearly variegated in their points of emphasis. As Yukl states, "Leadership has been defined in terms of traits, behaviors, influence, interaction patterns, role relationships, and occupation of an administrative position."[5] Defining leadership requires ongoing academic research, scholarly debate, and practical application.

One also finds many astute definitions of leadership authored by highly regarded figures in study of leadership. For instance, Peter Drucker defines leadership as "the lifting of a man's vision to higher sights, the raising of a man's performance to a higher standard, the building of a man's personality beyond its normal limitations."[6] According to John Maxwell, a popular guru of Christian leadership, "The true measurement of leadership is influence—nothing more, nothing less."[7] In his classic study of spiritual leadership, Oswald Sanders postulates that "Leadership is influence, the ability of one person to influence others."[8] In the same vein, Henry and Richard Blackaby state, "Spiritual leadership is moving people on to God's agenda."[9] J. Robert Clinton defines leadership as "a dynamic process in which a man or woman with a God-given capacity influences a specific group of God's people toward His purposes for the group."[10] Amplifying Clinton's definition, Banks and Ledbetter hold that,

---

1 (2008): 36, accessed November 19, 2023, https://www.regent.edu/acad/global/publications/elj/issue1/elj_v1is1.pdf; quoted in Oliver Rigaud, "A Christian Servant Leadership Model and Training for the Adventist Church in France" (D.Min. thesis, Andrews University, 2012), 94.

3. Warren Bennis and Burt Nanus, *Leaders: Strategies for Taking Charge*, 2nd ed. (New York: Harper Business, 1997), 4.

4. Gary Yukl, *Leadership in Organizations*, 8th ed. (Boston: Pearson, 2013), 3, 11.

5. Yukl, *Leadership in Organizations*, 2.

6. Peter F. Drucker, *The Practice of Management* (London: Heinemann, 1955), 138.

7. John C. Maxwell, *The Irrefutable Laws of Leadership Workbook* (Nashville: Thomas Nelson, 1998), xiv.

8. J. Oswald Sanders, *Spiritual Leadership: Principles of Excellence for Every Believer* (Chicago: Moody Press, 1967), 27.

9. Henry T. Blackaby and Richard Blackaby, *Spiritual Leadership: The Interactive Study* (Nashville: Broadman & Holman, 2006), 20.

10. J. Robert Clinton, *The Making of a Leader: Recognizing the Lessons and Stages of Leadership Development*, Second Edition (Colorado Springs: NavPress, 2012), 14.

"From a Christian point of view, it is only when the direction and method are in line with God's purposes, character, and ways of operating that godly leadership takes place."[11] George Barna affirms, "A Christian leader is someone who is called by God to lead; leads with and through Christ-like character; and demonstrates the functional competencies that permit effective leadership to take place."[12] Harvard scholar Gary Wills sees the leader as "the one who mobilizes others toward a goal shared by leader and followers. In that brief definition, all three elements are present. Leaders, followers, and goals make up the three equally necessary supports for leadership."[13]

Aside from the final definition by Wills, most of the others are slanted toward qualities of the leader. The definition proposed by Wills differs in its inclusion of the leader, followers, and a goal, with each of these playing an instrumental role in Christian leadership. Of the above definitions of Christian leadership, only the one by Henry and Richard Blackaby portrays the Holy Spirit as inherent, asserting that "spiritual leaders depend on the Holy Spirit."[14] A definition of leadership framed from a Spirit-empowered perspective provides a more fully developed conception of the role of the Holy Spirit in Christian leadership.

Spirit-empowered leadership is a type of leadership that is distinguished by a primary focus on the empowering presence of the Holy Spirit. The role of the Holy Spirit is primal in giving rise to, shaping, and sustaining Spirit-empowered leaders. Leaders of this brand have a particular *élan vital* (vital force), which they attribute to *charisma*, a gift of the Holy Spirit. Charismatic leaders commonly attest to having an inspiring vision and an uncanny ability to convince their followers to identify with the vision. Through their power of persuasion, such leaders can influence the followers' emotions (i.e., charisma). Herein lies a prerequisite of charismatic leadership: the leader's charisma must be recognized and confirmed by his or her followers, which suggests that there is more to Spirit-empowered leadership than the inspiring qualities of the leader. It is the followers who attest to and confirm that their leader qualifies as a charismatic leader.

The key attribute of a Spirit-empowered leader is empowerment by the Holy Spirit. As they are led by the Holy Spirit, charismatic leaders are empowered to

---

11. Robert Banks and Bernice M. Ledbetter, *Reviewing Leadership: A Christian Evaluation of Current Approaches* (Grand Rapids: Baker Academic, 2004), 17.

12. George Barna, *Leaders on Leadership: Wisdom, Advice and Encouragement on the Art of Leading God's People* (Ventura, CA: Regal, 1997), 25.

13. Garry Wills, Certain Trumpets: *The Call of Leaders* (New York: Simon & Schuster, 1994), 17.

14. Blackaby and Blackaby, *Spiritual Leadership*, 20.

mobilize a collective effort among followers to move in tandem, pursuing a shared vision or goal. Brian Dodd writes, "The Christian life is to be a Spirit-led life, and Christian leadership must be Spirit-led too."[15] As in subsequent sections of the book, leadership development in Spirit-empowered movements is activated and sustained by the leading of the Holy Spirit. Leadership formation occurs through a process, propelled by experiences with the Holy Spirit, in which an emerging leader is filled with or baptized in the Holy Spirit. Leadership emerges in this process as a grace gift (*charismata*), which is often accompanied by a calling that reveals one's purpose in the kingdom of God. Affirmation of one's leadership gifting comes as followers recognize an emerging leader's anointing, which in Weber's terminology serves as attribution of charisma. The leader is recognized as having a capacity to set an organization's direction, starting with a small group, youth group, or ministry, and expanding to a church, larger ministry, or network of churches. In a Spirit-empowered context, a leader is often gifted in the mediation of charisma, having an ability to impart (assist others in receiving) charismatic gifts, such as words of knowledge, speaking in tongues, interpretation of tongues, healing, or exorcism. A charismatic leader customarily gathers a leadership team that functions as a staff or accountability structure. This team plays versatile roles, including oversight, support, and succession arrangement. Also known as the charismatic aristocracy, the team assists the leader in steering the process of charismatic leadership development.[16]

Power

Power is the ability to influence others, a natural process in the fabric of organizational life. Getting things done requires power. Every day, managers in public and private organizations acquire and use power to accomplish organizational goals. It is incumbent upon a leader to understand how power is acquired, know how and when to use it, and be able to anticipate its probable effects. The concepts of power and leadership are closely linked; leaders use power as a means of attaining group goals. Learning how power operates in organizations helps a leader become better able to use that knowledge to become a more effective leader. In its simplest terms, power is the ability to influence someone else.[17]

---

15. Dodd, *Empowered Church Leadership*, 27.

16. Paul Joose, "Max Weber's Disciples: Theorizing the Charismatic Aristocracy," *Sociological Theory* 35, no. 4 (2017): 337–39.

17. Fred C. Lunenburg, "Power and Leadership: An Influence Process," *International Journal of Management, Business, and Administration* 15, no. 1 (2012): 2.

Power is more complex than what one can convey with a unitary definition. In 1959, John French and Bertram Raven proposed that there are five kinds of power in organizations: legitimate, reward, coercive, expert, and referent.[18] Legitimate power is based on a position of power in an organization. Reward power is displayed when a leader provides an employee with financial rewards such as a pay raise or bonus or non-financial benefits such as a promotion, a favorable work assignment, more responsibility, new equipment, and recognition. Coercive power is in play when a leader issues punishment or a threat to do so by means of reprimand, undesirable work assignment, withholding important information, demotion, suspension, or dismissal. Expert power is respected due to a person's ability to influence others because of recognized knowledge, skills, or abilities. This kind of power is increasingly important as organizations depend on high-tech expertise for normal operations. Referent power develops out of respect for a person who is admired for attractive characteristics and charisma.[19]

Diane Tracy, a New York management consultant, suggests a new concept of power in her bestselling book, *The Power Pyramid: How to Get Power by Giving It Away*. The new concept is referred to in leadership literature as "empowerment." The main idea is that a leader can achieve ultimate power by giving it to the people who work for him or her. Today, many organizations are recommending a flattening of the power pyramid. These leaders are beginning to see the need to involve organization members at all levels in making decisions and solving problems. Authentic power, according to Tracy, flows from the bottom up, rather than from the top down. She writes, "If you are successful in giving your people power, they will surely lift you on their shoulders to heights of power and success you never dreamed possible ...."[20] This approach has been shown to achieve better work outcomes.

John Wimber, founder and International Director of the Association of Vineyard Churches, has a significantly different take on power. His concept of "power evangelism" is derived from a Spirit-empowered (Pentecostal-charismatic) perspective. Wimber makes a distinction between authority and power. The Greek word for power (*dunamis*) means the ability to do something. It can be translated as force, strength, or power. The Greek word for authority (*exousia*) refers more

---

18. John R. P. French, Jr., and Bertram Raven, "The Bases of Social Power," in *Studies in Social Power*, ed. Dorwin P. Cartwright (Ann Arbor: University of Michigan, 1959), 150–67.

19. Lunenburg, "Power and Leadership," 2–4.

20. Cited in Lunenburg, "Power and Leadership," 6–7.

closely to the permission or legitimation to do something. Wimber holds that the ability to do something flows from the authority one possesses. Authority can be delegated, as was the case when Jesus sent out his disciples with authority over evil spirits, instructing them to heal the sick (Mark 6:7; Luke 10:9).[21] Wimber is keen to point out that the word for "power" in the New Testament synonymous with a miracle. Having deposed Satan, Jesus gave his disciples authority to perform acts of power: to proclaim the good news, to baptize and teach, to drive out demons, to heal the sick, to speak in new tongues, to raise the dead; to disciple the nations, and to represent Jesus to the world (Matt. 10:8; 28:18–20; Mark 16:15–21; John 20:21; also 1 John 3:1; cf. 2 Cor. 5:21; Eph. 2:4–6; Luke 10:19; Acts 1:8). According to Wimber, the Church has the authority and power to announce and demonstrate the Kingdom of God through power evangelism, which "transcends the rational through the demonstration of God's power in signs and wonders and introduces the numinous of God. This involves a presentation of the good news of God's reign accompanied with the manifest presence of God. Power evangelism is spontaneous and is directed by the Holy Spirit."[22]

To summarize, in Spirit-empowered leadership, all the above perspectives on power are in play, not only the primal sense of "supernatural" kingdom power, as conceived by Wimber, but also the "natural" organizational aspects illuminated by the work of researchers such as Lunenburg, French and Raven. French and Raven's typology of power will serve as a backdrop for our analysis of the dark side of power in charismatic leadership.

Spirit

To put it simply, Spirit-empowered leadership is leadership empowered by the Spirit. But what does this mean? What Spirit? A natural mystical force? To be clear, when we use the term "Spirit-empowered," we have in mind the Holy Spirit, who is set apart, holy, sinless, and pure. The adjective "holy" denotes that the Spirit is divine, rather than a natural mystical force. The Holy Spirit is God, the third member of the Trinity in perfect union with the Father and the Son. As such, the Spirit has attributes and abilities that belong only to God. He participates in creation (Gen. 1:2), reveals God, exalts Christ, calls and commissions leaders, and inaugurates the Church on the day of Pentecost. He is

---

21. All citations of Scripture in this book use the New International Version of the Bible, fully revised edition, 2011.

22. John Wimber, "Power Evangelism," *Renewal Journal* 22 (July 2011), accessed November 18, 2023, https://renewaljournal.com/2011/07/22/power-evangelism-byjohn-wimber/.

the source of power for the mission of the Church. He is involved in the process of salvation, regenerating sinners, teaching believers, and sanctifying those who seek after holiness.[23]

The Holy Spirit is also the giver of spiritual gifts: "Now to each one the manifestation of the Spirit is given for the common good" (1 Cor. 12:7). The gifts listed by Paul in 1 Corinthians 12:8–10 include wisdom, knowledge, faith, healing, miraculous powers, prophecy, discernment of spirits, speaking in tongues, and interpretation of tongues. Paul uses the image of the body to illustrate how spiritual gifts function as a unit. "Just as a body, though one, has many parts, but all its many parts form one body, so it is with Christ. For we were all baptized by one Spirit so as to form one body—whether Jews or Gentiles, slave or free—and we were all given the one Spirit to drink" (1 Cor. 12:12–13). Here we see Christ and the Spirit working in perfect unity. As John the Baptist stated, "I baptize you with water, but he [Christ] will baptize you with the Holy Spirit" (Mark 1:8).

Where does leadership fit into this picture? Leadership is both a spiritual gift (Rom. 12:8) and a position of influence and responsibility. Paul designates five leadership gifts in Ephesians 4:11: apostles, prophets, evangelists, pastors and teachers. Those who occupy these gifts or positions have a specific purpose: "to equip his [God's] people for works of service, so that the body of Christ may be built up until we all reach unity in the faith and in the knowledge of the Son of God and become mature, attaining to the whole measure of the fullness of Christ" (Eph. 4:12–13). We are wise to give special emphasis to unity and maturity as the end of leadership in the church. Leaders are gifted by the Spirit with a special calling to serve God's people by preparing them for service to Christ and building them up until they become mature. From a New Testament perspective, all Christian leaders are charismatic in the sense that the Holy Spirit has gifted and called them to serve Jesus Christ and his people.

Methodology

A methodology is a set of concepts, ideas, and procedures that inform the design of a research project. Ideally, a methodology is based on a theory that has been tested and shown to be valid. The purpose of a methodology is to provide a framework for analysis. There is a difference between methods and methodology. Methods are the procedures followed in gathering evidence; a methodology,

---

23. Keith Warrington, *Pentecostal Theology: A Theology of Encounter* (London: T&T Clark, 2008), 46–47.

on the other hand, is theorized because it consists of an underlying theory that informs an approach to a research project. To summarize, methods relate to specific procedures or steps taken to do the research, while methodology supplies the theoretical basis for using these methods as discourse tools in a research project.

The methodology of this book is grounded in a sociological theory of Max Weber (1864–1920). Weber came from a highly cultured segment of the German upper middle class. He was brought up in Berlin and studied law, receiving an appointment of Privatdozent at the University of Berlin. He diverted from the legal field at a relatively early age, however, when he accepted a position as professor of economics at the University of Freiburg and soon thereafter succeeded Karl Knies as Chair of Economics at Heidelberg. After only a brief tenure in this position, he suffered a severe breakdown of health that forced his resignation from his professorship and kept him out of productive work for about four years. During the most productive years of his life, he lived as a private scholar in a state of semi-invalidism in Heidelberg. During the latter part of the First World War, however, he accepted a temporary teaching appointment at the University of Vienna. Finally, in 1919, he took on a regular appointment to the Chair of Economics at Munich. He died suddenly of pneumonia in the second semester of his incumbency there, at the height of his intellectual powers.[24]

What is particularly interesting is Weber's concept of *charisma*, which he defines as "the gift of grace," derived from the vocabulary of early Christianity.[25] Weber applies the term *charisma* to "a certain quality of an individual personality by virtue of which he is set apart from ordinary men and treated as endowed with supernatural, superhuman, or at least specifically exceptional powers or qualities." These qualities are "not accessible to the ordinary person, but are regarded as of divine origin or as exemplary, and on the basis of them the individual concerned is treated as a leader."[26] Charismatic leaders are the objects of complete personal devotion. In fact, their charismatic authority depends on the absolute trust of followers who are bonded in an emotional form of communal relationship. In return, charismatic leaders demand new obligations, as in the case of Jesus, who says in the Sermon on the Mount, "You have heard that it was said… But I tell you … (Matt. 5:27–28, 31–32, 33–34, 38–39, 43–44). However, unlike Jesus, when a

---

24. Talcott Parsons, "Introduction," in Max Weber, *The Theory of Social and Economic Organization*, ed. Talcott Parsons, trans. A. M. Henderson and Talcott Parsons (New York: The Free Press, 1947), 4–5.

25. Weber, *Theory of Social and Economic Organization*, 328.

26. Weber, *Theory of Social and Economic Organization*, 358–59.

charismatic leader's status dissipates, it is as if their exceptional powers or qualities have deserted them. They can lose their charismatic authority if followers do not benefit from their leadership.[27] Hence, Weber holds that charismatic authority "lasts only so long as the belief in the charismatic inspiration remains."[28] For Weber, the key to sustained charismatic leadership is that followers must sustain their attribution. Weber postulates three types of authority, which are based on the following:

1. **Rational**; resting on a belief in the "legality" of patterns of normative rules and the right of those elevated to authority under such rules to issue commands (legal authority);
2. **Traditional**; resting on an established belief in the sanctity of immemorial traditions and the legitimacy of the status of those exercising authority under them (traditional authority); or finally
3. **Charismatic**; resting on devotion to an individual person's specific and exceptional sanctity, heroism, or exemplary character, and of the normative patterns or order revealed or ordained by him (charismatic authority).[29]

While rational authority is conveyed by virtue of a legally established order and traditional authority is transmitted according to a traditionally sanctioned position, charismatic authority is attributed to a leader by those who are subject to charismatic authority, that is, by followers or disciples.[30]

According to Talcott Parsons, two points stand out in Weber's treatment of charismatic authority. As a source of legitimate authority, charisma is (1) a revolutionary force tending to upset the stability of institutionalized orders, (2) which cannot itself become the basis of a stabilized order without undergoing profound structural changes. As a result of these changes, charisma tends to morph into either the rational-legal or the traditional type.[31] This process is known as "routinization." A crisis is presented for charismatic authority when the time comes for the designation of a successor. Hence, the problem presented by succession pertains to not only who qualifies as the successor, but also what constitutes the pattern of determination of the legitimacy of the next leader's status, both of which are crucial for all charismatic movements. The functional problem is that of maintaining the authority of the original point of reference—as a divine mission—and yet meeting the changed conditions with new leadership.

---

27. Weber, *Theory of Social and Economic Organization*, 358–63.
28. Weber, *Theory of Social and Economic Organization*, 362.
29. Weber, *Theory of Social and Economic Organization*, 328.
30. Weber, *Theory of Social and Economic Organization*, 359.
31. Weber, *Theory of Social and Economic Organization*, 66.

The leader himself or herself may have the primary role in designating his or her successor and the pattern of succession, or in varying ways and degrees the decisions may be participated in by the members of the administrative staff (charismatic aristocracy) or the total membership of the group of followers.[32]

For Weber, the fundamental question is whether the administrative staff will tend to take on either the character of a band of patrimonial retainers and hence lead in the traditional direction or that of a group of officials who lead in a rational-legal direction.[33] The relevance of the patterns described by Weber is apparent in the next section on the charismatic leadership theory.

Charismatic Leadership Theory

Max Weber established a foundation for charismatic leadership theory. He defines "charisma" as an occurrence of being "set apart from ordinary people and treated as endowed with supernatural, superhuman, or at least specifically exceptional powers or qualities...regarded as of divine origin or as exemplary, and of the basis of them the individual concerned is treated as a leader."[34] Weber argues that the "usefulness of the above classification can only be judged by its results in promoting systematic analysis."[35] Generations of scholars engaged in the social sciences have debated Weber's theory, and in the field of leadership studies a branch has emerged designated as charismatic leadership theory. Stated succinctly, this theory envisions an organizational structure in which an influential leader uses charisma to motivate followers to act toward a common goal. This shared goal or vision cultivates a strong foundation around the charismatic leader and molds the group together to be more effective.

It was not until the 1970s that Weber's theory of charismatic leadership was taken up by theorists of organizational leadership. Robert House formulated a theory of charismatic leadership starting from the premises of Weber's sociological concepts.[36] House hypothesized that, based on certain leader behaviors, followers attribute extraordinary or heroic leadership ability to their leaders. Other researchers worked with House's theory to define key characteristics of charismatic leadership. House and Shamir, House, and Arthur

---

32. Parson, "Introduction," Weber, *Theory of Social and Economic Organization*, 66.
33. Weber, *Theory of Social and Economic Organization*, 67.
34. Weber, *Theory of Social and Economic Organization*, 358–59.
35. Weber, *Theory of Social and Economic Organization*, 328.
36. Robert J. House, "A 1976 Theory of Charismatic Leadership," in *Leadership: The Cutting Edge*, ed. J. G. Hunt and L. L. Larson (Carbondale, IL: Southern Illinois University, 1977).

delineated the following characteristic behaviors of a charismatic leader: (1) articulates an ideological vision,[37] (2) refers to distal rather than proximate goals, (3) behaviorally models the values implied in the vision by personal example, (4) expresses high-performance expectations of followers, (5) communicates a high degree of confidence in followers' ability to meet such expectations, and (6) demonstrates behaviors that selectively arouse unconscious achievement, power, and affiliative motives of followers when these motives are specifically relevant to the attainment of the vision.[38]

Conger and Kanungo expanded the terrain of charismatic leadership theory by developing a widely accepted framework, holding that charismatic leadership is typified by four key characteristics: (1) possessing and articulating a vision, (2) being willing to take risks to accomplish the vision, (3) exhibiting sensitivity to the needs of followers, and (4) demonstrating novel behavior.[39] Charismatic leadership theory not only utilizes Weberian categories for analysis of charisma, but also posits criteria for differentiating between healthy and defective charismatic leadership. Informed by the findings of David C. McClelland in his study of the inner dimensions of power, House and Howell defined two types of charismatic leadership: personalized and socialized.[40] The categories of personalized and socialized charismatic leadership will serve as criteria for our analysis of the dark side of Spirit-empowered leadership in the final section of this chapter.

House and Howell defined *socialized* charismatic leadership as positive leadership that is (1) based on egalitarian behavior, (2) serves collective interests and is not driven by self-interest of the leader, and (3) develops and empowers others. McClelland and his colleagues reported that socialized leaders tend to be altruistic, work through legitimate established channels and systems of authority, when such systems exist, and are self-controlled and follower-oriented rather than narcissistic. House and Howell defined *personalized* charismatic leadership as negative leadership that (1) is based on personal dominance and authoritarian behavior, (2) serves the self-interest of the leader

---

37. An ideological vision specifies a better future in terms of such values as human rights, peace, freedom, order, equality, and attainment of status and privileges that are claimed to the moral right of followers.

38. Robert J. House and Jane M. Howell, "Personality and Charismatic Leadership," *Leadership Quarterly* 3, no. 2 (1992): 83.

39. Jay A. Conger and Rabindra N. Kanungo, ed., *Charismatic Leadership: The Elusive Factor in Organizational Effectiveness* (San Francisco: Jossey-Bass, 1988).

40. David C. McClelland, *Power: The Inner Experience* (New York: Irvington, 1975); House and Howell, "Personality and Charismatic Leadership," 81–108.

and is self-aggrandizing, and (3) is exploitative of others. Personalized leaders rely on personal approval or rejection of followers to induce others to comply with their wishes. They show disregard for the rights and feelings of others, and they tend to be narcissistic, impetuous, and impulsively aggressive. These two types of charismatic leadership are not mutually exclusive; a leader can simultaneously display characteristics of both leadership types.[41] More about these types of charismatic leadership will be conveyed at the close of this chapter. For now, it suffices to say that charismatic leadership theory serves our purpose of identifying, understanding, and evaluating common patterns of leadership in global, Spirit-empowered movements.

Thesis

The research findings of House and Howell and Conger and Kanungo provide sufficient data from which to advance a thesis. The major claim of this study is that Spirit-empowered leadership is essentially charismatic in its structure and operation. Charismatic leadership is conceived of as a gift given and sustained by the Holy Spirit. Hence, it is endowed and empowered by the Spirit, rather than acquired by human effort and skill. However, those entrusted with it must steward it so that it serves and upbuilds the vitality and mission of the Christian community. At times, this will demand that leaders face the dark side of a Spirit-empowered community of faith and hold accountable those who betray the fiduciary trust of leadership by falling into moral failure, financial malfeasance, or abuse of power. It behooves educators and thought leaders to develop a leadership development strategy that addresses these issues proactively rather than reactively.

A secondary claim of this study is that Spirit-empowered leaders are called to equip their colleagues, followers, and students for discernment of charismatic leadership. Discernment is the ability to distinguish between good and evil, pride and humility, and glorifying God and seeking self-interest. Spirit-empowered leaders should be open to accountability. Leaders gain from having their leadership evaluated according to its concurrence with two touchstones: the Bible and the Holy Spirit. It is incumbent upon educators to equip students to exercise discernment in evaluating the authenticity of their leaders.

---

41. House and Howell, "Personality and Charismatic Leadership," 84.

Touchstones: Bible and the Holy Spirit

A *touchstone* is a standard or criterion by which something is judged or recognized. The term is derived from an ancient practice (dating to 600 BCE) of testing the quality and value of precious metals by means of a touchstone and an acid test. First, the jeweler rubs a tiny part of the jewelry on the touchstone. This leaves a streak on the stone. The jeweler must be careful not to damage the customer's jewelry. He or she then takes a test needle and rubs the streak, applying an acid solution to the streak. For higher karat levels the solution is *aqua regia* (a mixture of hydrochloric and nitric acid). The jeweler looks for color changes and watches how quickly the streak disappears. The purer the gold—the higher the karat level—the stronger the acid required to change its character and dissolve the streak.[42]

You might ask what this has to do with the Bible and the Holy Spirit, and here is the point. Both the Bible and the Holy Spirit can serve as touchstones with which we can apply an acid test of discernment regarding questionable biblical interpretations and spiritual phenomena. The biblical scholar Richard Longenecker was the first to bring this to my attention. He argues that the New Testament—building on the Hebrew Scriptures—serves as the touchstone for assessing genuine Christian social ethics. Let me assure you that all of us will, at times, need a standard for discerning what is true from what is false. That standard is as close at hand as one's Bible. As Longenecker says, "The Bible presents the proclamation of God's definitive word to humankind in the person and ministry of Jesus Christ of Nazareth and the paradigm of how the implications involved in God's revelatory and redemptive activity were begun to be spelled out in the apostolic period."[43] The assumption here is that we have a rule of faith, a basic summary or paradigm of authentic biblical doctrine, which was worked out in the apostolic period. In other words, the "apostles' teaching" set an authoritative standard that serves as a touchstone for discernment today. To use this touchstone and apply it as an acid test requires knowledge of the Bible *and* "intimate acquaintance with the same Spirit who inspired the biblical writings."[44] Knowledge of the Bible and

---

42. For more information, see Walo Wälchli, "Touching Precious Metals," *Gold Bull* 14, no. 4 (1981): 154–58, accessed November 18, 2023, https://link.springer.com/content/pdf/10.1007/BF03216559.pdf.

43. Richard N. Longenecker, *New Testament Social Ethics for Today* (Grand Rapids: Eerdmans, 1984), 22.

44. Longenecker, *New Testament Social Ethics for Today*, 22.

intimate acquaintance with the Holy Spirit—these are quintessential criteria for Spirit-empowered leaders to use in coming to terms with the complexities of the varying ideologies and competing lifestyles of today.

Charismatic Leadership in the Old Testament

Let me begin by saying that the Bible is largely a book about leadership. It narrates the stories of Spirit-empowered leaders who were chosen, equipped, and sent by God to carry out his plan of redemption and renewal. Although, as David G. Firth observes, there is no one word in Hebrew that equates with our word *leadership*; the importance of leadership is a central concern of the Old Testament.[45] My contention is that leadership is a charismatic gift empowered by the Holy Spirit. We will approach our brief study of leadership in the Bible in the spirit of Paul's hermeneutical aim of interpreting narratives in the Old Testament as "examples" that were "written down as warnings for us, on whom the culmination of the ages has come" (1 Cor. 10:11). We can learn a great deal from the Old Testament about how to practice charismatic leadership with integrity and wisdom.

The Holy Spirit was active in the Old Testament. The Spirit of the Lord not only hovered over creation (Gen. 1:2), but he also empowered leaders. John H. Walton writes, "The Spirit of the LORD often legitimized leaders in the Old Testament, whether judges or kings."[46] Moses could be considered the paradigmatic Spirit-empowered leader of the Old Testament. Specifically, it was through Moses that God enacted the mediation of Spirit-empowerment in the commissioning of charismatic leaders.[47] We see this when God commissioned seventy elders for leadership in Numbers 11.[48] In Numbers 11:17, God says to Moses, "I will come down and speak with you there, and I will take some of the power of the Spirit that is on you and put it on them.

---

45. David G. Firth, "The Spirit and Leadership: Testimony, Empowerment, and Purpose," in *Presence, Power, and Promise: The Role of the Spirit of God in the Old Testament*, ed. David G. Firth and Paul D. Wegner (Downers Grove: IVP Academic, 2011), 259.

46. John H. Walton, "The Ancient Near Eastern Background of the Spirit of the Lord in the Old Testament," in *Presence, Power and Promise: The Role of the Spirit of God in the Old Testament*, ed. David G. Firth and Paul D. Wegner (Downers Grove: InterVarsity Press Academic, 2011), 48.

47. Jiří Moskala, "The Holy Spirit in the Hebrew Scriptures," *Journal of the Adventist Theological Society* 24, no. 2 (2013): 51–52.

48. On Numbers 11 and the role of the Spirit in the commissioning of the seventy elders, see Christopher J. H. Wright, *Knowing the Holy Spirit through the Old Testament* (Downers Grove: InterVarsity Press Academic, 2006), 44–62.

They will share the burden of the people with you so that you will not have to carry it alone." The seventy elders received the same Spirit as Moses and with it the gift of leadership for the purpose of assisting Moses. Then they prophesied as confirmation of their call to leadership (Num. 11:25b), but two of the elders who were not present also received the gift of the Spirit and prophesied as a confirming sign (Num. 11:26). When others objected, Moses replied, "Are you jealous for my sake? I wish that all the LORD's people were prophets and that the LORD would put his Spirit on them!" (Num. 11:29). This same pattern appears in the commissioning of Joshua. "So the LORD said to Moses, 'Take Joshua son of Nun, a man in whom is the spirit of leadership, and lay your hand on him. Have him stand before Eleazar the priest and the entire assembly and commission him in their presence'" (Num. 27:18–19).

Early in the Old Testament, a pattern unfolds in relation to the role of the Holy Spirit in empowering charismatic leaders. According to Tamás Czövek, an ordained minister in the Reformed Church in Hungary and Professor of Old Testament at the Pentecostal Seminary in Budapest, in a biblical context, charisma is an "extraordinary quality of a leader, which, on the narrative's level, is recognized as superhuman and supernatural by the narrator and the characters." The leader offers a resolution to a particular crisis by virtue of his or her charisma.[49] Leslie Hoppe, Professor of Biblical Studies at Catholic Theological Union, notes that the rule of the judges was thoroughly personal—independent of any hierarchical structure. This pattern of leadership was "charismatic." He explains, "Charismatic leaders do not owe their position to any socio-political structure but to the personal, physical, and psychological attributes that set them apart from the commonplace. Ancient Israel identified the source of these attributes as the 'Spirit of the Lord' and so regarded the judges as divine agents with supreme authority."[50]

The Spirit of the Lord commissioned four leaders in the book of Judges. Each commissioning is narrated with this formulaic phrase: "the Spirit of the LORD came upon [name of leader]." These leaders are Othniel (Judg. 3:10), Gideon (Judg. 6:34), Jephthah (Judg. 11:29), and Samson (Judg. 14:6, 14:19, 15:14).[51] The Spirit enables strong and effective leadership, but, as Wonsuk Ma points out, the leadership

---

49. Tamás Czövek, *Three Seasons of Charismatic Leadership: A Literary-Critical and Theological Interpretation of the Narrative of Saul, David, and Solomon* (Milton Keynes, UK: Paternoster, 2006), 29–30.

50. Leslie Hoppe, *Joshua, Judges, with an Excursus on Charismatic Leadership in Israel* (Old Testament Message) (Wilmington, DE: Michael Glazier, 1982), 214.

51. Moskala, "The Holy Spirit in Hebrew Scriptures," 34.

style of some of judges gives reason for pause, due to their failure to internalize the transformative work of the Spirit.[52] Walton holds that Israelite theology of the Spirit's endowment of leaders represents a qualified agency, in that these leaders can "still manifest human inadequacies and failure, thereby mitigating the results."[53] Accordingly, Hoppe points out a shortcoming of the charismatic leadership of the judges, namely that the judges were unable to unite *all* the tribes in a common effort. The leader who formed the most extensive tribal league was Deborah, who marshalled only six tribes. Further, according to Malamat, the leadership of each judge was temporary, raising residual concerns about succession.[54]

However, with the rise of Saul and David, an attempt was made to institutionalize the charisma of leadership.[55] We see a poignant example of the divine intent pertaining to charismatic leadership when Samuel prophesied that Saul would meet a company of prophets on the road, be filled with the Spirit of God, prophesy with them, and become a changed person (1 Sam. 10:6). And it came to pass (10:10–11), albeit with a tragic flaw in the case of Saul, which Wonsuk Ma construes as unrealized character development.[56] When David was anointed by Samuel "from that day on, the Spirit of the LORD came powerfully upon David" (1 Sam. 16:13), whereas soon afterward "the Spirit of the LORD had departed from Saul" (1 Sam. 16:14). The sobering twist of the demise of Saul's leadership should warn us against presuming upon the Holy Spirit. Leadership is a sacred trust that can be forfeited by a lack of faithfulness. Charismatic leadership is likely to lose its grip when a leader focuses more on his or her own power than on trusting in the Holy Spirit. This is exactly what happened to Saul when he felt threatened by David. As Czövek explains the Saul syndrome, "Once a charismatic leader or movement becomes static, he or she is in need of a dynamic start-over and the intervention of God's dynamic and uncontrollable Spirit... Because charismatic leaders are led by the very dynamic Spirit of God who does not know stasis, a charismatic should never sit back but be open to the Spirit's guidance."[57]

---

52. Wonsuk Ma, "The Tragedy of Spirit-Empowered Heroes: A Close Look at Samson and Saul," *Spiritus: ORU Journal of Theology* 2, no. 1–2 (2017): 23.

53. Walton, "Ancient Near Eastern Background of the Spirit of the Lord," 61.

54. Abraham Malamat, "Charismatic Leadership in the Book of Judges," in *Magnalia Dei, The Mighty Acts of God: Essays on the Bible and Archaeology in Memory of G. Ernest Wright*, ed. Frank Moore Cross, Werner E. Lemke, and Patrick D. Miller, Jr. (Garden City, NY: Doubleday, 1976), 161–63.

55. Hoppe, *Joshua, Judges, With an Excursus on Charismatic Leadership in Israel*, 215.

56. Ma, "The Tragedy of Spirit-Empowered Heroes," 35.

57. Czövek, *Three Seasons of Charismatic Leadership*, 218.

Isaiah and Ezekiel are two examples of the Holy Spirit's role in the commissioning of these major prophets. Isaiah's commissioning is a classic visionary call narrative. In the thick of a vision, Isaiah saw the Lord "high and exalted, seated on a throne," with his train filling the temple and seraphs flying about, calling to one another, "Holy, holy, holy, is the Lord Almighty; the whole earth is full of his glory." Over the din of rumbling earthquakes, Isaiah heard the voice of God beckoning, "Whom shall I send? And who will go for us?" Isaiah responded, "Here I am. Send me!" (Isa. 6:1–8). This story resonates with many of us who have a visionary call narrative of our own. Later in Isaiah, we see evidence that Isaiah clearly comprehended the implications of his calling to prophetic leadership. He exclaimed, "The Spirit of the Sovereign LORD is upon me, because the LORD has anointed me to proclaim good news to the poor. He has sent me to bind up the broken-hearted, to proclaim freedom for the captives and release from darkness for the prisoners, to proclaim the year of the Lord's favor..." (Isa. 61:1–2a). In a charismatic context, a call to ministry often comes with a miraculous experience, such as a vision. Additional evidence of similar experiences that Spirit-empowered leaders have encountered is included in the second part of this book.

The prophet Ezekiel experienced a grand vision of four living creatures and the glory of the Lord. He saw the living creatures moving and rising from the ground. "Wherever the spirit would go, they would go, and the wheels would arise along with them because the spirit of the living creatures was in the wheels" (Ezek. 1:20). Seeing the glory of the Lord, Ezekiel fell facedown, and then the Lord spoke, calling the prophet, feeding him a scroll, and sending him to speak his words to the Israelite captives (Ezek. 1:28; 2:3, 9; 3:4). So, what does this have to do with us? The place of visions and dreams in contemporary Spirit-empowered leadership should be affirmed and encouraged as authentic. There are many instances of mystical experience in Scripture, and as I understand 1 Corinthians 10:11, the experiences of the faithful in the past are meant to be examples for today. Here is the takeaway point: This is still happening today. David Tasker says it well: "When times become tough and political or religious leaders are not giving clear enough leadership, then God empowers men and women to become his mouthpieces in giving an otherwise bewitched population a healthy dose of reality ..., wooing a disenchanted people back to the only One who can save them. What is more relevant to the twenty-first century than that?"[58]

---

58. David R. Tasker, "Ruach Elohim: The Holy Spirit in the Old Testament," *Ministry:*

There is a pattern of leadership development in the Old Testament that later evolved into the method of mentoring leaders in rabbinic Judaism. The biblical method of developing a leader is based on the practice of an emerging leader following a master-leader to learn by observation and service. The purpose of the master-servant relationship is to mentor the emerging leader for the next generation of leadership, and training and mentoring someone may take many years. For example, Joshua spent years with Moses, during which the younger Joshua observed the elder Moses in preparation for Joshua's future leadership. In a sense, Joshua served as an apprentice under Moses. According to A. K. Fountain, "Joshua was Moses' servant for almost all of the wilderness period, which is approximately thirty-eight years."[59] After spending sufficient time watching Moses and learning from him, Joshua was well prepared to assume leadership and bring the tribes of Israel into the Promised Land. The Lord confirmed, "As I was with Moses, so I will be with you; I will never leave you nor forsake you" (Josh. 1:5).

A second example is the younger Elisha following and learning from the elder Elijah (1 Kings 19:19–21). For years, Elisha served as an attendant to Elijah, but the true purpose of this master-servant relationship was to mentor the emerging leader. Elisha served an apprenticeship under Elijah until Elijah was taken up into heaven.[60] Receiving a double measure of Elijah's mantle (charisma), Elisha not only continued the ministry of Elijah, but also expanded the one-on-one model of mentoring by gathering a "company of prophets" (2 Kings 2:3, 7, 15). Elisha's type of leadership development was continued by later prophets and may have set an Old Testament precedent for the disciples of Jesus.

Charismatic Leadership in the New Testament

Jesus is the quintessential Spirit-empowered leader. From the moment of conception, Jesus was filled with the Holy Spirit,[61] as prophesied in the Old Testament (Isa. 42:1 and Matt. 12:18; Isa. 61:1 and Luke 4:1).

International Journal for Pastors 85, no. 1 (January 2013): 19, https://www.ministrymagazine.org/archive/2013/01/ruach-elohim:-the-holy-spirit-in-the-old-testament.

59. A. K. Fountain, "An Investigation into Successful Leadership Transitions in the Old Testament," *Asian Journal of Pentecostal Studies* 7, no. 2 (2004): 196.

60. Fountain, "An Investigation into Successful Leadership," 196.

61. Gregory A. Smith, "The Holy Spirit in the New Testament," *Scholar's Crossing*, Faculty Publications and Presentations, Liberty University 68 (2000): 1.

- Jesus was conceived by the Holy Spirit (Matt. 1:1–20; Luke 1:35).
- The Holy Spirit descended on Jesus as a dove during his baptism (Matt. 3:16; Mark 1:10; Luke 3:21–22; John 1:32).
- John the Baptist, also Spirit-filled, declared that Jesus would baptize with the Holy Spirit and fire (Mark 1:8; Luke 3:16; John 1:33).
- The Holy Spirit led Jesus into the desert to be tempted by the devil (Matt. 4:1; Mark 1:12–13; Luke 4:1–2).
- Lastly, Jesus carried out his ministry in the anointing of the Holy Spirit (Luke 4:14, 18), casting out demons by the power of the Holy Spirit (Matt. 12:28).

Seeing the results of the mission of the seventy-two, full of joy through the Holy Spirit, Jesus praised the Father for revealing these things to his little children (Luke 10:21).

The leadership of Jesus was rooted in the Old Testament. He utilized a mentorship model. He called twelve apostles and taught them as he traveled, taught, and performed acts of power. Jesus clearly stated that he did not come to abolish the law, prophets, and writings of the Old Testament but to fulfill them (Matt. 5:17). During the Feast of Tabernacles, "Jesus stood and said in a loud voice, 'Let anyone who is thirsty come to me and drink. Whoever believes in me, as the Scripture has said, rivers of living water will flow from within them.' By this he meant the Spirit, whom those who believed in him were later to receive. Up to that time the Spirit had not been given, since Jesus had not yet been glorified" (John 7:37–39).

Just prior to his crucifixion, Jesus prepared his inner circle of leaders (apostles) to sustain his movement after he ascended to the right hand of the Father. In his Upper Room discourse (John 13–17), Jesus promised his apostles (sent ones) that he would send "another advocate" (*paraclete*) (John 14:16) who would empower them to continue his mission. There are five references to the Holy Spirit in John 14–16 (14:16–17, 26–28; 15:26; 16:7–8, 13). The advocate is a person, not merely a force or power. Jesus refers to the advocate with a masculine pronoun, that is, as "he" and "him." According to Gary Burge, this "shows that for John, 'spirit of truth,' meant more than a mere tendency or influence."[62] The Holy Spirit is another helper of the same kind as Jesus. Christ is the first advocate or paraclete; the Holy Spirit is the same kind of advocate, although different, still the same. Jesus is the archetype. Just as Jesus taught and mentored the apostles, so the second advocate, the Holy Spirit, will continue to teach them Jesus' words, guide them into truth, and

---

62. Gary M. Burge, *The Anointed Commentary: The Holy Spirit in the Johannine Tradition* (Grand Rapids: Eerdmans, 1987), 142.

sustain their mission. Jesus promised that he would not abandon his apostles but would continue to lead them even though the world would not see him. The Holy Spirit would call to remembrance the teaching of Jesus and "he will tell you what is yet to come" (John 16:13).

Jesus spoke these words prior to his crucifixion, and John recorded them in writing about thirty years after Pentecost. John's perspective on the Holy Spirit was shaped by his memory of the miracle of Pentecost and the post-resurrection appearances of the risen Christ. After his glorification (crucifixion and resurrection), Jesus appeared to the apostles and interpreted the Scriptures, opening their minds to see that he fulfilled Old Testament prophecies of the Messiah (Luke 24:44). He appeared to the inner circle, showed them his hands and feet, commissioned them, and breathed upon them, saying, "Receive the Holy Spirit. If you forgive anyone's sins, their sins are forgiven; if you do not forgive them, they are not forgiven" (John 20:22). This experience was a foretaste of Pentecost, when the Holy Spirit filled all believers. Further, prior to Pentecost, Jesus assured his inner group of leaders that they would receive the promise of the Father: "But you will receive power when the Holy Spirit comes on you; and you will be my witnesses in Jerusalem, and in all Judea and Samaria, and to the ends of the earth" (Acts 1:8). The stage is now set for the story of Pentecost.

Spirit-empowered leadership in the New Testament church commenced with the outpouring of the Holy Spirit during the Feast of Pentecost. Authored by Luke, a doctor and companion of the apostle Paul, the Pentecost account is divided into three parts: (1) the empowering presence of the Holy Spirit, (2) Peter's sermon and the crowd's response, and (3) the emerging shape of the early Christian community.[63] To understand the significance of the Pentecost event for Christian leadership, it is important to set the scene. The occasion is the Jewish Feast of Pentecost, beginning on the fiftieth day after Passover. Ben Witherington, a noted New Testament professor, estimates that there could have been as many as 180,000 to 200,000 in attendance, with most in the temple precincts.[64] The following description of the Pentecost event in Acts 2 is based on Julianne Cenac's division of the text.

---

63. Julianne R. Cenac, "Leader Emergence and the Phenomenological Work of the Holy Spirit in Acts 2," *Journal of Biblical Perspectives on Leadership* 3, no. 1 (Winter 2010): 127.

64. Ben Witherington III, *The Acts of the Apostles: A Socio-Rhetorical Commentary* (Grand Rapids: Eerdmans, 1997), 156.

Manifestation of the Holy Spirit

As the followers of Jesus were all together in one place, they experienced a powerful manifestation of the Holy Spirit. With tongues of fire hovering above each of them, they were filled with the Holy Spirit and began to speak in the languages of those who had come from near and far to observe the Feast. The crowd was perplexed and wondered what was going on. Some evidently accused the apostles of being drunk, prompting Peter to proclaim that the strange goings on constituted the fulfillment of the prophecy of Joel 2:28–32.

Peter's Sermon

Peter's explanation of the manifestation of the Holy Spirit was grounded in a hermeneutical strategy of making textual connections between present experience and the manifestations of the Spirit in biblical history. With intertextual citations of Joel 2:28–32, Psalm 16:8–11, and Psalm 110:1, Peter provided an interpretation of the manifestation of the Spirit that had just occurred, claiming that what happened concurred with how God conferred his Spirit on certain leaders in the Old Testament, calling them into leadership and endowing them with a special gift of power and ability. Peter conferred on Jesus the ultimate title of Lord and Christ, which God confirmed by raising Jesus from the dead. "Exalted to the right hand of God, he has received from the Father the promised Holy Spirit and has poured out what you now see and hear" (Acts 2:33). Setting up the response, Peter drove the point home: "Therefore, let all Israel be assured of this: God has made this Jesus, whom you crucified, both Lord and Messiah" (Acts 2:36). For us, the takeaway from Peter's sermon is the connection it makes between the fulfillment of Old Testament prophecy in Jesus and Spirit empowerment. Peter's use of Joel's prophecy makes it clear that Pentecost stands in continuity with the charismatic activity of the Spirit in the Old Testament times. Further, Peter's sermon sets the scene for the emergence of Spirit-empowered leadership.

Shaping of the Christian Community

The audience's response was undoubtedly prompted by a stinging sense of guilt on the part of those who may have taken part in the frenzied crowd who clamored, "Crucify him! Crucify him" (Luke 23:21). Cut to the heart, they pleaded, "Brothers, what shall we do?" Peter exhorted them, "Repent and be baptized, every one of you, in the name of Jesus Christ for the forgiveness of your sins. And you will receive the gift of the Holy Spirit. The promise is for you and your children and for all who are far off—for all whom the Lord our God will call" (Acts 2:37–39). The response was overwhelming. With 3,000 converts, the leaders organized the ministry of the newborn church of Jerusalem, apportioning people into house groups in which they were discipled for growth in the faith. From the beginning, demonstrations of charismatic power abounded, especially prophecy, miracles of healing, exorcism, prayer and worship, breaking of bread, and sharing of possessions.

The Acts 2 event constitutes the *charismatic birthright* of Spirit-empowered leadership. Through the outpouring of the Holy Spirit, the leaders of the new Christian movement underwent a dramatic transformation. As they were baptized in the Spirit, they were equipped to mediate the mystical transformation experience to their followers. Here we see a fundamental connection between the dynamic experience of the apostles and that of other leaders throughout the biblical narrative, as covered above, who were endowed with charismatic authority and empowerment. The position of leadership was confirmed by virtue of the filling of the Holy Spirit filling and the gifting of charisma, a special grace, power, or ability. Cenac suggests that here we have "a glimpse into the God-ordained purposes of leadership, particularly when the Holy Spirit is imparted or employed."[65] The transformation of Peter, as evidenced by the boldness of his Pentecost sermon, shows that the key to leadership in a Lukan context is Spirit-empowerment. The empowering presence of the Spirit enabled Peter with gifts and abilities he did not demonstrate prior to Pentecost. In the book of Acts, leadership is not about the leader himself or herself, but rather the Holy Spirit who transforms the leader with power, wisdom, and skill to do God's work among God's people. Cenac contends, "This assertion turns the traditional thinking of leadership upside down."[66] Innate traits may be helpful, but they do not make one a Christian leader, especially not a leader in Spirit-empowered movements, simply because in this realm, leadership is derived from charismatic experience and gifting. We shall see many examples of this in the historical sketches of Spirit-empowered leaders to follow.

The mediation of Spirit empowerment should be seen as a transformative process through which the outflow of charisma occurs. Prime examples of this process include Peter's housetop vision in Joppa (Acts 10:9–23a), the ensuing Gentile Pentecost in the home of Cornelius (Acts 10:23b–24), and the Jerusalem Council (Acts 15:1–35). Through these events, the gift of

---

65. Cenac, "Leader Emergence": 132.
66. Cenac, "Leader Emergence": 134.

leadership becomes something that is mediated through spiritual experience. Seen in a wider context, the gift of leadership is conveyed through the power of the Holy Spirit working in and beyond previously held cultural and theological limitations. As the Bible is interpreted for the community, the message bears fruit in the transformation of listeners who are open to receive and embrace it. Spiritual gifts are activated through a process of transmission. This process is an essential dynamic of Spirit-empowerment not only in the book of Acts, but also in contemporary contexts. Charisma is received, transmitted, and shared, releasing new dimensions of leadership. As the gifting of charismatic leaders is acknowledged collectively by the people who follow them, their charisma is mediated (shared) among the faithful.[67] The point here is that Spirit-empowered leadership flows through an interactive process in which the Holy Spirit distributes spiritual gifts for the common good (1 Cor. 12:7), including the gift of leadership (Rom. 12:8). This underlines a key point in Weber's theory of charismatic leadership. The ultimate indicator of sustainable charismatic leadership is that followers continue to affirm the charisma of a leader. Weber himself acknowledged that the source of his theory was early Christianity. From this source, he derived his view that charismatic leadership hinges on the attribution of charisma by the followers, that is, on a collective affirmation of a given leader's gifting. The implications of this crucial point will be fleshed out as the book proceeds.

The Shadow Side of Charismatic Leadership

Two Pentecostal scholars weighed in on the body of research on charismatic leadership theory. Roger Heuser and Byron D. Klaus, formerly faculty members of Southern California College (now Vanguard University), an affiliate of the Assemblies of God, published an article titled "Charismatic Leadership Theory: A Shadow Side Confessed." While acknowledging that charismatic leaders often succeed in accomplishing extraordinary feats, there is also "a potentially darksome side to leaders who employ leadership charism." Pointing to recent research by leadership theorists, Heuser and Klaus contend that a charismatic leader whose interior life is unexamined can "potentially take on a dark side that is eventually projected on to the

---

67. Roberta Bivar Campos, "Sharing Charisma as a Mode of Pentecostal Expansion," *Social Compass* 61, no. 3 (2014): 279.

entire organization." Such leaders "come to a place where they embrace dispositions and practices that are not from God."[68] It is evident to Heuser and Klaus that the Pentecostal-charismatic leaders are at the forefront of a global movement that is authentically liberating, yet "it also yields a potential opportunity for abusive leaders to thrive." They raise concerns about "non-accountable dynamic leaders who fashion a following with the 'sound bites' of God-like utterances in the context of manipulative phenomenology, thus creating an image of powerful ministry leadership."[69] Hence, the authors conclude, "The mixed bag of phenomenal growth world-wide and the shadow side of charismatic leadership is a paradox that needs to be acknowledged and subsequently addressed."[70]

Stephen Fogarty, Principal of Alphacrucis College in Australia, adopts the terminology of Conger (1990) in his analysis of the "dark side" of charismatic leadership.[71] Fogarty's analysis is particularly relevant to our study because he is affiliated with the Spirit-empowered movement. While acknowledging the strong positive effects that charismatic leaders can have on organizations, Fogarty states that charismatic leaders can also produce significant negative outcomes to the detriment of both the leader and the organization. Working from House and Howell's typology of positive socialized and negative personalized charismatic leadership, Fogarty compares the characteristics and consequences of personalized and socialized charismatic leadership and then offers strategies for minimizing the risks of the dark side of charismatic leadership.

Fogarty observes that *personalized* charismatic leaders are typically authoritarian and narcissistic. They pursue goals that serve their own interests, and they manipulate followers to get their way. Hence, they can be exploitative. They have an extreme need for power. They demand that followers identify with and support their leadership. They display low regard for legitimate channels of authority, and they are likely to pursue courses of action that enhance their power within the organization and attract credit for their achievements.[72] In contrast, *socialized* charismatic leaders govern in an egalitarian manner

---

68. Roger Heuser and Byron Klaus, "Charismatic Leadership Theory: A Shadow Side Confessed," *Pneuma: The Journal of the Society for Pentecostal Studies* 20, no. 2 (1998): 166.

69. Heuser and Klaus, "Charismatic Leadership Theory," 168.

70. Heuser and Klaus, "Charismatic Leadership Theory," 169.

71. Jay A. Conger, "The Dark Side of Leadership." *Organizational Dynamics* 19, no. 2 (1990): 44–55, accessed March 24, 2024; https://doi.org/10.1016/0090-2616(90)90070-6.

72. Stephen G. Fogarty, "The Dark Side of Charismatic Leadership," *Australian Pentecostal Studies* 13 (2010): 10.

and serve the interests of the organization and their followers. They seek to empower followers and govern through established channels to accomplish their goals. Their relationship with followers is focused less on the personality of the leader and more on the leader's message about the organization and its ideals and goals. Followers can place constraints on the leader's influence. These leaders are considered non-exploitative because they are concerned with meeting the needs of their followers.[73]

Fogarty summarizes the negative consequences of personalized charismatic leaders: they tend to have an undue need for power, negative life themes, and narcissistic tendencies, contributing to a view of the world where personal safety is achieved through the domination of others. The negative consequences include unethical and destructive leadership behavior. Unethical charismatic leaders have a desire to produce dependent and compliant followers. The resultant outcomes include the nurture of blind loyalty and the suppression of criticism. When these behaviors become systematic and repeated, they are classified as destructive.[74]

Fogarty offers a strategy for minimizing the risks presented by the dark side of charismatic leadership. The long-term solution would be cultivating socialized instead of personalized charismatic leaders. However, this is not always feasible, given the need for more immediate countermeasures. Fogarty draws upon the research of Diane Chandler, Professor of Leadership Studies at Regent University, who finds that leadership failure can be attributed to (1) unresolved childhood needs, (2) personality determinants, (3) moral values and character weakness, and (4) internalized success stressors.[75]

In view of Chandler's findings, Fogarty offers three proactive safeguards that are intended to maximize the unique contributions of the charismatic leader while minimizing potential negative consequences. First, Fogarty suggests that an effective *accountability structure* should be put in place at the time of appointment of the leader. Effective accountability measures might include careful oversight by a board of directors, agreement on financial and decision-making parameters, and enactment of a system of checks and balances. Leaders who are held accountable are more likely to consider the consequences of unwise actions and consider the interest of the organization

---

73. Fogarty, "The Dark Side of Charismatic Leadership," 10.

74. Fogarty, "The Dark Side of Charismatic Leadership," 12–13.

75. Diane J. Chandler, "The Perfect Storm of Leaders' Unethical Behavior: A Conceptual Framework," *International Journal of Leadership Studies* 5, no. 1 (2009): 74.

and its members. Second, Fogarty commends a viable *support system* for the leader. This could include personal confidantes, developing mentoring relationships, formal and informal training (including education in ethics), and the provision of personal and professional development opportunities. A support system can prevent the demise of an otherwise successful leader due to isolation. Third, Fogarty insists that the *selection process* should include a validated assessment tool that differentiates between socialized and personalized charismatic leaders. Other assessment tools could measure such leadership orientations as the need for power, negative life themes, and narcissism.

Succession of leadership in charismatic circles is often hampered by a lack of insight into the dynamics of power motivation. It would be in the organization's best interest to transfer leadership to a leader with a socialized power motivation corresponding to Jesus's teachings on servant leadership (Matt. 20:25–28). As Fogarty states, "A socialized charismatic leader is likely to create an organizational culture which is egalitarian, non-exploitative, and altruistic."[76]

Conclusion

This introductory chapter began by defining three terms that are at the heart of the topic: leadership, power, and Spirit. Max Weber's theory of charismatic leadership serves as our theorized methodology for critical analysis of Spirit-empowered leadership. The thesis, the major claim of the book, is that Spirit-empowered leadership is essentially charismatic in its structure and operation. The secondary claim of this study is that it is incumbent upon Spirit-empowered leaders to equip their colleagues, followers, and students to analyze and assess charismatic leadership. Spirit-empowered leaders should be open to accountability. They gain from being evaluated according two touchstones, the Bible and the Holy Spirit. In the interest of establishing criteria for accountability, we delved into the patterns and principles of charismatic leadership in the Bible, adducing from the Old and New Testaments how charismatic leadership can be practiced with integrity and wisdom. Finally, we explored the problem of the shadow side of charismatic leadership and proposed countermeasures. Building on this introduction, the next chapter discusses three problems that gave rise to the research design of the book. These problems are categorized as *lacunas*, that

---

76. Fogarty, "The Dark Side of Charismatic Leadership," 15–16.

is, under-discussed issues in the study of Spirit-empowered leadership. The next chapter describes each lacuna, analyzes its cause, clarifies its impact on the practice of leadership, and proposes solutions.

2

LACUNAS IN THE STUDY OF SPIRIT-EMPOWERED LEADERSHIP

A *lacuna* is an empty space or a hole where something should be. In Latin, *lacuna* means "pit or hole." Its plural can be rendered as *lacunae* or *lacunas*. The term lacuna is often used to refer to missing parts of books or manuscripts due to lost pages, intentional censorship, or accidental omissions. In the study of anatomy, a lacuna is a hollowed-out place or a cavity within a bone. Given the current context of organizational change, Gordon contends that leadership lacunas have been shown to have problematic consequences for leadership theory.[1] Spirit empowered leadership is not immune to the problem of lacunas. The author finds that certain issues are under-discussed in the study of Spirit-empowered leadership and therefore qualify as lacunas. This chapter deals with three lacunas that are of pressing concern in Spirit-empowered leadership, namely, spiritual formation, moral integrity, and power distance. These lacunas impinge directly on the viability of the genre of Spirit-empowered leadership. Hence, they should be addressed as top priorities in the development of the next generation of leaders in the Spirit-empowered movement.

Spiritual Formation

The first leadership lacuna has to do with spiritual formation. According to Mary Kate Morse, "Christian spiritual formation is the process of being conformed to the image of Jesus Christ for the glory of God and for the sake of others" (2 Cor. 3:17–18)… "The focus of spiritual formation is the Holy Spirit, who guides the ongoing journey towards union with God."[2]

---

1. Raymond D. Gordon, "Conceptualizing Leadership with Respect to its Historical-Contextual Antecedents to Power," *The Leadership Quarterly* 13, no. 2 (April 2002): 151.

2. Mary Kate Morse, "Evangelism, Discipleship, and Spiritual Formation," accessed November 25, 2023, https://www.missioalliance.org/evangelism-discipleship-and-spiritual-formation-which-is-what/.

The students I taught at Hillsong College in Australia were extraordinary. They were brilliant thinkers and avid Spirit-filled servants of Christ with much potential for leadership. Many came from abroad to do the Bachelor of Theology degree. Sadly, the college overworked them, requiring twenty hours of volunteer ministry on top of the full-time course of study and twenty hours of outside employment needed for financial support. It was clear that many students displayed symptoms of burnout, depression, and anxiety, which was made more acute by the constant hype of living the Hillsong dream of unquenchable praise and exhilaration. When the indications of student burnout were brought to the attention of the Hillsong leadership, they took the matter seriously and conducted a student survey, which revealed a gap in the spiritual practices promoted by Hillsong. The missing element was quiet time for spiritual formation.

During my time in Australia (circa 2008-10), I was teaching a class on Christian spirituality at the Hillsong campus in Baulkham Hills, near Sydney. Doing a literature search for a prospective text yielded an array of texts by well-known authors, including Dallas Willard, author of *The Great Omission*, which brought to light the root cause of the missing element in the spiritual formation of my students. Willard's main point is that churches in the Western world have neglected the training of disciples due to two great omissions from the Great Commission. Whereas Jesus directed the Early Church to pursue the goal of making disciples from all nations, teaching them to observe his teaching and baptizing them in the name of the Father, Son, and Holy Spirit, over the centuries the Christian Church drifted in another direction. First, in place of Christ's plan, Christians omitted the making of disciples, relegating discipleship to the preserve of a mature class of believers. Second, instead of training new believers prior to baptism, Christians omitted the step of teaching them to do what Jesus did and relegated it to after baptism, if at all. Having made these two omissions, converts were not trained how to live as Christ lived and taught. Hence, Willard states, "When confronted with the example and teachings of Christ, the response today is less one of rebellion or rejection than one of puzzlement."[3] While spiritual formation is not a new topic within the Church at large, it is a relatively new topic in Spirit-empowered churches, except perhaps for Catholic charismatic communities.

In many Pentecostal and charismatic churches, an intentional process of spiritual formation is not to be found. Teaching is rarely focused on spiritual

---

3. Dallas Willard, *The Great Omission: Reclaiming Jesus' Essential Teachings on Discipleship* (Oxford, UK: Monarch Books, 2006), 6.

disciplines. Rather, the preferred style of spirituality tends to be emotive, kinesthetic and performative with primary emphasis on Spirit-baptism as the chief means of spiritual formation. Frank Macchia finds that "the result is that their chief pneumatological emphasis accents power encounters and signs and wonders, but spiritual formation can become neglected in the process."[4] Macchia explains that the Pentecostal belief in Spirit-baptism as the medium of power encounters normally involves speaking in tongues, prophecy, and divine healing. He then asks, "What do such power encounters or crisis experiences have to do with spiritual formation or one's journey toward deeper union with Christ?" He acknowledges that crisis moments and sudden awakenings that are typical of Pentecostal spirituality "can eclipse the process involved in spiritual formation."[5] Further, he states, "The result was a fateful separation of Spirit baptism from both initiation to Christ and sanctification. Spirit baptism became power detached from union; power detached from purity."[6] Macchia goes on to stress the importance of closing this breach. He sees the problem and advances a lucid theological analysis, but there is something missing in his analysis in that he does not present classic spiritual disciplines as the solution.[7]

According to Charles Dawes, "The lack of a formation process within the Pentecostal movement is disastrous for the spiritual vibrancy of those associated with the movement."[8] Due to a historic demonstration of exclusivity toward other Christian traditions, Pentecostals are left with a narrow understanding and experience of spiritual formation. To make matters worse, some leaders of Spirit-empowered churches have raised concerns about and objections to spiritual formation.[9] Historically, Pentecostals have had serious reservations about Roman Catholic spiritual practices and doubted their efficacy in producing spiritual maturity. In failing to incorporate ancient practices into their worship, some Pentecostals sacrificed a rich legacy of spiritual formation experience. Dawes states, "My tradition provided a model of longer, louder, and lower when it came to prayer. The longer you prayed, the more mature you were in the faith. The volume of your prayer determined validity, and finally the posture in which

---

4. Frank D. Macchia, "Spirit Baptism and Spiritual Formation: A Pentecostal Proposal," *Journal of Spiritual Formation and Soul Care* 13, no. 1 (2020): 44.

5. Macchia, "Spirit Baptism and Spiritual Formation," 47.

6. Macchia, "Spirit Baptism and Spiritual Formation," 49.

7. Macchia, "Spirit Baptism and Spiritual Formation," 58.

8. Charles T. Dawes, "The Jesus Prayer for Pentecostals: A Fresh Proposal for Spiritual Formation in the Pentecostal Church" (D.Min. diss., George Fox Evangelical Seminary, 2013), 13.

9. Jeremy Feller and Christo Lombaard, "Spiritual Formation Towards Pentecostal Leadership as Discipleship," *KOERS: Bulletin for Christian Scholarship* 3, no. 1 (2018): 7.

you prayed was important."[10] Pentecostal spirituality teems with experience and momentum globally, but this expansion needs to be undergirded with spiritual formation practices that connect to the broader Christian tradition while preventing one's Pentecostal heritage from being compromised. Dawes makes a case for the use of the Jesus Prayer as a means of formation for Pentecostals. He highlights the similarities between Eastern Orthodox and Pentecostal spirituality and compares the Jesus Prayer and Pentecostal prayer, commending the Jesus Prayer as a spiritual formation practice for the Pentecostal community.[11]

Willard defines spiritual formation as "the process of shaping our spirit and giving it a definite character. It means the formation of our spirit in conformity with the Spirit of Christ."[12] He urges that the gifts of the Holy Spirit should be actively pursued, received, and cultivated. However, he cautions that "the gifts by themselves do little to form the spirit and character of those who exercise them. Most importantly, he states that gifts of the Spirit are not substitutes for spiritual formation." Spiritual formation requires a clear goal, which is, as Willard states, the inner formation of Christlikeness.[13] Spiritual formation also requires means or practice for attaining the goal. These means include practices known as spiritual disciplines. The term discipline comes from the same word as disciple. As disciples of Jesus, we discipline ourselves to do what Jesus did as well as what he taught.

Spiritual disciplines have been practiced for centuries as methods of pursuing the outcome of Christlikeness. From personal experience, the author has come to see that there is great value in educating students concerning the spiritual disciplines of the Christian tradition and guiding them in these classic practices. As he lectures on the biblical and historical roots of spiritual disciplines and coaches his students in the practice of contemplative prayer, *lectio divina*, meditation on icons, daily examen, and the Jesus Prayer, they invariably experience renewal of their spiritual vitality. The outcome is a sense of wonderment and joy at the perceptible acceleration in their spiritual formation. The author is convinced that although exuberant praise and worship are wonderful and exhilarating, they cannot make up for a lack of time spent in the prayer closet (Matt. 6:5–8). If we truly desire to influence the spiritual vitality of our students for the better, we will prioritize spiritual disciplines as crucial to the process of spiritual formation.

---

10. Dawes, "Jesus Prayer for Pentecostals," 13.
11. Dawes, "Jesus Prayer for Pentecostals, 15–16.
12. Willard, *The Great Omission*, 53.
13. Willard, *The Great Omission*, 116.

The claim I wish to make is that spiritual formation is necessary for the development of Spirit-empowered leaders. According to Dale Coulter, spiritual formation in the context of the Spirit-empowered movement should be concerned with the work of the Holy Spirit in the process of forming believers in the image of Christ.[14] This is a holistic process, informing the mind, conforming behavior, and transforming the inner being toward the image of Christ (Col. 3:9–10). Johnson and Moore define spiritual formation as "the redemptive, grace-filled, Spirit-guided process of conforming the human heart, mind, and actions to the image of Christ in light of the coming Kingdom, to the glory of God, and for the sake of the world."[15] Spiritual formation is a continuous process of growth throughout the human lifespan. In the Spirit-empowered movement, three considerations are weighed in evaluating a candidate's qualifications for leadership. The first is the candidate's competency or skill set. The second is the candidate's gifting. The third is the candidate's calling. Underlying all three is the character of a candidate. The issue of character should be a primary concern in Spirit-empowered leadership. Leadership development must address all three factors—skills, gifts, and calling—but character is most fundamental because of the role it plays in reflecting the image of Christ. Therefore, given that the goal of spiritual formation is union of the whole person with Christ, Feller and Lombaard assert that "spiritual formation for the whole person is necessary for Pentecostal leadership."[16] Hence, spiritual formation should be a key factor in the development of Spirit-empowered leaders.

In the final part of this book, I propose a plan for the development of emerging Spirit-empowered leaders that incorporates the process of spiritual formation, based on the premise that intentional participation in spiritual formation is essential for the growth of spiritual maturity, the transformation of character, and the maintenance of sustainable leadership.

Moral Integrity

The second lacuna in Spirit-empowered leadership is the *moral integrity* of its leaders. All too often another story of moral failure on the part of a well-known

---

14. Dale M. Coulter, "The Whole Gospel of the Whole Person: Ontology, Affectivity, and Sacramentality," *Pneuma: The Journal of the Society for Pentecostal Studies* 35, no. 2 (2013): 161.

15. Bob L. Johnson and Rickie D. Moore, "Soul Care for One and All: Pentecostal Theology and the Search for a More Expansive View of Spiritual Formation," *Journal of Pentecostal Theology* 26, no. 1 (2017): 132.

16. Feller and Lombard, "Spiritual Formation towards Pentecostal Leadership," 6.

and highly respected Christian leader comes out in the media. The impact of such failures on our morale is harmful and devastating. Most disturbing is the effect that moral failures of leaders have on the trust level of followers. I have seen this up close in my role as chair of the ethics committee of the ministerium of my denomination. When it is brought to light that a leader has been living a double life, appearing in public as a model of moral integrity while in private engaging in unethical conduct, followers of the fallen leader experience a betrayal of trust, which it is. The damage done is even more profound because the moral failure of leaders often calls into question the credibility of the beliefs of followers, congregants, and the public. The process of healing in recovery is difficult, can require lengthy counseling, and should not be rushed. If we cherish the value of faithfulness as crucial in Christian faith, we will prioritize moral integrity as a non-negotiable of Spirit-empowered leadership.

"Integrity" is defined in the *Cambridge English Dictionary* as the quality of being honest and having strong moral principles, hence, moral uprightness.[17] Integrity is consistency between what one professes to be true and how one behaves. Moral integrity is a matter of abiding by accepted standards of moral conduct. According to Jerry E. White, "Integrity is both a character trait and a practical discipline. All our talents, success, and skills amount to nothing without personal integrity."[18] For leaders, the ever-present challenge is to maintain integrity in relationships with co-workers. To meet this challenge, leaders should own the basic assumption that leadership is a sacred trust grounded in a divine calling. To be a Spirit-empowered leader is a sacred responsibility. While leadership is a special calling, it is also a practical occupation governed by normative standards of ethical conduct. Members of the profession are expected to meet standards of moral integrity and are accountable for violation of these standards. A Christian leader is ultimately accountable to God for maintaining his or her integrity.

Moral failure has been a recurring problem for leaders in the Spirit-empowered movement since its beginning. A few examples will suffice to verify this point. These examples have led many interested observers to ponder the root causes of the breakdown of moral integrity, develop proactive solutions for the problem of moral failure, and instill the value of moral integrity in emerging Spirit-empowered leaders.

---

17. "Integrity," *Cambridge English Dictionary*, accessed November 18, 2023, https://dictionary.cambridge.org/us/dictionary/english/integrity.

18. Jerry E. White, "Leading with Integrity," *Christian Leadership Challenge*, accessed November 18, 2023, https://ym.christianleadershipalliance.org/page/leadingwithintegrity.

Examples of Moral Failure in the Spirit-Empowered Movement

Charles Fox Parham was a leading figure of early Pentecostalism. He published the first Pentecostal periodical, organized interstate Pentecostal meetings, and issued the first Pentecostal ministerial credentials. Parham fell from prominence due to an alleged moral failure. He and an accomplice were arrested in San Antonio on July 23, 1907, and charged with sodomy, a felony under Texas law. Rumors of Parham's "awful sin" had been circulating since earlier that year, leading to his disfellowship in the early summer from the Texas branch of the Apostolic Faith organization that he had founded. The arrest was based on the testimony of a lone witness, the landlady of the boarding house where Parham stayed. The story of Parham's arrest was carried in the religious and secular press, impugning his stature as a founding father of Pentecostalism.[19]

A catalogue of the most egregious examples of moral failure in the Spirit-empowered movement would have to include Ted Haggard. In November 2006, Haggard resigned as senior pastor of the 14,000-member New Life Church in Colorado Springs and as head of the National Association of Evangelicals. He was alleged to have engaged in immoral exploits. Though Haggard denied the accusation at first, he eventually owned up to the allegations. A letter from Haggard was read to the New Life Church on November 5 in which the founding pastor admitted that he was "guilty of sexual immorality" and "a deceiver and a liar." He said, "There is a part of my life that is so repulsive and dark that I've been warring against it all of my adult life." In January 2009, Brady Boyd, who succeeded Haggard as senior pastor at New Life Church, disclosed that Haggard had an illicit relationship with a member of the church that "went on for a long period of time."[20]

Brian Houston served as co-pastor with his wife Bobby of Hillsong Church in Sydney, Australia, from 1997 to 2009. His father, Frank Houston (d. 2004), was exposed in 1999 as a child molester by one of his victims. After trying unsuccessfully to pay off the victim with $10,000, Frank Houston confessed to that incident, but it was only the tip of the iceberg. A Royal Commission investigation in October 2014 found that Frank had molested at least seven boys, and Brian Houston testified before the commission that he had no

---

19. James R. Goff, Jr., *Fields White unto Harvest: Charles F. Parham and the Missionary Origins of Pentecostalism* (Fayetteville: University of Arkansas Press, 1988), 136–39.

20. "Disgraced Pastor Faces More Gay Sex Allegations," Associated Press, January 24, 2009; Steve Rabey, "Editor Decries Pentecostal Shrugs over Moral Failures," *Christian Century* (June 15, 2010): 117–18.

doubt there were others. The pedophilia began when Frank Houston was a Pentecostal leader in New Zealand. Subsequently Brian Houston resigned from Hillsong after internal investigations reported he had engaged in inappropriate conduct of "serious concern" with two women.[21]

The most recent scandal involved Robert Morris, founding pastor of Gateway Church in Dallas, who led the megachurch for decades before his resignation after allegations of sexual abuse came to light. His downfall occurred after Cindy, Morris's accuser came forward with her story that Morris began sexually abusing her in the early 1980s when she was twelve years old and he was in his twenties. After the allegations were made public, Morris admitted to his congregation that he was "involved in inappropriate sexual behavior with a young lady." Overwhelming public backlash ensued, and Morris ultimately decided to resign from the church on June 18, 2024.[22]

What can we learn from these vexing incidents in the history of Spirit-empowered leadership? First, we can learn from history by knowing about it. The stories of moral failure, painful and disappointing as they may be, need to be told. Second, there is much to be learned from the scholarship of leadership studies. The following section reviews the findings of scholars who help us to discern roots of the problem and diagnose points of vulnerability in leaders who have compromised their moral integrity. Third is the exploration of a proactive solution for preventing future recurrence of moral failure.

Roots of the Problem

Diane Chandler, in an article on the unethical behavior of leaders, explores the question of how leaders can make poor ethical decisions. She discerns a pattern of intrapersonal and interpersonal factors that contribute to moral failure. The intrapersonal factors include unresolved childhood needs, personality determinants, moral values, character weakness, and internalized

---

21. "Hillsong Leader Brian Houston Breaks Silence on Pedophile Father," *The Daily Telegraph*, Sydney, October 13, 2014, accessed November 18, 2023, https://www.dailytelegraph.com.au/news/nsw/hillsong-leader-brian-houston-breaks-silence-on-paedophile-father-it-was-wrong-not-to-report-him/news-story/ 6530b4352962bc835e8fb2f906d657cf; "Hillsong's Brian Houston Resigns from Megachurch," *The Daily Telegraph*, March 23, 2022, accessed November 18, 2023, https://www.theguardian.com/world/2022/mar/23/hillsongs-brian-houston-resigns-from-megachurch.

22. Ryan Osborne, "'We Are Deeply Sorry': Gateway Church Cancels Major Conference in Wake of Robert Morris Resignation." WFFA Dallas, August 15, 2024, accessed November 18, 2023, https://www.wfaa.com/article/news/local/gateway-church-robert-morris-allegations-gateway-conference-canceled-investigation-tony-evans/287-07160d0d-3d05-4058-b4c4-c3df32cb0d5a.

success stressors.[23] These factors are more likely to be in play when a leader has an inordinate desire to be in charge. They are conducive to rationalization of unethical behavior, propensity to deception, and the "Bathsheba Syndrome" of moral lapse and cover-up. The interpersonal factors include unrestrained charisma, abuse of personalized power, deficiencies in interpersonal skills, and lack of accountability and support systems. Chandler's analysis of charisma is particularly relevant to Spirit-empowered leadership. She holds that charismatic leaders tend to lead by casting a compelling vision, relying on an expressive style of communication, taking personal risks, and projecting high expectations of followers. When a charismatic leader curries inordinate allegiance, he or she can lapse into moral indiscretion if systems of accountability are not in place or the leader is averse to honest and well-intended critique. According to Howell and Avolio, "Unethical charismatic leaders select or produce obedient, dependent, and compliant followers." In so doing they hinder followers from expressing alternative views and inhibit feedback and accountability. The downside of this pattern is that a leader's moral deviation goes unchallenged.

In his article, "Bridging the Gap between Pentecostal Holiness and Morality," Tham Wan Yee examines the problem of moral failure in Pentecostalism, attributing it to a gap between "what is preached and what is practiced,...a sharp divergence between creed and character, or between beliefs and behavior."[24] As he peers deeper into the root of this syndrome, Yee diagnoses the problem as a lack of a proactive plan for moral development. He states, "Pentecostals are strong in preaching against immorality but have a weak educational and organizational structure for moral development." He proceeds to suggest "reasons why Pentecostals have so easily failed in the department of moral character development among their constituents."[25] Yee surmises that the chief reason is that spirituality is seen as being on a higher plane than morality to the extent that Pentecostals assume that morality will be an automatic product of spirituality.[26] The result is a bifurcation of power and purity. In holding that the outcome of Spirit baptism is an enduement of power, with a vague link to holiness, leading scholars in the Assemblies of God such

---

23. Diane J. Chandler, "The Perfect Storm of Leaders' Unethical Behavior," *International Journal of Leadership Studies* 5, no. 1 (2009): 74.

24. Tham Wan Yee, "Bridging the Gap Between Pentecostal Holiness and Morality," *Asian Journal of Pentecostal Studies* 4, no. 2 (2001): 156.

25. Yee, "Bridging the Gap," 162.

26. Yee, "Bridging the Gap," 163.

as Robert Menzies have distanced holiness from the ambit of Pentecostal experience. Yee argues that "such a dichotomy, however unintentional, has often placed power away and ahead of purity."[27] The same cannot be said of the Wesleyan wing of Classical Pentecostalism, which has maintained a high view of sanctification. Yet the relaxation of its historic stipulation of sanctification as a precondition for Spirit baptism may have had a similar albeit lesser effect of placing power ahead of purity.

In *Understanding Ethical Failures in Leadership*, Terry Price argues that ethical failures in leadership are fundamentally cognitive, not volitional. He writes, "Leader immorality is more a matter of belief and knowledge than a matter of desire and will." Price holds that ethical failures in leadership are primarily due to mistaken moral beliefs: "Leaders can believe, based on the importance of the collective ends they seek to achieve, that they are justified in making exceptions of themselves and in excluding others from the protections of morality."[28] Exception-making occurs when a leader holds a mistaken belief that their actions can be excepted from the scope of normal moral requirements. Price asks, "Why would leaders mistakenly believe that they are justified in making exceptions of themselves?"[29] He explains that leaders tend to think about their behavior in ways that allow for deviations from generally applicable moral requirements, justifying the making of exceptions on the basis of the demands placed on them by the complex situations they face. They tend to believe that they are justified in violating generally applicable moral requirements because they are over-ridden by other values to which they are committed, such as the importance of their work. The result is the inevitability of moral fallibility. Price acknowledges that current leaders display a "robust awareness of fallibility as moral agents" and acceptance of "the specific inclinations behind immoral social practices." Yet, in the final analysis, Price comes down on the side of moral leadership, calling for "contemporary leaders to adopt a principle of inclusiveness at the margins of moral community, even though this principle is in direct conflict with many of our most common presuppositions about the nature of leadership."[30]

---

27. Yee, "Bridging the Gap," 165.

28. Terry L. Price, *Understanding Ethical Failures in Leadership* (Cambridge: Cambridge University Press, 2006), 1.

29. Price, *Understanding Ethical Failures*, 7.

30. Price, *Understanding Ethical Failures*, 10.

Proactive Solution

It's important to explore proactive solutions for preventing future recurrences of moral failure among emerging Spirit-empowered leaders. To begin, we can rule out moral legalism as a solution for moral failure. Restrictions against drinking alcohol have not prevented leaders for lapsing in their sobriety. Strict sexual moral prohibitions of marital infidelity and same sex relationships have not prevented leaders form cheating on their spouses or engaging in same sex dalliances. Legal penalties for extortion and cheating on tax reports have not kept leaders from financial fraud and facing criminal charges. The most efficacious proactive solution is to develop leaders who model moral integrity in their personal lives and organizational relationships. The foundation of moral integrity is the leader's character, as displayed in thoughts, decisions, and actions that are consistent with accepted standards of Christian ethics, such as love, mercy, justice, righteousness, faithfulness and trustworthiness. Perhaps the ideal traits of Christian character are summed up in the fruit of the Spirit: love, joy, peace, patience, kindness, goodness, faithfulness, gentleness, and self-control. How does one develop these qualities of Christian character?

The Bible supplies an answer to this question. The starting place of Paul's theory of moral integrity is the mind, that is, moral apprehension (Rom. 12:2). In depicting the locus of renewal in the mind, Paul is in effect asserting that belief or intellectual apprehension is a crucial prerequisite for moral development. Yet, belief by itself is not the whole picture. Belief must be activated by an act of the will (decision) and then translated into action. Moral integrity emerges as a person responds to real moral challenges with apprehension of God's will, decision to comply with the will of God, and corresponding moral action. We will incorporate this basic biblical schema into a case study.

Let's consider a hypothetical situation in which a leader is presented with a moral dilemma due to an unkept promise. He or she had previously committed to an appointment with a staff member for guidance and mentoring. Then a wealthy congregant invited the leader to accompany him on a luxury cruise on the family yacht, and the leader immediately accepted the offer. Shall the leader tell the truth that a better offer has been received, or fabricate an excuse along the lines of a rationalizing his or her change of plans as a ministry opportunity? At this point the leader can engage the cognitive dimension by reflecting on what is the right thing to do, interpreting the moral situation, and considering how it might be resolved.

The *affective dimension* or evaluation stage kicks in when the conscience is activated with impulses such as guilt feelings, ethical values, allegiances or commitments. Sticking with our hypothetical, the leader has put himself in a bind. He is torn between his desire for a pleasurable experience on the congregant's yacht and his allegiance to the ethical principle of telling the truth. He feels like he may lose faith with his staff member if he tells the truth, yet he does not want to own up to his duplicity in opting for the cruise over mentoring the staff member. A Christian reflects on his or her allegiances by processing the feelings evoked by the moral situation. A strong anchor to the moral teachings of the Scriptures is of inestimable value in navigating the waters between the cognitive and affective dimensions and positioning one for safe harbor (no pun intended) in the behavioral dimension.

The above processing acts as safe passage to the *behavioral dimension* that takes one into the realm of the will, the instrument of acting on a decision. Not all decisions result in action. In fact, in some cases non-action could be the most moral course of action; yet in other cases action will be the appropriate response. In both cases, in the decision stage a person is faced with choosing an act of the will to do the right thing and doing it.[31] In the case of our hypothetical, a decision has been made, and action is required to untangle the double-booking. The use of moral dilemma stories is an effective method for instructing emerging leaders on the development of moral integrity. After posing a dilemma, like the above hypothetical story, the instructor would ask the leaders in training, "what would you do and why? How would you navigate each of the dimensions?"

If emerging leaders can be trained to process moral situations by working through the above three dimensions using moral dilemma stories, they would be in a better position to deal with real life moral dilemmas. In a lab setting, they would practice a sequence of moral reasoning, comprised of the cognitive, affective, and behavioral dimensions, equipping them with a method of working through the stages of apprehension, evaluation, and decision. The outcome of our approach is internalization of a biblical pattern of making moral choices. It is through the accumulation of one's choices that a person advances in moral character with the end in view of building one's moral house on a solid foundation, as in Christ's image of the rock (Matt. 5:24–27). The end in view is that moral character is the accretion of moral actions over a period of time.[32]

---

31. Yee, "Bridging the Gap," 168–70.
32. Yee, "Bridging the Gap," 171.

Leadership is a sacred trust grounded in a divine calling. To be a Spirit-empowered leader is a sacred responsibility. Failure to uphold moral integrity represents a recurrent trend in Spirit-empowered leaders that has the effect of eroding trust and calling into question the credibility of the religious convictions of followers. The root of the problem was found to lie in a pattern of intrapersonal and interpersonal factors that contribute to moral failure. The intrapersonal factors include unresolved childhood needs, personality determinants, moral values and character weakness, and internalized success stressors. The interpersonal factors include unrestrained charisma, abuse of personalized power, deficiencies in interpersonal skills, and lack of accountability and support systems. Both sets of factors are exacerbated by an inordinate desire for power which opens the door for unethical leaders to prey on obedient, dependent, and compliant followers by inhibiting feedback and accountability. The downside of this pattern is that a leader's moral deviation goes unchallenged. Proactive solutions are advanced, the most efficacious of which is to develop leaders who model moral integrity in their personal lives and organizational relationships.

Power Distance

The third lacuna in Spirit-empowered leadership is *power distance*. In any organization with leaders and followers, such as a church, school, or mission agency, there are relative levels of power and authority. Power distance refers to the relationship between leaders and followers and how they interact with each other. Leadership scholars differentiate between high and low power distance. In an organization with high power distance, leadership is more likely to function as a hierarchy where everybody has a place, authority does not require further justification, and high-ranking individuals are respected and looked up to. In an organization with low power distance, leadership is more likely to function as a democracy in which the aim is to distribute power equally. Due to the premium placed on equality and collaboration, additional justification is often needed for the exercise of authority. In general, more autocratic or authoritarian leadership[33] flourishes when power distance is high and democratic leadership thrives when

---

33. Authoritarian leadership, as it is defined by the author in this study, is in play when a leader assumes absolute control over decision-making, eschews consultation with subordinates and communication with followers, and demands unquestioning obedience. See Ella Pizzolitto, Ida Verna, and Michellna Venditti, "Authoritarian Leadership Styles and Performance: A Systematic Literature Review and Research Agenda," *Management Review Quarterly* 73 (2023): 841–71; https://doi.org/10.1007/s11301-022-00263-y.

power distance is low. In autocratic leadership, much of the power is concentrated in the hands of a few leaders or even one person. In democratic leadership, power is distributed throughout an organization by means of collaborative processes of consultation, decision-making, and shared governance.

This section poses a question concerning high and low power distance. Is one or the other more appropriate for Spirit-empowered leadership? In the Spirit-empowered movement we find some leaders who opt for high power distance and others who opt for low power distance. Should one be preferred over the other? Answers to the question are not imposed on the readers; instead, we let readers decide for themselves. Our aim is to present an exposition of the dynamics of power distance and discuss critical issues that are relevant to Spirit-empowered leadership.

Theory of Power Distance

The concept of power distance originated with research conducted by the Dutch social psychologist Geert Hofstede. His area of specialization focused on how values in the workplace are influenced by culture. Hofstede defines culture as "the collective programming of the mind distinguishing the members of one group or category of people from others."[34] Along with his research team, Hofstede formulates six dimensions of national culture, which are the following:

1. Power Index
2. Individualism versus Collectivism
3. Masculinity versus Femininity
4. Uncertainty Avoidance Index
5. Long-Term Orientation versus Short-Term Normative Orientation
6. Indulgence versus Restrain

Hofstede's six dimensions have been applied worldwide in both academic and professional management settings. Hofstede analyzed a large database of employee value scores collected within IBM between 1967 and 1973. The data covered more than seventy countries, from which Hofstede first used forty countries with the largest groups of respondents and afterwards extended the analysis to fifty countries and three regions. Subsequent studies validating the earlier results include such respondent groups as commercial airline pilots and students in twenty-three countries, civil service managers in fourteen countries, "up-market" consumers in fifteen countries, and "elites" in nineteen countries.

---

34. G. H. Hofstede, "National Culture," *Hofstede Insights,* May 11, 2022, accessed November 18, 2023, https://hi.hofstede-insights.com/national-culture.

In the 2010 edition of Hofstede's *Cultures and Organizations: Software of the Mind,"* scores on the six dimensions are listed for seventy countries, partly based on replications and extensions of the IBM study on different international populations and the work of other scholars.[35]

Our primary interest pertains to how Hofstede conceives of the first dimension of national culture, the power index. Hofstede sees power distance as related to the inequalities that exist in different societies, which he defines as "the extent to which a society accepts the fact that power in institutions and organizations is distributed unequally."[36] The power gap raises the question of the extent to which subordinates are or are not free to express disagreement with supervisors and supervisors are or are not expected to consult with their subordinates in the decision-making process. Levels of power distance are determined by how willing employees are to accept a situation in which a boss has more power than they have. Hofstede found that in high power distance countries, it is considered important to consult the boss before taking on a major task or making decisions, while in low power distance countries employers expect subordinates to rely on their skills to initiate actions on their own.[37] The power distance dimension of a country has an effect on the styles of leadership that are applicable in its society.

Expanding upon the work of Hofstede, the GLOBE Project created a tool for measuring how a society practices power distance and how the society values it (how it should be).[38] GLOBE attested to find a universal desire to see power distance reduced in society, based on the premise that low power distance is intrinsic to the human spirit and high-power distance is associated with authoritarian values, low economic production, and low quality of life. Whereas Hofstede depicted how power distance was practiced in an organization, the GLOBE instrument prescribed how people should engage in work and leadership. In discussing effective leadership behaviors, the GLOBE project asserted that democracy, the middle class, and immigrant flows had moved societies toward lower power distance. GLOBE found that "regardless of the religion, any society that has neither a democratic tradition nor an established middle class will have a relatively high level

---

35. Hofstede, "National Culture."

36. Geert H. Hofstede, *Culture's Consequences: Comparing Values, Behaviors, Institutions and Organizations across Nations* (Thousand Oaks: Sage, 2001), 45.

37. Hofstede, *Culture's Consequences*, 87.

38. R. J. House, M. Javidan, P. Hanges, P. Dorfman, and Gupta V. ed., *Culture, Leadership and Organizations: The GLOBE Study of 62 Societies* (Thousand Oaks: Sage, 2004).

of power distance."[39] GLOBE observed that while Hofstede's power distance index calibrated how power distance is practiced, it did not assess how it is valued (how it should be).[40] GLOBE showed that high-power distance cultures reinforce social conformity, especially among those of lower socioeconomic status. In contrast, those who have lower levels of power distance expect to voluntarily participate in societies and organizations. Further, GLOBE found that the correlation between low power distance and financial stability in the middle class was related to a desire to have a voice in decision-making processes in organizations and society. Given this correlation, GLOBE reasoned, it follows that it is incumbent upon an ethical leader to reduce power distance in their organizations and societies.

Research on power distance since Hofstede, such as GLOBE, has observed correlations between power distance and patterns of leadership in relation to work-related processes and outcomes, including well-being, attitude-behavior, emotions, justice, abusive supervision, leadership, feedback/performance ratings, human resource management practices, organizational innovation, venture creation, ethics and corporate social responsibility.[41] We will touch on some of the findings of this body of research. The consensus is that power distance is associated with lower levels of well-being at the national level, yet higher job satisfaction at the individual level. Followers in high and low power distance contexts prefer different leader behaviors. Leaders in high power distance cultures seem to engender more mimicry in followers; whereas transformational leadership styles are more likely to thrive and impact follower outcomes in lower power distance cultures. New ideas for organizational innovation are often negated in high power distance cultures because they seem to threaten the social hierarchy. Ethics violations are generally more common in high power distance countries, probably because there are fewer checks and balances on those in power.[42] In terms of power distance and leadership, with greater power distance, leaders have more influence on followers because followers defer to the leader, have greater respect for leaders, develop more formalized relationships, and internalize leader expectations to a greater extent. Undoubtedly, power distance affects how leaders and followers tend to interact. The research on transformational leadership, inaugurated by Bass in 1985,[43] indicates that the prototype of a transformational

---

39. House, et al., *Culture, Leadership and Organizations*, 526.

40. House, et al., *Culture, Leadership, and Organizations*, 543.

41. Michael A. Daniels and Gary J. Greguras, "Exploring the Nature of Power Distance." *Journal of Management* 40, no. 5 (2014): 1208–11.

42. Daniels and Greguras, "Exploring Power Distance," 1209–11.

43. Bernard M. Bass, *Leadership and Performance beyond Expectations* (New York: Free Press,

leader contrasts with typical leadership styles in high power distance societies. Transformational leaders prefer charismatic influence, inspirational motivation, and intellectual stimulation of followers. The evidence suggests that high power distance exacerbates the effect of transformational leadership. This could be because both subordinates and supervisors in high power distance cultures may feel a level of discomfort with feedback, interpreting it as disrespectful to the leader. As such, research demonstrates that upward feedback in high power distance contexts tends to be more lenient.[44]

Power Distance in Spirit-Empowered Leadership

We can draw implications for Spirit-empowered leadership from the research of Hofstede and the GLOBE project. In scanning the global breadth of the Spirit-empowered movement, one finds that power distance in Spirit-empowered leadership generally correlates with a given context, depending on the high or low power distance of the national culture. In the case of Nigeria, which is rated as a having high power distance national culture, if we were to take Benson Idahosa, Enoch Adeboye, or David Oyedepo as representative cases of African Spirit-empowered leadership, we would find that the level of power distance in these Spirit-empowered leaders falls in line with the national culture. These leaders exhibit an autocratic leadership style in which the general overseer makes decisions in a unilateral fashion with a minimal degree of accountability.[45] Being a Pentecostal pastor in Africa can be a source of considerable power and respect, comparable to the prestige of a traditional "big man."[46] In recent decades Pentecostal-charismatic leaders in Africa have extended their influence by means of popular culture, entertainment, and mass media. Some churches operate publishing houses, radio and television stations. Several purchase time on public stations to broadcast videotaped services, sermons, and choir performances.[47] Pentecostal-charismatic gospel songs are often played at non-religious events,

---

1985).

44. Daniels and Greguras, "Exploring Power Distance," 1215–17.

45. Grace Ogechukwu Okoranta, "The Impact of Leadership Styles in the Pentecostal Churches on the Growth of the Gospel in Kaduna State." (M.A. thesis, Ahmadu Bello University, Zaria, Nigeria, 2015), xiii.

46. John F. McCauley, "Pentecostalism as an Informal Political Institution: Experimental Evidence from Ghana," *Politics and Religion* 7 (2014): 765–70.

47. Martin Lindhardt, "Introduction: Presence and Impact of Pentecostal Charismatic Christianity in Africa," in *Pentecostalism in Africa: Presence and Impact of Pneumatic Christianity in Postcolonial Societies*, ed. Martin Lindhardt (Leiden: Brill, 2015), 22.

such as electoral campaigns.[48] The blurring of boundaries between religion and secular entertainment is not limited to Africa. Lindhardt states that it is present in other parts of the world, particularly Latin America, where Pentecostals take advantage of access to mass media. For example, the Universal Church of the Kingdom of God in Brazil runs its own television station. Yet African Pentecostal-charismatic celebrities far outnumber those in Latin America.[49] Lindhardt holds that their power and influence is facilitated "not only by their skills as public entertainers and by their increased access to the media, which allows for new kinds of careful staging of personal charisma," through which they project an image of success in material affairs, allegedly due to successful management of spiritual forces. In short, these celebrities claim to be channels of extraordinary spiritual powers, deserving respect and awe.[50]

In the case of Norway, which is rated as a low power distance country, the level of power distance accorded to its Spirit-empowered leaders does not entirely fall in line with the national culture. One might expect that Pentecostal leaders in Norway would prioritize democratic values. However, this is only partially the case. In Norwegian Pentecostalism it is up to the pastoral leader to set the direction for the Pentecostal congregation by setting goals within a biblical perimeter, yet at the same time leadership rests more on persuasion than position. The Norwegian Pentecostal leader depends on the community's recognition of his or her authority and as such there is a dialectic relationship between agency and structure involving an appropriate level of accountability that hinges on the leader's ability to adapt to the organization.[51] At first glance, it appears that Pentecostal leadership in Africa and Norway largely falls in line with the power distance of the respective national cultures. Yet, upon closer examination the picture is not so clear. In the context of Norway, a low power distance country, the verdict is mixed concerning the affinity between Pentecostal leadership and democratic principles and values. Åkerlund holds that while Pentecostalism is democratic in the sense that charisma is open to everyone, stratification occurs in that some members are seen as more exemplary than others. He writes, "In this aspect, charismatic leaders in Pentecostalism have roles parallel to saints in the Catholic tradition."[52] The role of a Pentecostal leader is bolstered by a particular approach to the Bible. Åkerlund explains, "When the charismatic

---

48. Lindhardt, "Presence and Impact," 23.

49. Lindhardt, "Presence and Impact," 25.

50. Lindhardt, "Presence and Impact," 27.

51. Åkerlund, *A Phenomenology of Pentecostal Leadership*, 72.

52. Åkerlund, *A Phenomenology of Pentecostal Leadership*, 42.

leader transforms the biblical text into something alive and tangible, he or she replaces the authority of Scripture itself."[53] In Pentecostal preaching, a pastor customarily relies on private spiritual impressions from the Spirit to understand the deeper meaning and relevance of a text, thereby enhancing his or her authority as one who deciphers the Word of God. Åkerlund avers, "The unstable nature of charismatic leadership moderates the autocratic tendencies in Pentecostal leadership."[54] Thus, Åkerlund finds a latent tension in Pentecostal leaders between a radical open egalitarianism (all have the same access to the empowering Spirit) and the notions of hierarchy and submission (the Spirit has empowered some to lead and others to follow).[55]

One finds the same sort of equivocation regarding the compatibility of Pentecostalism and democracy in scholarly studies of other regions. Paul Freston observes that Latin American growth in Evangelical Protestantism, and particularly Pentecostalism, can be seen as coinciding with processes of democratization and re-democratization.[56] Martin Lindhardt, in his study of "Pentecostal Politics in Neo-Liberal Chile," notes that the British sociologist David Martin acknowledges that Pentecostal religion teaches skills that are functional in terms of democratic participation. These include the ability to express oneself in public and to organize church events, and the capacity to create voluntary associations.[57] Martin characterizes Protestantism, including Pentecostalism, as an anti-hierarchical religion where "like-minded" individuals constitute a kind of egalitarian community. This, he claims, is more modern and democratic than the hierarchical and absolutist "old-fashioned" Catholic Hispanic culture, which has been challenged in Latin-American societies by the growth of Protestantism not only religiously, but also politically and socially. Lindhardt observes that in Pentecostalism the distinction between ritual experts (priests) and lay people is not as marked as in the Catholic Church.[58] Lay Pentecostals participate actively in ritual life, for instance, as preachers in religious and in public squares, as faith healers, as narrators of testimonies, and as prophets and Sunday school teachers. Furthermore, Pentecostalism promotes values such

---

53. Åkerlund, *A Phenomenology of Pentecostal Leadership*, 42.

54. Åkerlund, *A Phenomenology of Pentecostal Leadership*, 43.

55. Åkerlund, *A Phenomenology of Pentecostal Leadership*, 43.

56. Paul Freston, ed. *Evangelical Christianity and Democracy in Latin America: Evangelical Christianity and Democracy in the Global South* (New York: Oxford University Press, 2008), 3.

57. David Martin, *Pentecostalism: The World Their Parish* (Malden, MA: Blackwell, 2002), 88.

58. Martin Lindhardt, "Pentecostalism and Politics in Neo-Liberal Chile," *Iberoamericana: Nordic Journal of Latin American and Caribbean Studies* 42, no. 1¬2 (2012): 73.

as individual autonomy, self-esteem and self-expression that are compatible with democratic principles and with Enlightenment notions of personhood that inform modernist democratic ideologies. Lindhardt also refers to the work of Peter Berger, who finds an "exceptionally high" affinity between Pentecostalism and modern democracy.[59] The waves of democratization that have swept Latin America during recent decades have been accompanied by the continuing growth and outreach of Pentecostal churches. Leading researchers have reported that Latin American Pentecostals have positive attitudes towards democracy.[60] In particular, studies of Pentecostalism in a variety of Latin American countries show that relationships between spouses tend to become more democratic (based on dialogue and consensus) after conversion to Pentecostalism.[61] In other words, Pentecostalism contains several democratic elements or features.

However, even though there may be a certain affinity between Pentecostalism and modern democracy in terms of values, notions of individual autonomy, and the organizational and rhetoric skills required of competent participants, Lindhardt argues that certain disaffinities need to be taken into consideration. Unholy alliances between Pentecostal leaders and authoritarian regimes such as Augusto Pinochet's military government in Chile (1973–1990) seem to support a view of Pentecostalism as a conservative and authoritarian religion, whose marked otherworldliness, or anti-worldliness, finds consonance with political systems where popular political mobilization is discouraged. Hence, Lindhardt concludes that although Pentecostalism may contain certain democratic qualities, there is also a striking compatibility with autocratic leadership and a neo-liberal social order where political apathy is widespread and where a privatized rather than a communal and associative sense of progress predominates.[62] Wolfgang Vondey concedes that there is a measure of support for democratic values in Pentecostalism, yet he also detects "unresolved tensions" between egalitarian ideals and the institutionalization of the movement, resulting in racial and gender discrimination, exclusive fellowship, and hierarchal forms of leadership and administration. Hence, Vondey states that one cannot "speak in general terms

---

59. Lindhardt, "Pentecostalism and Politics in Neo-Liberal Chile," 74.

60. Michael Dodson, "Pentecostals, Politics and Public Space in Latin America," in *Power, Politics and Pentecostals in Latin America*, ed. Edward L. Cleary and Hanna W. Stewart-Gambino (Boulder, CO: Westview Press, 1997), 25–26; Freston, *Evangelical Christianity and Democracy in Latin America*, 228.

61. Lindhardt, "Pentecostalism and Politics in Neoliberal Chile," 74; David Martin, *Tongues of Fire: The Explosion of Pentecostalism in Latin America* (Oxford: Blackwell, 1990), 180.

62. Lindhardt, "Pentecostalism and Politics in Neoliberal Chile," 61.

of Pentecostalism as an egalitarian movement....It is therefore more accurate to speak of Pentecostalism as an egalitarian movement in development."[63]

We can conclude that in the regions of the world where Spirit-empowered Christianity is vigorously flourishing, namely the Global South, the tendency is toward leadership styles that exhibit high power distance. It would then follow that Spirit-empowered leadership, as it expands in the West through the phenomena of reverse mission and migration, will increasingly gravitate toward higher power distance. Is this a positive development? That depends on how one regards the mixed bag of correlations, reported above by Daniels and Gregarus, between power distance and patterns of leadership in relation to work-related processes and outcomes. On the positive side of the equation, leaders who operate with higher power distance have more influence on followers because followers defer to the leader, have greater respect for leaders, develop more formalized relationships, and internalize leader expectations to a greater extent. On the negative side, higher power distance militates against collaboration and consultation between leaders and followers. Both subordinates and supervisors in high power distance cultures may feel a level of discomfort with feedback, interpreting it as disrespectful to the leader. Research demonstrates that upward feedback in high power distance contexts tends to be more lenient, that is, more accepting of unilateral practices of autocratic leaders. As an overall result, higher power distance is correlated with conformity to strict social roles, maintenance of the status quo, limited social progress, and a tenuous sense of well-being.[64]

The best prospect for meeting the leadership challenge of power distance lies in an amplification of the democratic impulses of Pentecostalism in the process of leadership development in the Spirit-empowered movement. The author's conviction is that the challenge implicit in a drift toward higher power distance can be met by training emerging leaders to follow the path of transformational leadership, with its preference for charismatic influence, inspirational motivation, and intellectual stimulation of followers.

Conclusion

This chapter took note of three lacunas that impinge directly on the well-being of the genre of Spirit-empowered leadership and argued that these gaps should therefore be addressed in development of the next generation of leaders

---

63. Wolfgang Vondey, *Pentecostalism: A Guide for the Perplexed* (London: Bloomsbury, 2013), 125–26.

64. Daniels and Greguras, "Exploring Power Distance," 1207.

of the Spirit-empowered movement. Building on our discussion of the defining characteristics of Spirit-empowered leadership and three lacunas in Spirit-empowered leadership, the next part of the book presents historical sketches of Spirit-empowered leaders whose influence has proven to be formative in shaping the contours of contemporary Spirit-empowered leadership in its diverse global contexts. I will present evidence in the historical sketches, showing that successive waves of Spirit-empowered leaders not only manifested the defining characteristics delineated in chapter 1, but also were beset with the nagging challenges engendered by the lacunas set forth in chapter 2.

PART TWO

HISTORICAL SKETCHES OF SPIRIT-EMPOWERED LEADERS

Two questions come to the fore in this part of the book concerning the historical genealogy of Spirit-empowered leadership. How has this genre of leadership developed over time? To what extent has the prototype of Spirit-empowered leadership preserved its *élan vital* as the Pentecostal-charismatic movement assumed different historical, cultural, and theological variations? We will attempt to answer these questions by means of diachronic analysis of historical sketches of specific Spirit-empowered leaders. Leaders were selected based on their influence in shaping the leadership practices in four eras in the history of global Spirit-empowered leadership—precursors, early Pentecostal leaders, neo-Pentecostal leaders, and Global South charismatic leaders.

As we survey the succession of leaders in four historical phases, two formative dynamics in the emergence of Spirit-empowered leadership will be observed. First, the essential factor in the formation of a Spirit-empowered leader is the primacy of experience of the Holy Spirit. Spirit-empowered leadership originates with an experience of spiritual empowerment imparted through a transformative encounter with the Holy Spirit. This encounter is customarily associated with healing, prophecy, exorcism, calling, trance, and/ or vision. Second, the driving force in historical development of the tradition of Spirit-empowered leadership has been explosive growth, increasingly tending toward transcendence of pre-existing denominational forms. An analogy can be drawn with the expansion of the Christian movement from its origins as a sect within Judaism to a universal faith encompassing the Gentile world. The breakthrough to global expansion of the New Testament church can be traced to visionary experiences of the leading apostles, Peter and Paul, through which the Holy Spirit-empowered a new global dimension of mission. As the early Christian movement grew by means of an outward flow from its point of origin in the Land of Israel to diverse global regions, so has the Spirit-empowered movement expanded beyond its historical roots in Western holiness traditions and emerged as the driving force of the explosive growth of Christianity in the Global South.

The purpose of the following chapters is to trace the development of patterns of Spirit-empowered leadership as exemplified by specific leaders. Much can be learned about leadership from case studies of influential Christian leaders.[1] This part of the book is organized in four chapters, each covering a historical phase of Spirit-empowered leadership. Chapter 3 provides historical sketches of notable evangelical and holiness leaders who are recognized as "precursors of Pentecostalism"—John Wesley, Edward Irving, Charles Finney, Phoebe Palmer, John Christian Arulappan, and John Alexander Dowie. Chapter 4 focuses on "seminal leaders of the early Pentecostal movement"—Charles Parham, William Seymour, Aimee Semple McPherson, Francisco Olazábal, Pandita Ramabai, Lillian Trasher, C. H. Mason, Garfield Haywood, and Mok Lai Chi. In chapter 5, the focus is on "neo-Pentecostal leaders" of charismatic movements with a global reach, including Kenneth Hagin, Oral Roberts, David Yonggi Cho, Derek Prince, and Léon-Joseph Suenens. Chapter 6 looks at "charismatic leaders of the Global South" who made important contributions to the growth of subaltern Spirit-empowered movements that blossomed in the 1970s and 1980s with the advent of modern digital technologies—Peter Anim, Benson Idahosa, David Oyedepo, Edir Macedo Bezerra, and Mike Velarde. Finally, based on the findings of the historical sketches, there is a summative assessment of the historical development of the essential characteristics of Spirit-empowered leadership as well as the ongoing challenges posed by the lacunas in the areas of spiritual formation, moral integrity, and power distance.

---

1. J. Robert Clinton, *Leadership Emergence Theory: A Self-Study Manual for Analyzing the Development of a Christian Leader* (Altadena, CA: Barnabas Resources, 1989), 70–71.

3

PRECURSORS

Pentecostals trace their origin to the New Testament apostles and the experience of speaking in tongues on the day of Pentecost, recorded in Acts 2. However, the history of the modern-day Pentecostal movement has its roots in the late nineteenth century. Prior to the Azusa Street Revival in 1906,[1] reports surfaced of Spirit baptism, sanctification subsequent to conversion, and outbreaks of charismatic gifts. Revivals spontaneously generated by the Holy Spirit surfaced in disparate geographical regions. Below are historical sketches of six leaders who are widely recognized as precursors of Pentecostalism, beginning with John Wesley.

John Wesley (1703–1791), Anglican clergyman, co-founder of the Methodist movement with his brother Charles and a central figure in the Evangelical Awakening in England, devoted his life to the cause of holiness of heart and life. After concluding studies at Oxford University, he made a failed attempt as a missionary in the colony of Georgia. He experienced a spiritual renewal when his heart was strangely warmed during the reading of the preface of Luther's *Commentary on Romans* at the famous Aldersgate meeting of 1738. Because of disenchantment with traditional church ministry, following in the footsteps of George Whitefield, he disavowed a settled pastorate and opted to preach to masses of unchurched commoners in parish cemeteries, factories, and fields, itinerating widely to follow up on converts. Wesley was an avid reader, drawing on eclectic sources, with broad interests in the church fathers, health, and social ministries. He organized class meetings, small groups for study, accountability, worship, and outreach. He trained lay leaders, both men and women, to lead class meetings and serve as preachers. Wesley envisioned holiness as consisting of Christian perfection, or perfect love. According to Henry Knight, Wesley

---

1. The Azusa Street Revival is commonly regarded as the historic event that launched the Classical Pentecostal Movement and its trademark practices of speaking in tongues, healing, and prophecy. It occurred in Los Angeles over a period of three to five years and was known for its interracial composition and the global missionary impulse that it unleashed. See Vinson Synan, *The Holiness-Pentecostal Tradition: Charismatic Movements in the Twentieth Century* (Grand Rapids: Eerdmans, 1971, 1997), 84–142.

viewed salvation as both instantaneous and a process, entailing conversion (justification and new birth) and growth in sanctification (holiness) until a second work of transformation (perfect love).[2] Kenneth Collins sees justification

Figure 1: John Wesley

Portrait of John Wesley, William Hamilton, 1788, oil on canvas. Courtesy National Portrait Gallery, London; Wikimedia Commons, PD-US.

and entire sanctification as the "two principal foci of the Wesleyan way of salvation."[3] Wesley viewed the Holy Spirit as pervasively at work throughout the process of salvation. However, he shied away from correlating sanctification with receiving the Holy Spirit, explaining, "If they like to call this 'receiving the Holy Ghost' they may: only the phrase, in that sense, is not scriptural, and not quite proper; for they all 'received the Holy Ghost' when they were justified. For God then 'sent forth the Spirit of his Son into their hearts, crying Abba Father.'"[4] Wesley tended to use the term "baptized in the Spirit" in reference to justification rather than sanctification, but he did not scrupulously observe the distinction, leaving the door open for Wesley scholars to advance differing interpretations.

Wesleyan Pentecostals view Wesley as the spiritual and intellectual father of Pentecostalism.[5] Support for this view mainly rests on John Fletcher whose theology of sanctification was linked to Spirit baptism. As a leader, Wesley was a dominant force, exemplifying high power distance, and setting an example of strenuous labor and unwavering commitment to his cause. He exercised tight control over a regimented structure of class meetings, chapels, and

2. Henry Knight, *From Aldersgate to Azusa Street: Wesleyan, Holiness, and Pentecostal Visions of the New Creation* (Eugene, OR: Pickwick, 2010), 22.

3. Kenneth J. Collins, *John Wesley: A Theological Journey* (Nashville: Abingdon, 2003), 264.

4. Thomas Jackson, *Works of John Wesley*, Letters: vol. 12, Letter 416; cited in Mark K. Olson, "John Wesley's Doctrine of Baptism with the Holy Spirit: An Exegetical Study," *wesleyscholar.com.*, accessed August 16, 2025, https://wesleyscholar.com/john-wesley's-doctrine-of-the-baptism-with-the-holy-spirit-an-exegetical-study-part-two_ftn17.

5. Synan, *Holiness-Pentecostal Tradition*, 1.

itinerating lay preachers. Wesley never intended for the Methodist movement to separate itself from the Anglican Church. Although critical of the middle way of Anglicanism, he remained a loyal son of the church of his parents. In this respect, Wesley differs significantly from the leaders of Pentecostal denominations and charismatic networks.

Edward Irving (1792–1834) was a complex and controversial Church of Scotland minister who is best known for his interest in charismatic gifts and unconventional theological views.[6] Irving was pastor of the Regent Square Church in London. In 1830, Irving received news of miraculous happenings in Scotland. It was reported that "the Holy Ghost came with mighty power upon [Mary Campbell] as she lay in her weakness, and constrained her to speak at great length, and with superhuman strength, in an unknown tongue, to the astonishment of all who heard, and to her own great edification and enjoyment in God." Irving was also told that James and George Macdonald in Port Glasgow were noted for a healing ministry, particularly the healing of their sister Mary Campbell herself.[7] Convinced of the supernatural origins of these manifestations, in 1831 Irving made space in the Sunday services of his Regent Square Church in London for the exercise of charismatic gifts, including speaking in tongues with extemporaneous interpretation in English. By the end of the year, the Trustees requested that these phenomena be restricted,

Figure 2: Edward Irving
Portrait of Edward Irving, artist unknown, ca. 1823, watercolor. Courtesy National Portrait Gallery, London; Wikimedia Commons, PD-US.

but Irving refused, averring that he would never "gainsay or impede the work of speaking with tongues and prophesying which God had begun amongst us."[8] This eventuated in his dismissal by the fifty-fifth London Presbytery in 1832 for heresy. Thereafter, Irving left with eighty of his followers and founded Newman Street Church (London). After Irving's death in 1834, his followers

---

6. Margaret Oliphant, *The Life of Edward Irving*, 5th ed. (London: Hurst and Blackett, 1862), 1; Arnold Dallimore, *The Life of Edward Irving: The Forerunner of the Charismatic Movement* (Edinburgh: Banner of Truth, 1983), 3.

7. Oliphant, *The Life of Edward Irving*, 287–89.

8. Oliphant, *The Life of Edward Irving*, 340.

founded the Catholic Apostolic Church, also known as the Irvingite Church. This much can be said concerning Irving's leadership: he was obedient to what he perceived to be a heavenly vision of the restoration of charismatic gifts, for which he contended valiantly. As he suffered for his convictions at the hands of incredulous ecclesiastical authorities, so did many Pentecostals.

Charles Finney (1792–1875), a leading American figure in the Second Great Awakening and evangelical social reform movements of his day, is recognized as a forerunner of the mass evangelism of Billy Graham.[9] He strived for the abolition of slavery, women's rights, temperance, and peace. He opposed the federal policy of Indian removal and the Mexican American War. He formulated a higher law argument, which justified non-compliance with fugitive slave laws and endorsed the participation of his students in the Underground Railroad.[10] Finney's writings, especially his *Lectures on Revivals of Religion* (1835), have been translated into several languages and are still published and sold today. In 1835, Finney accepted the position of Professor of Theology at Oberlin College (Oberlin, Ohio) with the proviso that the faculty and not the trustees would have jurisdiction over admissions. He did this for

Figure 3: Charles Grandison Finney

Portrait of Charles Grandison Finney, artist unknown, 19th century. Courtesy Christian History, vol. 7, 4:2; Wikimedia Commons, PD-US.

the purpose of keeping the door open for African American applicants. His purpose in committing much of his life to theological education at Oberlin was to train the next generation of revivalists and social reformers. Due to Finney's leadership of theological education at Oberlin, a generation of men and women were trained as revivalists, abolitionists, teachers, and public servants.

Finney's chief theological legacy was his doctrine of entire sanctification (perfection). According to Timothy Smith, Finney "proclaimed, as Wesley

---

9. William G. McLoughlin, *Modern Revivalism: Charles Grandison Finney to Billy Graham* (New York: Ronald Press, 1959), 11, 510.

10. Eric N. Newberg, *Charles G. Finney and the Civil War: How Evangelical Religion Affects American Politics* (Lewiston, NY: Edwin Mellen Press, 2017), 1.

refused to allow his preachers to say, that the entire sanctification of the believer's moral will was achieved through the baptism of the Holy Spirit."[11] Finney straightforwardly affirmed the doctrine of sanctification through baptism of the Holy Spirit, stating, "Every individual Christian may receive and is bound to receive this gift of the Holy Ghost at the present moment."[12] Finney's equation of sanctification with Spirit baptism may have been borrowed from Wesley's colleague John Fletcher. Finney's conception of role of the Spirit baptism in sanctification was extensively embraced in nineteenth century American Methodism. Finney also set a theological precedent for the future development of the central doctrine of Spirit baptism in the Wesleyan wing of Pentecostalism, which was popularized at the Azusa Street Revival by William Seymour, who claimed that Spirit baptism is "a gift of power upon the sanctified life."[13]

Phoebe Palmer (1807–1874) was a pivotal figure in the Holiness movement.[14] Her work as a revivalist began when she became the leader of "The Tuesday Meeting for the Promotion of Holiness," which met in the parlor of her home in New York City.[15] Although these meetings were originally designed for women only, men soon came in droves as well. Sarah Lankford, Phoebe's sister, who claimed to have experienced entire sanctification prior to Phoebe, was holding a women's prayer meeting in the home they shared at 54 Rivington Street. After her own sanctification experience, and Sarah's move away from New York City, Phoebe began to lead this assembly. In 1839, Phoebe was appointed to preside over her own "mixed" class meeting. She was the first woman to be appointed to this type of leadership role in American Methodism.[16] Dieter points out that "the leadership role exhibited by Phoebe Palmer and Sarah Lankford in the Tuesday Meetings and subsequent Holiness evangelism came at a time when the whole question of women's rights was being agitated."[17] In the years prior to 1840, Palmer was active in various church-related activities. In addition to the Tuesday Meeting, she also led camp meetings and revivals throughout America, Canada, and England. The

---

11. Timothy L. Smith, "The Doctrine of the Sanctifying Spirit: Charles G. Finney's Synthesis of Wesleyan and Covenant Theology," *Wesleyan Theological Journal* 13, no. 1 (Spring 1978): 100.

12. Smith, "The Doctrine of the Sanctifying Spirit," 11.

13. Cecil M. Robeck, *The Azusa Street Mission and Revival: The Birth of the Global Pentecostal Movement* (Nashville: Nelson, 2006), 123.

14. Melvin E. Dieter, *The Holiness Revival of the Nineteenth Century* (Metuchen, NJ: The Scarecrow Press, 1980), 62.

15. Robeck, *Azusa Street Mission and Revival*, 123.

16. Kendra Weddle Irons, "Phoebe Palmer: Chosen, Tried, Triumphant: An Examination of Her Calling in Light of Current Research," *Methodist History* 37, no. 1 (October 1998): 30.

17. Dieter, *The Holiness Revival*, 42.

Figure 4: Phoebe Palmer

Portrait of Phoebe Palmer, from Richard Wheatley, *The Life and Letters of Mrs. Phoebe Palmer*, 1881, vi. Courtesy Internet Archive; Wikimedia Commons, PD-US.

influence of Palmer's leadership crossed denominational lines. According to Thomas Oden, in developing her doctrine of holiness, Palmer "deeply affected four worldwide religious traditions: Wesleyan, Holiness, Pentecostal, and Charismatic."[18]

Palmer was arguably a leading theologian of the Holiness movement. According to Knight, she followed John Fletcher and other early Methodists as well as Finney in equating entire sanctification with the baptism of the Holy Spirit.[19] Her original theological contribution was her "altar theology" of sanctification, which was based on the biblical premise that the altar sanctifies the gift. From this she reasoned that Christ was both the sacrifice for sin and the altar upon which a believer could offer up his/her whole heart in return for entire sanctification as a gift for faith.[20]

John Christian Arulappan (1810–1867). Of the precursors, one of the best known, yet least recognized for sponsoring the exercise of charismatic gifts of the Holy Spirit is John Christian Arulappan, who was born into a Christian family in Tirunelveli, India.[21] His family sent him at the age of fifteen to study at the Christian Missionary Society (1790–1838) with Carl T. E. Rhenius, who arrived in India in 1814 as the first CMS missionary.[22]

---

18. Thomas C. Oden, ed., *Phoebe Palmer: Selected Writings* (New York: Paulist Press, 1988), 4.

19. Knight, *From Aldersgate to Azusa Street*, 59.

20. Dieter, *The Holiness Revival*, 27.

21. Stanley M. Burgess and Gary B. McGee, "Tirunelveli and Travancore (1860–1880)," in *New International Dictionary of Pentecostal and Charismatic Movements*, ed. Stanley M. Burgess and Eduard M. van der Maas (Grand Rapids: Zondervan, 2002), 118. Hereafter, NIDPCM.

22. Carl Theophilus Ewald Rhenius (1790–1838) was born in West Prussia. He studied at a missionary seminary in Berlin and was sent by the Christian Missionary Society to Madras, India. He distinguished himself as a linguist by mastering Tamil. In 1820 the CMS transferred him to Palayankottai, Tirunelveli, where he proved to be a zealous evangelist and somewhat of a maverick, insisting that the local evangelists, who reported more than 3,000 converts in ninety villages, could be ordained without the presence of a bishop. The CMS leadership disagreed and after extended debate in 1835 severed the connection with Rhenius, who is remembered as one of the fathers of the church in Tirunelveli. Hans-Werner Genischen, "Rhenius, Carl Theophilus Ewald," *Biographical Dictionary of Christian Missions*, ed. Gerald H. Anderson (New York: Macmillan Reference USA, 1998), 565–66.

In 1833, Arulappan came into contact with Anthony Norris Groves (1795–1853), an independent British Brethren missionary from England.[23] Arulappan traveled with Groves to the Nilgiri Hills, preaching in transit. This was the beginning of Arulappan's extensive itinerant ministry. Arulappan refused to receive any remuneration from Groves and thereafter lived "by faith," relying on support from locals alone. He soon returned to Tirunelveli, practicing an anti-establishment form of Christianity that challenged the conventions of conservative evangelicalism, like the radical evangelicals who were the forebears of Pentecostalism. For instance, Arulappan rejected the prevailing view that only ordained clergy possessed the right to administer the sacraments of Baptism and Holy Communion.

Arulappan preached that all followers of Christ, regardless of race or caste, could receive the empowerment of the Spirit and share in the priesthood of all believers. Further, he insisted that faith missions were open to all and did not rely on a stipend from church headquarters. He also advocated open worship services that included the breaking of bread, a simple biblical exposition based on the pattern of the early "apostolic" teaching, and a communitarian lifestyle. Following the example of Rhenius and Groves, in 1842 Arulappan organized an agricultural self-supporting village for Christians that included a boarding school, printing press, itinerant preaching base, a church, and periodic conventions for Bible training. Arulappan and his colleagues were responsible for establishing churches and schools in the area. By 1859, there were thirty-three self-supporting villages and around 800 converts.[24] These and later churches followed social codes suited to Indian culture and were independent of foreign mission authorities. They represented the first truly indigenous churches in India in modern times. The main features of the revival that began under Arulappan's leadership from

---

23. Anthony Norris Groves (1795–1853), an English Protestant missionary, studied theology at Trinity College Dublin and in 1829 launched the first Protestant mission to Arabic-speaking Muslims in Baghdad, but left after a short stay due to political conflict and the death of his wife and newborn baby. In 1833 he visited missionaries in India and in 1836 returned to establish a missionary team in southern India, pioneering new ventures in Tamil Nadu, the southernmost state of Indian and the home of the Tamil people. Groves advocated for the New Testament as the manual of missionary methods, predating Roland Allen by eighty years. He passed on his principles to John Arulappan, one of his Indian disciples. Following the example of Groves, Arulappan worked as a faith missionary and planted a network of indigenous Indian fellowships. "Anthony Norris Groves: The First Brethren Missionary to India," accessed March 3, 2024; https://borivaliassembly.net/ministry-corner/anthony-norris-groves/.

24. Allan Heaton Anderson, *To the Ends of the Earth: Pentecostalism and the Transformation of World Christianity* (Oxford: Oxford University Press, 2013), 19–20.

1860–1865 consisted of confessions of sin, emphasis on holiness, restoration of the offices of apostle and prophet, manifestations of the charismatic gifts, and concern for the poor.[25] Women played leadership roles, which was unusual in nineteenth century India, but a portent of the work and ministry of Pandita Ramabai forty years later. According to Anderson, this was one of the earliest "Pentecostal" revivals in the nineteeth century of which we have any knowledge in which many charismatic gifts were reported.[26] Arulappan died in 1867 after a short illness. His followers were actively responsible for an outbreak of revival in nearby Travancore (Kerala) in 1873–1875 among Syrian Orthodox, previously affiliated with Mar Thoma Church, founded according to tradition by the apostle Thomas.[27]

John Alexander Dowie (1847–1907) is widely regarded as a precursor of Pentecostalism. Dowie was born in Edinburgh, Scotland, and emigrated with his parents to Australia at age fourteen. Sensing a call to pastoral ministry, he became a Congregational minister, holding a succession of pastorates, ultimately landing in the prestigious Collegiate Church in Newton, a suburb of Sydney. There, according to Edith Blumhofer, he adopted the message of divine healing.[28] A turning point in Dowie's life occurred when his daughter died, leading Dowie to redouble his resolve to make divine healing the central focus of his ministry. He established the Free Christian Church in Melbourne, founded the Divine Healing Association (DHA), and from this base conducted healing crusades throughout Australia and New Zealand. In the summer of 1886, he experienced a vision, instructing him to carry "leaves of healing from the Tree of Life to every nation."[29] In 1888, he travelled across the United States, holding crusades and establishing branches of DHA in virtually every major American city, including Philadelphia.

In 1894, Dowie set up his headquarters in Chicago, Illinois, and converted his private residence into a healing home, where sick people could study and receive prayer for healing. This did not sit well with the State Board of Health, which brought charges of practicing medicine without a license against Dowie and had him arrested and jailed, yet the charges were ultimately dismissed. In

---

25. Burgess and McGee, "Tirunelveli and Travancore (1860–1880)," 118.

26. Anderson, *To the Ends of the Earth*, 21–25.

27. Anderson, *To the Ends of the Earth*, 25.

28. Edith Blumhofer, "John Alexander Dowie," in *NIDPCM*, ed. Stanley M. Burgess and Eduard M. van der Maas (Grand Rapids: Zondervan, 2002), 586.

29. Grant Wacker, Chris R. Armstrong, and Jay S. F. Blossom, "John Alexander Dowie: Harbinger of Pentecostal Power," in *Portraits of a Generation: Early Pentecostal Leaders*, ed. James R. Goff and Grant Wacker (Fayetteville: University of Arkansas Press, 2002), 4.

1900, Dowie announced plans for the establishment of a religious community in Zion City, north of Chicago. With the completion of Shiloh Tabernacle and the official incorporation of the city, 2,000 people moved to Zion City.

This community grew to 6,000 in the next few years, attracted by economic benefits, such as guaranteed employment and profit-sharing from Zion businesses.[30] Dowie grew increasingly eccentric, announcing that he was the prophesied Elijah, the Restorer. In 1904, he told his followers to anticipate the full restoration of apostolic Christianity and revealed that he had been divinely commissioned to be the "first apostle of the Lord Jesus Christ in the Christian Catholic Apostolic Church in Zion." Subsequently, he signed his name, "John Alexander, First Apostle."[31] In 1905, due to the strain of opposition coming from within and without, he suffered a stroke. In 1906, he appealed to Wilbur Glenn Voliva, his overseer for Australia, to take charge of Zion City with full power of attorney. Voliva sided with the residents of Zion

Figure 5: John Alexander Dowie

Postcard of John Alexander Dowie, no date, photographer unknown. Courtesy Newberry Library; Wikimedia Commons, PD-US.

City, who at this time had come to the painful realization that their leader had driven the city into irreparable financial ruin. Voliva had the distasteful task of informing Dowie that he had been removed from office. With his health declining and Zion City in disarray, Dowie died on March 9, 1907.[32]

Although Dowie denounced the nascent Pentecostal movement just before his death, thousands of his followers left his organization to join the ranks of various Pentecostal groups. Many Pentecostal churches in North America, Europe, New Zealand, Australia, and especially South Africa trace their origins

---

30. Wacker, et al., "John Alexander Dowie," 7.

31. Wacker, et al., "John Alexander Dowie," 8.

32. Wacker, et al., "John Alexander Dowie," 9–10.

to this enigmatic leader.[33] Blumhofer writes, "Dowie's end-time expectations, his message of divine healing, and his restorationist vision made him an important forerunner of Pentecostalism. Many of his followers accepted Pentecostal views; some became prominent leaders in a movement that regarded itself as an end-time restoration."[34] Examples of leaders influenced by Dowie include Marie Burgess, John G. Lake, Gordon Lindsay, William Hammar, and J. Roswell Flower.[35] Further, there is evidence of historical connections between Dowie and African Pentecostalism. Brian Stanley has tracked the influence of Dowie in the emergence of Pentecostalism in South Africa. He reports that when Bengt Sundkler, conducting his pioneering research on Zionist churches among Zulus and Swazis in the 1950s and 1960s, asked about the origination of their movement, Zionist leaders characteristically gave the answer, "John Alexander, First Apostle."[36] Philip Jenkins concurs that the roots of African Zionism can be traced to Dowie. He asks, why is this church called Zion Christian Church? We might think it obvious: some early founder read his or her Bible and took the title of that great city in the Holy Land. In fact, this African Zion is named not for Jerusalem but for Zion, Illinois. The ZCC traces its origins to John Alexander Dowie (1847–1907)." He continues, "there is remarkably little in the ZCC thought world that does not stem from Dowie himself, that 'primitive' Scot. This includes the concept of the church's leaders as exalted or even messianic prophets, the centrality of healing and prophecy and the acceptance of polygamy. Even the church's prohibition of alcohol, smoking and pork can be traced to Dowie."[37] The rapid growth of the Christian Catholic Church in South Africa and Faith Tabernacle in Nigeria was relatively short-lived. Dowie fell out of favor with the Aladura churches in Nigeria and many of the African members transitioned to Pentecostalism.[38]

---

33. D. William Faupel, "Theological Influences on the Teachings and Practices of John Alexander Dowie," *Pneuma: The Journal of the Society for Pentecostal Studies* 29 (2007): 227.

34. Blumhofer, "John Alexander Dowie," *NIDPCM*, 587.

35. Wacker, et al., "John Alexander Dowie, *Portraits of a Generation*, 1.

36. Brian Stanley, "From Plato to Pentecostalism: Sickness and Deliverance in the Theology of Derek Prince," *Studies in Church History*, vol. 59 (Cambridge University Press, 2022), 398, https://doi. org/10.1017/stc.2022.19.

37. Philip Jenkins, "South African Zionists, Notes from the Global South," *Christian Century* (June 14, 2011): 45.

38. Adam Mohr, "Zionism and Aladura's Shared Genealogy in John Alexander Dowie," *Religion* 45, no. 2 (2015): 247, accessed November 19, 2023, https://www.tandfonline.com/doi/abs/10.1080/ 0048721X.2014.992105. The term *aladura* means "the praying people." It is a title given to indigenous religious movements that emerged in western Nigeria, the most well-known of which are Christ Apostolic Church (1922), Cherubim and Seraphim (1925), Church of the Lord (1930), and Celestial Church of Christ (1947).

Conclusion

It is evident that the Pentecostal Revival did not emerge suddenly from heaven as an entirely new phenomenon. We have seen how leaders of the nineteenth century played the role of precursors, setting the stage for the full-blown emergence of the Pentecostal Revival. The precursors of Pentecostalism discussed above clearly manifested several of the defining characteristics of Spirit-empowered leadership, primarily the core doctrine of baptism in the Spirit. A few may have been prone to missteps in theological formation and leadership identity. For example, Irving clearly transgressed the boundaries of normative Christology, holding that Christ was incarnate in sinful flesh, and Dowie espoused an exaggerated sense of self-importance, proclaiming himself to be Elijah the Restorer. While clearly not the norm, these aberrations do reappear at times at the margins of Spirit-empowered leadership. The next section focuses on the leaders who were instrumental in giving rise to and guiding the early Pentecostal movement.

4

Early Pentecostal Leaders

The origins of Early Pentecostalism can be dated back to the turn of the twentieth century. The emergence of Spirit-empowered leadership came to full flowering with the emergence of prominent leaders, whose ministries are discussed below: Charles Parham, William J. Seymour, Aimee Semple McPherson, Francisco Olazábal, Pandita Ramabai, Lillian Trasher, Charles H. Mason, Garfield Haywood, and Mok Lai Chi. The primary formative leaders of the earliest phase of North American Pentecostalism were Charles Parham and William Seymour. These seminal leaders set patterns governing the praxis of Spirit-empowered leadership. We will begin with Charles Parham, the so-called "projector" of early Pentecostalism. A more extensive analysis will be presented of Seymour's leadership, given his role in the Azusa Street Revival (1906–1908)[1] and the legacy of diversity in Spirit-empowered leadership that he left for his contemporaries and successors. Less extensive analyses will be afforded to other early Pentecostal leaders who carried on Seymour's legacy of Spirit-empowered leadership.

Charles F. Parham (1873–1928) served as an erstwhile mentor of William J. Seymour. The two met 1905 in Houston, Texas, when Parham admitted Seymour as a special student to his Apostolic Faith Bible Training School. Years before, Parham had operated a similar venture in Topeka, Kansas. Some background information may prove to be instructive. By September of 1900 Parham had been convinced that *xenolalia* (the ability to speak in a foreign language without having to learn it) constituted the "Bible evidence" of the Baptism of the Holy Spirit.[2] He had arrived at this conviction the previous summer after accompanying Frank Sandford to his "Holy Spirit and Us Bible

---

1. Azusa Street Revival occurred in Los Angeles over a three-year period, 1906–1908, in an abandoned building formerly used as a stable, in which three meetings per day were conducted seven days a week. The primary leader was William J. Seymour (1870–1922), an African American holiness preacher. Seymour assembled an interracial leadership team. The revival was publicized by the *Apostolic Faith*, with an estimated readership of 50,000. The distinguishing mark of Azusa Street was the practice of speaking in tongues, which was seen as evidence of baptism in the Holy Spirit.

2. Goff, *Fields White unto Harvest*, 15.

School" in Shiloh, Maine. There Parham witnessed speaking in tongues for the first time. He returned to Topeka in the fall of 1900 and organized his own school after the model of Sandford's school.

By this time Parham was wedded to the notion of tongues as the evidence of Spirit baptism, which would later become the signature doctrine of Classical Pentecostalism. At the end of the year, Parham gave his students an assignment.

Figure 6: Charles Parham
Photo of Charles Parham, prior to 1910. Wikimedia Commons, PD-US

They were to ascertain the true evidence of Spirit baptism from Acts 2, the account of the Christian Pentecost. Parham absented himself, leaving his students to complete their assignment. He returned on January 1, 1901, to find that one of his students, Agnes Ozman, was primed to receive the baptism of the Holy Spirit with tongues as the package deal. Parham recalls, "Humbly in the name of Jesus, I laid my hand upon her head and prayed. I had scarcely repeated three dozen sentences when a glory fell upon her, a halo seemed to surround her head and face, and she began to speak in the Chinese language, and was unable to speak in English for three days."[3] In her own account, presented to the Stone Church in Chicago in 1908, Ozman states, not mentioning Parham by name, "We were urged to seek for and to receive the promised baptism in the Holy Spirit.... I was the first one to speak in tongues in these last days." Ozman insisted that January 1, 1901, was not the first time she had spoken in tongues. "Indeed, three weeks before this, while three of us girls were in prayer, I spoke three words in another tongue." She again spoke in tongues when Parham laid his hands on her, this time for a much longer duration, and within two days Parham and thirteen other students had also spoken in tongues.[4] According to Vinson Synan, "This event is commonly regarded as the beginning of the modern Pentecostal movement in America."[5] Parham went on to appoint himself as the "projector" of the Apostolic Faith movement, holding significant revival campaigns in Kansas and Texas. In the estimation of James R. Goff, "On the eve of the great revival at Azusa Street,

---

3. Sarah Parham, *The Life of Charles F. Parham* (Baxter Springs, KS: Apostolic Faith Bible College, 1930), 52.

4. Agnes Ozman, "The First One to Speak in Tongues," *Latter Rain Evangel* (January 1909): 2.

5. Synan, *The Holiness-Pentecostal Tradition*, 91.

Parham stood as the Pentecostal movement's greatest preacher and teacher, and clearly ranking as its most recognized personality."[6] Unfortunately, Parham's life turned into a cautionary tale, as he forfeited his leadership position due to a number of missteps, including a foiled attempt to take over the Azusa Street Revival, an alleged moral failure, and a fundraising scam concerning the lost ark of the covenant.

Putting aside Parham's foibles, we see an enduring pattern in his leadership. Parham exemplified the essential factor in the formation of a Spirit-empowered leader, which is the primacy of experience of the Holy Spirit. At Sandford's school he witnessed students speaking in tongues. We could say that his leadership began with this experience of supernatural power imparted through a transformative personal encounter with the Holy Spirit. He acted on this experience, and the rest is history. However, there is a dark side to Parham's exercise of leadership. His desire for power got the best of him and spilled over into behavior that was destructive. This is a temptation that every Spirit-empowered leader must overcome.

William J. Seymour (1870–1922) was an African American holiness preacher and student at Charles Parham's school in Houston, Texas. In accordance with the Jim Crow laws of the American South, Seymour could not sit in the classroom with the white students, so he sat outside the door overhearing the proceedings. When Seymour received an invitation via Julia Hutchins to go from Houston, Texas, to Los Angeles, California, in 1906, Parham loaned him money for the train fare and sent Seymour off with his blessing. Despite some early squabbles in Los Angeles, Seymour soon gathered a following, preaching the full gospel, including tongues speaking. By April 1906, the Azusa Street Revival had caught fire and was burning brightly. Seymour had it in his mind to ask his mentor, Charles Parham, for guidance and encouragement. In October 1906, Seymour pumped up interest in Parham in preparation for his highly anticipated visit to the mission. He writes, "This man has preached in different languages over the United States, and men and women of that nationality have come to the altar and sought God. He was surely raised up of God to be an apostle of the doctrine of Pentecost."[7] Seymour's hope for fatherly affirmation was of course dashed when Parham castigated Seymour and his leadership team for the interracial interactions he observed during the revival meetings. Nonetheless, the fact remains that Parham and Seymour both made

---

6. James R. Goff, Jr., "Charles F. Parham and His Role in the Development of the Pentecostal Movement: A Reevaluation," *Kansas History* 7 (Autumn 1984), 232.

7. "The Pentecostal Baptism Restored," *The Apostolic Faith* 1, no. 2 (October 1906): 1.

significant contributions as seminal leaders of the early phase of the Pentecostal movement. Parham bequeathed to Seymour the doctrine of speaking in tongues as the Bible evidence of the baptism of the Holy Spirit.[8] Seymour bequeathed to the Pentecostal movement what he had received from Parham, plus his own contribution, a prodigious ecstatic spirituality with leveling tendencies toward racial integration that Parham could not abide.[9]

Seymour's style of leadership differed appreciably from Parham's. According to Mel Robeck, Seymour envisioned the Apostolic Mission as a multiracial, multiethnic congregation.[10] Seymour's vision was clearly stated in the September 1906 issue of the mission's newspaper, which stated, "The work began among colored people. God baptized several sanctified wash women with the Holy Ghost, who have been much used of Him. The first White woman to receive the Pentecost and gift of tongues in Los Angeles was Mrs. Evans who is now in the work in Oakland. Since then, multitudes have come, God makes no difference in nationalities, Ethiopians, Chinese, Indians, Mexicans, and other nationalities worship together."[11] Seymour's experiences as an African American, raised as a child of former enslaved people in Louisiana, shaped the vision of Azusa and led to the formation of an interracial leadership team. Seymour exuded an aura of humility. He was described by first-hand observers as humble, quiet, soft-spoken, unassuming, and gentle. In contrast, Parham sought to grasp power at Zion City, Illinois, in 1907 after the demise of its eccentric founder, John Alexander Dowie. Robeck suggests that perhaps Seymour's humility may have been shaped by societal norms to which he was subjected as an African American.[12] This was the era of racial segregation. Seymour strategically assembled an interracial leadership team, made up of men and women. The original team consisted of Florence Crawford, Clara Lum, Glen A. Cook, G. W. Evans, and Hiram Smith. Later, Seymour added Phoebe Sargent, Sister Prince, May Evans, Thomas Junk, and Jennie Evans Moore. The publication of *The Apostolic Faith* was a cooperative effort, edited by Clara Lum, who proofread Seymour's submissions and anonymously wrote many of the articles herself.[13]

---

8. Goff, "Charles F. Parham and His Role," 236.

9. Dale T. Irvin, "Pentecostal Historiography and Global Christianity: Rethinking the Question of Origins," *Pneuma: The Journal of the Society for Pentecostal Studies* 27, no. 1 (Spring 2005): 40–41.

10. Robeck, *Azusa Street Mission and Revival*, 88.

11. *The Apostolic Faith* 1, no. 1 (September 1906), 3.

12. Robeck, *Azusa Street Mission and Revival*, 93.

13. Robeck, *Azusa Street Mission and Revival*, 99. Robeck describes the roles played by members of the staff, 101–105.

Seymour's role as leader entailed writing articles for *The Apostolic Faith*, regular preaching, leadership of the staff, setting doctrinal standards, and church discipline. Seymour spent hours each day in prayer and Bible study. He led the meetings in a manner reminiscent of the Welsh Revival (1904–1905), which dispensed with an order of service and designated speakers. Seymour would open a meeting with prayer and reflections on Scripture and then bow his head and turn the proceedings over to the direction of the Holy Spirit, which gave rise to spontaneous testimonies, extemporaneous singing, confession of sin, prophecies, and various spiritual manifestations, particularly baptism in the Spirit with "Bible evidence" of speaking in tongues. There was a tarrying room upstairs in the mission for those who had not yet experienced entire sanctification. Seymour and his team held to a three-stage *ordo salutis* (order of salvation), involving conversion, entire sanctification, and baptism in the Spirit. The results of the Azusa proceedings are documented in the plethora of testimonies published in *The Apostolic Faith*, many of which attested to a missionary call confirmed by the gift of the language of the people group to which one was called.

Given the flood of people who gathered for countless meetings between 1906 and 1908, the challenge of managing the ministry was significant. However, the greatest challenge to Seymour's leadership

Figure 7: William Seymour

Photo of William Joseph Seymour, ca. 1922. Courtesy of Azusa Street Mission Foundation; Wikimedia Commons, PD-US.

was posed by three fellow leaders, Charles Parham, Florence Crawford, and William Durham. As noted above, Parham castigated Seymour and his team for the intermingling of the races during the meetings. For unclear reasons, Crawford abruptly walked out on the ministry along with Clara Lum, taking the mailing list for the ministry with them. This left Seymour without the ability to continue publication of the newspaper. Durham forced out Seymour, changed the locks on the building, and took over his leadership of the mission. All this misery had the effect of seriously compromising Seymour's ability to continue as the leader of the revival, eventually leading him to revise the doctrine of evidence and to institute love as the true evidence of Spirit baptism. However, the setbacks Seymour experienced have not diminished the legacy of his leadership.

The Azusa Street Revival became a crucial locus for the Pentecostal movement as it mushroomed around the globe. New Testament principles of spiritual empowerment, coupled with the experience of the baptism of the Holy Spirit, developed during the formative years at the Azusa Street Mission, provided the essential theological pattern.[14] Widespread circulation of literature coming from the pens of Pentecostal editors quickly carried the message overseas. Hundreds of potentially influential leaders from around the globe traveled to Azusa Street or one of the other urban centers, experienced Spirit baptism for themselves, and then returned to their place of origin to contextualize the Pentecostal message within their own cultural matrix.[15] The largest measure of credit for the global mission of Pentecostalism should be accorded to the Holy Spirit. Yet William Seymour deserves some credit too, not for being a dominant leader, but rather for his interracial vision, humble demeanor, and servant leadership.

Aimee Semple McPherson (1890–1944), known to those familiar with her as Sister Aimee, was a gifted evangelist, prolific writer, founder of the International Church of the Foursquare Gospel, and a proficient leader. She married a Pentecostal evangelist, Robert Semple, and they accompanied William H. Durham on evangelistic tours in the northern United States and Canada until they were called to be faith missionaries to China. Tragically, Robert Semple fell ill with malaria in Hong Kong and died in 1911, widowing Aimee— who months later gave birth to a daughter, Roberta. She returned to New York City, where she served in a Salvation Army mission. There she met Harold McPherson, married, and gave birth to a son, Rolf. In 1915, Aimee embarked on her evangelistic ministry, with a tent and a "gospel car," travelling the country and proclaiming that "Jesus saved" and calling upon her listeners to "prepare to meet your God."[16] Soon she gained nationwide recognition, and in 1917 she began publication of her trademark periodical, *Bridal Call*. McPherson defined the theological focal point of her ministry as "heralding the imminent arrival of

---

14. Cecil M. Robeck, Jr., "Azusa Street Revival," in *NIDPCM*, ed. Stanley M. Burgess and Eduard M. van der Maas (Grand Rapids: Zondervan, 2002), 344–50.

15. Douglas Petersen, "The Azusa Street Mission and Latin American Pentecostalism." *International Bulletin of Missionary Research* 39, no. 2 (2006), 66.

16. Matthew Sutton, *Aimee Semple McPherson and the Resurrection of Christian America* (Cambridge: Harvard University Press, 2007), 192.

Christ, the bridegroom of the church."[17] In the May 1918 issue of *Bridal Call*, she stridently rebuked the "learned divine," the educated (ostensibly) male preacher who advocated "no tears, these are undignified, no shouting, this is excitement."[18] What civilization needed, she proclaimed, was not cold warnings against "this new religion where people shout and dance and sing" but encouragement to embrace emotional fervor as a return to "old time religion."[19]

In 1919, McPherson received official credentials as an "evangelist" of the Assemblies of God (AG). In the early 1920s, she began to build an institutional structure designed to promote a moderate, inclusive, upbeat Pentecostal gospel. In 1922, she returned her evangelist credentials to the Assemblies of God, effectively establishing her position as an independent Pentecostal pastor, in part as the result of her persistent desire to form partnerships with churches that were traditionally unsupportive of the sorts of charismatic gifts Pentecostals advocated.[20] She chose Los Angeles for the home base of her ministry, in 1923 completing the Angelus Temple, a "modern structure" that allowed McPherson to "make church-going an entertainment instead of a mere habit."[21]

Figure 8: Aimee Semple McPherson

Photo of Aimee Semple McPherson, ca. 1910, photographer Albert Witzel. Courtesy of Witzel Studios; Wikimedia Commons, PD-US.

As her Los Angeles-based ministry developed, McPherson developed a strategy for social reform, which started with the extension of sympathy and

---

17. Edith Waldvogel Blumhofer, *Aimee Semple McPherson: Everybody's Sister* (Grand Rapids, Eerdmans, 1997), 119.

18. Aimee Semple McPherson, "Topics of the Day," *Bridal Call* (May 1918): 7.

19. McPherson, "Topics of the Day," 7.

20. Blumhofer, *Aimee Semple McPherson*, 176–77.

21. Blumhofer, *Aimee Semple McPherson*, 4.

hospitality to those among her devoted followers who were rejected by society. For example, as Sutton notes, McPherson's hospitality ministry took special care when it came to extending sympathy to unwed mothers.[22] The advance of McPherson's institutional network hit an obstacle in 1926, when her public image was tarnished by widespread skepticism and criminal charges related to her story of having been kidnapped, which were dropped in January 1927. To celebrate, McPherson set out on an eighty-day national "vindication tour."[23] To expand her ministry, she incorporated the International Church of the Foursquare Gospel as a denomination and founded the Angelus Temple commissary, an institution designed to modernize her approach to social work and joined the Los Angeles Chamber of Commerce. When the Stock Market crashed in 1929, the Commissary offered significant help to the city's needy and destitute, and by the end of 1931 it had emerged as the "best-known" source of relief for a suffering Los Angeles public.[24] McPherson held multiple leadership roles. As Grant Wacker explains, she balanced the positions of "denominational head and administrator, a local pastor in Los Angeles, a radio personality, and an itinerant evangelist and divine healer."[25] McPherson established the City Sisters, who were tasked with the alleviation of suffering for all regardless of race or creed. "White or black, Catholic or Protestant, Jew or Gentile," she wrote, "it matters not, wherever there is trouble and a heart is bowed with sorrow, there go the white-clad Sisters of Love with their sunny smiles and their ready aid."[26]

As much as McPherson was a social reformer of sorts, she was also devoted to Pentecostal theology. As Robeck points out, she did much to popularize the restorationist view of church history. In her sermon, "Lost and Restored," she shared her vision of the Pentecostal renewal of the dispensation of the Holy Spirit. She also founded educational institutions, including a Bible School for training ministers. As her health began to falter in 1944, in the interest of succession she named her son Rolf as Vice President of Foursquare. The day after preaching in the Oakland Civic Auditorium on September 26, she was found dead. The impact of the life of Aimee Semple McPherson was truly impressive. Robeck

22. Sutton, *Aimee Semple McPherson*, 62–63.

23. Blumhofer, *Aimee Semple McPherson*, 297, 300.

24. Michael E. Engh, "'A Multiplicity and Diversity of Faiths': Religion's Impact on Los Angeles and the Urban West, 1890¬1940," *The Western Historical Quarterly* 28, no. 4 (1997): 480.

25. Grant Wacker, *Heaven Below: Early Pentecostals and American Culture* (Cambridge: Harvard University Press, 2001), 145.

26. Aimee Semple McPherson, "The Commissary," *Bridal Call Foursquare* 24 (June 1929): 6.

sized up her contributions, crediting her as a "colorful, sometimes controversial, figure. But she was also an extremely gifted communicator and organizer; a competent musician; a prolific writer; in many ways a servant of the people, especially the poor; an installer of vision who challenged her followers to trust in Jesus Christ, "the same yesterday and today and forever" (Heb. 13:8), a theme prominently displayed in many Foursquare churches today." Robeck opines that McPherson "was undoubtedly the most prominent woman leader Pentecostalism has produced to date,"[27] although the same could possibly be said of Pandita Ramabai and Lillian Trasher.

Francisco Olazábal (1886–1937) was the most effective Hispanic preacher of the early Pentecostal movement. Wilson writes, "Known affectionately as 'El Azteca,' the well-educated, physically imposing, and unusually effective evangelist dominated his devoted following."[28] According to Gaston Espinosa, "The key to Olazábal's success and rise to prominence was his healing ministry and his ability to exercise charisma."[29] Olazábal was born into a traditional Roman Catholic family in Veran, Sinaloa, Mexico. In 1898, his mother converted to evangelical Protestantism and became an itinerant evangelist. Francisco went north in 1903 to visit relatives in San Francisco, California, and rededicated his life to Christ due to the influence of George and Carrie Judd Montgomery. After earning a B.A. at the Wesleyan School of Theology in San Luis Potosi, Mexico, and serving various pastorates, in 1912 he entered Moody Bible Institute, where he studied under Reuben A. Torrey, read Charles Finney's *Lectures on Revival of Religion*, and refined his English language skills. After Moody, he served the Church of the Open Door in Los Angeles, was ordained to the Methodist ministry in 1916, and assumed the responsibility of overseeing churches in California.

During this time, Olazábal reconnected with the Montgomery's, who had become Pentecostals, and was persuaded that baptism in the Holy Spirit was a second step in the order of salvation and that healing was available to all who ask for it in faith. These beliefs were confirmed when the Montgomery's

---

27. Cecil M. Robeck, Jr., "Aimee Semple McPherson," in *NIDPCM*, ed. Stanley M. Burgess and Eduard M. van der Maas (Grand Rapids: Zondervan, 2002), 858.

28. Everett Wilson, "Francisco Olazábal," in *NIDPCM*, ed. Stanley M. Burgess and Eduard M. van der Maas (Grand Rapids: Zondervan, 2002), 936.

29. Gaston Espinosa, "Francisco Olazábal: Charisma, Power, and Faith Healing in the Borderlands," *Portraits of a Generation: Early Pentecostal Leaders*. ed. James R. Goff and Grant Wacker (Fayetteville, University of Arkansas Press, 2002), 179.

and others prayed for Olazábal's wife Macrina and she was healed.[30] Olazábal subsequently underwent baptism in the Holy Spirit and in 1917 affiliated with the Assemblies of God and received ministerial credentials. After conducting an evangelistic campaign for Alice Luce, leader of the Spanish-speaking division of the AG, Olazábal saw the need for a Latino Bible Institute and was encouraged by the AG General Presbyter, who confided, "A movement is afoot in Texas to establish a Bible training school for the American work. It would be a splendid thing if it might include a Spanish department."[31] Olazábal moved to El Paso, Texas, and opened a Mexican mission to reach the immigrants coming across the border. Initial results of 400 converts were impressive but scuttled when a conflict arose with H. C. Ball and Alice Luce, who doubted his organizational capability. Following escalation of the conflict, Olazábal resigned in December 1922. Asked why he resigned, he replied, "The gringos have control."[32] According to Arlene Walsh, Miguel Guillen provides an alternative account, holding that Olazábal was forced out of the AG due to ethnocentric prejudice on the part of White officials who were threatened by his powerful presence and success in expanding the Mexican Pentecostal community.[33] Sadly, this incident is reminiscent of a conflict involving William Seymour and Mexicans during the Azusa Street Revival, which led to the expulsion of the Mexican contingent from the mission.[34]

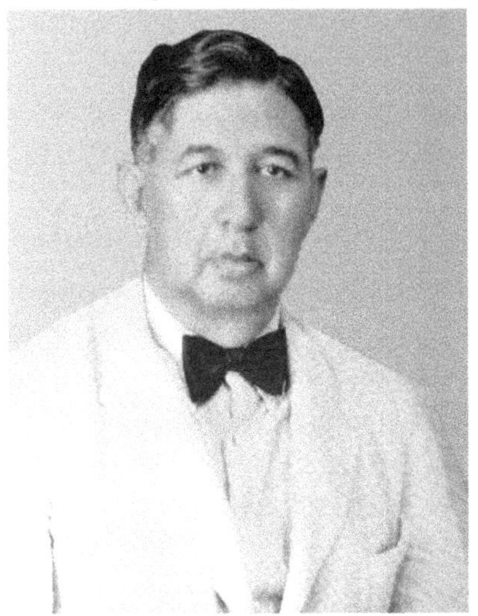

Figure 9: Francisco Olazábal

Photo of Francisco Olazábal, ca. 1938. Courtesy of American Historical Society, PD-US.

In 1923, Olazábal formed and led the Latin American Council of Christian Churches, which eventually grew to a network with 150 churches and 50,000

---

30. Gaston Espinosa, "Latino Pentecostal Healing in the North American Borderlands," *Global Pentecostal and Charismatic Healing*, ed. Candy Gunther Brown (Oxford: Oxford University Press, 2011), 135.

31. Henry C. Ball, "Mexican Work," *Weekly Evangel* (June 12, 1920): 10–11.

32. Espinosa, "Francisco Olazábal," 183.

33. Arlene Walsh, "Henry Ball, Francisco Olazábal, Alice Luce, and the Assemblies of God Borderlands Mission," *From Aldersgate to Azusa Street: Wesleyan, Holiness, and Pentecostal Visions of the New Creation* (Eugene, OR: Pickwick, 2010), 271.

34. Espinosa, "Francisco Olazábal," 179.

members. From then on, he focused on conducting evangelistic and healing crusades in California, Texas, the Midwest, the East Coast, and Puerto Rico. In 1927, congregants of Aimee Semple McPherson directed her attention to Olazábal's successful healing crusades in Los Angeles. After personally attending one of his services, McPherson called him the "Mexican Billy Sunday" and arranged to speak at one of his meetings with Olazábal as interpreter. Shortly afterward she extended an invitation for Olazábal and his council to merge with the Foursquare denomination. He took the matter to the leadership of the council, and they soundly rejected the proposal. This did not set well with McPherson, who was indignant that a Mexican denomination made up of "migrant farm laborers, maids, ditch diggers, and the like" would refuse her generous offer. She upbraided Olazábal and demanded that he return the love offering she had raised for him. He insisted that love offerings are never returned. At that, McPherson told Olazábal to get out of her office and never return.

Fortunately, the best was yet to come for Olazábal, as he embarked upon a transnational ministry, beginning in Chicago with a campaign that attracted 3,000 per night for several weeks. In 1931, he conducted a revival in Spanish Harlem (New York City) at Bethel Temple with Spanish, English, and Italian services, which were attended by as many 100,000, drawn by reports that countless people had been healed of major illnesses and medical conditions. This much is certain: The revival converted thousands to Pentecostalism because by 1932 the membership of Bethel Temple had grown to over 1,500, making it one of the largest churches in New York City.[35] In 1934, Olazábal conducted the first island-wide mass revival in Puerto Rico, holding services in tents, churches, civic auditoriums, and sports arenas, with estimates of attendees reaching as high as 20,000. Tragically, at the height of his popularity, Olazábal died in a car accident in 1937. Throughout his thirty-year career, Olazábal attracted 250,000 Mexicans, Puerto Ricans, Anglo-Americans, Italians, and Blacks to his healing evangelism crusades. As to the significance of Olazábal as a leader, he contributed to the establishment of at least fourteen denominations, but most impressive of all, his ministry "crossed linguistic and racial boundaries in a day when the Ku Klux Klan, white superiority, and racial segregation shaped the racial and social imagination of a large segment of Anglo-American society."[36] Along with his formidable contribution to early Pentecostal leadership, his story is a painful reminder of the ethnocentric attitudes in early Pentecostalism

---

35. Espinosa, "Latino Pentecostal Healing in the North American Borderlands," 139.
36. Espinosa, "Francisco Olazábal," 187.

that blocked Olazábal and other deserving Hispanics from full inclusion in the ranks of leadership.

Pandita Ramabai (1858–1922), Indian reformer and founder of the Mukti mission, is perhaps one of the most significant woman leaders in the early Pentecostal movement. Allan Anderson notes that the revival movement she led was obscured in the histories of Pentecostal origins because she did not start a Pentecostal denomination or believe in the doctrine of initial evidence—and perhaps—because the Mukti revival was not situated in the Western world.[37] As a young woman, Ramabai appropriated human-rights teaching from the ancient Hindu Vedas to oppose unjust religious, political, and economic practices of her own day—especially lack of education, inadequate health care, child marriages, and harsh practices towards widows.[38] Ramabai was a consummate scholar, fluent in Sanskrit, Kannada, Hindi, Bengali, Marathi, English, Hebrew, and Greek. Eventually her search for social justice and compassion led her to the Anglican Community of St. Mary the Virgin in Wantage, England,

Figure 10: Pandita Ramabai

Photo of Pandita Ramabai Dongre Mehavi, 1898. Photo in Pandita Ramabai Sarasvati and Manoramabai, *The Widow's Friend*, 1903. Courtesy of *One More Voice* and Hathi Trust, PD-US.

where she embraced Christian faith and was baptized in 1883.[39] After returning to India in 1898, Ramabai founded the famous Mukti Sadan (House of Salvation) in Kedgaon, outside of Pune, in Maharastra State in western India, a community dedicated to the care and education of child widows of all castes and religions.[40]

---

37. Allan Anderson, *Spreading Fires: The Missionary Nature of Early Pentecostalism* (London: SCM Press, 2007), 6.

38. Eric J. Sharpe, "Ramabai Dongre Medhavi (Pandita Ramabai Sarasvati)," in *Biographical Dictionary of Christian Missions*, ed. Gerald H. Anderson (Grand Rapids: William B. Eerdmans Publishing Company, 1999), 557.

39. Uma Chakravarti, *Rewriting History: Life and Times of Pandita Ramabai* (New Delhi: Zubaan, 2013), 413; Augustine Kanjamala, *The Future of Christian Mission in India: Toward a New Paradigm for the Third Millennium* (Eugene, OR: Pickwick Publications, 2014), 57.

40. Sharpe, "Ramabai Dongre Medhavi," 557.

It was at Mukti Mission that dispossessed women and children (especially child widows and orphans) experienced one of the most significant outpourings of the Holy Spirit in modern times. In January 1905, Ramabai issued a call for prayer. Five hundred and fifty women met twice daily for intercessory prayer. In June, thirty young women went out to preach the gospel in nearby villages. On June 29, 1905, evidence of an outpouring of the Holy Spirit was reported, with several "slain in the Spirit" and others experiencing manifestations of the Spirit such as ecstatic speech, trembling, shaking, intense confession of sins, ecstasy, clapping, shouting of praises, exorcism, and the Pentecostal experience referred to as "baptism in the Holy Ghost and fire."[41] Soon the Mukti women were praying for more than 29,000 individuals by name daily. The revival continued into 1906, when participants may have also experienced *glossolalia* (speaking in tongues). Several of the missionaries at Mukti, including Minnie Abrams (Methodist Episcopal) and Albert Norton (Methodist, later independent), who had received Spirit baptism, worked closely with Ramabai. In 1907, Ramabai wrote that even the most refined and educated English men and women came under God's power, losing control over their bodies, shaking like reeds, and stammering words in various unknown tongues, entering into communion with God. So far as we know, Ramabai did not speak in tongues, but commended the experience to others.[42]

Numerous miracles are attributed to Ramabai's ministry, including finding locations for water wells in times of drought. The Mukti Mission broadened its outreach to include ministry to blind people, preschool education, an early hospital, and vocational and industrial support services. The Mukti Revival was holistic in the sense that it aimed to provide a "total environment" for its community by offering training in "income-generating skills." After the revival, the Mukti Mission expanded to include "a rescue mission, a hospital, an oil-press, a blacksmith forge, a printing press, a complete school that provided college entrance, a school for the blind, and training departments in teaching, nursing, weaving, tailoring, bread and butter making, tinning, laundering, and masonry. It would not be an exaggeration to rank Pandita Ramabai as

---

41. Wessly Lukose, *Contextual Missiology of the Spirit: Pentecostalism in Rajasthan, India* (Oxford, UK: Regnum Books International, 2013), 82.

42. Edith L. Blumhofer, "Consuming Fire: Pandita Ramabai and the Global Pentecostal Impulse," in *Interpreting Contemporary Christianity: Global Processes and Local Identities*, ed. Kalu Ogbu (Grand Rapids: Eerdmans, 2008), 220–221. In her study on Pandita Ramabai and Indian Revivals, Edith Blumhofer also recounts that there were Spirit manifestations including speaking in tongues in the 1873 revival.

one of the most amazing women of modern times, and one of the principal modern pioneers in emergent Pentecostalism, given that the Mukti Revival in India, led by her, can be viewed as the origin of Indian Pentecostalism, in that it preceded the Azusa Street Revival.[43] In support of this view, one can point to Minnie Abrams, one of the missionaries who collaborated with Ramabai in Mukti. Abrams contacted her friend and former Bible school classmate in Valparaiso, Chile, Mrs. Willis Hoover, and shared a report of the revival in Mukti contained in a booklet she (Abrams) wrote in 1906, titled *The Baptism of the Holy Ghost and Fire*.[44] As a result of Abrams' booklet, the Methodist churches in Valparaiso and Santiago were stirred to expect and pray for a similar revival, which began in 1909. Some have claimed that Chilean Pentecostalism has its roots in the Mukti Revival rather than in the Azusa Street Revival, and further that it was specifically a Methodist revival that did not promote a doctrine of "initial evidence."[45]

Lillian Hunt Trasher (1887–1961) belongs to a select group of early Pentecostal missionaries known for their enduring achievements in global evangelism and holistic ministry.[46] Over the years, the services provided by Trasher's orphanage in Assiut, Egypt, encompassed basic care for abandoned children, spiritual formation, education, and social welfare. Trasher gained wide recognition as a leading figure in the global expansion of Pentecostal missions.[47] Her letters to the *Pentecostal Evangel* publicized her work among Egyptian widows and children, earning her the title of "Nile Mother." The children who grew up and were educated in Trasher's orphanage later served as leaders of the Pentecostal movement in Egypt as well as the Egyptian government, gaining international fame for Trasher.[48]

---

43. Lukose, *Contextual Missiology of the Spirit*, 9.

44. In its second edition later that year, the booklet included a discussion of the restoration of speaking in tongues, the first written Pentecostal theology of Spirit baptism.

45. Allan Anderson, "Pandita Ramabai, the Mukti Revival and Global Pentecostalism," *Transformation* 23, no. 1 (2006): 47; M. Adhav Shamsundar, *Pandita Ramabai* (Madras: Christian Literature Society, 1979), 216.

46. Gary B. McGee, "Pentecostal Mission Strategies: A Historical Review," *Missionalia* 20, no. 1 (1992): 22; Gary B. McGee, "'The Lord's Pentecostal Missionary Movement': The Restorationism Impulse of a Modern Mission Movement," *Asian Journal of Pentecostal Studies* 8, no. 1 (2005): 57–58.

47. The entire issue is devoted to Thrasher's life and ministry. *Assemblies of God Heritage* 4, no. 4 (Winter 1984–85), accessed November 19, 2023, http://www.agheritage.org/pdf2/Heritage/Winter-1984¬1985. See Wonsuk Ma, "When the Poor Are Fired-Up," *Transformation* 24, no. 1 (January 2007): 33.

48. Scott Shemeth, "Lillian Hunt Trasher," in *NIDPCM*, ed. Stanley M. Burgess and Eduard van der Maas (Grand Rapids: Zondervan, 2002), 1153.

Trasher was born in Jacksonville, Florida, on September 27, 1887. Her mother, originally a Quaker, raised Lillian in the Roman Catholic tradition. After a conversion experience in 1905, Lillian enrolled in God's Bible School in Cincinnati, Ohio, but soon dropped out to work in a North Carolina orphanage, operated by evangelist Mattie Perry. From there she went to Greenville, South Carolina, to study at Altamont Bible and Missionary Institute, later known as Holmes Bible College, where she was baptized in the Spirit.[49] Trasher attended a Church of God (Cleveland, Tennessee) congregation in Dahlonega, Georgia, where she became a Pentecostal and planned to marry a Pentecostal pastor, Tom Jordan. However, after sensing a call to the mission field, she broke off the engagement in spite of the disapproval of her parents. After meeting George S. Brelsford, a missionary on leave from his work in Assiut, Egypt, Lillian weighed the possibility of joining Brelsford and randomly opened her Bible to Acts 7:34, "I have indeed seen the oppression of my people in Egypt. I have heard their groaning and have come down to set them free. Now come, I will send you back to Egypt." This settled the matter. Accompanied by her sister Jennie, Lillian left for Egypt in 1910 as an independent missionary.[50]

Residing with other missionaries at Brelsford's mission in Assiut, Trasher began to study Arabic, waiting for direction. Soon thereafter she ministered to a dying woman who had a small baby who was an orphan. Lillian assumed care of the baby, and this led to the establishment of what is known today as the Lillian Trasher Memorial Orphanage.[51] By 1914, Lillian had set up a school and Bible study program for the eight orphans in her care, and by 1918, she had fifty orphans and eight widows in a new widows' dormitory. In 1918, Jennie and Lillian returned to the United States, after anti-English riots in the wake of World War I sparked an attack on the orphanage.

In 1919, Lillian affiliated with the Assemblies of God and went on a speaking tour of Assemblies of God churches, raising significant funds for the orphanage.

---

49. Harold D. Hunter, "Pentecostal Social Engagement: Excerpts from Around the World," in *Engaging the World: Christian Communities in Contemporary Global Societies*, ed. Afe Adogame, Janice McLean, and Anderson Jeremiah, Regnum Edinburgh Centenary Series (Minneapolis: Fortress Press, 2014), 21, 44.

50. Glenn W. Gohr, "Lillian Trasher: Serving the Widows and Orphans of Egypt," *AG News*, December 23, 2021, accessed November 19, 2023, https://news.ag.org/en/articles/news/2021/12/this%20week%20in%20ag%20history%20dec%2021%201935.

51. Lillian Trasher, *The Birth of Assiout Orphanage or Why I Came to Egypt in 1910* (Springfield, MO: The General Council of the Assemblies of God, Inc., n.d.), 2–3, 7–8. See Jerome Beatty, "Nile Mother," *The American Magazine* (June 1939): 55, 56, 180; Jerome Beatty, *Nile Mother: The Story of Lillian Trasher* (Springfield, MO: The General Council of the Assemblies of God, Inc., n.d.), 22.

In 1920, Lillian returned to Egypt; by 1921, she was caring for 150 orphans and, by 1924, 300 children. She raised funds on a faith basis, sharing many stories of miraculous provision of financial and material support, even during the years of the Great Depression. In 1935, she attested that "we are being fed like the sparrows, who have no barns or storerooms. Seven hundred little ones. We are still looking to the Lord for our hourly needs.... Pray for me and children."[52] In June 1933, Trasher had conveyed in a letter that she was in "very much need of prayers" because of Muslim unrest directed toward missionaries. Much of this discontent was related to an incident that came to be known as the "Port Said orphanage scandal of 1933," which erupted after a Muslim orphan named Turkiyya Hasan received a spanking at the Swedish Salaam Orphanage in Port Said for showing disrespect to a visiting missionary. When news of this punishment spread, Islamic activist groups like the Muslim Brotherhood, established in 1928 by Hassan al-Banna, made Turkiyya's spanking a rallying point for the cause of curtailing missionary activity, claiming that missionaries beat her when she refused to convert to Christianity. Trasher insisted that this was not the case. Rather, she alleged that the girl had been disciplined after being "haughty and rude" to a missionary who was visiting the orphanage in Port Said. Nonetheless, the story of a forced conversion sparked controversy that resulted in the removal of Muslim girls from the Swedish Salaam Orphanage and relocation to a Muslim orphanage in Cairo. In response, Trasher feared that "the officials may take away all of our Muslim children and they may even send me home."[53] In another letter sent in July, Trasher reported that despite the admiration of Egyptian government officials for the work and care she provided, the government had removed seventy Muslim children from her orphanage and relocated them to a Muslim orphanage.[54]

Despite the setback, Trasher pressed on, working until 1954 without a furlough. By the time of her death on December 17, 1961, the residents at Lillian Trasher's orphanage had increased to 1,200 children. "Mamma Lillian" was buried in the orphanage's cemetery on the same day that she died, in accordance with Egyptian law. A Muslim village official previously stated, "I believe that when she dies, in spite of the fact that she

---

52. Lillian Trasher, "Assiout Orphanage: A Testimony to God's Faithfulness," *Pentecostal Evangel* (December 21, 1935): 11.

53. Lillian Trasher, *Letters from Lillian* (Springfield, MO: Assemblies of God Division of Foreign Missions, 1983), 20–21.

54. Trasher, *Letters from Lillian*, 22.

is a woman and a Christian, God will take her to paradise."[55] On the day of her burial, according to Hans Kommers, "In every window, every balcony the procession passed, people stood remembering this great woman who had *loved so deep* and *given so much*."[56] Today, the Assemblies of God of Egypt oversees the orphanage, with eighty-five percent of the funding coming from churches in Egypt.[57]

Trasher's accomplishments have drawn the attention of contemporary scholars. Two examples will suffice. Beth Baron writes, "Trasher ran the Asyut Orphanage (which was later named for her) as a faith-based institution for half a century. It grew into a virtual village, housing at its height some 1400 orphans and widows and proved quite exceptional."[58] In a recent article, Egyptian scholars compared the level of care in three orphanages in Assiut—Lillian Trasher, El-Hanan, and El-Safa dar. They described the existing Lillian Trasher Orphanage Center as a "big institution containing a lot of facilities and buildings," serving males and females with an extensive complex consisting of an administrative building, living quarters for males and females, each building containing a TV room, toilet in each floor, internal kitchen, hospital, church, primary school teaching children who are residents in the orphanage and other children from neighboring areas, main kitchen, carpentry workshop, farm, bakery, playground and swimming pool in addition, wide spaces between buildings.[59] The authors summed up their findings, observing that three-quarters of the studied orphans were from Lillian Trasher.[60]

The significance of Lillian Trasher's mission in Egypt is due not only to her enduring achievements as a global Pentecostal missionary, but also because of her resonance with broader currents in the history of Christian mission. The anti-missionary movement in Egypt during the early 1930s altered Protestant missionary orphanages in the country into institutions open only to Christian

---

55. Shemeth, "Lillian Hunt Trasher," *NIDPCM*, 1153.

56. J. Hans Kommers, "Attaining the Correct Balance: Exploring the Challenges and Spirituality of Single Women Missionaries in the Victorian Era," *In die Skriflig* 54, no. 1, (2020): 6, accessed November 18, 2023, https://www.scielo.org.za/pdf/ids/v54n1/37.pdf.

57. McGee, "The Lord's Pentecostal Missionary Movement," 57¬58.

58. Beth Baron, "Mama Trasher and the Assiout Orphanage," paper presented at the conference "Competing Kingdoms: Women, Mission, Nation, and American Empire, 1812–1930," Rothmere American Institute, University of Oxford (April 2006), 23.

59. Bakheeta Abd El-Aziz Mohammed, Yasser Mohamed Badereldin, and Amera Ezzat Abd El-Naser, "Psychological Aspects among Children and Adolescents of Orphanages at Assiut City," *Assiut Scientific Nursing Journal* 6, no. 14 (August 2018), 89.

60. Mohammed, Badereldin, and El-Naser, "Psychological Aspects among Children," 95.

and Jewish children. According to Renee Ann Torres, Trasher embodied not only the characteristic Pentecostal focus on evangelization, but also reigning nineteenth century concepts of the scope of women's work.[61] As Beth Baron contends, women missionaries like Lillian Trasher were "engaged from the outset in social welfare projects, starting or working in schools, hospitals, clinics, and orphanages that consistently fused social work and proselytizing."[62] Thus, in one sense Trasher's ministry to orphans exemplified a larger trend of social work in Christian missions that was popular among modernist and liberal Christian missionaries. In another sense, Trasher and her colleagues at the orphanage in Assiut stood against religious modernism and steadfastly continued the work that was deemed appropriate for Pentecostal women missionaries. Moreover, Trasher's orphanage, along with other faith missions, continued to grow in the interwar period, eschewing retrenchment espoused by their liberal counterparts. Some organizations like the YWCA became more secular, focusing on humanitarianism and civil rights. Others, like the Assemblies of God, retained their Pentecostal zeal inflamed by the spirit of women leaders like Lillian Trasher.[63]

Charles Harrison Mason (1866–1961) was one of the most significant leaders in the modern Pentecostal movement. Like William Seymour, he was raised in the Reconstruction Era South, a child of tenant farmers. In 1880, he was miraculously healed of yellow fever and baptized by his half-brother, I. S. Nelson, pastor of the Mt. Olive Baptist Church near Plummersville, Arkansas. In 1893, he experienced sanctification after reading the autobiography of Amanda Berry Smith, the first African American woman to serve as an international evangelist. Ithiel Clemmons notes that Smith's story attracted many Blacks into the Holiness movement, including Mason, who went on to team up with Charles Price Jones, with whom he co-founded the Church of God in Christ (COGIC).[64] In 1906, news about the Azusa Street Revival struck a chord with Mason, and he travelled to California, where he received the baptism of the Holy Spirit and spoke in tongues under the ministry of his fellow African American, William Seymour. Mason's experience of the "third

---

61. Renee Ann Torres, "Emissaries for the Lord: American Protestant Women Writers and Missionaries 1930s," (Master's thesis, Washington State University, 2017), 103–104.

62. Beth Baron, "Nile Mother: Lillian Trasher and the Orphans of Egypt" *Competing Kingdoms: Women, Mission, Nation, and the American Protestant Empire, 1812–1960* (Durham: Duke University Press, 2010), 262.

63. Torres, "Emissaries for the Lord," 107–108.

64. Ithiel Clemmons, "Charles Harrison Mason," in *NIDPCM*, ed. Stanley M. Burgess and Eduard M. van der Maas (Grand Rapids: Zondervan, 2002), 865–866.

blessing" caused a breach with Jones and a separation, with Mason going his own way, reorganizing the COGIC as an interracial Holiness Pentecostal body with himself as General Overseer.

According to David Daniels, Mason's goal was "to overcome racial prejudice and institutional racism by erecting a racially inclusive organization."[65] To this end, Mason sought legal incorporation, enabling him to ordain ministers of all races, allowing them to perform marriages and receive legal benefits. This led several White ministers to affiliate with Mason's group in order to obtain credentials from COGIC. However, this was short-lived (1909–1914), when about 350 White ministers left to join the newly founded Assemblies of God. Serious concerns have been raised about the hardships imposed upon Blacks by the location of the organizational meeting of the AG in Hot Springs, Arkansas, which was attended by 400 preachers, only two of which, Mason and Garfield Haywood, were Black. Nevertheless, despite the departure of most of the White ministers in COGIC, Mason maintained cordial relationships with the founding leaders of new Pentecostal denominations, including E. N. Bell, Joseph King, and A. J. Tomlinson.[66]

After the declension, Mason continued to steer an interracial course, stating in the church manual that "its Overseers, both colored and white, have equal power and authority in the church."[67] Like many Holiness and Pentecostal preachers of his day, Mason was a pacifist who objected to World War I on the grounds of conscience. He was singled out by the FBI for investigation and was jailed in Lexington, Mississippi, for preaching against the war. Mason "denounced the arrogance of a nation that persisted in blood spilling to rescue people abroad as a despicable cover for oppression of Americans at home." He charged that it was "the rich man's war and a poor man's fight."[68] Mason proved to be an adaptable leader. With the influx of rural Blacks to urban cities after World War I, Mason rethought the mission of COGIC, shifting to a "decidedly urban episcopal leadership model."[69] Largely due to Mason's leadership, at his death in 1961, COGIC had grown

---

65. David D. Daniels, "Charles Harrison Mason: The Interracial Impulse in Early Pentecostalism," in *Portraits of a Generation: Early Pentecostal Leaders*, ed. James R. Goff and Grant Wacker (Fayetteville: University of Arkansas Press, 2002), 256.

66. Clemmons, "Charles Harrison Mason," *NIDPCM*, 866.

67. Cited in Daniels, "Charles Harrison Mason: The Interracial Impulse in Early Pentecostalism," 255.

68. L. F. Thurston, "C. H. Mason: Sanctified Reformer," *From Aldersgate to Azusa Street: Wesleyan, Holiness, and Pentecostal Visions of the New Creation* (Eugene, OR: Pickwick, 2010), 234.

69. Thurston, "C. H. Mason: Sanctified Reformer," 233.

to one of the largest Pentecostal bodies in the world, with 482,679 members and 5,500 congregations.

Garfield Thomas Haywood (1880–1951), preeminent African American leader and theologian in the early Oneness Pentecostal movement,[70] served as the pastor of Christ Temple Apostolic Faith Church in Indianapolis, Indiana, and general secretary of the Pentecostal Assemblies of the World. He was born to formerly enslaved people who moved their family to Indianapolis. Haywood dropped out of high school to support his family and worked as a cartoonist for two Black newspapers, the *Indianapolis Freedman* and the *Indianapolis Recorder*, both of which addressed issues related to racial discrimination.[71] After marrying Ida Howard in 1902, he went to work at an iron foundry, where he met Oddus Barbour, who had received Pentecostal Spirit baptism. Accompanying Barbour to the downtown Indianapolis storefront mission led by Henry Prentice, an Azusa Street veteran, both Haywood and his wife were baptized in the Holy Spirit in 1908.[72] Haywood soon sensed a call to preach the gospel. When Prentice moved to New York City, he designated Haywood as his successor. Due to his preaching and teaching gifts, innovation, and charismatic personality, Haywood grew the racially mixed congregation to more than 400 members.[73]

According to Johnny King, Haywood was first introduced to the idea baptism in the name of Jesus in 1910 by the Persian evangelist, Andrew Urshan, who remarked that Haywood was "rather friendly about it."[74] However, when Glenn Cook, a leader of the emerging Oneness Pentecostal movement

---

70. The Oneness Pentecostal Movement originated in 1914 as an offshoot of the mainstream of American Pentecostalism. At the time, most of the early Pentecostal denominations adhered to the doctrine of the Trinity. A split occurred within the Assemblies of God when a group of Pentecostals rejected the Trinity and insisted that baptism should only be in the name of Jesus. Because they rejected these doctrines, they split from the Assemblies of God to form their own denomination. Today, there are approximately 24 million people in the Pentecostal Oneness movement, which consists of various denominations. The United Pentecostal Church International (UPCI) is the largest Oneness Pentecostal denomination.

71. David D. Bundy, "G. T. Haywood: Religion for Urban Realties," in *Portraits of a Generation: Early Pentecostal Leaders*, ed. James R. Goff and Grant Wacker (Fayetteville: University of Arkansas Press, 2002), 238.

72. Johnny King, "G. T. Haywood," in *Brill's Encyclopedia of Global Pentecostalism* (hereafter *BEGP*), ed. Michael Wilkinson, Connie Au, Jörg Haustein, and Todd M. Johnson (Leiden: Brill, 2021), 277–278.

73. Estrelda Alexander, "G. T. Haywood and the Emergence of Oneness Pentecostalism," *From Aldersgate to Azusa Street: Wesleyan, Holiness, and Pentecostal Visions of the New Creation* (Eugene, OR: Pickwick, 2010), 277.

74. King, "G. T. Haywood," 278.

approached Haywood and argued in favor of the tenets of the "new issue," Haywood was skeptical. Yet, after praying about it, Haywood was convinced of its validity and was rebaptized in the name of Jesus and subsequently rebaptized most of the members of his congregation.[75] Between 1910 and 1925, Haywood published *The Voice in the Wilderness* advocating Pentecostal doctrine. He also served as editor of *The Christian Outlook*, which was created by a merger of two other Oneness periodicals. In 1911, Haywood joined the new Los Angeles-based Oneness Pentecostal denomination, the Pentecostal Assemblies of the World (PAW), and was appointed to a leadership position. Nevertheless, Haywood maintained cordial relationships with Trinitarian Pentecostals, such as Roswell Flowers, and like C. H. Mason, he attended the organization meeting of the Assemblies of God in 1914 and spoke at local AG churches and larger meetings. In 1915, Haywood was ordained by the PAW and acquired a large building with seating for 600 to accommodate an annual "Apostolic Convention." As a measure of the stature of Haywood's leadership, when the PAW was legally incorporated in 1919, its headquarters relocated to Indianapolis, Indiana. According to Bundy, the convention and its publications contributed to the recognition of Haywood as a nationally significant Pentecostal leader.[76] He was in demand as a revival speaker throughout the United States and Canada. From 1919 onward, the history of the PAW and Haywood were linked, as Haywood served as administrator, theologian, author, composer, and mission executive. As administrator, he dominated decision-making, setting the trajectory of the PAW strategic plan. He authored thirteen books, composed over one hundred hymns, and created paintings for the walls of Christ Temple. As theologian, he communicated the authoritative message of Oneness Pentecostal theology. As mission executive, he organized the mission program of the PAW, sending missionaries to Liberia, South Africa, India, Japan, Egypt, China, and the Caribbean.[77]

Haywood was a multi-talented leader. He used a movie camera to record his trip to the Holy Land and used the footage to educate his congregation. At the time of his death, Christ Temple was the largest church in Indianapolis with 1,500 members. Haywood openly supported the ministry of women, allowing them to preach from the pulpit of his congregation and encouraging them to be involved in church planting. Despite his impressive gifts, Haywood's

---

75. King, "G. T. Haywood," 278.
76. Bundy, "G. T. Haywood," 246.
77. Bundy, "G. T. Haywood," 250.

leadership did not go unchallenged. Not everyone took kindly to his stance on women in leadership, liberal views on divorce and remarriage, and his arbitrary style of leadership. Delegates from the Eastern District questioned the financial structure of the denomination and called for increased accountability by creating an associate board of bishops. Samuel Grimes was elected to replace Haywood as editor of *The Christian Outlook*, lessening the sway over the PAW formerly held by Haywood. With Haywood in a number of leadership positions, a shift occurred in the complexion of the PAW from an organization that was "predominately white to one where blacks represented the majority of its membership."[78] Unfortunately, the experiment in racial unity did not prevail, as a split occurred in 1924 when Whites broke away to form the Pentecostal Ministerial Alliance, which eventually became the United Pentecostal Church International. The split resulted in a larger Black majority in the PAW, yet still maintaining a commitment to racial equality.[79] The next year Haywood was elected as Presiding Bishop, serving from 1925 to 1931. Haywood vehemently held to the conviction that divine healing precluded the use of modern medicine. He succumbed to a hereditary condition.[80]

Haywood died of heart disease on April 11, 1931, at the age of fifty-one. His funeral was covered by the national press. About 10,000 converged in Indianapolis to pay final respects and celebrate his legacy. King credits him having "the most wide-ranging theological vision" of "any first-generation Pentecostal leader from either the Trinitarian or Oneness wings of the movement." The city of Indianapolis renamed the street where Christ Temple is located as Bishop Garfield T. Haywood Memorial Way.[81]

Mok Lai Chi (1868–1926), an elite former schoolteacher and government interpreter, was the *de facto* leader of the first indigenous Chinese Pentecostal church in Asia.[82] In 1892, Mok established the Morrison English School in Hong Kong, which was sponsored by the London Missionary Society, the Church Missionary Society, and the American Board of Commissioners for Foreign Missions (ABCFM). Mok had by 1895 dedicated himself to

---

78. Morris E. Golder, *The Life and Works of Bishop Garfield Thomas Haywood, 1880–1931* (Indianapolis: Indiana University, 1977), 64.

79. Talmadge Leon French, "Early Oneness Pentecostalism, Garfield Thomas Haywood, and the Interracial Pentecostal Assemblies of the World" (Ph.D. thesis, University of Birmingham, 2011), 281.

80. French, "Early Oneness Pentecostalism," 282.

81. King, "G. T. Haywood," *BEGP*, 278¬279.

82. Connie Au, "Mok Lai Chi," *BEGP*, ed. Michael Wilkinson, Connie Au, Jörg Haustein, and Todd M. Johnson (Leiden: Brill, 2021), 432.

Christian ministry, serving as treasurer, deacon, and elder of the Chinese Congregational Church, which was organized by Charles R. Hager, a missionary of the ABCFM, and led by Yung Park, its Chinese pastor. As noted by Connie Au, this church was the birthplace of Pentecostalism in Hong Kong.[83] When Alfred and Lillian Garr, who had received a missionary calling at the Azusa Street Mission, arrived in Hong Kong on October 8, 1907, they preached at the Congregational Church, with Mok as interpreter, holding nightly meetings. Within six months, the Pentecostal congregation numbered sixty Chinese converts; however, at this point the American missionaries had not learned Chinese, so they were dependent on Mok for communicating the Pentecostal message. Mok stated, "To get at the Chinese, one must speak the language. Both preaching and teaching must be done in the Chinese language. The time being short, the saints have to go to work at once. They have to work through interpreters. The writer is now acting as interpreter for Bro. Garr and his two sons for Sister Garr."[84]

When opposition mounted from other missionaries in Hong Kong, the Pentecostal group was ejected from the ABCFM church and relocated upstairs to the much smaller site of Mok's school.[85] From this point on, according to Anderson, Mok led the Pentecostal mission.[86] Garr himself later acknowledged that Mok was "head of the work here."[87] In June 1908, the Garr's returned to the United States, grieving over a stillborn baby and the sudden death of their African American assistant, Maria Gardner, and her child. With the encouragement of Thomas J. McIntosh, from 1908 to 1917 Mok published *Pentecostal Truths* (PT), a Chinese Pentecostal newspaper with short portions in English.[88] Each issue contained three pages in Chinese and one in English. To enable millions of illiterate people, especially women and children, to *know* the crucial revival message, Mok deliberately wrote in simple Chinese and distributed the newspaper free of charge, relying on voluntary donations for printing and postage. This newspaper spread not just in Hong Kong, but to China, Australia,

---

83. Connie Au, "Elitism and Poverty: Early Pentecostalism in Hong Kong (1907¬45)," *Global Chinese Pentecostal and Charismatic Christianity* (Leiden: Brill, 2017), 67–68.

84. Connie Au, trans., *Pentecostal Truths* 2, no. 8 (October 1909), 1, accessed November 18, 2023, https://pentecostalarchives.org/?a=d&d=PTHK190910-01&e=-------en-20--1--img-txIN-----------.

85. Anderson, *Spreading Fires*, 112.

86. Anderson, *Spreading Fires*, 118.

87. Anderson, *Spreading Fires*, 113.

88. See https://pentecostalarchives.org/collections/pentecostaltruths/index.cfm; accessed November 18, 2023. The translation of the original Chinese texts of 15 issues was done by Connie Au. Robert Yeung translated four issues (4/1909, 11/1914, 3/1915, and 4/1917).

Canada, America, and Singapore. Mok frequently included news of western Pentecostal periodicals such as *Confidence, Bridegroom's Messenger,* and *Apostolic Faith* to connect Chinese Christians with the global revival network. He also corresponded with the editors of these newspapers so that the West could also know the latest development of the revival in China.[89]

In March 1909, Mok and four members started an outreach project for the local people in Wan Chai, which was, according to Mok, "a vast and crowded area, full of commercial and industrial companies but also poor people. For the sake of saving the lost souls to fulfil God's commandment, we, as a Mission, have rented a house on the ground floor at 6 Cross Street" in Hong Kong's city center.[90] The meetings attracted crowds in the narrow streets every night, many of whom were low-wage workers. Besides conversions, healings also occurred. Mok and his team also launched missions in villages. His wife accompanied him on short trips; on long journeys, he traveled with Brother Cheng, who gave up his business for the gospel. Au contends that the Wanchai Mission linked social transformation and personal empowerment for deprived people in the forgotten parts of Hong Kong. With neither financial support from foreign missionary societies nor sophisticated mission planning, Mok and Cheng preached the gospel to the poor in Hong Kong with enthusiasm and simple determination. Although early Pentecostalism in Hong Kong was first established by the elite, it grew among the poor and for the poor.[91]

In February 1910, the work was renamed the Hong Kong Pentecostal Mission. Mok stressed that it was "a Christian mission founded by Chinese themselves. It was not a branch of a foreign mission set up in my country."[92] In January 1914, he added that the church was "not founded by Westerners. All deacons and workers are volunteers and Chinese."[93] The mission promulgated its own detailed statement of faith in 1910, which distinguished it from other churches and missionary societies.[94] On April 18, 1910, the Pentecostal Mission opened a Pentecostal English School with Anna Deane that offered free education for Chinese women and girls in the afternoon and a kindergarten for

---

89. Au, "Mok Lai Chi," *BEGP*, 433.

90. *Pentecostal Truths* 2–3 (March 1909), 4, accessed November 18, 2023, https://pentecostalarchives.org/?a=d&d=PTHK190903-01&e=-------en-20--1--img-txIN------------.

91. Au, "Elitism and Poverty," 78–79.

92. Au, "Mok, Lai Chi," BEGP, 432.

93. *Pentecostal Truths* 36 (January 1914): 1, accessed November 19, 2023, https://pentecostalarchives.org/?a=d&d=PTHK191401-01&e=-------en-20--1--img-txIN------------.

94. Au, "Elitism and Poverty," 72–73.

young children in the morning. Girls of all ages and boys below ten years old were accepted. Deane was the head teacher and Rosa Pittmann, Cora Fritsch, and Pun Yan Chi were voluntary assistants.

Deane had been a teacher for twenty-one years in the United States and taught English using effective methods. Besides learning English, the pupils were taught about Christian values through Mok's daily preaching as the superintendent of the school. As far as many Chinese were concerned, English was a means of gaining upward social mobility and a prosperous future. However, as far as Mok was concerned, English was a means of gaining converts, as he clearly stated: "We are not making money by teaching them English, but we do want to see their souls saved."[95] Mok's social prestige gave him enormous privilege in society, but he was not indifferent to the injustices suffered by ordinary people. He was very concerned about the high rent imposed on tenants by covetous businessmen in Hong Kong and China and was elected president of the Chinese Tenant Protective Association. He protested the unjust system on behalf of several hundred thousand residents. Eventually, he successfully pushed the government to pass legislation on renting. Some members of the association wanted to erect a statue of him, but he declined, as he simply wanted to "remove the pain of our people, not for the vague glory."[96]

Anderson credits Mok as "the leader of the first Pentecostal church in China and obviously a very influential Pentecostal pioneer." Yet he laments that Mok has been "left out of popular histories and his contribution forgotten—despite the fact that he led the first Chinese Pentecostal church, published the first Chinese Pentecostal periodical *Pentecostal Truths*, and conducted outreach and planted churches not only in Hong Kong but also in areas surrounding Canton and Macao." Further, Anderson writes, "There is evidence that Mok's influence extended way beyond South China into North China, and the largest indigenous Pentecostal church in China, the True Jesus Church traces its beginnings to his influence."[97]

Conclusion

We could have included important founding leaders of Pentecostal denominations in our historical sketches of early Pentecostal leaders, such

---

95. *Pentecostal Truths* 3–4 (March–April 1910): 1, 4, accessed November 19, 2023, https://pentecostalarchives.org/?a=d&d=PTHK191003-01&e=-------en-20--1--img-txIN-----------.

96. Au, "Elitism and Poverty," 81.

97. Anderson, *Spreading Fires*, 123.

as Joseph King (Pentecostal Holiness Church), Ambrose Jessup Tomlinson (Church of God), Roswell Flower (Assemblies of God), Eudorus Bell (Assemblies of God), and Andrew Urshan (United Pentecostal Church). However, the trajectory of the author's argument led elsewhere. From the vantage point of the cross-cultural contours of global Spirit-empowered movements of today, it seemed fitting to select leaders whose legacies were most prescient of the future. The profiles of Parham, Seymour, McPherson, Olazábal, Ramabai, Trasher, Mason, Haywood, and Mok resonate with future trends toward globalization and cultural diversity. These early Pentecostal leaders appropriated and adapted the prototype established by Parham and Seymour, namely, the core experience of baptism in the Spirit as the vital force of leadership empowerment. Nevertheless, the historical record also discloses evidence of flaws in leadership, namely, racial discrimination, rivalry, scandals, and authoritarian decision-making. Cases in point include Parham's mockery of racial intermingling at Azusa; his attempted takeover of Zion City; moral failure and purported discovery of the Ark of the Covenant; the absconding of the Azusa mailing list by Florence Crawford and Clara Lum; Aimee Semple McPherson's racially charged berating of Olazábal as well as her scandalous disappearance; the arbitrary leadership style of Garfield; and the omission of Mok, the indigenous leader of the mission in Hong Kong, from popular histories of Pentecostalism in China, perhaps due to his association with the True Jesus Church and its preference for baptism in Jesus' name. The lacunas discussed in chapter 2—spiritual formation, moral integrity, and power distance—were in play from the beginnings of Pentecostalism. At this incipient stage in its development, Spirit-empowered leadership exhibited a co-mixing of positive and negative aspects, which in our summative analysis will be termed personalized and socialized styles of charismatic leadership.

The next stage in the history of Spirit-empowered leadership still sees that the same blend of prototype and foible prevailing in the neo-Pentecostal stream of Spirit-empowered leadership, yet with new variations and innovations.

5

Neo-Pentecostal Leaders

A new phase in the Spirit-empowered movement emerged in the 1960s with the rise of a "neo-Pentecostal" generation of leaders. Whereas the first phase of Pentecostal leaders fit into Niebuhr's category of Christ against Culture, the neo-Pentecostal leaders assumed a culture-accommodating stance, akin to the category of Christ Transforming Culture.[1] These leaders espoused what came to be known as Word of Faith and Prosperity theologies. They proved to be quite at home with this world and its perks. The neo-Pentecostal leaders gradually replaced the more otherworldly focus of classical Pentecostalism with a focus on imparting the secrets of a better life in the here and now. They shared a conviction that material success is a virtue, and from that assumption, they advanced the claim that faith can overcome the obstacles to health and prosperity. Below we will survey five such leaders who were exceptionally influential in promoting the health and wealth message.

Kenneth Hagin (1917–2003) is widely recognized as the father of the Word of Faith Movement.[2] He was born a sickly child in 1917 and went to school in McKinney, Texas. At the age of fifteen, he fell gravely ill, and on the way to the hospital his vital signs failed three times during which he had a vision of the horrors of hell, leading to his conversion on April 22, 1933. During this experience, his mind was fixed on the words of Jesus in Mark 11:24: "Therefore I tell you, whatever you ask for in prayer, believe that you have received it, and it will be yours." After Hagin recited this verse, both his heart condition and an incurable blood disease were healed within eight months. Soon afterward Hagin started preaching.[3] He encouraged his followers to hope for the prosperity and healing that

---

1. H. Richard Niebuhr, *Christ and Culture* (New York: Harper & Brothers, 1951). Niebuhr proposed five models: (1) Christ against culture; (2) Christ of culture; (3) Christ above culture; (4) Christ and culture in paradox; and (5) Christ the transformer of culture.

2. Keith Warrington, "Healing and Kenneth Hagin," *Asian Journal of Pentecostal Studies* 3, no. 1 (2000), 119.

3. R. M. Riss, "Kenneth E. Hagin" in *NIDPCM*, ed. Stanley M. Burgess and Eduard M. van der Maas (Grand Rapids: Zondervan, 2002), 687.

God promised in the Bible, with the proviso that they would have to believe that they have received them already. In 1937, he was baptized in the Holy Spirit and served as pastor of five Pentecostal churches. In 1963, Hagin left the Assemblies of God and established his own ministry, based in his Garland, Texas, home which by means of distribution of his audio tapes and books, grew into a massive global movement. In 1974, he founded Rhema Bible Training center, which by 2000 had graduated 16,500 students. In 1979, Hagin moved his operation to Broken Arrow, a suburb of Tulsa, Oklahoma, and founded the Kenneth E. Hagin Evangelistic Association, publishing *Word of Faith* magazine with an eventual circulation of 540,000. In that same year, he established a Prayer and Healing Center as a place where the sick could come to build their faith and to receive healing. Hagin's Word of Faith theology consists of two major themes: divine healing and God's desire to materially bless believers. He proposed a faith theory, portraying faith as a seed that is planted. He taught that "seed faith" must be exhibited as a concrete conviction expressed in a public confession. Hagin differentiated between *Logos* and *Rhema*. "Logos" is an objective word, but "Rhema" implies that Logos becomes one's specific testimony and conviction. When Logos becomes Rhema, the seed of faith is planted. It should be noted that confession of one's faith was an important teaching of nineteenth century evangelicalism. For instance, this view of faith is found in Charles Finney and Phoebe Palmer, two of the precursors of Pentecostalism discussed above.

Figure 11: Kenneth Hagin
Photo of Kenneth Hagin, 13 August 2003. Courtesy of Rhema Ministries, Kenneth Hagin Ministries; Wikimedia Commons, CC BY-SA 4.0.

Hagin played a key role in the development and expansion of prosperity theology. He consistently taught and preached that God will bless his people in every area of their lives if they put full confidence in him and his promises. Hagin's Rhema Bible Training Center (RBTC) is known for its international influence, attracting leaders from across the globe who return to their countries of origin and start ministries modelled after the Rhema prototype.[4] Hagin's

---

4. Simon Coleman, "The Faith Movement: A Global Religious Culture," *Culture and Religion* 3, no. 1 (2002): 7.

protégés include Kenneth Hagin, Jr., Kenneth Copeland, Fred Price, and Ulf Ekman, a RBTC graduate, and founder of *Livets Ord* ("Word of Life")—which was one of Europe's largest charismatic churches, located in Uppsala, Sweden. According to Michael McClymond, Hagin was primarily known as a teacher and author rather than as a healing evangelist.[5] His ministry reports and some sixty-five million copies of his books have been disseminated. As of 2019, RBTC had more than 80,000 alumni, some of whom have established Word of Faith churches and/or parachurch evangelistic ministries. Rhema campuses exist today in several countries outside the United States.[6] Still known among his followers as "Papa Hagin" or "Brother Hagin," although diseased he continues to influence the Pentecostal world.[7] The prosperity emphasis in global Pentecostalism today stems from Hagin's nearly seventy-year-long preaching and teaching ministry. Hagin could be considered the most powerful theological influence of the Prosperity Gospel. Before his death in 2003, Hagin Sr.'s son, Kenneth Hagin, Jr., was already established as heir apparent.[8]

From the 1980s onward, Hagin's "health and wealth" message suffered relentless attacks from various detractors, including Hank Hanegraaff, John MacArthur, Jr., Gordon Fee, and Daniel McConnell. These critics pointed to obvious instances where Hagin plagiarized the writings of evangelist E. W. Kenyon (1867–1948), despite Hagin's claim that his ideas came to him directly from God. Detractors have upbraided Hagin for teaching that believers become "little gods" and that Jesus after his death and prior to his resurrection suffered the torments of hell within the realm of the dead. One key objection has been that—in borrowing ideas from Kenyon—Hagin taught not Christian "faith cure" but an esoteric "mind cure" doctrine of the kind associated with Mary Baker Eddy, founder of Christian Science.

Granville Oral Roberts (1918–2009), America's premier healing evangelist and founder of Oral Roberts University was born in Ada, Oklahoma and raised in poverty. At the age of seventeen, he was stricken with tuberculosis, but through the evangelistic ministry of George W.

---

5. Michael McClymond, "Kenneth Hagin." *BEGP*, ed. Michael Wilkinson, Connie Au, Jörg Haustein, and Todd M. Johnson (Leiden: Brill, 2021), 270.

6. McClymond, "Kenneth Hagin," 270.

7. David T. Amano, "The African Background of the Prosperity Gospel," *Theologia Viatorum* 45, no. 1 (2021), 3.

8. Cephas Tushima, "Leadership Succession Patterns in the Apostolic Church as a Template for Critique of Contemporary Charismatic Leadership Succession Patterns," *HTS Theological Studies* 72, no. 1 (2016): 6–7.

Moncey, he was healed of tuberculosis and cured of stuttering. At that time, he heard the voice of God saying, "Son, I am going to heal you and you are going to take My healing power to your generation,"[9] and from there, Roberts went on to preach a message of salvation and healing. In 1936, he was ordained by the Pentecostal Holiness Church and commenced his ministry of healing evangelism in 1947 in Enid, Oklahoma. His first of many books was entitled, *If You Need Healing—Do These Things!* He launched a radio program, distributed a monthly magazine, *Healing Waters* (renamed *Abundant Life* in 1956), and from his headquarters in Tulsa, Oklahoma, he travelled across America holding healing crusades in a portable tent that seated 12,500. In 1955, Roberts took a bold step broadcasting a weekly television program, which took viewers inside his tent to see Roberts in action and hear his message. Paul Chapell observes, "Through this program the healing message was literally lifted from the Pentecostal subculture of American Christianity to its widest audience in history."[10] By 1962, *Abundant Life* had a circulation of 600,000. Between 1947 and

Figure 12: Oral Roberts

Photo of Granville Oral Roberts, ca. 1970. Copyright: Oral Roberts University, Holy Spirit Resource Center. Used with permission.

1968, Roberts conducted more than 300 major crusades, personally praying for millions of people. His healing message was broadcasted on more than 500 radio stations and major television networks. During the 1950s, his public ministry was racially integrated, despite the severe opposition that he faced for seating Blacks and Whites together.

---

9. David Edwin Harrell, Jr., *Oral Roberts: An American Life* (Bloomington: Indiana University Press, 1985), 5.

10. Paul G. Chappell, "Granville Oral Roberts," in *NIDPCM*, ed. Stanley M. Burgess and Eduard M. van der Maas (Grand Rapids: Zondervan, 2002), 1024.

Healing and prosperity were the consistent keynotes of Roberts's message. Because of his impoverished upbringing, he was sensitive to the misery of poverty. He brought hope to the poor and the sick, proclaiming that God had better things in store. Roberts was among the first, along with Kenneth Hagin, to teach the "seed faith" principle, that a generous financial donation could function as an expression of faith and bring greater financial blessing in the future.[11] As early as 1954, he was teaching his followers to expect a sevenfold return from their contributions to his ministry. Oral Roberts was a leading proponent of prosperity gospel preaching with his "seed faith theology." Roberts' law of seed-faith is based on three main principles:

1. Believers should turn their lives completely to God and recognize that God is the source of all their needs; if they bless any one person, God—not the person—is the source of the blessing.
2. According to Roberts, the principle of sowing and reaping is that whatever any believer gives freely to God will be returned to him or her in many folds.
3. The seed of anything, such as compassion, talent, time, love, money, and kindness, will be received back from God.[12]

Oral Roberts engaged in several educational initiatives, some more successful than others. In 1965, he established Oral Roberts University (ORU), a coeducational liberal arts college located in Tulsa. Dedicated in 1967 by Billy Graham, ORU is considered by many to be the premier charismatic university in America. It was accredited in 1971 and, as of 2023, almost 6,000 students were enrolled. However, some of Roberts's initiatives did not prove to be sustainable. In 1979 Roberts established the O.W. Coburn School of Law,[13] but he could not preserve its financial viability, and in 1986 the ORU Board of Regents of Oral Roberts University voted to transfer the law school to Christian Broadcasting Network University (CBNU), along with its approximately 190,000 library volumes worth an estimated $10 million.[14] In

---

11. Michael McClymond, "Granville Oral Roberts," in *BEGP*, ed. Michael Wilkinson, Connie Au, Jörg Haustein, and Todd M. Johnson (Leiden: Brill, 2021), 553.

12. Oral Roberts, *The Miracle of Seed-Faith* (Tulsa: Oral Roberts Evangelistic Association, 1970), 37.

13. The O. W. Coburn School of Law was the law school of Oral Roberts University. The school was named after donor Orin Wesley Coburn, the founder of Coburn Optical Industries and the father of future U.S. politician Tom Coburn. "Oral Roberts University O. W. Coburn Law School | Tulsa," Lawyer.com, accessed March 15, 2024, https://www.lawyer.com/lawschool/lawschool.php?lid=LAW259.

14. "Oral Roberts University Gives Its Law School to CBN University," *Christianity Today*, February 7, 1986, accessed March 15, 2024, https://www.christianitytoday.com/ct/1986/february-7/oral-roberts-university-gives-its-law-school-to-cbn.html. In 1990, CBNU became Regent University.

1981 Oral Roberts founded the City of Faith Medical and Research Center at a cost of $250 million, based on the integration of medical science and healing prayer in the treatment of the whole person. When the medical school went bankrupt in 1989, it was closed, yet ORU retained the building, now known as CityPlex, housing several medical offices and labs.

The above setbacks notwithstanding, Roberts left an important legacy in his pioneering effort to merge modern medicine with healing prayer as an outgrowth of his version of prosperity theology. Roberts' understanding of prosperity, including emotional as well as physical wellness, higher education, and ecumenical openness, differed from the narrow focus on money espoused by other televangelists. As compared with Billy Graham's evangelism, McClymond holds that Roberts's healing-and-prosperity evangelism offered a more encompassing message regarding God's blessing and wellness in one's soul, body, emotions, relations, and finances thus exemplifying an enduring ideal of the Pentecostal "full gospel."[15]

Oral Roberts established himself as a core leader of the charismatic movement. According to historian Vinson Synan, Roberts was considered the most prominent Pentecostal in the world. His message was increasingly aimed at the emerging charismatic renewal in Catholic and Protestant circles. He organized ecumenical and layperson's seminars at Oral Roberts University to promote the work of the Holy Spirit. Daniel Isgrigg aptly observes that "at every turn in the development of his ministry, Roberts' focus on baptism in the Spirit propelled him to each new adventure, including his launch into healing evangelism, influence within the charismatic renewal, and the founding of Oral Roberts University."[16] Throughout his meteoric career, Roberts remained true to his Pentecostal roots. Yet he did something in 1968 that shocked even his staunchest supporters, when he joined Boston Avenue Methodist Church and assumed the title of Elder in the Oklahoma Conference of the Methodist Church. Many have pondered Roberts' motivation for this move. One could surmise that Roberts' Methodist affiliation was related to his desire to reach a wider audience and perhaps a broader fundraising base. However, in 1987 the Methodist Church withdrew its affiliation with ORU, leading to the resignation of its Methodist faculty. In the previous year Roberts had organized International Charismatic Bible Ministries, forming a support

---

15. McClymond, "Oral Roberts," *BEGP*, 554.

16. Daniel D. Isgrigg, "Oral Roberts: A Man of the Spirit," *Spiritus: ORU Journal of Theology* 3, no. 2 (2018): 326.

group of charismatic leaders who were attuned to Roberts' prosperity theology. At this point, Roberts' support base shifted from mainline charismatics to leaders in the Word of Faith movement. In 1991, Oral Roberts put in motion his succession plan, having the trustees elect him as Chancellor and his son Richard as president of the university. In 1993, Oral Roberts retired and moved to California. Despite his best efforts, Richard Roberts could not raise funds on the level that his father had done. Increasingly the University lived on borrowed money, so much so that the debt soared to over $50 million. In 2007, Richard was asked to resign. Oral Roberts died on December 15, 2009, at ninety-one years of age. He was one of the most prominent American religious leaders of his time, second only to Billy Graham.

Throughout Roberts' career, one can detect a pattern of expanding influence. He played a leading role in configuring transnational networks of global Pentecostals. He directly inspired and supported—including financially—Pentecostal churches in Africa, including some of the pioneers of neo-Pentecostalism, such as the late Archbishop Benson Idahosa of Nigeria.[17] According to Asamoah-Gyadu, Oral Roberts played a pioneering role in world Pentecostalism in the following areas: the organization of mass evangelistic crusades that focused on healing; the publication of popular books focusing on miracles, especially faith healing; the preaching of financial "sowing and reaping"; the use of modern media, especially televangelism and the distribution of books; the formation of the transnational charismatic group, the Full Gospel Businessmen's Fellowship International, which is now also a global movement; and the neo-Pentecostal gospel of prosperity in which material things, especially wealth, became a prime indicator of God's blessing.[18] Oral Roberts visited South Africa in 1955, where it was reported that his meetings attracted up to 125,000 people, and his team recorded more than 20,000 conversions to Christ. He visited Nigeria and Ghana too, popularizing the idea of the "healing crusade" in Africa. He also played a formative role in the use of media for mediating spiritual power. He appeared on national television stations in Ghana and Nigeria, and his programs enjoyed wide viewership. Roberts sent his published books to those who wrote to him. In Africa, one of the most popular of his publications was *Your Miracle Is on the Way*. When audiocassette tapes came into vogue, young Christians in Africa,

---

17. J. Kwabena Asamoah-Gyadu, "'Your Miracle Is on the Way': Oral Roberts and Mediated Pentecostalism in Africa," *Spiritus: ORU Journal of Theology* 3, no. 1 (2018): 9.

18. Asamoah-Gyadu, "Your Miracle Is on the Way," 9–10.

fascinated with the then new media resource, received recordings of Oral Roberts' sermons.[19]

Today, the media has become part of the self-definition of the global Pentecostal-charismatic movement. However, in Africa, Pentecostalism as a media-driven religious phenomenon cannot be explained in terms of historical development without the story of Oral Roberts. His media ministry influenced many of the pioneering founders of neo-Pentecostal churches in Africa, and he must be credited with the Pentecostal-charismatic theology of seed sowing in which it is believed that a person's blessing is directly related to the level of giving in tithes, offerings, and gifts "sown" in the lives and ministries of the anointed of God.[20]

In terms of indigenous progenitors, the late Archbishop Benson Idahosa ranks highest among the personalities driving the emergence of the contemporary Pentecostal movement and its trendy prosperity message in Africa. Archbishop Idahosa was a protégé of Oral Roberts, and Idahosa and his wife, Margaret, were both recipients of honorary doctorates from Oral Roberts University. His encounter with Roberts led Idahosa to found All Nations Bible School in Benin City, Nigeria. Many contemporary Pentecostal pastors trained in that institute. In 1988, Oral Roberts visited West Africa, including Ghana. A report in the publication *West Africa* put the figure attending this crusade, held at the sports stadium in the capital Accra, at about 70,000 people. Oral Roberts may no longer be on Africa's television screens, but the principle of seed faith that he popularized and that informs much of what is entailed in the gospel of prosperity continues to circulate among Christians interested in that sort of discourse.[21]

Whatever protestations one may have about the role of North American influences in the rise of Pentecostalism in Africa, the effect of Oral Roberts in reshaping the nature of African Pentecostal discourses, theologies, and practices cannot be denied. One of the most enduring legacies of Oral Roberts in Africa is his influence on the preaching of prosperity messages, especially the formulaic theologies of sowing and reaping. Oral Roberts will remain a historical figure of great importance in the development of world Pentecostalism, including its African versions.[22] As to leadership style, Oral Roberts is known for taking charge of every part of the organization. To maintain message control, he served

---

19. Asamoah-Gyadu, "Your Miracle Is on the Way," 12–13.
20. Asamoah-Gyadu, "Your Miracle Is on the Way," 13–14.
21. Asamoah-Gyadu, "Your Miracle Is on the Way," 20.
22. Asamoah-Gyadu, "Your Miracle Is on the Way," 25.

as editor-in-chief of *Abundant Life*. Many of his strategic decisions were allegedly informed by direct communication from God. For instance, concerning his decision to cease the nationally televised program, in retrospect he wrote, "The Lord let me see that that phase of our ministry was ended."[23]

David Yonggi Cho (1936–2021), founding pastor of the world's largest church, Yoido Full Gospel Church, was a leading figure in the Church Growth movement. He was raised as a Buddhist but converted to Christianity when he was healed of tuberculosis. He aspired to become a medical doctor but had a vision of Jesus dressed as a fireman, who called him to preach and filled him with the Holy Spirit. Cho moved from Pusan to Seoul in 1956 and entered the Full Gospel Bible Institute run by the Assemblies of God (AG). The AG officially began its ministry in Korea in 1953 by gathering those who had come into the Pentecostal faith. Cho soon received recognition for his skills in English and began working as an interpreter for missionaries while studying at the Bible Institute. After his graduation in 1958, Cho opened a tent church in Daejo Dong with Ja Sil Choi, his classmate, a former registered nurse, and his future mother-in-law. Cho preached a message of hope to slum dwellers suffering during a time of post-war devastation.[24]

Cho had an up and down relationship with the Assemblies of God. When people from evangelical denominations who did not believe in healing came to teach at the Full Gospel Bible Institute, Cho came under fire and was divested of his AG ministerial license, and consequently his church became an independent church. This parting of the ways was precipitated by pastors in the denominational headquarters and missionaries who criticized Cho for leading healing services in a tent church. Yet this was not the case with John W. Thurston, an American missionary who previously served in West Africa. He encouraged Cho's healing ministry, worked alongside him in the tent church, and introduced him to the writings of Oral Roberts on healing.[25] Cho later explained how he was influenced by Roberts:

> In my earlier days of my pastoral duties, my dream was to become someone like Pastor Oral Roberts. Thus, I read his books imagining I would be someone like him one day— Even though I liked Billy Graham's message, I still believe that my mission is to witness the Bible and spread the healing of Jesus Christ. Therefore, I expressed my vision as I

---

23. Oral Roberts, "We Are Returning to Television," *Abundant Life* (February 1969): 2–7.

24. Young-hoon Lee, "The Life and Ministry of Yonggi Cho and the Yoido Full Gospel Church," *Asian Journal of Pentecostal Studies* 7, no. 1 (2004): 5.

25. Myung Soo Park, "David Yonggi Cho and International Pentecostal/Charismatic Movements," *Journal of Pentecostal Theology* 12, no. 1 (2003): 115.

watched Oral Roberts preaching on TV. "Lord, make me be filled with your Spirit. Let me preach, tell and show your healing works as Pastor Oral Roberts."[26]

Cho's theology was influenced by Oral Roberts, especially his teaching on the threefold blessing (body, soul, and spirit), as Cho clearly states in his preface to the Korean version of Roberts' autobiography, *Expect a Miracle*:

> I have many co-workers in Jesus Christ both in and out of this country. Among them. Pastor Oral Roberts is a co-worker that I love and look up to—personally, I have received many challenges from Roberts, his emphasized message, "Dear friend, I pray that you may enjoy good health and that all may go well with you, even as your soul is getting along well" (3 John 1:2) has become the testimony in my pastoral career—I love Pastor Oral Roberts with all my heart. He has prayed for my pastoral career and life and kept encouraging me.[27]

In 1958, Cho launched his ministry in a tent in an impoverished Seoul area. While working as an interpreter for Sam Todd, an American healing evangelist, Cho was introduced to the prosperity teachings of Oral Roberts.[28] In 1962, Cho established a 1,500-seat revival center in downtown Seoul and named it the Full Gospel Central Church. The church grew at a fast pace: from 500 (1962), 3,000 (1964), 8,000 (1968), 10,000 (1973), to a staggering 100,000 in 1979, 200,000 in 1980, 500,000 in 1985, 700,000 in 1992, 755,000 in 2007, and to 838,000 when Cho retired in 2011.[29] In 1966, Cho was selected as General Secretary of the Korean AG. Cho enumerated seven key components of church growth, including the following: (1) leadership, (2) Holy Spirit, (3) prayer, (4) the sermon, (5) cell groups, (6) mass media, and (7) the kingdom of God.[30] Cho claimed that the Holy Spirit is his partner and senior pastor, and he attributed the unprecedented growth of his church solely to the work of the Lord.[31] In every service of the Yoido Full Gospel Church (YFGC), re-named in the 1990s, Cho prayed for the sick right after the sermon. Cho put more emphasis on

---

26. Oral Roberts, *Expect a Miracle*, Korean ed. (Seoul: Word of Seoul, 1998), words of recommendation, quoted by Park, "David Yonggi Cho and International Pentecostal/Charismatic Movements," 116.

27. Oral Roberts, *Expect a Miracle*, Korean ed., preface.

28. Dwight J. Wilson, "Paul Yonggi Cho," *Dictionary of Pentecostal and Charismatic Movements* (Grand Rapids: Zondervan, 1988), ed. Stanley Burgess, Gary McGee, and Patrick Alexander, 161–62.

29. Wonsuk Ma, "The Future Growth of Global Christianity and Yoido Full Gospel Church: Its Potential Role in the New Context," *Great Commission Research Journal*, 10, no. 1 (Fall 2018): 12.

30. David Yonggi Cho, "Church Ministry Taking Steps with the Holy Spirit: Interview with the Rev. Cho," in *Charis and Charisma: David Yonggi Cho and the Groth of Yoido Full Gospel Church*, ed. Sung-hoon Myung and Young-gi Hong (Oxford: Regnum Books, 2003), 37–40.

31. Ma, "Future Growth of Global Christianity and Yoido Full Gospel Church," 23.

divine healing than on speaking in tongues. Divine healing is one of the most significant factors for the YFGC's remarkable growth. Thousands of church members testify to their experiences of healing through Cho's prayer.[32]

Cho began participating in international Pentecostalism more actively in the 1960s. He attended the fifty-year anniversary of the Assemblies of God in the United States in 1964 as a representative of the AG in Korea. Since then, he has traveled all over the United States to lead revival meetings. In May 1967, he attended the Pentecostal World Conference in Rio de Janeiro as a representative from Asia, and he led meetings for one hundred days in different parts of the world. He became the president of the AG Council in Korea in 1966 and became an adviser to the Pentecostal World Conference. He hosted the meeting for the AG Northeast Asian region in Korea in 1969. Not only leaders from Asia, but also leaders from the United States including Thomas Zimmerman (president of the AG Council) and Philip Hogan (director of the Mission Department) also participated in this meeting. Through these events, Cho was able to expand his world stage. Cho hosted the Pentecostal World Conference in 1973 in Seoul to coincide with the dedication service for his church. Pentecostals from all over the world attended this conference, and on the last day of the conference, Cho held the dedication service for the Full Gospel Central Church. Through this event, Cho secured his place as a stellar leader in world Pentecostalism.[33]

Figure 13: David Yonggi Cho

Photo of David Yonggi Cho, 14 September 2021. Copyright: Yoido Full Gospel Church. Used by permission.

Cho's church was widely viewed as a model of the cell group structure. Inspired by Exodus 18:21–22, Yoido Full Gospel Church adopted a cell group system in 1964. A cell group is essentially a church within a church that grows without limit by means of multiplication. The YFGC cell group system began

---

32. Sang Yun Lee, "Yonggi Cho," *BEGP*, ed. Michael Wilkinson, Connie Au, Jörg Haustein, and Todd M. Johnson (Leiden: Brill, 2021), 127.

33. Park, "David Yonggi Cho," 120.

with twenty cell groups, and since then has grown to well over 10,000 cell groups (not including twenty independent churches). Cho believed that women would make ideal cell leaders, having both the time and the desire to make home visits, something that many men, for reasons pertaining to the gender norms of Korean culture, were not likely to do. His decision to appoint women as cell leaders of groups with male members went against the grain of Korean culture, yet it proved to be a crucial factor in the growth of the church. Further, it had the effect of elevating the status of Korean women.[34]

In the 1980s, Cho built relationships with leaders of charismatic renewal movements, with whom he shared theological affinities. Charismatic leaders emphasized the Holy Spirit but did not insist upon speaking in tongues as proof of baptism in the Spirit. Cho nurtured a relationship with Pat Robertson, founder of the Christian Broadcasting Network and host of the 700 Club, a syndicated cable TV program. In 1979, Cho invited Robertson for the anniversary of the Yoido Full Gospel Church. Robertson was originally a Baptist but became a charismatic after experiencing the baptism of the Holy Spirit. He founded Regent University in 1979 and ran for the U.S. presidency in 1988. The relationship between Robertson and Cho eventuated in the formation of a sister-school relationship between Regent University founded by Robertson and Hansei University founded by Cho.[35]

Cho developed the theology of the "fivefold gospel" and the "threefold blessing," which have served as driving forces in the growth of the YFGC. The core doctrines of Cho's fivefold gospel, dating from 1974, include salvation, baptism in the Spirit, divine healing, the second coming, and blessing. The threefold blessing, dating from the tent-church phase of Cho's ministry, constitutes Cho's pastoral theology. Based on 3 John 2, Cho taught that blessings included salvation, prosperity in all things, and a healthy life. This was a message that struck a contextual chord with people who were suffering from poverty and sickness in the post-Korean War society. Nonetheless, mainstream Korean denominations accuse Cho of preaching Christian shamanism.[36]

Cho's theology gained international appeal, mainly due to the church growth training he offered to local pastors.[37] After receiving Cho's church growth training, the annual growth of the Australian Assemblies of God skyrocketed

---

34. Young-hoon Lee, "Life and Ministry of Yonggi Cho," 7.
35. Park, "David Yonggi Cho," 122.
36. Sang Yun Lee, "Yonggi Cho," *BEGP*, 127.
37. Ma, "Future Growth of Global Christianity," 14.

from two percent to thirty percent.[38] Similar stories were heard in Africa, Latin America, and various parts of Asia. Cho's church also produced published material to share its church growth principles. The most significant program that the church instituted to propagate church growth was Church Growth International in 1976. The YFGC annual conferences and seminars have drawn megachurch pastors and those who desire to learn from successful practitioners. These mechanisms widely disseminated the key "ingredients" of YFGC's strategy for church growth.[39] Equally significant is the fact that the teaching of megachurch leaders throughout the world confirmed that the church in any context can experience growth. However, varying social contexts do require careful adjustment of church growth principles. The fruit of YFGC's concerted efforts is seen in the rise of the megachurch movement. YFGC's experience has inspired, challenged, and helped many church leaders around the world to grow their churches. Leadership succession is one of Cho's most important legacies. In 2008, Cho enacted a transition plan for the succession of leadership at YFGC to Young-hoon Lee. According to the plan, for an interim period Cho and Lee shared leadership of the home church in Seoul and on occasion collaborated in international ministry. The exemplary leadership succession from Cho to Lee was a significant accomplishment. Yonggi Cho died on September 14, 2021.

Derek Prince (1915–2003) was born in Bangalore, India, to a British army family and was educated at Eton College and King's College, Cambridge. He was elected a philosophy Fellow of King's in March 1940, specializing in Plato. During World War II, he enlisted with the Royal Army and while in military training in Scarborough, England, he visited a small Elim Pentecostal church and was converted and baptized in the Holy Spirit, accompanied by speaking in tongues. Shortly afterward he was shipped out to North Africa. During a leave in Palestine, he was baptized in the Jordan River by Saul Benjamin, a Pentecostal missionary whom Prince had met in Jerusalem.[40] After the war, Prince was assigned to a duty station in Palestine. In February 1946, he married a Danish Pentecostal missionary, Lydia Christensen, moved to Ramallah, and shared in her ministry to the Arab population and in parenting her eight adopted daughters, of whom six were Jewish, one was Arab, and one was English. Christensen ushered Prince into the circle of Pentecostal missionaries.

---

38. Ma, "Future Growth of Global Christianity," 15.

39. Ma, "Future Growth of Global Christianity," 16.

40. Stephen Mansfield, *Derek Prince: A Biography, Father, Statesman, Teacher, and Leader* (Lake Mary, FL: Charisma House, 2005), 98.

After the British Mandate terminated in May 1948 and full-scale warfare ensued between five Arab nations and the new state of Israel, the Pentecostal missionaries fled their posts and the Prince family landed in London, where Derek planted a Pentecostal church. For eight years he served as a pastor of this congregation, mostly made up of Jamaicans. In 1957, Derek and Lydia went to Kenya, Africa, as Assembly of God missionaries, stationed at Kisumu in western Kenya, where Prince became principal of the Assemblies of God's Nyang'ori Teacher Training Center. At Kisumu, he became involved in healing and deliverance ministry. In 1959, Derek and Lydia adopted their ninth child, an African baby girl. Later, the Princes relocated to Canada and then to the United States. Derek launched an international teaching ministry, through which he propounded his distinctive view that even Spirit-filled Christians could be prone to demonic infestation and need deliverance.[41] Prince came to see that while the spirit of a Spirit-filled person was immune, his or her body and soul could be susceptible to the haunting presence of demons.[42] His conviction that even Spirit-filled Christians might be demonized marked a subtle difference from Classical Pentecostal doctrine, which held that Spirit-baptized persons were not susceptible to demonic possession.[43] Subsequently Prince moved to Fort Lauderdale, Florida, where he joined a cadre of charismatic teachers known as "the Fort Lauderdale Five," leaders of the Shepherding Movement.[44] Subsequently, his influence on the global charismatic movement became quite significant. Eventually he returned to Jerusalem and with his second wife, Ruth, and they built a home, dedicated as a place of intercession, fellowship, and the promotion of "understanding and reconciliation between Jews and Christians."[45] For the last twenty years of his life, Derek Prince divided his time between Fort Lauderdale and Israel until his death on September 24, 2003, in Jerusalem.[46]

---

41. Brian Stanley, "From Plato to Pentecostalism: Sickness and Deliverance in the Theology of Derek Prince," *Studies in Church History* 58 (2022): 10, accessed November 19, 2023, https://doi.org/10.1017/stc.2022.19.

42. Mansfield, *Derek Prince*, 209.

43. David Edwin Harrell, Jr., *All Things Are Possible: The Healing and Charismatic Revivals in Modern America* (Bloomington, IN: Indiana University Press, 1979), 185.

44. S. David Moore, "Shepherding Movement," in *NIDPCM*, ed. Stanley M. Burgess and Eduard M. van der Maas (Grand Rapids: Zondervan, 2002), 1060–1062.

45. Derek Prince, "Home to Jerusalem, Part 9, Derek Prince's Life Story," video filmed in 2001 in Jerusalem, https://www.youtube.com/watch?v=AEOtOkEPBII.

46. For autobiographical information, see Derek Prince, *Jubilee 1995 Celebration: 50th Year in Ministry*, 1¬23. For biographical information on Derek Prince, see Linda Howard, "A New Beginning," *Charisma* (April 1984): 38¬–43; and Mansfield, *Derek Prince*.

The leadership style of Derek Prince was unlike other neo-Pentecostal luminaries in that Prince did not wield his influence primarily through large public crusades or mass healing meetings. David Harrell comments that he was "never a revivalist," but rather a lecturer and teacher whose refined Cambridge accent, "education and studious manner always set him somewhat apart" from the Pentecostal mainstream.[47] A prolific popular writer, Prince published more than forty books by 1984; by his death, the total had reached over eighty.[48] From 1979, he broadcast an American daily radio program *Today with Derek Prince*, which was eventually circulated internationally in thirteen languages. His global influence appears to have been most extensively mediated through the international cassette and book ministry that he established in late 1983.[49] He visited Ghana in 1987 and secured widespread acceptance of his deliverance ministry at a time when it was still controversial within Pentecostal circles in Ghana.[50] Opoku Onyinah describes Prince as "the mentor" of this kind of ministry in Ghana.[51] He was particularly influential on both Owusu Tabiri, a leading figure in developing Ghana's "prayer camps," specializing in spiritual warfare in the early 1990s, and Aaron Vuha of the Evangelical Presbyterian Church.[52]

Several popular charismatic Protestant practitioners of deliverance ministry trace their understanding of demonization and its remedy to Prince. They include the New Zealand Anglican Bill Subritzky; the British founder of Ellel Ministries, Peter Horrobin; and the Southern Baptists Frank and Ida Mae Hammond, authors of the intriguing handbook, *Pigs in the Parlor: A Practical Guide to Deliverance*, which claims over one million copies sold worldwide.[53] Prince

---

47. Harrell, *All Things Are Possible*, 182, 184–85.

48. Derek Prince, *Life's Bitter Pool: From Bitterness to Joy* (Harpenden, UK: Derek Prince Ministries, 1984), 43; "About Derek Prince," online at https://www.derekprince.org/Groups/1000103610/DPM_USA/About/About_Derek_Prince/About_Derek_Prince.aspx; accessed January 18, 2021.

49. Prince's obituary in *King's College Cambridge Annual Report* (2004), 50, notes the particular significance of audiocassettes for the dissemination of his teaching.

50. Paul Gifford, *African Christianity: Its Publica Role* (Bloomington: Indiana University Press, 1989), 100, 346–47.

51. Opoku Onyinah, *Pentecostal Exorcism: Witchcraft and Demonology in Ghana* (Leiden: Brill, 2012), 172.

52. Gifford, Paul, Ghana's *New Christianity: Pentecostalism in a Globalizing African Economy* (Bloomington, Indiana University Press, 2004), 89; see also E. Kingsley Larbi, *Pentecostalism: The Eddies of Ghanaian Christianity* (Accra: Centre for Pentecostal and Charismatic Studies, 2001), 393.

53. James M. Collins, *Exorcism and Deliverance Ministry in the Twentieth Century: An Analysis of the Practice and Theology of Exorcism in Modern Western Christianity* (Eugene, OR: Wipf & Stock, 2009), 64-5, 87–90; Frank Hammond and Ida Mae Hammond, *Pigs in the Parlor: A Practical Guide to Deliverance* (Kirkwood, MO: Impact Christian Books, 1990).

himself never produced a full practical guide to techniques of deliverance. The Hammonds' handbook was written at his suggestion and followed his teaching closely, reproducing verbatim the prayer that Prince recommended for use when conducting an exorcism.[54] It coached deliverance practitioners on how to purge the afflicted of indwelling demons by vomiting them up, a practice that bears close parallels with some accounts of exorcism in early modern Europe.[55] Brian Stanley claims that the source of Prince's distinctive view of deliverance can be located in his Cambridge research on Plato. He argues that Prince's later teaching on deliverance resembles the language of Plato's *Phaedo*. The *Phaedo* proclaimed a disjunction between two spheres of existence, the changing world of the visible and "the unchanging things you can only perceive with the mind."[56] Similarly, Prince, in *Blessing or Curse: You Can Choose*, stated, "The things that belong to the visible realm are transitory and impermanent. It is only in the invisible realm that we can find true and abiding reality. It is in this realm, too, that we discover the forces which will ultimately shape our destiny, even in the visible realm."[57]

Prince's demonology promised Christians in Africa and other parts of the non-Western world an explanation for their continuing predicaments in the final years of the twentieth century. Deliverance ministry emerged as a ubiquitous feature of contemporary global neo-Pentecostalism, and no single theological lineage can be identified as common to its manifold occurrences. David Maxwell's study of the Zimbabwe Assemblies of God indicates the growing salience from the 1980s onwards of a preoccupation with deliverance and of analogous ideas of ancestral curses as the likely explanation of the intractable poverty of individuals, but without attempting to construct a genealogy of such ideas.[58] Brian Stanley more precisely finds the prevalence of deliverance ministry in Prince's impact on leading teachers of demonology in Africa.[59] Paul Gifford, Kwabena Asamoah-Gyadu, and Opoku Onyinah have all identified Prince as being of unusual importance for West African Pentecostalism. The common idea in Africa and elsewhere, among those who received Prince's message, is the association of physical ailments with the curse of chronic poverty.

---

54. Hammond and Hammond, *Pigs in the Parlor*, 154–55.

55. Hammond and Hammond, *Pigs in the Parlor*, 222.

56. Stanley, "From Plato to Pentecostalism": 17–18.

57. Derek Prince, *Blessing or Curse: You Can Choose*, 3rd ed. (Baldock: Derek Prince Ministries-UK, 2007), 36.

58. David Maxwell, *African Gifts of the Spirit: Pentecostalism and the Rise of a Zimbabwean Transnational Religious Movement* (Oxford, Oxford University Press, 2006), chapter 8.

59. Stanley, "From Plato to Pentecostalism": 18–20.

Léon Joseph Suenens (1904–1996) is recognized as an influential leader of the early phase of the Catholic Charismatic Renewal (CCR). Educated at the Pontifical Gregorian University in Rome, Suenens was ordained in Malines (Mechelen), Belgium in 1927, where he taught philosophy until 1939. He served as vice-rector and rector of the University of Louvain and auxiliary bishop of Malines from 1940 to 1961, when he was appointed archbishop of Malines-Brussels; in 1962, he was made cardinal by Pope John XXIII.[60]

Suenens played a leading role in the Second Ecumenical Council of the Vatican (Vatican II), shaping the agenda and advocating for reform. He urged the expansion of lay charismata, ecumenical cooperation, and issues of social and humanitarian concern. In 1972, Suenens personally encountered the Catholic Charismatic Renewal. He was immediately taken by this encounter, appealing as it did to his keen desire to see the church flourish as in a new Pentecost through the work of the Holy Spirit. For Suenens, this amounted to a lifelong goal. Subsequently, he visited the University of Notre Dame and met

Figure 14: Cardinal Léon Joseph Suenens

Photo of Cardinal Léon Joseph Suenens, 19 November 2014. Wikimedia Commons, CC BY-SA 4.0.

with the American leaders, whom he invited to a conference in Malines, which led to the publication of *Theological and Pastoral Guidelines on the Catholic Charismatic Renewal.*

Suenens invited the Americans Stephen Clark and Ralph Martin to establish the CCR International Information Office in Brussels (later moved to Rome). Initially, Cardinal Suenens described the Renewal as a "moving of the Holy Spirit" and as "a high voltage current of Grace which is coursing through the Church." Cardinal William Levada sizes up the significance of Suenens and the CCR:

---

60. David D. Bundy, "Léon Joseph Suenens," in *NIDPCM*, ed. Stanley M. Burgess and Eduard M. van der Maas (Grand Rapids: Zondervan, 2002), 1108–1109.

> How could a cardinal with a face that did not show many emotions, with a straight and immobile stature, with a grave and steady voice, find himself at ease in the midst of a crowd that sang, danced, clapped hands and spoke in tongues? Was it a late life conversion to fantasy and imagination in a man who had been until then too rational and responsible? No. Rather, he perceived in this revival a return to the church of the Acts of the Apostles about which he had always dreamed—with a taste for the Scriptures, spontaneous prayer, joy, a sense of community, the stirrings of the Spirit, the proliferation of charisms. The renewal gave the legitimate role of the heart and the body back to the spiritual life of Christians.[61]

According to the recollection of Pope Francis, Suenens described the charismatic renewal as the following:

> not a specific Movement; the Renewal is not a Movement in the common sociological sense; it does not have founders, it is not homogeneous, and it includes a great variety of realities; it is a current of grace, a renewing breath of the Spirit for all members of the Church, laity, religious, priests and bishops. It is a challenge for us all. One does not form part of the Renewal, rather, the Renewal becomes a part of us, provided that we accept the grace it offers us.[62]

Suenens made a singular contribution to the CCR by explaining the renewal to the Pope and by alerting the leadership of the Church to what Levada characterizes as their "amnesia" about the gifts of the Holy Spirit to the church: the eucharist, the Blessed Virgin Mary, the pope as visible center of unity, the scope of Catholic teaching and practice.[63]

From 1974 to 1986 Suenens composed a series of six "Malines Documents," which still serve as a guide to the CCR, with poignant insight into its possibilities and its needs. Suenens authored *Charismatic Renewal* (1974), with Kilian McDonnell as lead consultant, followed by *Ecumenism and Charismatic Renewal* (1978). In 1979, he wrote *Charismatic Renewal and Social Action: A Dialogue* in collaboration with his longtime friend, Dom Helder Camara of Brazil. In 1982, he wrote *Renewal and the Powers of Darkness* with a foreword by Cardinal Joseph Ratzinger, later, Pope Benedict XVI. The final two "Malines

---

61. William J. Levada, Archbishop Emeritus of San Francisco, "Pentecostal Catholics—A History of the Catholic Charismatic Renewal," Archdiocese of San Francisco, Catholic Charismatic Renewal, accessed November 18, 2023. https://www.sfspirit.com/renewal-history.html. For the full text of Archbishop Levada's keynote address of May 31, 1996, delivered at the Cleveland symposium, see *Origins*, CNS Documentary Service (June 20, 1996) 26: no. 5, "The Charism of Cardinal Suenens."

62. Pope Francis, quoting Cardinal Suenens, in "Address of His Holiness Pope Francis to the Renewal in the Holy Spirit Movement," *The Holy See*, July 3, 2015, accessed November 18, 2023, https://www.vatican.va/content/francesco/en/speeches/2015/july/documents/papa-francesco_20150703_movimento-rinnovamento-spirito.html.

63. Levada, "Pentecostal Catholics (Suenens)."

Documents" treat two specific issues the renewal had to deal with: an over-reliance on introspection, in *Culte du Moi et Foi Chrétienne* (1985), and the controversial phenomenon of *Resting in the Spirit* (1986), sometimes also referred to as "slaying in the Spirit."[64]

Ultimately, Cardinal Suenens became concerned about trends in the CCR, perceiving a tendency to act independently of the Church in the manner of a parachurch body. As a result, he felt the need to bring the CCR into complete integration with the ecclesial structure of the Church, and in 1976 he mandated that in Belgium only priests could lead prayer groups.[65] With his retirement in 1979, Suenens began to pull back from active leadership in the CCR, yet this does not diminish the extent of his contribution. He succeeded in gaining the endorsement of the CCR from the Pope, locating its office close the seat of ecclesial power, and setting the table for engagement of leading Catholic scholars with the renewal. As of 2013, the Catholic Charismatic Renewal had grown to over 160 million members.

Conclusion

The neo-Pentecostal leaders surveyed above carried on the prototype of early Pentecostal leadership, yet they added new theological accents and methods. The primary point of continuity with early Pentecostal leaders was their conception of leadership as the direct outflow of baptism in the Spirit. The leadership journey of Hagin, Roberts, Cho, Prince, and Suenens began with a life-changing experience of Spirit baptism, followed by calling and empowerment for leadership. The primary point of discontinuity in these four leaders (and their followers) was a surmounting of the narrow cultural ethos of Classical Pentecostalism. They cast off the shackles of social disenfranchisement and deprivation. The common thread in neo-Pentecostalism consisted of a broader outlook and appeal, a rising above disenfranchisement and deprivation. Their message was essentially world-affirming in the sense that they were focused on the good things in life, such as health and wealth, flourishing and growth. They organized impressive ministries and educational institutions. For Hagin, the key idea was faith and establishment of Rhema Training Institute; for Roberts, it was seed faith theology and the founding of Oral Roberts University; for Cho, the breakthrough came with the theology of threefold blessing, the growth of the largest church in the world, and a worldwide training program that

---

64. Levada, "Pentecostal Catholics (Suenens)."
65. Bundy, "Léon Joseph Suenens," *NIDPCM*, 1109.

mentored like-minded leaders; for Prince, his keynote was a diagnosis of the root of spiritual brokenness and a cure that comes through healing of the mind through intercession and prayer, not to mention an innovating delivery system with worldwide reach; and for Suenens, his encounter with and investigation of the Catholic Charismatic Renewal laid a foundation upon which successive Catholic scholarship and ecumenical initiatives would be built.

The neo-Pentecostal leaders accomplished much in broadening the appeal of charismatic gifts. However, that is not to say that they were without their flaws. These leaders did not always foresee the drawbacks of their ambitious visions and plans for expansion of their ministries. Because they were susceptible to over-reach, they often cast caution to the wind, promised more than could be realistically achieved, and embarked on grandiose projects requiring intense fundraising campaigns, which left their staff, supporters, and followers in a state of exhaustion. Lacking the capacity for empathy, they could not comprehend the dark side of their leadership. A few examples will suffice. To begin, not everyone that was prayed for was healed, leaving those who weren't healed in a state of despair. Second, the line between psychiatric disorder and demonic possession was blurred, tending at times to demean the role of the professional therapist. Third, a tinge of anti-intellectualism narrowed the space allowed for critical scholarship in pulpit ministry and educational institutions. Finally, returning to the three lacunas discussed above, in neo-Pentecostal movements, there was a neglect of the spiritual disciplines, recurrent lapses in moral integrity, and a penchant for high power distance in ministry leadership. Nonetheless, despite these gaps, each of these leaders should be credited with equipping a generation of successors who would pass the torch to the next phase in the history of Spirit-empowered leadership.

6

Global South Charismatic Leaders

Pentecostals and charismatics represent a large share of the astounding growth of Christianity in the Global South. The impressive growth of Spirit-empowered movements signifies a massive shift in the cartography of world Christianity. In 1995, Lamin Sanneh observed that Christianity was undergoing a radical shift of huge proportions and significance in the sense that it was ceasing to be a Euro-American religion and was becoming decidedly global.[1] Philip Jenkins corroborated Sanneh's observation and prognosticated that whereas in 1900; eighty-three percent of the world's Christians lived in Europe and North America; and in 2050, seventy-two percent of Christians will live in Africa, Asia, and Latin America. Hence, if we imagine a typical Christian back in 1900, we might think of a German or an American. In 2050, we should rather turn to a Ugandan, a Brazilian, or a Filipino.[2]

Andrew Walls, a leading historian of Christian mission, holds that the demographic shift in world Christianity noted above constitutes "the most striking change in the religious map of the world for several centuries." One part of the globe has seen the most substantial accession to the Christian faith since the conversion of the northern barbarians; another, the most considerable recession from it since the rise of Islam. The most obvious center of accession is sub-Saharan Africa, in which even a century ago the Christian population was statistically marginal; the most obvious center of recession is Western Europe, which a century and a half ago would certainly have been identified as the most dynamic and significant center of Christianity. Walls asks, "Yet how is the contemporary student of Christianity to understand this important

---

1. Lamin Sanneh, "Global Christianity and the Re-education of the West," *Religion Online,* accessed November 18, 2023, *https://www.religion-online.org/article/global-christianity-and-the-re-education-of-the-west/.*

2. Philip Jenkins, *The Next Christendom: The Coming of Global Christianity* (New York: Oxford Academic Press, 2011), xi.

motor of modern Christianity?"[3] Walls argues that Christianity has become a genuinely multicultural world religion, thriving profusely in the idioms of other languages and cultures, marked by a lively cross-cultural and interreligious sensibility, unburdened by the heavy artillery of doctors and councils, and otherwise undaunted by the scandalous paucity of money, trained leadership, infrastructure, and resources. Nothing better demonstrates the newness of world Christianity than the fact that in indigenous communities of faith fresh energy and intelligence is being devoted to the production of new hymns, music, and artistic and liturgical materials; to the creation of fresh categories for doing theology; to the retrieval of threatened cultural resources; to the application of faith to public issues; and to the promotion of ecumenical interchange and partnership. At the forefront of these developments are innovative, charismatic leaders who are not bound by the restrictions of past forms.

This chapter provides an overview of five such Spirit-empowered leaders—three African leaders, followed by one leader from South America, and another from the Philippines—who are representative of the new wave of charismatic leaders who have made formative contributions to transformations in the shape of global Christianity.

Peter Anim (1890–1984) is regarded as a progenitor of Pentecostalism in Ghana. The major classical Pentecostal denominations in Ghana today are the Church of Pentecost, the Apostolic Church of Ghana, the Christ Apostolic Church, and the Assemblies of God. The first three have origins in the work of this remarkable Ghanaian, who is credited not only as the pioneer of Spirit-empowered leadership in Ghana, but also for contributing to the social and political development of Ghana.[4]

The region witnessed a major outbreak of the deadly influenza epidemic in 1918 and a concomitant economic recession. Western medicine and mission churches were unable to handle the crisis. Africans were convinced that the epidemic had an important spiritual dimension and set up fellowships to pray for divine intervention. Peter Newman Anim (1890–1984), formerly known as Kwaku Anim Mensah (also known as Kwaku Manasseh) was born in the Volta region of Ghana. In 1917, Anim discovered a copy of "The Sword of the Spirit," a publication of the Faith Tabernacle church in Philadelphia, Pennsylvania, which

---

3. Andrew Walls, "Structural Problems in Mission Studies," *International Bulletin of Missionary Research* 14, no. 4 (October 1991): 152.

4. Peter White, "Centenary of Pentecostalism in Ghana (1917–¬2017): A Case Study of Christ Apostolic Church International," *HTS Theological Studies* 75, no. 4 (2019), 7.

was circulating in his country. Faith Tabernacle was an offshoot of Dowie's Zion City, which emphasized healing and baptism by immersion. In 1921 Anim received healing from guinea worm infection and protracted stomach ailments. Anim resigned from the Presbyterian church to become an independent healing preacher. He gathered a large following in Asamankese, located in an Eastern Province of Ghana, affiliating for a short time with Faith Tabernacle in Philadelphia. At this time, similar developments were taking place in Nigeria, where David Odubanjo became the leader of a Faith Tabernacle offshoot. Ultimately, relations between the Faith Tabernacle in Philadelphia and its branches in West Africa deteriorated for three main reasons. First, in over four years, none of the American leaders had visited West Africa, which cast doubt on their commitment. Second, there were doctrinal differences over speaking in tongues, a practice that was embraced by the Africans but rejected by the Americans, who like the Zionists in Chicago, considered it a satanic delusion. Third,

Figure 15: Peter Anim

Photo of Apostle Peter Newman Anim, ca. 1935, photographer unknown. Courtesy of Believers Portal, Christ Apostolic Church International.

in 1926 the Philadelphia church's leader, Pastor James Ambrose Clark, was excommunicated for matrimonial affairs. Anim and the Nigerian leaders severed the connection with Faith Tabernacle.

At the same time, another periodical began circulating in West Africa, *The Apostolic Faith*, published in Portland, Oregon, by Florence Louise Crawford, who previously served on the leadership team of the Azusa Street Revival in Los Angeles.[5] After the break with Philadelphia, Anim found the teachings of the Apostolic Faith in line with his own practices and took the name Apostolic Faith for his movement. Anim states, "I was forced with the necessity of contending for a deeper faith and greater spiritual power that what my primary religious experience was able to afford, and I began to seek with such trepidation to know

---

5. Florence Crawford and Clara Lum left the Azusa Street mission to start a work in Portland, Oregon. They began publishing *The Apostolic Faith* from their new home. It is believed by many that, without permission, they took the mailing lists from the mission, in effect limiting the mission and William Seymour from keeping in contact with subscribers and raising contributions, thereby contributing to the demise of the revival. See Robeck, *Azusa Street Mission and Revival*, 286–87.

more about the Holy Ghost."[6] In correspondence with Odubanjo, he discovered that Faith Tabernacle in Nigeria was seeking affiliation with the Apostolic Church in Britain to assist in addressing the difficulties the African leaders were having with the colonial administration. In 1931 Anim and two of his leaders met up with three leaders of the British Apostolic Church, who were travelling from England, and accompanied them from Accra to Lagos. According to Anim's own account, in 1932 during prayers in a village, some of his key leaders experienced baptism in the Spirit and the practice of speaking in tongues quickly spread in what was called the "Holy Ghost Dispensation."

> At these meetings a great number of our Sisters received a mighty Baptism of the Holy Ghost, speaking in tongues, prophesying together with the manifestation of all other signs of the Apostolic promises, Acts 1–4; 10:44–46....Prayer was continued and the Sisters filled with the Holy Ghost were moved to lay hands on the Brothers and some were Baptized by the Holy Ghost.... Here we realized in fact our paramount call to the Apostles of the Faith as recorded in St. Mark 16:15–20, and from that period the name of the Church had a worldwide fame.[7]

Ghanaian scholars argue that Anim's organization was "Pentecostal" before the arrival any missionary presence,[8] and affiliated with the Apostolic Church after a brief visit from their missionary in Nigeria in 1935. Anim negotiated for missionaries to be sent to Ghana to assist the growing number of churches, and the Apostolic Church sent James McKeown in 1937. McKeown (1900–1989) contracted malaria soon after his arrival and was taken to hospital for treatment, an act that Anim and his followers regarded as deviating from their conviction of divine healing without the use of medicine. This conflict resulted in Anim and some of his followers withdrawing from the Apostolic Church two years later to form the Christ Apostolic Church (CAC). The CAC continued its opposition to the use of medicine well into the 1970s. After Anim was forced into a premature retirement in 1957, his position as leader was reinstated because of prophecy. Anim then continued as leader of the CAC in Ghana until his death at the age of ninety-four.

In its short history, the CAC suffered several schisms from which it never fully recovered, and it was soon overtaken by the rapidly growing and well-organized Church of Pentecost. Nevertheless, Anim remains the widely acknowledged

---

6. Peter Anim, *The History of How the Full Gospel Church Was Founded in Ghana* (Accra: Christ Apostolic Church, n.d.), 1.

7. Anim, *History of How the Full Gospel Church Was Founded in Ghana*, 3.

8. E. Kingsley Larbi, "Peter Newman Anim," in *Dictionary of African Christian Biography*, accessed November 18, 2023, https://dacb.org/stories/ghana/anim-peter/.

pioneer of Ghanaian Pentecostalism. His philosophy of leadership is reflected in the constitution of the Christ Apostolic Church International (CACI), which espouses the fivefold ministry of apostle, prophet, evangelist, pastor, and teacher.[9] According to Larbi, Anim succeeded in establishing a self-governing, self-financing, self-propagating, and self-theologizing Pentecostal denomination. Although Anim did not build a solid financial base for his organization, he laid a foundation for his successors to build upon.[10]

Benson Idahosa (1938–1998), founder of Church of God Mission International, is recognized as the father of Pentecostalism in Nigeria. In 1971, he received a diploma in Divinity from Christ for the Nations Institute in Dallas, Texas. In 1981, he received a Doctor of Divinity degree from the Word of Faith College in New Orleans, and in 1984, he received a Doctor of Law degree from Oral Roberts University. He was the founding president of the Pentecostal Fellowship of Nigeria (PFN) and a member of the College of Bishops of the International Communion of Christian Churches. He held the honorary position of President of All Nations for Christ Bible Institute.

Born to non-Christian parents in a predominantly non-Christian community in Benin City, Nigeria, he was rejected by his father, John, for being frail and sickly. He constantly had fainting spells as a child, and during one of these spells, his mother Sarah abandoned him at a rubbish heap, presuming that he was dead. Hours later he came to, began wailing, and was rescued by his mother.[11] He grew up in a poor household. Like most of the surrounding houses, his family home was a mud house. He was denied access to education until he was fourteen years old, when he was able to attend a local Anglican school. At age nineteen, he was converted to Christianity, joined an Assemblies of God congregation, and was mentored by Pastor Opko. The influence of Opko impacted the future orientation of Idahosa's missional ministry. Ruth Garlock writes, "With Pastor Opko's encouragement, he began organizing teams of workers, whose duty was mainly to pray and singing gospel songs to create awareness of Jesus Christ, within the neighborhood where they intend to evangelize and going into the villages around Benin City to preach the gospel that radically changes the life of his hearer."[12] Idahosa was very active in evangelization and after experiencing

---

9. Peter White, "A Century of Pentecostalism in Ghana," *HTS Theological Studies* 77, no. 4 (2019), 4.

10. Larbi, "Peter Newman Anim," n.p.

11. Ruthanne Garlock, *Fire in His Bones: The Story of Benson Idahosa* (Tulsa: Praise Books, 1998), 2–5.

12. Garlock, *Fire in His Bones*, 62.

a revelation of divine calling into ministry, he led outreaches from village to village, before establishing a church in a store in Benin City.[13]

Idahosa was initiated into the experience of baptism in the Spirit through the mediation of Pastor Opko. During this experience Idahosa felt submerged in the presence of the Holy Spirit. Soon afterward he sensed greater power in his preaching through which he gained his most significant convert, his future wife, Margaret Izevbigie (later Margaret Idahosa), who confessed faith in Jesus after she witnessed the miracle of her niece being raised from the dead during Benson's prayer. On the merit of his success in leading outreaches, in 1965 Idahosa was asked to head up Calvary Fellowship, providing a golden opportunity to showcase his leadership gift.[14] At this time, Idahosa received a divine calling for an expansion of his influence. He heard the Lord say, "I have called you that you might take the gospel around the world in my name.... Preach the gospel and I will confirm my Word with signs following."[15] In 1968, Idahosa raised the funds for construction of his first church building, named the "Mother Church," changing its name to the Church of God Mission International in 1974.[16]

Idahosa benefited from the help of significant allies, the first of which was a Welsh Pentecostal missionary to Nigeria, S. G. Elton, who was affiliated with the Latter Rain Movement.[17] According to Kalu, Elton put Idahosa in touch with Gordon and Freda Lindsay, who not only provided funds to pay for the roofing of Idahosa's church, but also offered him a scholarship to study at Christ for the Nations Bible Institute in Dallas, Texas. Another ally was T. L. (Tommy Lee) Osborn, from whose publications and personal correspondence Idahosa borrowed the model of open-air crusades.[18] He also adopted Osborn's trademark prosperity theology. Probably the most significant of Idahosa's allies was Oral Roberts. In imitation of Oral Roberts, whom Idahosa revered as a mentor, Idahosa ventured into higher education, establishing Christian Faith University

---

13. V. I. Iyawe, *Archbishop Benson Idahosa: Achievements and Legacies of a Colossus* (Benin City, Nigeria: Gift-Prints Associates, 1999), 1.

14. Usman I. Habib, "A New Paradigm of Leadership Development: Church of God Mission International" (Ph.D. diss., University of Manchester, 2014), 60.

15. M. A. Ojo, *The End-Time Army: Charismatic Movements in Modern Nigeria* (Trenton: Africa World Press, 2006), 61.

16. Garlock, *Fire in His Bones*, 128.

17. Ogbu Kalu, *African Pentecostalism: An Introduction* (New York: Oxford University Press, 2008), 91.

18. B. A. Idahosa, *4 Facts You Need to Know* (Benin City: Gift-Prints Associates, 1995), iv–vii.

as an extension of his mission.[19] Asamoah-Gyadu suggests that Idahosa's venture into higher education was based on the example of Oral Roberts, who claimed that the idea for ORU came to him via divine revelation. Asamoah-Gyadu cites the website of Benson Idahosa University: "After the establishment of the Church of God Mission in the 1960s, Archbishop Benson Idahosa *received specific directions from God* to venture into the area of education" (italics are Asamoah-Gyadu's). Ultimately, the name of Idahosa's university was changed to Benson Idahosa University. In 1992, Idahosa applied to the Minister of Education for a license to operate a private university, and a team of academics and professionals was assembled to prepare a feasibility report and develop a master plan for the proposed university. Operating as the Institute of Continuous Learning (ICL), the proposed University organized academic and professional programs for young students. In February 2002, ten years after the application to start a private University, the Nigerian Federal Government, acting through the National Universities Commission (NUC), granted Benson Idahosa University a license to operate. The University started operating as a fully licensed institution in March 2002 with an initial student enrollment of 400, with two registered faculties (the Faculty of Arts, Social Sciences, and Education and the Faculty of Basic and Applied Sciences).[20] Margaret Idahosa was designated as Chancellor, a position she held until recently, and Faith Emmanuel Idahosa (FEB), son of Benson and Margaret, became the university's second president. Along with his duties as President of Benson Idahosa University, FEB is also the President of Big Ben's Children Hospital, Vice President of Faith Mediplex group of hospitals, Vice President of All Nations for Christ Bible Institute International, and Vice President of the Archbishop Idahosa Foundation and Idahosa World Outreach.[21]

Benson Idahosa's leadership style developed as he adapted his institutions to the Nigerian context, deploying strategic initiatives of fervent prayer, aggressive evangelism, and the Holy Spirit's power to perform miracles

---

19. Asamoah-Gyadu, "Your Miracle Is on the Way," 17.

20. Asamoah-Gyadu, "Your Miracle Is on the Way," 24.

21. Asamoah-Gyadu, "Your Miracle Is on the Way," 16–18; Henry Kwadwa Amoako, "Biography of Faith Emmanuel Idahosa," *African Research Consult*, accessed November 18, 2023, https://african-research.com/research/biography/the-marvelous-son-of-the-late-archbishop-benson-idahosa-bishop-feb/.

around the central theme: "Evangelism is our supreme task."[22] Idahosa boldly challenged local customs as inimical to the gospel, such as the practice of men shaving their heads in deference to the death of Oba of Benin, the traditional monarch.[23] Idahosa challenged the resort to indigenous occult powers as a means of protecting people from harm. This message found a receptive audience, as evidenced by the rapid growth of his church, necessitating a relocation to a new facility on Airport Road in 1986. The new headquarters of Idahosa's ministry, Faith Miracle Center, was a cathedral with seating for 10,000 people. Idahosa's Church of God Mission International has branched the world over, from Europe to Africa to Asia to America. Idahosa launched Idahosa World Outreach television ministry (IWO TV), with the intention of reaching a potential viewing audience of fifty million people. According to his associate, Bishop Ojo,

> His teaching was quite different from what was in vogue then. He began the television ministry in Nigeria. We used to go to the television station to preach live on the set. Then people criticized him for using the television. Some began to call the television devil's box. Idahosa brought drum set and guitars and they called us disco church. There is no minister in Nigeria to compare to him when he was alive. Benson Idahosa was a bulldozer. He was a pioneer. He cleared the way. All of those who condemned him and criticized him have now eaten their words.[24]

By 1971, Idahosa had established churches all over Nigeria and Ghana. Known for his boldness, power, and prosperity-based preaching, as well as an unstoppable faith in the supernatural, he was instrumental in fomenting a major wave of revival, as many conversions from animism to Christianity occurred between the 1970s and 1990s in Nigeria. Among his many accomplishments, he founded the Pentecostal Fellowship of Nigeria and like Anim popularized the fivefold ministry, comprised of apostles, prophets, evangelists, pastors, and teachers, thereby instilling what Kalu characterizes as an autocratic conception

---

22. P. Obadan, *The Legend: Archbishop Prof. Benson Idahosa 11 September 1938–12 March 1998* (Benin City: Glopet Limited, 2006), 13.

23. Obadan, *The Legend*, 192–93.

24. Church Gist, "Abacha I Did Not Come to Pay Homage, I have Come to Advise You. You Cannot Stay Here without My Prayer: An Interview with Archbishop Joseph Imariabe Ojo," June 8, 2021, accessed November 18, 2023, https://churchgist.org/abacha-i-did-not-come-to-pay-homage-i-have-come-to-advise-you-you-cannot-stay-here-without-my-prayer-archbishop-benson-idahosa/.

of leadership.[25] Many prominent Nigerian pastors, including Ayo Oritsejafor, David Oyedepo, Felix Omobude, Fred Addo, and Chris Oyakhilome, were Idahosa's protégés.[26]

David Olaniyi Oyedepo (1954–) was born to a Muslim father and a mother who was then a member of the Eternal Order of Cherubim and Seraphim movement in Nigeria. He was raised by his Christian grandmother, who inculcated in him a lifestyle of hard work, prayer, and spiritual disciplines, including tithing.[27] In 1969, at the early age of fifteen, Oyedepo received Jesus Christ as his personal Lord and Savior with the guidance of Betty Lasher, a schoolteacher on a mission assignment to Nigeria from the United States.[28] Subsequently, Oyedepo studied Architecture at Kwara State Polytechnic (now Kwara State University) and embarked upon a career as an architect. He worked briefly with the Federal Ministry of Housing in Ilorin, the Kwara State capital, before resigning to concentrate on Christian ministry. Later, he earned a doctorate in human development from Honolulu University.[29]

In May 1981, David Oyedepo experienced a call to ministry during an eighteen-hour vision. According to his account, he received from the Lord the assignment for his life and destiny. In the vision Oyedepo saw people hurting, depressed, oppressed, sick, beaten, battered, maimed, struggling, and in bondage and shame. While sobbing and crying, he heard the Lord tell him, "Now the hour has come for the liberation of mankind from the oppression of the devil through the preaching of the Word of faith and I am sending you to undertake this task."[30] Immediately after the vision, Oyedepo started Liberation Faith Hour Ministries, which he later renamed as Winners Chapel and, subsequently, Living Faith Church Worldwide. In 1983, about two years after the commencement of his ministry, though without formal theological

---

25. Ogbu Kalu, *African Pentecostalism*, 115.

26. Emmanuel Kingsley Kwabena Larbi, "The Development of Ghanaian Pentecostalism: A Study in the Appropriation of the Christian Gospel in Twentieth Century Ghana Setting with Special Reference to the Christ Apostolic Church, the Church of Pentecost, and the International Central Gospel Church" (Ph.D., diss., University of Edinburgh, 1996), 265.

27. Daniel Okpara, *15 Success Habits of Bishop David Oyedepo* (St. Peters, MD: Better Life Media, 2016), 54.

28. Christian Diet, "Biography of Bishop David Oyedepo," July 27, 2021, accessed November 18, 2023, https://christiandiet.com.ng/bishop-david-oyedepo-biography-ministry-lessons-from-his-life/.

29. Believers Portal, "Biography of Bishop David Oyedepo," September 8, 2016, accessed November 18, 2023, http://believersportal.com/biography-bishop-david-oyedepo/.

30. David Oyedepo, *Exploring the Secrets of Success* (Lagos, Nigeria: Dominion Publishing House, 1998), 1.

education, Oyedepo was ordained to pastoral ministry alongside his wife, Faith Abiola Oyedepo. Pastor Enoch Adeboye, General Overseer of the Redeemed Christian Church of God, officially commissioned Oyedepo into the Pentecostal ministry. In 1992, Oyedepo assumed the title of Bishop. He is presently the senior pastor of Faith Tabernacle, with a 50,000-seat church auditorium reputed to be one of the largest church auditoriums in the world according to the Guinness Book of Records.[31]

Since the commencement of his ministry in 1983, Bishop David Oyedepo has proven himself to be an extraordinary Spirit-empowered leader, achieving many notable accomplishments. In 1999, he directed the construction of Faith Tabernacle within a period of one year.[32] This feat stands out as a highlight of the boldness of Oyedepo's stature in the Spirit-empowered movement as a preacher of faith and divine guidance. Due to the continuous influx of worshippers every week and the extended service hours, Oyedepo's ministry is in the process of constructing a 100,000-seat auditorium called The Ark. On the same site, a complex of edifices can accommodate a 10,000-seat children's church, shopping mall, prayer booth, missions tower, and a host of other ministry functions.[33]

By the year 2000, the Winners Chapel had a network of 400 branches in Nigeria and thirty-eight other African countries.[34] Presently, the Living Faith Church global church network has a presence in 145 nations including European countries and the United States. This aggressive branch network model has earned the church the status of an international ministry with global impact. In 2020, the ministry planted about 10,000 churches all over Nigeria and beyond despite the COVID-19 pandemic that ravaged humanity during the year.[35] The church growth agenda of the ministry is rooted and powered by the cell group replication strategy set forth specifically in Acts 5:42: "Day after day, in the temple courts and from house to house, they never stopped teaching and proclaiming the good news

---

31. Okpara, *15 Success Habits of Bishop David Oyedepo*, 14.

32. Okpara, *15 Success Habits of Bishop David Oyedepo*, 14.

33. Vanguard Media, "Winners Chapel to Commence 100,000 Capacity Ark Auditorium Project Soon," January 24, 2021), accessed November 18, 2023, https://www.vanguardngr.com/2021/01/winners-chapel-100000-ark-auditorium/.

34. Paul Gifford, "Healing in African Pentecostalism: The 'Victorious Living' of David Oyedepo," in *Global Pentecostal and Charismatic Healing*, ed. Candy Gunther Brown (New York: Oxford University Press, 2011), 253.

35. Vanguard Media, "Despite Covid, We Planted 10,000 Churches without Raising an Offering—Bishop Oyedepo," December 12, 2020, accessed November 18, 2023, https://www.vanguardngr.com/2020/12/despite-covid-we-planted-10000-churches-without-raising-an-offering-%E2%80%95-bishop-oyedepo/.

that Jesus is the Messiah." The cell groups that meet weekly under the umbrella of Winners Satellite Fellowship are engaged in caring, feeding, and nourishing members. The resulting growth has bolstered the overall expansion of the ministry. One of the main objectives of the Winners Satellite Fellowship is to raise up a new generation of leaders who will start more Fellowship Centers, thereby leading to further growth. Blending faith and hard work, Oyedepo insists that the growth of the ministry is the will of God, yet this requires dedication and faithfulness from members for its accomplishment.

The Dominion Publishing House is another achievement of the leadership of Bishop David Oyedepo. Established in 1985, it has over five million publications in circulation to date with the bishop himself having over seventy titles apart from numerous periodical articles, all geared toward world evangelization and fulfillment of the liberation mandate given to Oyedepo.[36]

Figure 16: David and Florence Abiola Oyedepo

Photo of David Oyedepo, head overseer of Living Faith Church, with his wife Faith Oyedepo, wearing a full Nigerian artier, 17 June 2017. Wikimedia Commons, CC BY-SA 4.0.

Oyedepo's ministry is committed to providing educational opportunities. It presently runs two accredited universities—Covenant and Landmark—and is in the process of establishing a third in Abuja, the capital of Nigeria; all three institutions are debt free. Other educational institutions are affiliated with Oyedepo's ministry, such as Faith Academy, Covenant University Day Secondary School, and Kingdom Heritage Primary School, all of which are dedicated to the purpose of raising up a new generation of leaders who love God passionately.[37] Oyedepo is convinced of the crucial importance of knowledge, which especially in developing countries of Africa cannot be over emphasized as the means of the liberation through knowledge.

---

36. List of books by Oyedepo, accessed December 28, 2023, https://www.duifibooks.com/a/bishop-david-oyedepo/4257402/.

37. Morack Akin-David, *The Leadership Secrets of David O. Oyedepo: The Secrets of Men Are in Their Stories* (Lagos: BookAddict Publications, 2015), 37.

Bishop David Oyedepo's ministry has contributed immensely to Spirit-empowered leadership through the establishment of educational institutions and various leadership training seminars organized across Africa and in other nations of the world. The Word of Faith Bible Institute is the ministry's leadership training and spiritual center, dedicated to the mission of empowering members and non-members to fulfill God's call on their lives. The curriculum of this Bible institute is designed to teach leadership skills for ministry, society, economy, and other areas of human endeavor including relationships and family.[38] Through this movement, Bishop David Oyedepo has influenced many emerging leaders who have blazed new paths in African Pentecostalism, e.g., David Ibiyeomie of Salvation Ministries in Port Harcourt, Nigeria, and Paul Enenche of Dunamis International Ministries.[39]

Oyedepo's extraordinary success has been met with controversy. In March 1996, he heard the voice of the Lord telling him that the time to purchase an aircraft had come. He neither hesitated nor sought consultation but simply reported to church members what he had heard from the Lord and took up an offering, from which a jet aircraft was purchased and delivered debt free. Faced with questions from critics, Oyedepo retorted that the purpose of the jet was for the proclamation of the gospel in Africa and the world. He stated, "God told us we are going to fly; if He left us to plan to fly, it won't enter our budget in the next ten years. We are just changing planes like we change bicycles because His blessings make us rich and add no sorrow."[40] Some among his adherents might say that Oyedepo's lavish expenses were indicative of divine approval, and, further, that sensitivity to the voice and direction of the Holy Spirit is the secret to a world of outstanding success and unparalleled leadership in the kingdom. However, Oyedepo's critics would counter that his leadership and that of other prosperity preachers is flawed by autocratic impulses and avaricious desires.[41]

This much cannot be denied: Bishop David Oyedepo is a leader of leaders. Through his leadership training seminars, Sons of the Prophets' yearly conferences, and the Word of Faith Bible Institute, Bishop Oyedepo has

---

38. Akin-David, *Leadership Secrets of David Oyedepo*, 37.

39. LFS News, "Meet Eight Spiritual Sons of Oyedepo…," August 22, 2020, accessed December 28, 2023, https://lightfeatherstoriesw.home.blog/2020/08/22/men-of-god-mentored-by-bishop-david-oyedepo/.

40. Vanguard Media, "Why I Have a Fleet of Private Jets, Bishop Oyedepo Reveals," September 2, 2023, accessed December 28, 2023, https://www.vanguardngr.com/2023/09/why-i-have-a-fleet-of-private-jets-bishop-oyedepo-reveals/.

41. Isaac Boaheng, Clement Amoako, and Samuel Boahen, "A Critique of Prosperity Theology in the Context of Ghanaian Christianity," *Noyam: E-Journal of Humanities, Arts and Social Sciences* 4, no. 11 (November 2023): 1358–59; https://doi.org/10.38159/ehass.20234114.

developed a model for leadership development for a new generation of leaders, not only in Africa but also in other global contexts. His book *Exploits in Ministry* commends this model. It is divided into six parts, namely, the minister and his call, fundamentals of leadership in ministry, the ladder of exploits, structure of ministry, financing the ministry, and relationships in ministry. This book delineates the steps of the ministry leadership ladder, provides tools for emerging leaders to discover their authentic leadership styles, and encourages them to lead others with relative confidence, purpose, and impact.[42] The bishop's exceptional mastery of entrepreneurial Spirit-empowered leadership has become a role model for many budding leaders in Africa and beyond.

Edir Macedo Bezerra (1945–), self-appointed bishop of the Universal Church of the Kingdom of God (IURD) and owner and chairman of the second-largest television network in Brazil, was born in Rio das Flores, Brazil. He was raised as a Catholic until age seventeen, when he joined Umbanda, a syncretic Afro-Brazilian religion that blends African traditions with Roman Catholicism, Spiritism, and Indigenous American beliefs. He attended university in Rio de Janeiro, majoring in mathematics. He received a master's degree in theological studies through the Federation of Evangelical Religious Entities of Spain in Madrid. He also holds a doctoral degree in Theology and in Christian Philosophy and an honorary degree in Divinity from the Faculdade de Educação Teológica do Estado de São Paulo. He began a career as a civil servant in 1963, working for the state-run lottery of Rio de Janeiro, Loterj, and then at the Brazilian Institute of Geography and Statistics as a researcher in the economic census of 1970. In 1965, at the invitation of his sister, Macedo converted to Pentecostalism during revival meetings held by Bishop Robert McAlister, a Canadian missionary who had founded the Igreja Vida Nova (New Life Church). From McAlister, Macedo heard about prosperity theology, positive confession, spiritual warfare, and hereditary curses, a combination of ideas that had a formative influence on his ministerial formation.[43] In 1975, he founded a Pentecostal church with Romildo Ribeiro Soares. In 1977, God spoke to Macedo in a vision, instructing him to start a new church using the name Igreja Universal do Reino de Deus (IURD), Universal Church of the Kingdom of God.[44] The church was small in

---

42. David O. Oyedepo, *Exploits in Ministry* (Lagos, Nigeria: Dominion Publishing House, 2006), 98–126.

43. Paulo Ayres Mattos, "Edir Macedo," in *BEGP*, ed. Michael Wilkinson, Connie Au, Jorg Haustein, and Todd M. Johnson (Leiden: Brill, 2021), 401.

44. David D. Bundy, "Edir Macedo," in *NIDPCM*, ed. Stanley M. Burgess and Eduard M. van der Maas (Grand Rapids: Zondervan, 2002), 854.

its beginnings but grew steadily by means of aggressive evangelism and eventually morphed into a denomination, establishing churches in Portugal, Mozambique, Angola, Indonesia, the United States, and throughout Latin America and Europe. Today, the IURD has spawned an extensive global network of branches ranging from cathedrals and temples, such as the opulent Temple of Solomon in Sao Paulo that seats thousands, to local storefront churches and rented spaces.[45] Macedo's mission strategy proved to be highly effective. The IURD would move into a community, buy an old theater or church building, and invest heavily in local radio and television broadcasts. Some examples purportedly include a theater on Broadway in New York City, the former St. Mary Star of the Sea Parish in Boston, and the Astoria theater in London. In 1989, Macedo bought the commercial television network, Record TV, and in the same year founded Grupo Record. In 1992, he spent eleven days in jail due to an accusation of charlatanism. According to his autobiography, *Nothing to Lose*, Macedo's followers organized several protests, with his loyalists camping in front of the police precinct where he was held.[46] In 2007, he founded the twenty-four-hour free-to-air news channel, Record News. According to official statistics of the denomination, as of 1997, the IURD claimed to have 6,000,000 adherents and 1,500 congregations. Other sources place the membership between one and a half and two million. From March 2013 to 2015, Macedo was on the Forbes list of billionaires with reported assets of U.S. $1.1 billion, making him by far the richest pastor in Brazil and the world. He is a prolific author with thirty-four titles, many of which have sold 250,000 to 350,000 copies, published by the IURD publishing house, Editora Gráfica Universal in Rio de Janeiro.[47]

Macedo's theology is essentially neo-Pentecostal with emphasis on the work of the Holy Spirit and the usual doctrinal keynotes of healing, exorcism, and prosperity theology. He aggressively attacks traditional Afro-Brazilian religions in a controversial book, *Orixás, caboclos & guias. Deuses ou demônios?* (Orixás, Caboclos and Guides. Gods or demons?), published in 1988 with sales that have exceeded three million copies.[48] Macedo claims that demons can take

---

45. Kathleen Openshaw, "Universal Church of the Kingdom of God," *BEGP*, ed. Michael Wilkinson, Connie Au, Jörg Haustein, and Todd M. Johnson (Leiden: Brill, 2021), 645.

46. Teresa Malcolm, "March on Behalf of Macedo," *National Catholic Reporter* 32, no. 13 (January 26, 1996), 7.

47. Bundy, "Edir Macedo," *NIDPCM*, 854.

48. Vagner Gonçalves da Silva, "Neo-Pentecostalism and Afro-Brazilian Religions: Explaining the Attacks on Symbols of the African Religious Heritage in Contemporary Brazil," trans. David Allan Rodgers, *Mana* 3 (2007): n.p., accessed October 10, 2023, http://socialsciences.scielo.org/pdf/s_mana/v3nse/scs_a03.pdf.

over humans through the magical practices conducted by family members or close friends involved in demonic cults, and can even attack a person's kin even after they are dead. He claims that Afro-Brazilian religions present a diabolical threat from their performance of animal sacrifices, the trances caused by spirit possession, worshipping of the dead, and the use of magic to cause harm. Macedo provides numerous testimonies of former members of Afro-Brazilian cults who converted to IURD, including his testimony as a former participant of Umbanda as well as a handwritten notebook of "fundaments" (secret knowledge) given to the author by a former saint-mother. The only protection, according to Macedo, is to accept Jesus fully into one's heart and be filled with the Holy Spirit.[49]

Macedo's style of leadership is highly authoritarian, centralized and micromanaged. Each congregation in the IURD remains loyal to the church's organizational hierarchy, especially in matters of church finances. All IURD churches share one common focus: the material well-being of its members, who in turn support the church and its pastors. In all the churches within its global empire, the primary focus of the IURD is on success, health, and "the pursuit of material happiness."[50] In the IURD, the giving of money to the church is a central tenet of belief; it is, in fact, thought to be central to salvation. Virginia Garrard-Burnett points out that in the church's thirteen-point statement of belief, the issue of the giving of tithes appears before statements about the Lord's Supper or eternal life made possible through Jesus's sacrifice. Garrard-Burnett writes, "Tithes and offering are so sacred, as sacred as the Word of God. Tithes and offering signify the loyalty and love that the servant has toward the Lord. One cannot disassociate tithes and offering from the redemptive work of the Lord Jesus; they signify, in truth, the blood of the saved for those who need salvation."[51] Macedo calls this formula for earthly salvation "the miracle of the tithe."[52]

Members are urged to give a donation at every service they attend, and many of the faithful attend services multiple times per week, sometimes more than once a day, since each day symbolizes a different aspect of intercession: for health, family, money, jobs, etc. It is perhaps too glib an observation to make, that such

---

49. da Silva, "Neo-Pentecostalism and Afro-Brazilian Religions," n.p.

50. Virginia Garrard-Burnett, ed. "Neo-Pentecostalism and Prosperity Theology in Latin America: A Religion for Late Capitalist Society," *Iberoamericana. Nordic Journal of Latin American and Caribbean Studies* 42, nos. 1–2 (2012): 23.

51. Garrard-Burnett, "Neo-Pentecostalism and Prosperity Theology," 29.

52. See Virginia Garrard-Burnett, "Stop Suffering?: The Iglesia Universal del Reino de Dios in the United States" In *Conversion of a Continent: Contemporary Religious Change in Latin America*, ed. Timothy Steigenga and Edward L. Cleary, 218–38. (Ithaca, NY: Rutgers University Press, 2007), accessed March 21, 2024, https://doi.org/10.36019/9780813544021-012.

contributions do indeed produce prosperity—at least for the pastor and church administration, if not necessarily for the giver. Using the prosperity gospel as a platform, Macedo adeptly incorporates charismatic fervor, emphasis on the Holy Spirit, healing and exorcism from Pentecostalism, mystic and financial practices common to the Afro-Brazilian spiritism, and a hierarchical structure reminiscent of the Roman Catholic Church.[53] In addition to its outlets around the world, a university, and television and radio stations, the IRUD has also secured a strong political voice in Brazil. While many other churches in Brazil have chosen to not get involved in politics, the IURD has actively promoted candidates to public offices, from city councilmen to the national congress and president. In this way, the IURD has been successful at gaining legislation favorable to its interests and concessions to coveted radio and television stations, conceiving of its use of power as means of expanding the Kingdom of God on earth. As one could surmise, God's Kingdom is seen as synonymous with Macedo's Universal Church of the Kingdom of God.

Up until now, Bishop Macedo has been able to keep a tight grip on the leadership of his religious empire. Nevertheless, life is not easy for those who choose a career in Macedo's religious organization. The pastors are recruited from the lower classes and are offered a higher standard of living than they would otherwise have. In exchange for this security, the church demands blind loyalty from them. The pastors are subject to transfers from one church to another, sometimes even to other states or countries with no prior notice.[54] Though there have been many dissident pastors, most of these have been silenced either through financial payouts or legal threats. The few who insist on speaking out are outnumbered by the many pastors who will defend the church's practices. Perhaps the most serious problem faced by the IURD was when Sergio Von Helder, one of Macedo's pastors, desecrated an image of Brazil's patron saint on October 12, 1995, the patron saint's day. On a midnight television program, Von Helder slapped and kicked the statue of Our Lady of the Appearance, a Black likeness of the Virgin Mary. Few people saw the actual program, but another network sympathetic with the Catholic Church raised national ire by replaying the scene throughout the following day. IURD churches were attacked and stoned. Church members and pastors were threatened. Bishop Macedo went on national TV to ask forgiveness for his pastor's act and to say that the pastor

---

53. Ken Serbin, "Brazilian Church Builds an International Empire," *Christian Century* 113, no. 12 (April 10, 1996), 401.

54. Mattos, "Edir Macedo," *BEGP*, 402.

had been removed from his position.[55] Yet, even though what the pastor did was consistent with the fiery message Bishop Macedo himself preaches against the Catholic Church, he was removed to protect the church's public image. This illustrates the disposable way the IURD treats its clergy, maintaining them if they are useful to the "Kingdom," then disposing of them.

Serious concerns have been levelled against Macedo and the IURD.[56] The denomination has long been subject to charges of financial abuse and manipulation, both in Brazil and in other nations. Macedo has been accused of operating a cynical money-making scheme rooted in the prosperity gospel. Faithful members are told, in effect, that prayer and financial giving operate on the same crass principle as secular investments: the more one gives to the church, the more material benefit can be expected in this life. The church profits directly from the sale of promised miracles and blessings and from material products such as holy oils. Macedo has risen from humble origins to become a billionaire, with a lavish lifestyle; his holdings include Brazil's second-largest television network. Mattos concludes that the political influence of Macedo's IURD in all levels of the Brazilian society "has continuously grown up to now without any interruption."[57]

Mariano Zuniega Velarde (1939–), better known as Brother Mike Velarde, is the founder and "Servant Leader" of a Philippines-based Catholic charismatic movement called El Shaddai, which has an estimated following of from three to nine million.[58] A famous televangelist in the Philippines, he is also the owner of Amvel Land Development Corporation, a real estate company, and Delta Broadcasting System.[59] Finding a niche within the Catholic Charismatic Renewal, Velarde decided to remain within the Roman Catholic Church as a layperson.

Velarde became a Catholic charismatic-style preacher in 1982, when he started a radio program that soon gained a wide audience. In 1984, he founded the El Shaddai movement, which has become an eclectic expression of Philippine folk Christianity, the charismatic movement, and Roman Catholicism. Initially, Brother Mike reported that only "the poorest of the

---

55. Mattos, "Edir Macedo," *BEGP*, 402.

56. Openshaw, "Universal Church of the Kingdom of God," *BEGP*, 646–47.

57. Mattos, "Edir Macedo," *BEGP*, 402.

58. Katherine L. Wiegele, *Investing in Miracles: El Shaddai and the Transformation of Popular Catholicism in the Philippines* (Honolulu: University of Honolulu, 2005), 4.

59. Emma-Kate Symons, "Preacher Power," *Wall Street Journal* (May 14, 2010): n.p.

poor" attended El Shaddai's services.[60] The turning point in his career as a charismatic leader came when, once a month, he started calling together his faithful listeners for an outdoor prayer rally in a space near the radio station. When the crowd became too big for the space available, Velarde began to rent more spacious sites (from large stadiums to congress halls), until he found suitable accommodation in San Dionisio (Parañaque) in 2009. His new headquarters, with an estimated cost of about $21,000,000 (U.S. dollars), is called the House of Prayer, a megachurch-like structure located in Amyel Business Park. The facility covers 10,000 square meters, with 16,000 seats plus standing room for another 25,000 people. The temple was inaugurated by the former President of the Philippines, Gloria Macapagal Arroyo. Since then, the growth of the El Shaddai movement has been precipitous, both in the Philippines and through its diffusion, via the Philippine diaspora, around the world, to Europe, the Americas, Africa, and the rich Gulf countries.[61]

Velarde's leadership style is like other global charismatic founders of parachurch movements, particularly the 700 Club. In fact, Wiegele cites a source who claimed that Brother Mike's organizational terminology, fundraising methods, and theology were inspired by Pat Robertson's TV program.[62] As the head of El Shaddai, Brother Mike is assisted by a group of "disciples" that includes family members. He and the disciples choose men from among the members to serve as lay preachers, training them at the El Shaddai "College of Divine Wisdom," where they study the Bible and are taught evangelization methods, counseling skills and how to heal by praying over of hands. These preachers are assigned to preach at small gatherings in the Philippines and abroad and receive a stipend for doing so. Velarde appoints coordinators who are responsible for local organization and finances, operating along guidelines from the center. Interestingly, the coordinators are always women. In addition to the many employees who keep the organization and its media network functioning, volunteers serve in a range of capacities. Some distribute chairs or manage traffic at the Amvel compound during the gawain or clean the grounds afterwards. Women serve as ushers for Mass. They also assist in outreach programs. Men and women assist as lay ministers during communion, assist and prepare candidates for adult baptism and confirmation, and other El Shaddai liturgical events.

---

60. Symons, "Preacher Power," n.p.

61. K. L. Wiegele, "Catholics Rich in Spirit: El Shaddai's Modern Engagements," *Philippine Studies* 54, no. 4 (2006): 495–520.

62. Wiegele, *Investing in Miracles*, 18–26.

Those with communications skills help prepare newsletters and the El Shaddai magazine. Some lawyers offer free legal clinics, and doctors and dentists offer medical clinics.

The message of Brother Mike is like the prosperity gospel of Pentecostal televangelists, promising God's financial and physical blessings to all, if they remain faithful in attendance to gatherings, giving tithes and offerings, and displaying obedience. A vivid storyteller, Velarde peppers his talks with stories based either on his own experience or stories others have shared with him, incorporating bits of Filipino folk wisdom. A typical sermon might address the situation of Filipino families, remembering when young people ritually offered signs of respect to elders, and discuss how families are changing. Rather than framing himself as a culture warrior against modernity or contemporary mores, he tries to offer hope and ways forward, linking his stories with the biblical passage that opened the session. He cracks jokes and sings. The sermon would call the assembly to find ways to respect their elders, to remember that when you love your parents, you love God, and you put into practice the meaning of the love of God. A relentlessly positive message encourages believers to look at how God is present and working to bring better things in their lives. Esmeralda Fortunado-Sanchez writes,

> At the middle of his preaching, he asks the congregation to hold up their tithes and "love offerings" (additional donations beyond the 10% tithe) in the envelopes dedicated for that purpose. "Prayer requests" are always placed in the same envelope, and as they are held up, Brother Mike blesses them. To close, he makes the congregation repeat the theme of his healing message with a "prayer partner," while communicating his belief that people's generosity will be multiplied in miraculous ways, he regularly says that it means that in everything we do, God is always there.[63]

Velarde also employs the use of certain inanimate objects such as handkerchiefs, bankbooks, and umbrellas, which are held aloft during services. Such practices are not foreign to Filipino indigenous and folk religion. Thus, Velarde's brand of Catholic Charismatic Renewal is culturally relevant to many Filipinos.[64]

Velarde's practical theology consists of an organizational element that is typical of global Spirit-empowered leaders, the leadership team. Velarde is assisted by a group of disciples that include family members. He and the disciples choose

---

63. Esmeralda Fortunado-Sanchez and Thomas M. Landy, "El Shaddai and the Charismatic Transformation of Philippine Catholicism," *Catholic & Cultures*, S.J. Center for Religion, Ethics and Culture, College of the Holy Cross, n.p., accessed October 24, 2025, https://www.catholicsandcultures. org/philippines-el-shaddai-serves-largest-population-charismatic-followers.

64. Malou L. Aguilar, "Miracles Are His Business," *Asian Journal* (January 4, 2008): 1–2.

men from among the members to serve as lay preachers, training them at an El Shaddai-run College of Divine Wisdom, where they study the Bible and are taught evangelization methods, counseling skills, and the techniques of healing ministry—namely prayer with laying on of hands. The lay preachers are assigned to preach at small gatherings in the Philippines and abroad and receive a stipend for doing so. Each small group in El Shaddai has a coordinator responsible for local organization and finances, operating along guidelines from the center, and the coordinators are always women. In addition, men and women assist as lay ministers during communion, assist and prepare candidates for adult baptism, confirmation, and at El Shaddai liturgical events. Those with communications skills help prepare newsletters and the El Shaddai magazine. Some lawyers offer free legal clinics, and doctors and dentists offer medical clinics.[65]

Velarde stirred up two spates of controversy: first, when he was accused of supporting President Fidel Ramos in 1992, and second when he came under fire for his ownership of a TV broadcasting chain, which prompted a dispute between Velarde and Eddie Villanueva, leader of an independent global charismatic movement called Jesus is Lord. Despite these controversies, Velarde has earned the benevolent approval of the bishop of the diocese of Parañaque. Enzo Pace contends that the difference between Velarde and Villanueva concerns the way in which the two leaders operate in the political sphere. While Villanueva directly involved himself in electoral campaigns, Velarde chose a different tact. He realized the error of initial attempts he made to exploit his popularity as a religious leader in the political arena and adjusted the focus of his ministry, choosing to comply with the directives of the Filipino episcopate by avoiding direct involvement in the controversial political tussles that have characterized the Philippines in the last thirty years. Pace surmises that although Velarde has been keen to remain as a leader of a movement that remains within the Catholic Church, while at the same time embracing the transnational entrepreneurial persona and charisma of his counterpart, Eddie Villanueva.[66]

Conclusion

This chapter has followed the development of Spirit-empowered leadership across four historical stages: precursors, early Pentecostal, neo-Pentecostal,

---

65. Fortunado-Sanchez and Landy, "El Shaddai and the Charismatic Transformation of Philippine Catholicism," n.p.

66. Enzo Pace, "The Catholic Charismatic Movement in Global Pentecostalism," *Religions* 11, no. 351 (July 2020): 16.

and global charismatic. We have seen a continuous outpouring of Spirit baptism as the well from which Spirit-empowered leadership has flowed. From the outset, the type of leadership in the Spirit-empowered movement has been charismatic and ethnically diverse. We have also observed recurring leadership flaws, specifically tendencies toward authoritarian leadership and an affinity for prosperity theology. These commonalities have endured throughout the decades. We have also witnessed a momentous shift in geographical concentration with the diffusion of the Spirit-empowered movement from the West (Europe and North America) to the Global South (Africa, Latin America, and Asia).

These changes reflect what Jonathan Bonk calls a new development in "ecclesiastical cartography."[67] The map showing the concentration in world Christianity has shifted from north to south. Christianity is growing so rapidly in the Global South that Africa is becoming the home to the world's fastest growing Christian population. One might wonder what sort of Christianity is emerging. According to Philip Jenkins, in Africa, Asia, and Latin America, Christians live in settings closer to the social, cultural, and intellectual milieu in which the New Testament itself was written. For this reason, Jenkins argues, people in these regions read the Scriptures with a freshness and authenticity impossible in the prosperous societies of North America and Europe.[68] Many churches in the Global South take very seriously the supernatural worldview that pervades the Christian Scriptures, with the recurrent themes of demons, possession, exorcism, and spiritual healing. Yet at the same time, leaders of the Spirit-empowered movement in the Global South are engaging in social activism. Across Africa, Asia, and Latin America, churches seek both deliverance and liberation: deliverance from evil supernatural forces and liberation from oppressive social structures.[69] Such examples challenge our conventional division of religion into conservative and liberal forms, transcending Western preconceptions.

The expansion of global Christianity has brought with it a diversity of models of Spirit-empowered leadership. Part III of this book categorizes different types of leadership gifting, adapted from the biblical framework of Ephesians 4:11.

---

67. See Jonathan Bonk, "The Dictionary of African Christian Biography: A Proposal for Revising Ecclesiastical Maps," *Missiology: An International Review* 27, no. 1 (January 1999), 71–83.

68. Philip Jenkins, *The New Faces of Christianity: Believing the Bible in the Global South* (Oxford: Oxford University Press, 2006).

69. Donald E. Miller and Tetsunao Yamamori, *Global Pentecostalism: The New Face of Christian Social Engagement* (Berkeley: University of California Press, 2007).

The author is inclined to think that despite differences and contemporary modifications that have developed over time, these types are in tune with the charismatic core of Spirit-empowered ministry in the New Testament.

PART THREE

PARADIGMS OF GLOBAL SPIRIT-EMPOWERED LEADERSHIP

Spirit-empowered leaders employ different paradigms of ministry leadership. The aim of this part of the book is to identify, explain, and critique these paradigms. A paradigm is a typical example or pattern of something, that is, a model. Hans Kung offers perceptive thoughts on the concept of a paradigm. He writes, "A paradigm is not a theory or leading idea. It is an entire constellation of beliefs, values, techniques and so on shared by the members of a community."[1] In what follows, the author takes a typological approach, offering a synchronic analysis of prevalent models of Spirit-empowered leadership. He argues that Spirit-empowered leadership can be aptly categorized in terms of the five paradigms discussed below. This typology is offered with students and practitioners in mind, rather than experts in the field of leadership studies.

Chapters 7–11 delineate five paradigms of Spirit-empowered leadership: apostle, prophet, healing evangelist, pastorpreneur, and teacher-scholar.[2] These five paradigms are adapted from a popular formulation known as the Fivefold Ministry Gifts, based on Ephesians 4:11. While the term "fivefold ministry" does not appear in the Bible, it is commonly utilized as a framework for Spirit-empowered discourses on leadership. Examples of these discourses in various contexts are offered below.

Each of the following chapters follows a uniform structure or framework: (1) we set out the biblical premise of each paradigm, (2) describe the components or constituent ideas of each paradigm, (3) give examples of leading adherents of the paradigm, (4) conduct a formative assessment of each paradigm, and (5) conduct a summative assessment of the paradigms as a whole, assembling a synthesis of the overall continuity of the paradigms from Ephesians 4:12–16.

---

1. Hans Kung, *Theology for the Third Millennium: An Ecumenical View* (New York: Doubleday, 1988), 172.

2. Eric N. Newberg, "Paradigms of Global Spirit-Empowered Leadership," *Spiritus: ORU Journal of Theology* 7, no. 2 (2022): 169–98.

145

7

Apostle Paradigm

Our exposition of the apostle paradigm begins by raising a fundamental question: Are there modern-day apostles? The apostle is the first of the leadership gifts in Ephesians 4:11. There is no universal agreement in the Spirit-empowered movement concerning the inclusion of the "title" of apostle in contemporary leadership positions. There are, however, several Pentecostal and charismatic groups that view the apostolate as integral to their scheme of leadership. These include proponents of the New Apostolic Reformation (NAR), to be discussed below. Other groups, such as the American Assemblies of God, have chosen not to incorporate "apostle" in their leadership nomenclature, due to a concern voiced by Donald Gee, who stated, "It is a sorry fact that grave errors and extravagances quickly marred both the use of the prophetic gift and the office of the self-styled 'apostle' leader."[1]

While some Pentecostals are hesitant to endorse the office of apostle, nevertheless, there is wide agreement on the apostolic dynamic of Spirit-empowered Christianity. This agreement stems from the early Pentecostals who aspired to restore the apostolic faith and power of the New Testament church. The relevance of the apostle paradigm is evidenced, Warrington avers, by his observation that "many Pentecostal leaders function analogously to the early apostles in their leadership of churches and denominations."[2] Below is a description of the biblical grounds, components of the apostle paradigm, two case studies, and a brief formative assessment.

Biblical Patterns and Principles

The word "apostle" occurs seventy-nine times in the New Testament. It denotes a commissioned messenger or ambassador,[3] and the noun "apostle" (Greek

---

1. Donald Gee, *The Pentecostal Movement*, 117–118. Quoted in Keith Warrington, *Pentecostal Theology: A Theology of Encounter* (London: T&T Clark, 2008), 140.

2. Warrington, *Pentecostal Theology*, 140.

3. M. H. Shepherd, "Apostle," *The Interpreter's Dictionary of the Bible* (Nashville: Abingdon, 1962), 1: 172.

ἀπόστολος) is derived from the verb *apostello* (Greek ἀποστέλλω), which has a range of meanings in the New Testament. The term "apostle" designates an envoy sent out by a church as its representative, a missionary or preacher of the gospel, or the twelve, whom Jesus called and mentored. The tasks of an apostle vary but seem to be centered on the proclamation of the gospel and the planting and oversight of new churches (1 Cor. 9:5; 12:28; Eph. 3:5; 4:11).[4]

Hewett suggests two reasons for holding that Jesus did not establish an exclusive apostolate. First, Jesus allowed those who were not apostles to cast out demons in his name as he had instructed the twelve. Second, the twelve and "the seventy" (not designated as apostles) shared the same authority, abilities, and commission. Hence, both apostles and other disciples were empowered to preach the kingdom, heal the sick, and cast out demons.[5]

In the synoptic gospels, Jesus personally selected the twelve as apostles (Matt. 10:7–8; Mark 3:16–19; Luke 6:13–16). He then sent them out with instructions to proclaim the kingdom, heal the sick, and drive out demons. In the gospel of John, emphasis is placed on the sending motif in relation to Christ's mission as Logos and Son of God, and his sending of the twelve, without naming them as apostles per se.[6] Paul affirms that he too was chosen as an apostle by Christ in a post-resurrection appearance of Jesus on the road to Damascus (1 Cor. 15:8–9; Gal. 1:1; 2:6–9).

The main task of an apostle was to be a firsthand witness to the resurrection of Christ, with secondary tasks of preaching the gospel, performing signs and wonders, and planting churches. Paul describes the apostles and prophets as the Church's foundation of the chief cornerstone (Eph. 2:20). He describes other leaders as apostles, such as James, the brother of Jesus, and possibly Barnabas. He uses the word "apostle" in more than one sense, as referring not only to those appointed by Jesus, but also to those who served as emissaries of churches. Further, Paul differentiates between true and false apostles, with the false apostles consisting of his opponents. He does not reveal their identity, but resorts to ridiculing them (2 Cor. 11:5, 13; 12:11). According to Betz, we are left with the challenge of defining the criteria for true and false apostles. This challenge reared its head throughout Church history during controversies over heresy.[7]

---

4. Hans Dieter Betz, "Apostle," in *The Anchor Bible Dictionary*, ed. David Noel Freedman (New York: Doubleday, 1992), 1: 309.

5. J. A. Hewett, "Office of Apostle," in *NIDPCM*, ed. Stanley M. Burgess and Eduard M. van der Maas (Grand Rapids: Zondervan, 2002), 319.

6. Betz, "Apostle," 311.

7. Betz, "Apostle," 310–11.

The early Christian title of apostle presents several unresolved issues. Romans 16:7 contains a greeting addressed to two apostles, Adronicus and Junias, the latter of which may be a female name. This may indicate that there was a difference between the original twelve and later apostles, and further, that they were not the exclusive apostles. Among those who performed an apostolic function were James (1 Cor. 15:7; Gal. 1:19), Barnabas (Acts 14:4, 14; 1 Cor. 9:6), Andronicus and Junias (Rom. 16:7), possibly Silas and Timothy (1 Thess. 1:1; 2:7), and Apollos (1 Cor. 4:6, 9). It has been suggested that this latter group had the gift of apostleship (1 Cor. 12:28–29) but not the apostolic "office" that was conferred upon the twelve and Paul. Those who had the gift of an apostleship, then, were those who effectively preached the gospel message and confirmed it with signs and wonders.

The question remains as to whether people who carry out an apostolic function can be designated as apostles. Further, to what extent can we meaningfully speak of the apostolic office in our churches today? While we can affirm the uniqueness of the office of twelve (including Paul) in the New Testament, we can also affirm the apostolic ministry of those who are presently engaged in preaching the kingdom, healing the sick, driving out demons, and planting and overseeing churches. Despite those who contend that the office of apostle ceased and is no longer functioning, many Spirit-empowered leaders would argue from experience that the office of apostle is still open for business.

Components of the Apostle Paradigm

The apostle paradigm rests on the assumption that the function of the apostle extends beyond the context of the New Testament church. The strongest advocates for the contemporary office of apostle are affiliated with a movement known as the New Apostolic Reformation (NAR), a term coined by C. Peter Wagner (1930–2016), former Professor of Church Growth at Fuller Theological Seminary's School of World Missions. According to Wagner, the NAR is a made up of "loosely structured apostolic networks" emerging in "virtually every region of the world," constituting the "fastest growing segment of Christianity."[8] The NAR is largely—but not exclusively—made up of Pentecostals and charismatics. Wagner claims that around the year 2001, the Church entered the "second apostolic age."[9] He believes that in this second

---

8. C. Peter Wagner, *Churchquake! How the New Apostolic Reformation Is Shaking Up the Church as We Know It* (Ventura, CA: Regal, 1999), 6.

9. C. Peter Wagner, *Dominion: How Kingdom Action Can Change the World* (Grand Rapids:

apostolic age the offices and functions of apostle and prophet (Eph. 2:20) are being restored.

David Cannistraci defines an apostle as "one who is called and sent by Christ to have the spiritual authority, character, gifts, and abilities to successfully reach and establish people in Kingdom truth and order, especially through founding and overseeing local churches."[10] Cannistraci and Wagner believe that apostolic leaders will rise to prominence on the merit of their integrity, Christ-like character, and powerful supernatural gifting and authority. The extent of the NAR is far-reaching, with millions of participants accounted for in Africa, Asia, and Latin America.[11] When Wagner wrote *Churchquake!* in 1999, he contended that the NAR consisted of at least 40,000 apostolic churches representing approximately eight to ten million members in the United States.[12] He asserted that the NAR is rapidly growing in all of the six continents and is the "greatest change in the way of doing church since the Protestant Reformation."[13] In the Global South, a wide configuration of Pentecostal-charismatic churches are, as of 2013, aligned with the NAR, including the following groups: Judah Kingdom Alliance (JKA), New Covenant Ministries International (NCMI), Grace International (GI), Congress World Breakthrough Network (CWBN), and International Strategic Alliance of Apostolic Churches (ISAAC).[14] Taking into account the many independent or non-denominational churches that are affiliated with NAR-type networks, the movement boasts a staggering 369,000,000 participants.[15]

Perhaps the most intriguing aspect of the NAR is its version of dominion theology, rooted in the seven-mountain mandate, which originated in the Latter Rain Revival of 1948. Wagner states, "Several apostolic networks advocate forms of what some call 'dominion theology,' meaning that Christians are expected

---

Chosen Books, 2008), 22.

10. David Cannistraci, *The Gift of Apostle: A Biblical Look at Apostleship and How God Is Using It to Bless His Church Today* (Ventura, CA: Regal Books, 1996), 29.

11. R. Douglas Geivett and Holly Pivec, *A New Apostolic Reformation? A Biblical Response to a Worldwide Movement* (Wooster, MA: Weaver Book Company, 2014), 9.

12. Wagner, *Churchquake!* 8.

13. C. Peter Wagner, "Year in Review: The New Apostolic Reformation Is Not a Cult," *Charisma News* (August 24, 2011), accessed November 18, 2023, https://www.charismanews.com/opinion/31851-the-new-apostolic-reformation-is-not-a-cult.

14. Irving G. Chetty, "Origin and Development of the 'New Apostolic Reformation' in South Africa: A Neo-Pentecostal Movement or a Post-Pentecostal Phenomenon?" *Alternation* Special Edition 11 (2013): 194.

15. Todd M. Johnson and Ken R. Ross, ed. *Atlas of Global Christianity* (Edinburgh: Edinburgh University Press, 2009), 78–79.

to infiltrate social structures at all levels and, once there, use their influence to inculcate biblical values throughout their society."[16] Wagner outlines the strategy for marketplace transformation and appeals for leaders to take dominion over seven spheres or mountains of culture, encompassing the home: (1) church; (2) school; (3) government and politics; (4) media, arts, entertainment, and sports; (5) commerce; and (6) science and (7) technology.[17] Wagner describes how each of these seven mountains or spheres will become an "apostolic sphere." Apostles "are the only ones who will be able to change the power structure at the top of each mountain."[18] How will these apostles accomplish this? These seven spheres or mountains are perceived as having "principalities and powers that control" them. The only way to occupy them will be through high-level spiritual warfare, not political activism.[19]

Our primary concern relates to the shape of leadership in the NAR. The NAR is composed of "apostolic networks." Each network is led by an apostle whose ultimate authority is recognized by the collective of all participating churches and organizations within it. The apostles are the highest authorities and the ones who provide leadership and direction to the network. Using Ephesians 4 as a biblical justification, they assert their leadership role based on the spiritual gifts identified by Paul, who ranks apostles as the highest gift. Next to the apostles are the prophets who are God's spokespersons, imparting divine counsel and wisdom to God's people. These prophets, however, are accountable to the apostles while working alongside them to carry out the mission of the movement.

Who are the recognized apostles in the movement? The leading apostle of the NAR is the founder, C. Peter Wagner; others among the staff of recognized apostles are Doris Wagner (wife of Peter Wagner), Samuel Rodriguez, Ed Silvoso, Jim Ammerman, Cindy Jacobs (top-ranking female apostle), Os Hillman, Julius Oyet, Pat Francis, Bill Hamon, Lou Engle, Harry Jackson, Lance Wallnau, and John Benefiel. Todd Bentley ranks among the leading prophets.[20] In 1998, Wagner edited a book titled *The New Apostolic Churches*,

---

16. Wagner, *Churchquake!* 198.

17. C. Peter Wagner, *The Church in the Workplace: How God's People Can Transform Society* (Ventura, CA: Regal Books, 2006), 113.

18. Wagner, *Church in the Workplace*, 114.

19. For a critique of dominion theology, see Virginia Garrard, "Hidden in Plain Sight: Dominion Theology, Spiritual Warfare, and Violence in Latin America," *Religions* 11, no. 648 (2020), doi:10.3390/rel11120648.

20. Trevor O'Reggio, "The Rise of the New Apostolic Reformation and Its Implications for Adventist Eschatology," *Journal of the Adventist Theological Society* 23, no. 2 (2012): 135.

in which he lists nineteen groupings of proponents of the NAR. Their leaders included himself, John P. Kelly, John Eckhardt, Michael P. Fletcher, Wellington Boone, Larry Kreider, Roberts Liardon, Rice Brooks, Bill Hamon, Billy Joe Daugherty, Dick Iverson, Ralph Moore, David (Kwang Shin) Kim, Lawrence Khong, Paul Daniel, William F. Kumuyi, Eddie C. Villanueva, and Joseph C. Wongsak.[21]

What do apostles do? Cannistraci delineates seven responsibilities of an apostle. Apostles plant churches, oversee and strengthen churches, develop leaders, ordain elders and deacons, supervise and coordinate ministries, manage crises, and network with other leaders and their ministries. The roles they play can be synthesized as establishing, nourishing, communicating, teaching, preaching, writing, imparting, fathering, and networking.[22] What they don't do is micromanage a local church or ministry site. Apostles think of themselves as servants who lead by cooperation and consultation instead of control and domination.[23] Yet they see their authority as extensive, based on divine certification proven by an ability to draw large audiences, impart supernatural power, convey vision through revelation, pray for healing, cast out territorial spirits, decree judgment of evil and sin, and raise the dead.[24]

Of all the claims by Wagner, the most radical of all is the amount of trust and authority delegated by the Holy Spirit to local-level pastors and translocal-level apostles.[25] In the apostolic paradigm, the pastor (whether local or trans-local) sets the vision, focuses on leadership rather than management, makes policy decisions and delegates the rest, forms the management team, holds his or her position for life, and selects his or her successor.[26] It is up to the apostle himself or herself to start a network, and if this is done, the number of churches per network must be kept at a manageable level so the apostle can devote sufficient attention to mentoring upcoming charismatic leaders, thereby forestalling routinization of charisma. The same principle is applied to the multiplication of networks.[27] However, one must grant that in some cases the replacement of a traditional denominational structure with an apostolic network has proved to be a mixed blessing. Such was the case in Australia and South Africa.

---

21. C. Peter Wagner, *The New Apostolic Churches* (Ventura, CA: Regal Books, 1998), 4–6.
22. Cannistraci, *The Gift of Apostle*, 100–103.
23. Cannistraci, *The Gift of Apostle*, 147–149.
24. Cannistraci, *The Gift of Apostle*, 163–171.
25. Wagner, *Churchquake!* 75.
26. Wagner, *Churchquake!* 86–89.
27. Wagner, *Churchquake!* 146.

Australia and South Africa

Australia has been a hot spot for the apostle paradigm. David Cartledge, former president of Southern Cross College (now Alphacrucis College) in Sydney, Australia, played a leading role in the ascendancy of the apostle paradigm among Pentecostals in Australia. In *The Apostolic Revolution: The Restoration of Apostles and Prophets in the Assemblies of God in Australia*, Cartledge recounts the emergence of the apostle paradigm and its victory over democratic ecclesiology in the re-formed Assemblies of God of Australia (AGA), rebranded as the Australian Christian Churches (ACC). The gist of Cartledge's view of the gift of apostle is that the authority of the apostle is "a supernatural impartation that marks the leader out as one with abilities for leadership, creativity, persistence and faith that are not explainable by natural talents or political prospects. It is a process of the Spirit—a life changing anointing that promotes God's chosen leader to a place of divine opportunities."[28]

Cartledge argues that apostles should govern the Church because God has invested them with an impartation of authority for oversight. He cares little for democratic forms of leadership, impugning congregational government the source of "deacon possessed churches" who—in allowing for open debate— stirred up controversy, thereby inhibiting the growth and vitality of the church. Cartledge's central claim is that the endorsement of an apostolic paradigm of leadership in 1977, which he characterizes as a revolution, resulted in phenomenal growth and cultural influence throughout the nation of Australia.[29]

In his incisive study of the ecclesiology of the AGA, Shane Clifton, a former Professor of Theology at Alphacrucis College, critiques the premises of Cartledge's argument. He holds that it was "not exegetical but is derived from his experience within the AGA. He is arguing on the basis of pragmatism and church growth technique, and his reference to the Ephesians principle and offices of apostle and prophet is a creative justification for shifts that have already occurred with the AGA for practical, rather than theological reasons."[30] In short, Cartledge claimed that the move away from democracy and a centralized bureaucracy was the cause of AGA growth.[31] However,

---

28. David Cartledge, *The Apostolic Revolution: The Restoration of Apostles and Prophets in the Assemblies of God in Australia* (Chester Hill, Sydney, NSW: Paraclete Institute, 2000), 276.

29. D. Cartledge, *Apostolic Revolution*, 283.

30. Shane Clifton, *Pentecostal Churches in Transition: Analyzing the Developing Ecclesiology of the Assemblies of God of Australia* (Leiden: Brill, 2009), 173.

31. D. Cartledge, *Apostolic Revolution*, 178.

Clifton countered that it is more likely that the growth was the result of a number of underlying causes preceding the so-called revolution, including the strengthening of the local church autonomy, during the leadership of Andrew Evans as General Superintendent (1977–1999), an embrace of church growth principles, and among other things the writings of Peter Wagner and the emerging global influence of Hillsong Church.[32] One thing is certain. The influence of the NAR in the ecclesiology of Australian Assemblies of God can be documented. This influence was felt as far away as South Africa.

In South Africa, the largest Pentecostal church, the Apostolic Faith Mission of South Africa (AFM), approved a new Constitution in October 2000, adopting the apostolic paradigm as its polity. According to Matthew Clark, former head of New Testament at AFM Theological College in Auckland Park, Johannesburg, "The notion behind this change was that the 'real work' of God in the church was the result of anointed and visionary leadership, the influence and effect of strong leaders who would fulfil the role of apostles, 'fathers' and mentors in the church.... In the 1990s some influential AFM pastors began to take notice of the rapid growth of the Assemblies of God in Australia."[33] Influenced by David Cartledge's *The Apostolic Revolution* and previous developments with the AOG in Australia, the motive of the proponents of the new constitution in the Apostolic Church of South Africa was to be "released" from the "bonds" of restrictive Presbyterian-style church government, so they could freely follow their anointing and vision and accomplish great things for the Lord.[34] Clark holds that the implementation of this constitution had immediate implications and deleterious effects, detailed below.

The philosophy of church leadership within the denomination became a hybrid of democratic Presbyterian ecclesiology and New Apostolic thinking. In the area of leadership, there has been a clearly visible emphasis on the vision, authority, and privileges of leaders rather than on their commitment to faithful and sacrificial service to those they ostensibly lead and mentor, resulting in neglect of local churches under their leadership suffering from discipline issues or doctrinal problems. Some megachurch leaders instituted a headhunting policy, targeting medium and large local churches, persuading them to join their networks, resulting in some regions with one or two financially viable

---

32. Clifton, *Pentecostal Churches in Transition*, 157.

33. Matthew Clark, "Contemporary Pentecostal Leadership: The Apostolic Faith Mission of South Africa as Case Study," *Cyberjournal for Pentecostal Charismatic Research* 16 (January 2007): n.p.

34. Clark, "Contemporary Pentecostal Leadership," n.p.

(White Afrikaans) assemblies and many impoverished (Black) churches. Many medium and large local churches simply abandoned the challenges of regional racial unity in for the sake of joining networks consisting primarily of White Afrikaans' churches. The face of church government in the AFM has changed from being primarily collegial and Presbyterian to becoming authoritarian and Episcopalian.

Clark had significant misgivings concerning the swing of the AFM toward the NAR and advances two reasons for his misgivings. First, recent academic research in the AFM indicates that urban megachurches may not necessarily be the best vision-bearers of Pentecostalism. How viably can a seeker-sensitive, leader-oriented sub-group lead a Pentecostal movement into the twenty-first century, when for decades Pentecostals have found ministry expression in the New Testament model of participative and egalitarian "body ministry"? Second, he perceives that the change made in 2000 led to growing problems of pride, arrogance, abuse of authority, opportunism, and manipulative-ness among the pastorate of the movement. In support of his diagnosis, he points to explicit cases of conflict, discipline, and arbitration that have occurred in the church or been inflicted upon it. However, these outcomes could also be seen as partly due to the brash and opportunistic assertiveness, which is characteristic of aggressive Pentecostal expressions of ministry, often affirmed as an important leadership characteristic of the new paradigm.[35]

Rejoining Clifton's analysis of the Australian embrace of the NAR, perhaps there is some merit in his and Clark's claim that greater accountability and collegiality is afforded by democratic forms of ecclesiology. Clark's critique is based on his concern that the apostolic paradigm contradicts the principle of the priesthood of all believers. Clifton concurs with Veli-Matti Kärkkäinen[36] that traditional Pentecostal ecclesiology and its attendant congregational or presbyterial models "express better the mutuality demanded by church fellowship oriented to the Spirit."[37] The same view is held by Miroslav Volf,[38] who posits that "the universal distribution of the charismata implies common responsibility for the life of the church" and the "universal priesthood" is best protected by congregational models that require the election of officeholders

---

35. Clark, "Contemporary Pentecostal Leadership": n.p.

36. Veli-Matti Kärkkäinen, "Church as Charismatic Fellowship: Ecclesiological Reflections from Pentecostal-Roman Catholic Dialogue," *Journal of Pentecostal Theology* 18 (2001): 100–21.

37. Clifton, *Pentecostal Churches in Transition*, 177.

38. Miroslav Volf, *After Our Likeness: The Church as the Image of the Trinity* (Grand Rapids: Eerdmans, 1998), 230.

by the entire church.[39] These well-considered arguments of established Pentecostal theologians are worthy of deliberation.

Formative Assessment

Michael Brown, PhD New York University, a leader of the Brownsville Revival, offers a balanced assessment, acknowledging that there are no modern-day apostles akin to the twelve appointed by Jesus. However, if one takes the term "apostle" in its general sense as an emissary of the gospel, one can affirm that there are modern-day apostles. These apostles would be those who have pioneered movements and planted churches. Brown believes that the ascension leadership gifts in Ephesians 4:11, including the apostle, given to the Church by the risen Christ, were intended to continue until the Church arrives at maturity in the faith, which clearly is an ongoing process.[40] Perhaps it is best to think of the ministry of modern-day apostles as apostolic in the general sense adumbrated by Brown, rather than in terms that equate them with the twelve.

---

39. Clifton, *Pentecostal Churches in Transition*, 178.
40. Michael Brown, "Are There Modern-Day Apostles?" *Ask Dr. Brown Podcast*, May 24, 2016, accessed March 21, 2024, https://askdrbrown.org/library/are-there-modern-day-apostles.

8

Prophet Paradigm

Our exposition of the prophet paradigm leads with the question: Are there modern-day prophets? The prophet is the second of the leadership gifts in Ephesians 4:11. The prophet paradigm is premised on the assumption that prophecy is an essential component of Spirit-empowered leadership. This assumption is grounded in the tradition of biblical prophecy and the place of prophecy in the history of Pentecostalism. In the interest of understanding how the prophet paradigm is currently practiced, this chapter will (1) describe the biblical grounds and components of the prophet paradigm; (2) delineate two forms of prophecy, drawing correlations to leadership; and (3) offer a brief survey of prophecy in three African locales. Finally, this chapter concludes with a formative assessment of the paradigm.

Biblical Patterns and Principles

The Bible is filled with prophets and prophecy. The word "prophecy" displays a wide range of meanings throughout Scripture; therefore, a single definition cannot fit every context. However, in general terms, prophecy in the Bible can be construed as an oracle—a word spontaneously inspired by God and spoken by a human receptor and pertaining to a prediction of future events or a judgment on human sin or social injustice, and an impartation of divine anointing.

In the Old Testament, the Hebrew word *nabi*, meaning "one who is called to speak," is most often translated in English as "prophet." Three other Hebrew words, *roeh* ("seer"), *hozeh* ("visionary"), and *ish ha Elohim* ("man of God"), are used to describe persons who act as prophets. The latter title, "man of God," appears eighty times in the Bible, seventy-nine of which are in the Old Testament. It acknowledges the qualitative difference between all human beings and the few men and women who are specially chosen to speak on behalf of God. The author of 1 Samuel explains a shift occurring in Old Testament usage from *roeh* to *nabi*: "Formerly in Israel, if someone went to inquire of God, they would say 'Come, let us go to the seer,' because the

157

prophet [*nabi*] of today used to be called a seer [*roeh*]" (1 Sam. 9:9). Prophets in biblical Israel came from all walks of life, including shepherds, priests, agriculturalists, and scribes. According to Schmitt, "Divine inspiration is what made a person a prophet, and what caused the prophet to speak out, and what made others listen to the prophet as a legitimate spokesperson for the divine."[1] Lee Roy Martin says that a prophetic message originates in God, not in the prophet. Prophets often prefaced their proclamations with the messenger formula: "Thus says the Lord..." [*koh amar YHWH*]. At other times they concluded their message with the words, "...declares the Lord" [*neum YHWH*]. More than 240 times in the Old Testament, the prophetic message is characterized as "the word of the Lord," a designation that strengthens the prophetic claim to inspiration.[2] Hebrew prophets did more than predict the future; their messages called Israel to honor God. Their prophecies were not general pronouncements but specific words corresponding to a particular historical context. Prophets are raised up to call God's people to repentance and service on behalf of their covenant with the Lord.

In the New Testament, the Greek term for prophets (*prophetes*) means "one who speaks for." It refers to those who communicate a divine message, interpret the times, and impart divine truth.[3] Prophets announce the divine will. Their prophecies can be predictive or forthtelling. Prophets are not as common in the New Testament as the Old Testament, but they appear now and then:

- Predicting future events (Luke 2:28–35, Simeon) and (Acts 11:27–30, Agabus).
- Calling down divine judgment on sinners (Acts 5:1–11, Peter with Ananias and Saphira).
- Commissioning and sending missionaries (Acts 13:2).
- Interpreting the meaning of the outpouring of the Holy Spirit at Pentecost and the Gentile Pentecost (Peter's sermons in Acts 2:14–39 and 10:44–48).

The first prophet described as such in the New Testament is John the Baptist, a charismatic figure who resembled Elijah in his rustic lifestyle and penchant for speaking truth to power. He was alienated from conventional society and criticized local rulers, eventually paying with his life. Jesus himself is pictured

---

1. John J. Schmitt, "Preexilic Hebrew Prophecy," in *The Anchor Bible Dictionary*, ed. David Noel Freedman (New York: Doubleday, 1992), 5: 482, 488.

2. Lee Roy Martin, "Towards a Biblical Model of Pentecostal Prophetic Preaching," *Verbum et Ecclesia* 37, no. 1 (2015): 4.

3. M. Eugene Boring, "Early Christian Prophecy," in *The Anchor Bible Dictionary*, ed. David Noel Freedman (New York: Doubleday, 1992), 5: 496.

as a prophet in his identification with the call of Isaiah as one anointed by the Spirit to proclaim good news to poor and release to captives (Isa. 61:1–2; Luke 4:18–19). Jesus applied to himself the proverb of the prophet rejected in his hometown (Mark 6:4). Luke-Acts indicates that Barnabas was included among the prophets at Antioch (Acts 13:1–2), and the apostle Philip had four daughters, who prophesied (Acts 21:9).[4]

It should be noted that Paul was an advocate of prophecy (1 Thess. 5:19–20) and lists prophecy among the charismatic gifts. In fact, Paul designates prophecy as a gift to be sought above others (1 Cor. 14:5). It is significant that prophecy and leadership are found in the list of spiritual gifts in Romans 12:6–8. The linking of prophecy and leadership is far from coincidental. By definition, a leader shows the way for an organization to achieve its purpose. A prophetic leader is one who conveys a message from the Spirit to guide the organization in the achievement of its purpose. A prime example would be when the Lord called to Ananias in a vision and instructed him to go to the house where Paul was praying after his Damascus Road encounter with Jesus. The Lord said to Ananias, "Go! This man is my chosen instrument to proclaim my name to the Gentiles and their kings and to the people of Israel" (Acts 9:15). Ananias overcame his apprehension and did as he was told, and as he laid hands on Saul the former persecutor was filled with the Holy Spirit and received water baptism, paving the way for Paul's destiny as the premier church planter of the early Christian movement.

Components of the Prophet Paradigm

The prophet paradigm is based on the biblical assumption that "no prophecy of Scripture came about by the prophet's own interpretation of things. For prophecy never had its origin in the human will, but prophets, though human spoke from God as they were carried along by the Holy Spirit" (2 Pet. 1:20–21). The prophet paradigm is also informed by the Luke-Acts narrative of Pentecost in Acts 2 and 10 and the Pauline discourse on the charisms of the Holy Spirit in 1 Corinthians 12–14, including the charism of prophecy. The prevailing view of Pentecostals is captured by Amos Yong:

> From the days of Azusa Street onward, Pentecostals have understood the modern outpouring of the Holy Spirit as a fulfillment of prophecy. If the original day of Pentecost was foretold by Joel, it was only the "early rain" awaiting the abundant showers of a "latter rain" (Joel 2:23). Insofar as modern Pentecostalism was understood to fulfill this prophecy of a 'latter rain' revival anticipating the last days, the template

---

4. Boring, "Early Christian Prophecy," 497–500.

for organizing and explaining this later experience has been drawn from the early Christian experiences recorded in the book of Acts.[5]

Mark Cartledge notes that "a broad definition of prophecy should start with the revelatory experience through which Christians believe that God communicates."[6] Cartledge explains that this means that contemporary revelatory experiences (e.g., the word of wisdom, the word of knowledge, the discernment of spirits, and the interpretation of tongues) are integral to the practice of prophecy.[7] In the prophet paradigm, the prophetic mode of intermediation is epiphanic in the sense that the deity is revealed, not only through the revelatory message, but also through the divine presence that is experienced as an awe-inspiring power, which empowers the human recipient to speak the revelatory message.[8]

The charismatic manifestation of prophecy is thus an embodiment and expression of the divine presence that is experienced through a sacramental encounter with the Holy Spirit. According to Frank Macchia, Professor of Theology at Vanguard University, the speaker becomes a human channel of divine grace as the Spirit flows into and through one in an immediate, intimate and, sometimes, intense fashion. This observation has profound inferential significance in that, not only does the prophetic leader sacramentally participate in the divine presence, but also becomes a sacramental channel of the charism of prophecy through whom the hearers participate, sacramentally, in the divine presence.[9] The charismatic spirituality of the prophetic leader mediates a revelatory experience of divine presence in congregational settings, often presaged by visionary experiences, voices within or words coming to mind. A charismatic encounter is often a prerequisite for the manifestation of a prophetic revelation in the setting of worship, and the sharing of that prophecy serves to enliven a congregation with revelatory edification, encouragement, and consolation. Cartledge explains the context for prophecy in a hypothetical setting of worship in a contemporary church. He writes,

---

5. Amos Yong, *Spirit Poured Out on All Flesh: Pentecostalism and the Possibility of Global Theology* (Grand Rapids: Baker Academic, 2005), 83.

6. Mark J. Cartledge, *Practical Theology: Charismatic and Empirical Perspectives* (Eugene, OR: Wipf & Stock, 2018), 157.

7. M. Cartledge, *Practical Theology*, 157.

8. Samuel W. Muindi, "The Nature and Significance of Prophecy in Pentecostal-Charismatic Experience: An Empirical-Biblical Study" (Ph.D. diss., University of Birmingham, 2012), 2.

9. Frank D. Macchia, *Baptized in the Spirit: A Global Pentecostal Theology* (Grand Rapids: Zondervan, 2006), 74–75, 247–56.

Such meetings evince an openness with singing, glossolalia, and a longing to hear the word of God through Scripture and word gifts ... as the person feels "anointed" or "agitated" spiritually, a vision or a mental picture emerges suddenly in the person's mind; or sometimes a short phrase emerges ... the experience of prophecy flows out of prayer and worship as the person has a sense of "receiving" a message from an "external source" and which comes "suddenly" in this context ... the person who prophesies has opened up to the deeper level of the Spirit's purposes by means of worship, prayer, and glossolalia.[10]

Cartledge's hypothetical is exemplified below in the discussion of the thriving of the prophet paradigm in the Global South.

As Mel Robeck states, prophecy continues to play an important role in the spirituality of contemporary renewal movements.[11] However, the worldview of the Spirit-empowered movement not only makes room for the prophetic but also cherishes the prophetic as a core value in leadership, through which the Holy Spirit uses a human vehicle to speak a divine word. Prophetic revelations may come through visions, dreams, impressions, divine coincidence, or verbal proclamations. According to Opoku Onyinah, the functions of prophecy are to edify, encourage and comfort; provide correction and warning; and guide and direct ministers and leaders.[12]

Forms of Prophecy

According to Pentecostal sociologist Margaret Poloma, the major forms of prophecy found in contemporary Pentecostalism are twofold: (1) a democratized charism available to all Spirit-baptized persons and (2) an ecclesiastical office that is being restored to leaders.[13] The prophet paradigm of leadership directly pertains to the latter form, but the two are interconnected.

Democratized Charism

The form of prophecy as a democratized charism is aptly represented in Roger Stronstad's highly regarded work, *The Prophethood of All Believers*.

---

10. M. J. Cartledge, "Charismatic Prophecy: A Definition and Description," *Journal of Pentecostal Theology* 2, no. 5 (1994): 75.

11. Cecil M. Robeck, "Gift of Prophecy," in *NIDPCM*, ed. Stanley M. Burgess and Eduard M. van der Maas (Grand Rapids: Zondervan, 2002), 1010.

12. Opoku Onyinah, *Apostles and Prophets: The Ministry of Apostles and Prophets throughout the Generations* (Eugene, OR: Wipf & Stock, 2022), 62–65, 76.

13. Margaret Poloma, "The Millenarianism of the Pentecostal Movement," in *Christian Millenariansim from the Early Church to Waco*, ed. Stephen Hunt (Bloomington: Indiana University Press, 2001), 169.

Stronstad's thesis is that all believers are prophets, and the Church is meant to be a community of prophets. Jesus, "a prophet in word and deed," passed his prophetic mantle to his disciples, as Elijah did for Elisha.[14] At the end of his ministry, Jesus transferred the Spirit to the Church, empowering Christians to be mighty in word (prophetic speech) and power (signs and wonders).[15] As the prophethood of all believers was a lived reality in the Early Church, so it is now. Stronstad locates the basis for his thesis in "Luke's portrait of the people of God of the new age, who, by virtue of having the Holy Spirit poured forth upon them, have become the eschatological community of prophets upon whom Jesus, himself the eschatological prophet, has poured forth the Spirit of prophecy—both for their own generation, for their children's generation, and for each succeeding generation."[16]

Lee Roy Martin complements Stronstad's perspective by drawing upon the Old Testament to formulate a broad democratic vision of prophetic speech that also conceives of the Church as a community of prophets. Moses wished that all of God's people would be prophets (Num. 11:29), and Joel promised that the prophetic Spirit would be poured out on all people: "Your sons and daughters will prophesy, your old men will dream dreams, your young men will see visions. Even on my servants, both men and women, I will pour out my Spirit in those days" (Joel 2:28–29). The gospel narratives portray Jesus as the prophet par excellence, who calls his Church to be a prophetic community. For Pentecostalism, prophecy emerges not from individuals but from within the body of Christ. Therefore, the leader is one prophet among many.[17]

Ecclesiastical Office

Poloma credits the democratization of the charism of prophecy with contributing to the development of a second form of prophecy.[18] As waves of neo-Charismatic Renewal were sweeping through the globe in the 1990s, a trend emerged with the appearance of prophetic ministries and publications on the restoration of the ecclesiastical office of the prophet. Leaders of these ministries, such as Cindy Jacobs, Dutch Sheets, Chuck Pierce, Ted Haggard, and Bill Hamon, attested to having received a call to the office of prophet. They not only served as teachers

---

14. Roger Stronstad, *The Prophethood of All Believers: A Study in Luke's Charismatic Theology* (Sheffield: Sheffield Academic Press, 1999), 46.

15. Stronstad, *Prophethood of All Believers*, 81.

16. Stronstad, *Prophethood of All Believers*, 145.

17. L. R. Martin, "Towards a Biblical Model," 8.

18. Poloma, "The Millenarianism of the Pentecostal Movement," 6.

and role models of prophetic ministry but also insisted along with C. Peter Wagner that God was restoring the ecclesiastical office of prophet. Further, they claimed that as recipients of the leadership gift of prophet, they were divinely tasked with imparting prophetic messages on behalf of the church. Of these claimants, Bill Hamon stands out as a leading proponent. Cindy Jacobs, herself a widely acknowledged prophet, describes Hamon as a pioneer of prophetic leadership.[19] Hamon sees the office of the prophet as one of the five leadership gifts (Eph. 4:11) that Christ Jesus imparted for the building up God's people and maturing them to the full measure of Christ.[20]

There is an interconnection between the leadership office of the prophet, reserved for a select few, and the democratic charism, available to all believers. All Spirit-filled believers have the potential to move in the prophetic realm (Stronstad), but only some are accorded the leadership office of prophet (Hamon). The difference resides in the span of authority and influence. Individuals or groups of believers can edify one another with their prophetic words. Yet, a leader who is recognized as a prophet has a wider span of gifting and authority.[21] It is the second form of prophecy that has prevailed in the Global South.

Prophet Paradigm in the Global South

The prophet paradigm flourishes in Asia, Africa, and Latin America, yet African soil has proven to be the most fertile for the prophet paradigm. The advent of the office of prophet in African Christianity can be traced back to two points of origin. The first is the *Aladura* (praying) churches, which originated outside of a traditional missionary context. An example of a leader of an Aladura movement is Samuel Bilewu Joseph Oshoffa (1909–1985), the prophet-founder of the Celestial Church of Christ (CCC) in Nigeria in 1947. Oshoffa had visions in which God showed him how to organize a purified church based on a distinct liturgy, organizational structure, and code of rigorous ethical and doctrinal principles.[22] The second point of origin are the churches that remained in the orbit of Western missionaries. An example of a prophetic leader who traces his

---

19. Cindy Jacobs, *The Voice of God* (Ventura, CA: Regal Books, 1995), 28.

20. Bill Hamon, *Prophetic Destiny and the Apostolic Reformation* (Santa Rosa Beach, FL: Christian International Ministries, 1996).

21. Bill Hamon, *Apostles, Prophets and the Coming Moves of God: God's End-Time Plans for His Church and Planet Earth* (Shippensburg, PA: Destiny Image, 1997), 2.

22. Jeffrey D. Carter, "Celestial Church of Christ," in *NIDPCM*, ed. Stanley M. Burgess and Eduard M. van der Maas (Grand Rapids: Zondervan, 2002), 467.

heritage to missionaries is Ezekiel Guti (1923–2023), founder and leader of the Zimbabwe Assemblies of God. Guti established the Highlands Revival Centre, near Harare. His followers regard Guti as an apostle and prophet. He claimed over a million adherents in Zimbabwe. Churches affiliated with Guti are found in Malawi, Zambia, Mozambique, and other African countries. Outside of Zimbabwe his movement is known as Forward in Faith.[23]

Both above wings of Spirit-empowered Christianity in Africa embraced the prophet paradigm of charismatic leadership. The Kenyan scholar Samuel W. Muindi defines charismatic prophecy as an intense moment of participatory interface between the divine Spirit and the human spirit in which the divine Spirit infuses the human conscious dimension with revelatory impulses.[24] He holds that prophecy is basically a religious genre in the rubric of revelatory disclosures from the divine realm to the world of humanity and is thus an epistemic category of intermediation between divinity and humanity, as found among other intermediating functionaries such as diviners, shamans, mediums, or mystics.[25] This definition transcends the divide between African Initiated Christianity (AIC) and more traditional Pentecostal bodies. Following are two brief case studies of research on prophetic leadership in Ghana and Nigeria.

Ghana

In his study of prophetic ministry in Ghana, Daniel Nii Aboagye Aryeh of Perez University College in Ghana, defines the term "prophet" as referring to Christians who claim to have extra-sensory ability or perception enabling them to inquire and receive information from or by the Holy Spirit for seekers or inquirers. People who exhibit such prowess are either self-appointed or set apart as prophets by members of a church or ministry. They are seen as being able to diagnose the cause of illnesses and misfortunes, prescribe solutions, and predict present and future happenings and use this to the benefit of seekers or members.[26] Contemporary prophets in Ghana resonate with the role of medicine men, diviners, and seers in African traditional religion. The phenomenon of prophetic

---

23. David J. Garrard, "Ezekiel H. Guti," in *NIDPCM*, ed. Stanley M. Burgess and Eduard M. van der Maas (Grand Rapids: Zondervan, 2002), 683.

24. Muindi, "Nature and Significance of Prophecy," 2, 134.

25. Muindi, "Nature and Significance of Prophecy," 109.

26. Daniel Nii Aboagye Aryeh, "Academic versus Spiritual: Theological Education and the Anointing of the Holy Spirit in Contemporary Prophetic Ministries in Ghana," *Journal of Contemporary Ministry* 4 (2018): 63.

leadership attracts many to churches because Ghanaians are open to spiritual causality for the issues of life and willing to receive information concerning the future without investigating the source of power of the prophet. While Aryeh concludes that the prophet paradigm constitutes a culturally relevant conception of leadership in the African context, he does not condone the aversion of the leaders of contemporary prophetic ministries to the pursuit of formal theological education from accredited theological seminaries/institutions. He posits that academic education and the anointing of the Holy Spirit must complement each other. Hence, he proposes that budding prophets should seek personal mentorship and attend a Bible school.[27]

Joseph Quayesi-Amakye, Acting Dean of Central University College in Ghana, in his study of "Prophetic Practices in Contemporary Pentecostalism in Ghana," examines how Ghanaian Pentecostals engage in prophetic rituals as sources of victory and freedom in Christ. The rituals of Ghanaian Pentecostal prophets include the following: special anointing oils, blessed water, blessed herbal substances, deliverance (exorcism), and prophetic declarations. In these rituals, the blood of Jesus is employed as a metaphoric tool of destruction of evil for putting "a stop to the nonsense" of wicked forces. These rituals are carried out for spiritual protection, promotion, success, and security against enemies.[28] One such ritual involves the pouring of anointing oil on objects such as clients' bathrooms, toilets, garbage cans, floors, and entrances to homes; handkerchiefs; door keys and car keys; etc. Such "anointing" is meant to mark out clients and their property as beyond the attack of enemies.[29] In effect, prophetic symbolism transforms biblical acts into repeatable and transferable motifs with contemporary significance. Hence, a group may engage in "prophetic hours/walks" and "spiritual mapping" to re-enact Joshua's march around the city of Jericho (Josh. 1:2–5).

Asamoah-Gyadu contends that the phenomenon of "Pentecostal prophetism" was an innovation of Bishop James Saah of the Action Chapel International Accra, from whom it was replicated by other churches and ministries.[30] "Prophetic hours/walks" are a form of prayer that invokes divine judgment on one's enemies,

---

27. Aryeh, "Academic versus Spiritual," 75.

28. Joseph Quayesi-Amakye, "Prophetic Practices in Contemporary Pentecostalism in Ghana," *Canadian Journal of Pentecostal Charismatic Christianity* 6 (January 2015): 48.

29. Quayesi-Amakye, "Prophetic Practices," 49,

30. Quayesi-Amakye, "Prophetic Practices," 50–51; See J. Kwabena Asamoah-Gyadu, *Contemporary Pentecostal Christianity: Interpretations from an African Context* (Oxford: Regnum Books International, 2013), 35–57.

as Apostle Afotey Odai of the Maranatha Power Ministries told a pastors' conference at Kasoa on October 21, 2011, concerning how he dispossessed the "territorial powers" of Nungua-Accra, by walking through the township with his prayer team. In this case, the team anointed locations including a lagoon and commanded them to release their captives to Christ. Thus, prophetic enactments are embedded with prophetic assurances of territorial possession and occupation. In these cases, territorial possession entailed the transferring of physical, material, financial, physiological, and spiritual ownership from enemies to clients.[31] Thus, prophetic rituals and practices are meant not only to neutralize satanic powers but also to mediate and channel divine favor and assistance in clients' lives. The role of angels as divine couriers of victory in Christ is a crucial aspect in many of these rituals, which thrive on the belief of spiritual empowerment of believers. Spiritual empowerment supposes that Jesus differentiates between believers and their enemies. In prophetic circles, sermons are interrupted with reciprocating catchy interjections from congregants, like "Prophesy, you are Odii (prophet and seer)," "Prophesy to me," "Father, go deep," "You have seen correctly," or "A Daniel is in the house."[32] At times the prophets may move among the congregation to minister to parishioners' problems and offer solutions. The prophets are aided by assistants who carry bowls from which the prophets scoop and splash water or anointing oil onto the congregants. The eviction of a demonic presence may be carried out by the prophet or by the congregation, per the prophet's instruction. Prophetic eviction of demonic presence is often accomplished by the raising of arms, coupled with confessional declarations, such as "You spirit of poverty, sickness, disease, bad marriage, shame, embarrassment, disappointment, etc., today as I raise my hands to heaven, I command you in the name of the Lord Jesus Christ to leave me now." Or, they may say, "I command the fire of heaven to consume you right now... etc." Such prophetic declarations are understood as a display of spiritual empowerment.[33]

Nigeria

The same sort of culturally relevant phenomenon is found in Nigeria. According to Elizabeth Isichei, "When African prophets in Nigeria arose who spoke to these needs from the depths of their own religious consciousness, they counted their

---

31. Quayesi-Amakye, "Prophetic Practices," 51.
32. Quayesi-Amakye, "Prophetic Practices," 53.
33. Quayesi-Amakye, "Prophetic Practices," 54.

converts in hundreds of thousands."[34] The emphasis of the Nigerian prophets was on prayer as an act of speaking to God, a verbal means of communication with the divine, a way of making human concerns known in the spiritual realm. In the Nigerian Celestial Church of Christ, it is believed that "angels are messengers who carry prayers to God and blessings to human beings." Hence, God answers all prayers through angelic mediation. Ritual objects are thought to attract celestial angels and enhance the efficacy of prayer. Carter writes, "When members seek relief from a specific problem, whether it be personal, physical, or financial, the church will consult a prophet or prophetess who, after entering a trance, will frequently prescribe sprinkling (perhaps in the patient's bedroom), ingesting, or bathing in a specific type of water. When combined with prayer, these healing techniques are often successful for members of this church."[35]

"Like Prophets of Old, Nigerian prophetic leaders regard sound theology and proper ethics as the two handles of the plough which they must grasp firmly if they would plough a straight furrow for the Lord."[36] Analyzing the religious situation in Nigeria at the turn of the century, Luke Mbefo observes that there was dissatisfaction among members of the missionary churches. Their religious yearnings were not met adequately by the liturgical ceremonies of these churches. He writes the following:

> Their [members of mainline churches] expectations from the churches were not met. The missionaries of the older churches failed to address the type of questions the African situation raised for them: witchcraft, demon possession, haunting by evil spirits, the cult of ancestors; the use of protective charms, talisman; sorcery and the traditional dancing form of worship at the shrines. The tendency among the missionaries was to dismiss these questions as due to ignorance arising from a pre-scientific mentality.[37]

Prophets of these churches were gaining disciples when they established healing homes for sickness, promised children to barren women, or a hopeful future to the despondent. According to Mbefo, they have only to pray for you, and God will solve all your problems. An attentive listening to bidding prayers

---

34. Elizabeth Isichei, *A History of Christianity in Africa from Antiquity to the Present* (London: SPCK, 1995), 180–81.

35. Carter, "Celestial Church of Christ," 468–69.

36. H. O. Atansuyi, "Gospel and Culture in the Perspective of African Instituted Churches." *Cyberjournal for Pentecostal Charismatic Research*, n.p., accessed December 27, 2023, http://pctii.org/ccyerj/cyber3/aic.html.

37. Luke N. Mbefo, *The True African: Impulses for Self-Affirmation* (Onitsha, Nigeria: Spiritan Publications, 2001), 107, accessed December 27, 2023, https://archive.org/stream/trueafricanimpul00mbef/trueafricanimpul00mbef_djvu.txt

reveals that for most Nigerians, prayer means a catalogue of problems for God to solve. A church that refuses to address these problems is in perpetual danger of losing members.[38]

Temitope Balogun Joshua, popularly known as T. B. Joshua, was a Nigerian charismatic pastor, televangelist, and philanthropist. He was the leader and founder of Synagogue, Church of All Nations, a Christian megachurch that runs the Emmanuel TV television station from Lagos. In 1987, he visited a "prayer mountain" to seek the face of God. There, he fasted and prayed for forty days and forty nights. He wrote that in a heavenly vision he received divine anointing and a covenant from God to start his ministry. Thereafter, he laid the foundation of his ministry organization, "The Synagogue, Church of All Nations" (SCOAN), which released numerous videos claiming to document the healing of incurable disabilities and illnesses, including HIV/AIDS. The videos have generated a flurry of controversy and amassed hundreds of thousands of views. Many people have also claimed to have been healed through "Anointing Water" that has been prayed over by Prophet Joshua and given to those who were unable to physically attend his church in Lagos. His organization was caught up in controversy regarding the deliverance of those allegedly possessed by evil spirits during its services. He claimed to be a prophet and allegedly predicted such events as Michael Jackson's death, the attack during the Boston marathon in America, and the outcome of two African Cup of Nations (AFCON) final matches. T. B. Joshua also allegedly predicted the crash of Malaysian Airlines MH370 several months before the incident. T. B. Joshua authored and published several popular books.[39]

Formative Assessment

Lee Roy Martin observes that in pursuit of the prophetic ideal, Pentecostal preachers have traditionally relied upon the Holy Spirit to supply them with inspired messages appropriate to unique occasions. Pentecostal preachers, therefore, believe themselves to be proclaiming an inspired message, a word from the Lord, given for a specific time and place. However, a leader's claim of

---

38. Mbefo, *The True African*, 108.

39. SCOAN International, "Prophet T. B. Joshua," accessed December 27, 2023, https://www. scoan.org/about/prophet-tb-joshua/; Thomas Kingsley, "The Televangelist Who Claimed to Heal Aids and Counted Premier League Stars among His Followers," *Independent*, February 13, 2023, accessed December 27, 2023, https://www.independent.co.uk/news/uk/home-news/constance-marten-tb-joshua-mark-gordon-b2279954.html.

prophetic inspiration can open the door to abusive practices. The leader who claims divine inspiration may be tempted to assert infallibility and unquestioned authority. For this reason, a strong ecclesiology is required that insists upon accountability of leaders to the community of faith and includes a system for ensuring the theological orthodoxy and ethical integrity of ministers and leaders. With Martin, we concur that no prophetic leader should be allowed to operate outside the authority and accountability of the church as a whole.[40]

---

40. L. R. Martin, "Towards a Biblical Model," 5.

9

Healing Evangelist Paradigm

The evangelist is the third leadership gift in Ephesians 4:11. The Healing Evangelist Paradigm is rooted in the Pentecostal conception of the full gospel (i.e., inclusive of salvation and empowerment). Many early Pentecostal leaders coupled healing and evangelism as key components of the full gospel. Pentecostal evangelism involves more than simply seeking conversions. It entails empowerment with the Holy Spirt as the source for proclaiming Christ's victory over sickness and demonic oppression (i.e., healing). According to Allan Anderson, "The Pentecostal understanding of the full gospel meant that these 'signs and wonders' should accompany the preaching of the Word, and the divine healing in particular is an indispensable part of the Pentecostal evangelical methodology."[1] This chapter highlights the biblical grounds for a confluence of evangelism and healing, followed by a delineation of the components of the healing evangelist paradigm. This chapter also traces the succession of notable Pentecostal healing evangelists and the global mediation of the healing evangelist paradigm by Oral Roberts and David Yonggi Cho. The chapter closes with a formative assessment.

Biblical Patterns and Principles

The healing evangelist paradigm of Spirit-empowered leadership is grounded in a comprehensive biblical vision of health and wellness. From the beginning of the Spirit-empowered movement until today, its leaders have championed a holistic conception of evangelism. They have risen to prominence on the merits of their charismatic gifting and zeal for the ministry of healing. These leaders were known for accessing the power of Jesus and the Holy Spirit to free human beings from all aspects of suffering and sickness. Healing evangelists conceived of themselves as following in the steps of the disciples of Jesus who were given authority preach the kingdom of God and to heal the sick (Luke 9:1–2). They were convinced that

---

1. Allan Anderson, "Pentecostal Approaches to Faith and Healing," *International Review of Missionary Research* 91, no. 363 (2003): 525.

Jesus continues to make good on his promise: "But you will receive power when the Holy Spirit comes on you; and you will be my witnesses in Jerusalem, and in all Judea and Samaria, and to the ends of the earth" (Acts 1:8).

The origin of a word helps one to understand its root meaning and significance. The word "gospel," the modern form of the Anglo-Saxon word *god-spell*, is a Germanic rendering of the Latin *evangelium*. According to the article on "gospel" in the *Interpreter's Dictionary of the Bible*, the term was originally understood on a popular level as meaning "good tidings" or "good news" (Rom. 10:15). The Latin term goes back to the Greek *euangelion*, which in its religious sense is found only in the New Testament.[2] As a noun, *euangelion* is usually translated "gospel" but should probably be translated as "good news" because that is what the word literally means. When Jesus and the apostles used the word *euangelion* (good news, gospel), they were using a non-religious term from their cultural context. In classical and koine Greek, the secular term *euangelion* denoted the reward for good news, given either to the messenger or to the gods who have wrought a felicitous event. The word had political connotations at the time when it was borrowed by the writers of the New Testament, as it was commonly used with reference to an empire or kingdom and to its victories through which the power, order, and riches of an empire or kingdom were conveyed to those who were faithful or showed allegiance to that kingdom or empire. The corresponding verb *evangelize* (ευαγγελιζω) means "to announce proclaim or preach good news." An evangelist (εὐαγγελιστής) is one who brings good news. The Christian gospel announces the good news of Christ's victory over sin, death, and evil. Evangelism, according to L. Grant McClung, is "the act of proclaiming the good news of Jesus Christ in the power and anointing of the Holy Spirit with the intention that men and women will come to put their trust in Christ for salvation and serve him in the fellowship of his church."[3]

In framing a holistic understanding of the gospel, Pentecostals have tended to favor the account of Christ's evangelistic commission in Mark 16:15–18: "Go into all the world and preach the gospel to all creation. Whoever believes and is baptized will be saved, but whoever does not believe will be condemned. And these signs will accompany those who believe: In my name

---

2. Otto A. Piper, "Gospel (Message)," *Interpreter's Dictionary of the Bible: An Illustrated Encyclopedia* (Nashville: Abingdon, 1962), 2: 442.

3. L. Grant McClung, "Evangelism," in *NIDPCM*, ed. Stanley M. Burgess and Eduard M. van der Maas (Grand Rapids: Zondervan, 2002), 617.

they will drive out demons; they will speak in new tongues; they will pick up snakes with their hands; and when they drink deadly poison, it will not hurt them at all; they will place their hands on sick people, and they will get well." Pentecostals read the book of Acts as establishing the principle that divine healing opens the door for evangelism. This approach to evangelism, which prevails throughout the history of the Spirit-empowered movement, is labelled as "power evangelism" by John Wimber, founding Director of the Department of Church Growth at the Charles E. Fuller Institute of Evangelism. He writes, "By power evangelism I mean a presentation of the gospel that is rational but that also transcends the rational. The explanation of the gospel comes with a demonstration of God's power with signs and wonders." Power evangelism is a spontaneous, Spirit-inspired, empowered presentation of the gospel. Power evangelism is evangelism that is preceded and undergirded by a supernatural demonstration of God's presence.[4]

Healing is a pervasive theme in the Bible. It can be defined as the curing of a sick person and restoring him or her to health. In Hebrew the term for "healthy" or "whole" is a cognate of *shalom* (שָׁלוֹם), meaning "peace" or "harmony." The word for healing is *arukah* (אֲרוּכָה), meaning repair, recovery, or restoration of health. Because in biblical times sickness was considered a spiritual matter, healing could only be expected following a revival or revitalizing of the relationship between a person and God. The term commonly used in the Greek New Testament for healing is *iama* (ἴαμα), denoting a means of cure, remedy, or restoration of health. Another word is *iasis* (ἴασις), used in Luke 13:32 and in Acts 4:22 and 4:30, where Luke describes the miraculous physical restorations of the stooped woman (Luke 13:10–17), the man with dropsy (Luke 14:1–6), and a lame beggar (Acts 3:1–10). Paul's phrase, δὲ χαρίσματα ἰαμάτων ἐν τῷ (gifts of healing), suggests repeated phenomena of physical cures induced by one with the charismatic gift of healing. The idea is that certain Christians are endowed with a special capacity to mediate physical cures on a regular basis, derived from a grace-gift (i.e., a spiritual gift rather than a human ability).[5] In Lukan terminology, the healing activities of Jesus and his disciples are called "signs and wonders," recalling the signs and wonders accompanying

4. John Wimber, "Power Evangelism: Definitions and Directions," in *Wrestling with Dark Angels: Towards a Deeper Understanding of the Supernatural Forces in Spiritual Warfare*, ed. C. Peter Wagner and F. Douglas Pennoyer (Ventura, CA: Regal Books, 1990), 15, 24–29.

5. M. Dennis Hamm, "Gifts of Healing," in *The Anchor Bible Dictionary*, ed. David Noel Freedman (New York: Doubleday, 1992), 3: 89.

the exodus (Acts 7:36 and Exod. 7:3; Deut. 4:34; 6:22, 26:8). The healing and restoration of the sick constituted a significant aspect of the ministry of Jesus and subsequent apostolic practice. In the days following Pentecost, many healings took place at the hands of the apostles (Acts 2:43; 5:12; 8:7). In the ministry of Jesus, these healings were associated with the faith of the supplicant. As time passed, a standard formula developed, in which healings in the name of Christ were attributed to the expectant trust of the sufferer. R. K. Harrison notes that this standard format included techniques, such as anointing and prayer (James 5:14–15), that were employed by gifted leaders in the community as a means of healing disease.[6]

In the early Christian community healing was seen as a charismatic gift, included in the apostle Paul's list of spiritual gifts in 1 Corinthians 12:9, 28, and 30, along with the related terms, "faith" and "miraculous powers," evoking a sense of the abundance of supernatural gifting in the community. Nonetheless, careful attention to the application of these gifts in the practice of the early church shows that the accounts of healing seem to be restricted to leaders and well-known preachers of the gospel. Francis Martin draws four conclusions from New Testament portrayals of healing:

- The preaching of the word is itself sufficient to bring about healings, as confirmed in modern experience.
- Those who are sent to preach the gospel are often endowed with the gift of healing as part of their empowerment to bring people to salvation,
- God works healings though the ministry of the elders and the prayer of faith.
- There is a specific gift, possessed by some but not by others, that provides for healing both within and outside of the community and, in both instances, witnesses to the power of the resurrection to offset the moral and physical consequences of individual and communal sin.[7]

Components of the Healing Evangelist Paradigm

As early Pentecostals read the Bible, they assumed that the New Testament pattern of Holy Spirit-empowered evangelism and charismatic gifts including healing was directly applicable to their times. Their practices of ministry and theological perspectives were founded on a literal

---

6. R. K. Harrison, "Healing," *Interpreter's Dictionary of the Bible: An Illustrated Encyclopedia* (Nashville: Abingdon, 1962), 2: 548.

7. Francis Martin, "Gift of Healing," in *NIDPCM*, ed. Stanley M. Burgess and Eduard M. van der Maas (Grand Rapids: Zondervan, 2002), 697.

understanding of and commitment to Scripture. The same can be said of the Pentecostal approach to leadership. As the story of the New Testament church was dominated by leaders like Peter and Paul, who charted the course for the Early Church based on supernatural visions and power encounters with Jesus and the Holy Spirit, so it seemed that this should be the case with leadership in the Spirit-empowered movement. The biblical orientation of healing evangelists in the Spirit-empowered movement is indisputable. However, with the benefit of hindsight, we can see that the predisposition in favor of dominant leaders could have contributed to a neglect of Jesus' teaching on servant leadership. This was probably the case with Pentecostal healing evangelists, as seen below.

In her study of global Pentecostal and charismatic healing, Candy Gunther Brown finds that "Pentecostalism attracts adherents primarily through its characteristic healing practices."[8] Based on case studies of leading healing evangelists in a variety of global contexts, Brown argues that "divine healing is the single most important category—more important than glossolalia or prosperity—for understanding the global expansion of Pentecostal Christianity."[9]

Brown's viewpoint is confirmed by the findings of the 2006 Pew Spirit and Power survey of Pentecostals and charismatics in ten countries. The data revealed that in the United States, sixty-two percent of Pentecostals claimed to have witnessed or experienced divine healing, compared with forty-six percent of charismatics and twenty-eight percent of other Christians. The same pattern was found in three countries in Latin America, except that the percentage of Pentecostals who had witnessed or experienced divine healing was higher: seventy-seven percent in Brazil, seventy-seven percent in Chile, and seventy-nine percent in Guatemala. In Africa, the survey found that the percentage of Pentecostals who had witnessed or experienced divine healing was eighty-seven percent in Kenya, seventy-nine percent in Nigeria, and seventy-three percent in South Africa. In Asia, the percentage was slightly lower, with seventy-four percent in India, seventy-two percent in the Philippines, and fifty-six percent in South Korea.[10] This corroborates the finding of the Pew Study that a

---

8. Candy Gunther Brown, "Introduction: Pentecostalism and the Globalization of Illness and Healing," in *Global Pentecostal and Charismatic Healing*, ed. Candy Gunther Brown (Oxford: Oxford University Press, 2011), 8.

9. C. G. Brown, "Introduction," *Global Pentecostal and Charismatic Healing*, 14.

10. Pew Research Center, "Spirit and Power: 10 Country Survey of Pentecostals," October 5, 2006, accessed November 18, 2023, https://www.pewforum.org/2006/10/05/spirit-and-power/.

disproportionally higher percentage of Pentecostals and charismatics believe in praying for healing and deliverance than their non-Pentecostal-charismatic Christian counterparts.[11]

Pentecostal Healing Evangelists

This section briefly surveys a succession of Pentecostal healing evangelists, with the objective of tracing a chain of characteristic practices and influences of the healing evangelist paradigm.

John Alexander Dowie (1847–1907) directly influenced the emergence of Spirit-empowered healing evangelists.[12] In 1882, he began preaching divine healing and in 1890 established his headquarters near Chicago, eventually gaining worldwide fame for his eccentric ministry and rejection of medical science, resulting in battles with local authorities who accused him of practicing medicine without a license. In 1893, during the Chicago World's Fair, Dowie set up a booth for healing ministry. In 1896, he established his own church, the Christian Catholic Church, and purchased 6,000 acres north of Chicago, on which he built Zion City, a community of his followers. He published a magazine, *Leaves of Healing*, which promoted his itinerant speaking engagements as well as healing ministries that were spin-offs from Zion City. As a leader, Dowie presided over Zion City with an iron hand, appointing himself as the prophesied Elijah, the Restorer. In 1904, he proclaimed himself to be the first apostle of a renewed end-times church.[13] Although his prophecies came to naught, Dowie's global influence was extensive. According to David Edwin Harrell, Dowie was the first person to bring public attention to divine healing in twentieth-century America. Leading figures in the Pentecostal and charismatic healing movement were directly influenced by Dowie, including Gordon Lindsay, who names other leaders influenced by Dowie:

> Out of Zion came F. F. Bosworth, and his brother B. B. Bosworth, whose healing campaigns in the Twenties filled great auditoriums, seating many thousands of people. From Zion came John G. Lake with a message that stirred South Africa and resulted in the establishing of hundreds of churches that remain to this day .... Raymond T. Richey who was only a lad at that time, unconsciously absorbed the atmosphere of faith that pervaded the city, and later his healing ministry became the phenomenon of that time.... From the ministry of these men and others we might mention, there has arisen

---

11. Pew Research Center, "Spirit and Power," 18.
12. Harrell, *All Things Are Possible*, 13.
13. Blumhofer, "John Alexander Dowie," *NIDPCM*, 587.

a host of men of faith who have had powerful ministries. The Full Gospel movement [that] sprang into existence, coincidentally, as Dowie passed from the scene, owes Zion [City] a debt that it perhaps little realizes.[14]

Lindsay's claim of Dowie's global influence is confirmed by Adam Mohr, who documents Dowie's contributions to the Christian mission in South Africa. Mohr writes, "The evangelization of Africa was a particular priority of John Alexander Dowie, and in the first quarter of the 20th century, Dowie's version of Christianity—particularly divine healing without recourse to medicine—became incredibly popular in sub-Saharan Africa."[15]

John G. Lake (1870–1935), a protégé of Alexander Dowie, served as an elder in the Zion Catholic Apostolic Church. He was originally ordained to the Methodist ministry at age twenty-one but declined the appointment in favor of a business career, which was very successful. The turning point in his life occurred when his wife was healed of tuberculosis under Dowie's ministry. After receiving baptism in the Holy Spirit in 1907, Lake felt God directing him to Africa, so he left his business, distributed his funds, and set out for Africa believing that God would meet the needs of his family (wife and seven children). Lake was instrumental in establishing the Apostolic Faith Mission in South Africa and later starting healing centers in the northwest region of the United States. After five years as a missionary, Lake returned to Spokane, Washington, where he built a large charismatic church and itinerated as a healing evangelist. According to Gordon Lindsay, during this time "100,000 healings were recorded in five years."[16]

Figure 17: John G. Lake
Photo of John Graham Lake, ca. 1900-1905. Courtesy of John G. Lake Healing Rooms Ministries. Wikimedia Commons, PD-US.

Later he planted a church in Portland, Oregon, in which Lindsay was converted. Health issues prevented Lake from fulfilling his vision of a chain of healing institutions throughout the country.[17]

---

14. Harrell, *All Things Are Possible,* 14.

15. Mohr, "Zionism and Aladura's Shared Genealogy," 240.

16. Quoted in Harrell, *All Things Are Possible*, 15.

17. J. R. Zeigler, "John Graham Lake," in *NIDPCM*, ed. Stanley M. Burgess and Eduard M. van der Maas (Grand Rapids: Zondervan, 2002), 828.

Gordon Lindsay (1906–1973) was an important leader in the healing evangelist movement, publisher, and founder and director of Christ for the Nations Institute with his wife Freda Theresa Schimpf Lindsay (1914–2010). Gordon Lindsay's parents were members of Dowie's Zion City until its bankruptcy forced them to relinquish their shares and move. They ended up in Portland and attended an Apostolic Church pastored by John G. Lake, also a former resident of Zion City. Gordon Lindsay was converted at a meeting of Lake's healing ministry at which Charles Parham was the speaker. Lindsay subsequently joined the healing and evangelistic campaigns of Lake until he (Lindsay) began his own ministry in California. He returned to Portland and married Freda Schimpf at the Foursquare Gospel Church. In 1947, Lindsay signed on as manager of the evangelistic campaigns of William Branham and published the *Voice of Healing* to promote Branham's ministry. According to David Bundy, Lindsay fell out of favor with Branham when he reported on the campaigns of other healing evangelists. Thereafter, Lindsay focused on not only reporting the itineraries and results of healing evangelists but also on assessing the theological significance of the healing revival. He organized conventions of healing evangelists, until 1956 when he established Winning the Nations Crusade, which followed the model of T. L. Osborn's Native Church crusades, sending "deliverance teams" on missions across the globe. Lindsay was a prolific author, writing more than 250 books, articles, and pamphlets. In 1966, the Lindsays moved their headquarters to Dallas, Texas, and in 1967 renamed their work Christ for the Nations, Inc. In 1970, they opened Christ for the Nations Institute as a center for theological and spiritual formation for emerging leaders in the Spirit-empowered movement. David Bundy credits Gordon and Freda Lindsay for making major contributions to interdenominational and interconfessional understanding among Pentecostals and charismatics.[18]

Maria Woodworth-Etter (1844–1924) was one of the best-known healing evangelists at the turn of the twentieth century. She was affiliated with Winebrenner Churches of God from 1884 to 1904. She then worked independently until she signed on with Pentecostalism in 1912. Much of her notoriety stemmed from her practice of faith healing and display of charismatic gifts such as trances and slayings in the Spirit in her meetings. According to one estimate, a camp meeting led by Woodworth-Etter in

---

18. David D. Bundy, "Gordon and Freda Theresa Lindsay," in *NIDPCM*, ed. Stanley M. Burgess and Eduard M. van der Maas (Grand Rapids: Zondervan, 2002), 842.

Alexandria, Indiana, was attended by 25,000 people. The 8,000-seat tent that she used from 1889 was often not large enough to accommodate those who flocked to her meetings. Public attention and criticism were evoked by the huge crowds, spiritual fervor, and the perceived oddity of a woman preacher. Like Dowie, because of her practice of faith healing and eschewal of doctors, she was accused of practicing medicine without a license. Woodworth-Etter also operated in the gift of prophesy; her best-known prophecy was her prediction that the San Francisco Bay Area would be destroyed by an earthquake and tidal wave in 1890. Wayne Warner credits Maria Woodworth-Etter with taking "salvation, faith healing, and a subsequent spiritual experience of power

Figure 18: Maria Woodworth-Etter
Photo of Maria Beulah Woodworth-Etter, 1916. Wikimedia Commons, PD-US.

to the masses." She may not have been a theologian, but in the words of D. William Faupel, she deserves to be seen as "a monumental figure in terms of spreading the Pentecostal message."[19]

Smith Wigglesworth (1859–1947). By the end of the First World War, several healing evangelists achieved fame for their ministries, one of whom was Smith Wigglesworth. He was a plumber and volunteer in a Salvation Army mission in Bradford, England, who at age forty-eight, embarked upon a career as a healing evangelist. Shortly afterward (1907), he was baptized in the Spirit while attending the ministry of Alexander and Mary Boddy at Sunderland, a hub of Pentecostal missions. Wigglesworth claimed to have read nothing but the Bible. According to Warner, "Wigglesworth's ministry centered on salvation for the unconverted, healing for the sick, and a call for believers to be baptized in the Holy Spirit."[20] His practice was to conclude a sermon by praying for the sick, often weeping as he ministered. Yet he had a rough manner in dealing with

---

19. Wayne E. Warner, "Maria Woodworth-Etter," in *NIDPCM*, ed. Stanley M. Burgess and Eduard M. van der Maas (Grand Rapids: Zondervan, 2002), 1213.

20. Wayne E. Warner, "Smith Wigglesworth," in *NIDPCM*, ed. Stanley M. Burgess and Eduard M. van der Maas (Grand Rapids: Zondervan, 2002), 1195.

people who came for prayer. Warner records, "It was claimed that he would strike a person with his fist; a person suffering from stomach problems might receive prayer along with a sharp hit to the afflicted area. Others who were crippled (*sic*) were ordered to run across the platform after he prayed for them."[21] Despite some criticism from Pentecostal officials, Wigglesworth became one of the best-known evangelists in the Pentecostal movement, itinerating in many countries. He visited the United States in 1923, stopping over in the Springfield, Missouri, headquarters of the Assemblies of God. Stanley Frodsham, editor of the *Pentecostal Evangel*, recalled, "When in America, he filled the biggest halls, ministered to record crowds, prayed for thousands of people."[22] The author's assessment of Wigglesworth's tactics holds that occasional slapping during sessions of healing prayer is excessive and should not be replicated by emerging generations of healing evangelists.

George Jeffreys (1889–1962), founder and leader of the Elim Pentecostal Church, was baptized in the Spirit and healed of a speech impediment and partial facial paralysis in 1912. The next year, he teamed up with his brother Stephen Jeffreys (1876–1943) for a mission in Swansea, Wales, which brought the brothers to the notice of the wider evangelical community through reports in the *Life of Faith*, the official journal of the Keswick movement. Impressed by these reports, A. A. Boddy visited the mission and talked with the Jeffreys brothers, remarking "that the Lord needs evangelists in Pentecostal work today. There are many teachers and would-be teachers, but few evangelists. The Lord is giving an answer through this Revival to the criticism that the Pentecostal people are not interested in evangelistic work and only seek to have good times."[23] Boddy asked George Jeffreys to speak at the Sunderland Convention, which was well received. In 1915, George formed the Elim Pentecostal Alliance. Joined again by his brother Stephen, they travelled to London, Canada, and the United States, after which George embarked on a sustained period of evangelistic activity for ten years, planting new churches that flourished. According to D. W. Cartwright, "Everywhere there were huge crowds, dozens of healings, thousands of converts."[24] A highly successful campaign in Birmingham netted 10,000 converts.

---

21. Quoted in Warner, "Smith Wigglesworth," *NIDPCM*, 1195.

22. Quoted in Harrell, *All Things Are Possible*, 14.

23. Alexander A. Boddy, "The Welsh Revivalists Visited," *Confidence: A Pentecostal Paper for Great Britain* (Monkwearmouth, Sunderland, England, March 1913), 48.

24. D. W. Cartwright, "George Jeffreys," in *NIDPCM*, ed. Stanley M. Burgess and Eduard M. van der Maas (Grand Rapids: Zondervan, 2002), 807.

Jeffreys experienced great success as a healing evangelist and institution builder. During the peak of his ministry, he was seen as the greatest evangelist produced in Britain since Whitfield and Wesley. In the preface to Jeffreys's book on divine healing, *Healing Rays* (1935), the publisher credited the author for the pioneering leadership in advocating the foursquare gospel, which proclaims Christ as Savior, Healer, Baptizer in the Spirit, and Coming King. Donald Gee affirmed Jeffreys for "a voice like music, with sufficient Welsh intonation to add an inimitable charm. His platform personality at the time was magnetic. His face was appealing. Although lacking in academic training, he possessed a natural refinement that made him acceptable in all circles. He presented his message with a logical appeal and a note of authority that was compelling."[25] However, there was another side to Jeffreys. He could quibble over nonessential doctrinal points, such as church government. In 1939, when a ministerial conference declined to fall in line with his view, he resigned and founded the Bible-Pattern Church Fellowship, presumably laying claim to the correct view of the matter.

Aimee Semple McPherson (1890–1944). The most famous of the healing evangelists of the first half of the twentieth century was Aimee Semple McPherson, founder of the International Church of the Foursquare Gospel (ICFG). McPherson's leadership was expansive and prodigious. In 1917, she began publication of *Bridal Call*, a monthly magazine, about which Robinson writes, "Opening any issue at random, the reader would regularly learn of conversions, Spirit baptisms and healings."[26] While managing a megachurch, the Angelus Temple in Los Angeles, dedicated in 1923, she travelled widely holding tent meetings, proclaiming the foursquare gospel (Jesus as Savior, Baptizer in the Holy Spirit, Healer, and Coming King) to interracial audiences. She was the first woman to receive a license from the Federal Communications Commission (FCC) to operate a radio station, KFSG Los Angeles. For training new believers and budding ministers, in 1923 she established a school, the Lighthouse for International Foursquare Evangelism (LIFE) Bible College.

McPherson held regular healing services at Angelus Temple, during which she said she "felt the power of God working through me."[27] She dedicated a separate room, called the "powerhouse," where she and her followers gathered for the purpose of seeking the Holy Spirit's baptizing fire. Reports of miraculous

---

25. Donald Gee, *These Men I Knew*, 49; quoted in James Robinson, *Divine Healing: The Years of Expansion*, 1906–1930 (Eugene: Wipf & Stock, 2014), 115.

26. Robinson, *Divine Healing*, 198.

27. Amanda Porterfield, *Healing in the History of Christianity* (Oxford: Oxford University Press, 2005), 171.

healings in McPherson's ministry were published in the secular press, prompting an investigation by a group of doctors from the American Medical Association. Their report concluded that the healings they scrutinized were "genuine, beneficial and wonderful."[28] Despite the fame that healing brought to her ministry, McPherson downplayed its prominence in favor of emphasizing the balance of healing as one component of her conception of the foursquare gospel. McPherson's belief in healing through the Holy Spirit went back to Jesus and the apostles, as is generally the case with modern Pentecostals. Porterfield concludes that "McPherson's career epitomized the increasing prominence of faith healing."[29] Robinson depicts McPherson as the "harbinger of the post-war charismatic movement. Her drive to dispel the crass side of manifestations in some contemporary Pentecostalism, which marked the lowly social status of some adherents, was pitched to enable the merits of its doctrinal singularities to be given biblically reasoned consideration."[30]

Kathryn Kuhlman (1907–1976) was a fascinating modern healing evangelist. Dwight Wilson credits Kuhlman as the world's most widely known female evangelist.[31] She began her healing ministry at age sixteen, itinerating in Idaho, Utah, and Colorado. In 1935, she established the 2,000-seat Denver Revival Tabernacle and a burgeoning radio ministry. After a failed marriage, she restarted her ministry of miracle services. Healings were reported on a regular basis. In 1965, Kuhlman catapulted into prominence when she held services in the Pasadena Civic Center, seating 2,500. She later moved to the Los Angeles Shrine Auditorium, where for ten years she filled 7,000 seats, while also producing more than 500 telecasts for the CBS network.

In 1972, Oral Roberts University awarded Kuhlman with an honorary doctorate, in contrast to Wesleyan Pentecostals, who did not embrace her due to her divorce and her lack of emphasis on speaking in tongues. She eschewed the title of "faith healer," attributing her gift of healing as due to the Holy Spirit. Like other female Pentecostal ministers before her, Kuhlman did not start out with the intention of becoming a healing evangelist. The great crowds and opportunities came at the end of a lifetime of evangelism. "Like her two predecessors, Woodworth-Etter and Semple McPherson, she was a dynamic and

---

28. Quoted in Robinson, *Divine Healing*, 202.

29. Porterfield, *Healing in the History of Christianity*, 172.

30. Robinson, *Divine Healing*, 206.

31. Dwight J. Wilson, "Kathryn Kuhlman," in *NIDPCM*, ed. Stanley M. Burgess and Eduard M. van der Maas (Grand Rapids: Zondervan, 2002), 826.

Figure 19: Kathryn Kuhlman

Photo of Richard Roberts and Kathryn Kuhlman ministering, 15 January 1975. Courtesy of Oral Roberts Evangelistic Association; Wikimedia Commons, CC BY-SA 4.0.

successful soul-winner long before she was noted for her healing ministry."[32]

Kuhlman's greatest contribution was a particular praxis of healing, namely, her method of calling out specific disorders of people in the audience who were being healed. Kuhlman neither formed healing lines, nor laid hands on the heads of supplicants. Instead, she simply declared that healing was taking place in a particular seating area in which a seeker was located, a method some called the word of knowledge, and shared divinely imparted information regarding the Holy Spirit's healing activity. If an individual attested to experiencing a sensation and some change in symptoms, he or she might be invited to the platform to testify to their experience. Kuhlman customarily advised such people to seek the confirmation of a medical doctor before medicines or treatments were discontinued. Along with documented healings, another notable feature of Kuhlman's ministry was the phenomenon of people "going under the power" or being slain in the Spirit as she prayed for them. Wilson notes that this sometimes happened to dozens at a time and occasionally to hundreds at a time. Kuhlman's theology of miracles not only presented a new praxis of healing but also differed from Pentecostalism in her understanding of prayer. Hitherto, since the days of the Azusa Street Revival, classical Pentecostal prayer had been a loud and boisterous affair, punctuated by ecstatic effusions of glossolalia, shouting, running, and other outward displays. Kuhlman, in contrast, was often attacked by traditional Pentecostal detractors because her prayer and devotional life departed from these norms. Kuhlman may have set a precedent for what occurred years later at the revivals in Toronto and Pensacola.

Benny Hinn (1952–). In the 1990s, Benedictus "Benny" Hinn rose to prominence through his monthly Miracle Crusades and his half-hour television program, *This Is Your Day*, which aired three times daily on the

---

32. Wayne E. Warner, *Kathryn Kuhlman: The Woman behind the Miracles* (Ann Arbor: Servant, 1993), 154.

Trinity Broadcasting Network (TBN). Originally from Jaffa, Israel, Hinn's family relocated to Toronto to escape the ravages of the Six-Day War in 1967. In 1973, Hinn attended a Kathryn Kuhlman healing service in Pittsburgh, during which he heard an inaudible voice say to him, "My mercy is abundant to you." As he listened to the testimonies of those who had experienced healing, he declared, "I want what Kathryn Kuhlman's got."[33] From 1977 to 1981, Hinn worked with Kuhlman's healing ministry. Gohr states, "Kuhlman became an important role model for Hinn's healing ministry."[34] He went out on his own, preaching in Pentecostal churches in the Toronto area. Following the model of Kuhlman's meetings, Hinn shied away from laying hands on individuals and waited for them to approach the front and testify to their experiences of healing. Like Kuhlman, Hinn would induce supplicants to be slain in the Spirit, blowing the anointing, throwing his coat on people, and waving his arms over the crowd. Hinn proceeded to develop an international ministry, holding healing evangelist campaigns in many countries and establishing offices in Europe, Australia, New Zealand, New Guinea, India, Fiji, and the Philippines. For a while his theology bore the imprint of Kenneth Hagin's Word of Faith teachings, but he eventually distanced himself from positive confession, the health and wealth gospel, and irregularities in his doctrine of the Trinity.[35] In semi-retirement, Hinn continues to be highly influential and popular in the healing evangelist circuit.

Global Mediation of the Healing Evangelist Paradigm

Oral Roberts (1918–2009) had a deep influence on Pentecostalism in Africa by means of his healing evangelism campaigns in South Africa, Kenya, Ghana, and Nigeria and his worldwide media ministry of radio, television, and distribution of cassette tapes, books, and magazines. Through his campaigns and media, Oral Roberts inspired and influenced many leading Pentecostal leaders in Africa, including the late Archbishop Benson Idahosa of Nigeria, a protégé of Oral Roberts. Idahosa and his wife were both recipients of honorary doctorates from Oral Roberts University. It was Roberts's influence that led the Idahosas to establish All Nations Bible School in Benin City, Nigeria. Many contemporary Pentecostal pastors were trained in that institute, including Archbishop Nicholas

---

33. Glenn W. Gohr, "Benedictus 'Benny' Hinn," in *NIDPCM*, ed. Stanley M. Burgess and Eduard M. van der Maas (Grand Rapids: Zondervan, 2002), 714.

34. Gohr, "Benedictus 'Benny' Hinn," *NIDPCM*, 714.

35. Gohr, "Benedictus 'Benny' Hinn," *NIDPCM*, 714.

Duncan-Williams of Ghana, a word-of-faith preacher and pioneering founder of the Action Chapel International.[36]

Oral Roberts visited South Africa in 1955, and it was reported that his meetings attracted up to 125,000 people and reportedly gained more than 20,000 conversions to Christ. Roberts popularized the idea of the "healing crusade" in Africa. In 1988, Oral Roberts visited West Africa, including Ghana. A report in the publication *West Africa* put the figure attending his crusade in Ghana, held at the sports stadium in the capital Accra, at about 70,000 people.[37] His media ministry influenced many of the pioneering founders of neo-Pentecostal churches in Africa. Roberts is credited with originating the Pentecostal-charismatic theology of seed faith, which purports that a person's blessing is directly related to the level of giving in tithes, offerings, and gifts "sown" in the lives and ministries of the anointed of God. Asamoah-Gyadu concludes, "One of the most enduring legacies of Oral Roberts in Africa is his influence on the preaching of prosperity messages, especially the formulaic theologies of sowing and reaping. This legacy, however, leaves more questions than answers regarding its tendency to diminish the grace of God. Oral Roberts will remain a historical figure of great importance in the development of world Pentecostalism, including its African versions."[38] Roberts' international impact was not confined to Africa, but also extended to Asia through his relationship with David Yonggi Cho, pastor of the Yoido Full Gospel Church in Seoul, South Korea.

David Yonggi Cho (1936–2021). Of the Asian healing evangelists, David Yonggi Cho is considered by far the most influential in terms of the impact of his leadership. His charismatic leadership extended beyond Korea to the worldwide Spirit-empowered movement. Cho's full gospel theology clearly falls within the purview of the healing evangelist paradigm. Like other healing evangelists, Cho's experience of healing set the tone for his ministry of healing. He formulated an indigenous Korean theology that aligned the full gospel of Pentecostalism to the context of the Korean culture. Cho formulated two constructs that have been immensely significant in the development of an indigenized Korean theology. These are the threefold blessing (salvation, healing, prosperity) and the fivefold gospel (redemption, fullness of the Holy Spirit, blessing, divine healing, second coming). According to Hyeon Sung Bae, the fivefold gospel serves as the theological theory in Cho's doctrine of the full gospel, whereas the threefold

---

36. Asamoah-Gyadu, "Your Miracle Is on the Way," 7, 14.

37. Asamoah-Gyadu, "Your Miracle Is on the Way," 15.

38. Asamoah-Gyadu, "Your Miracle is on the Way," 25.

blessing is the practical application of it.[39] Cho writes, "The Gospel deals not only with the hope of eternal life and the salvation of spirit and soul but also with prosperity in life and physical health and wellness that would keep the balance between spirituality and reality."[40]

Cho conceived of the miracle of healing as "a sign of God's sovereignty in this present life" and "a sign of the coming of the kingdom of God to the earth." According to Sang Yun Lee, this means that the experience of healing can be seen as a means of experiencing the kingdom in the here and now of this life.[41] Whereas the Christian hope points to a future dimension, it also has a present reality. Cho's holistic message tracks with other healing evangelists in that it is based on 3 John 2: "Dear friend, I pray that you may enjoy good health and that all may go well with you, even as your soul is getting along well." Some have suggested that Cho derived his teaching on prosperity from Oral Roberts and that the provenance of his theology is found in American Pentecostalism. However, Cho himself insists that his brand of the full gospel is the product of a revelation he received in 1958, giving rise to his preaching and ministry since that time.[42] Allan Anderson paints a sympathetic picture of Cho, averring that no matter the source, his theology is typically Pentecostal and should be seen as a key factor in the worldwide growth of Pentecostalism.[43] There is little question concerning the influence of Cho as a pacesetter in the dissemination of the healing evangelist paradigm of Spirit-empowered leadership.

Reinhard Bonnke (1940–2019) was a renowned international evangelist who from his earliest days felt called to be a missionary to Africa. He was born in Königsberg, Germany, and was educated in Wales, where he met George Jeffreys. He attested that at age ten he received a call to minister "to the whole of Africa" with the assurance that "Africa will be saved." After marrying Anni Sülze in 1964, he pastored a small congregation of new converts in Flensburg and finally secured a placement with the Velberter

---

39. Hyeon Sung Bae, "Full Gospel Theology and a Korean Pentecostal Identity," *Asian and Pentecostal; The Charismatic Face of Christianity in Asia*, ed. Allan Andersson and Edmond Tang (Eugene, OR: Wipf & Stock, 2011), 432–33.

40. Yonggi Cho, *The Story of Fivefold Gospel for Modern People* (Seoul: Logos, 1997), 18.

41. Sang Yun Lee, "The Kingdom of God in Korean Pentecostal Perspective," in *Global Renewal Christianity: Spirit-Empowered Movements, Past, Present and Future*, Vol. 1: Asia and Oceania, ed. Vinson Synan and Amos Yong (Lake Mary, FL: Charisma House, 2016), 151.

42. David Yonggi Cho, *Salvation, Health and Prosperity* (Altamonte Springs, FL: Creation House, 1987), 11–12.

43. Allan Anderson, *Introduction to Pentecostalism: Global Charismatic Christianity* (Cambridge: Cambridge University Press, 2004), 232–33.

Mission (VM) as missionary to South Africa, relocating there with his pregnant wife and first child in 1967. After serving a year as an apprentice with the Apostolic Faith Mission (AFM) in Ermelo, he was assigned his first placement in Lesotho. Bonnke broke the mold of a White missionary by inviting Africans into his house, preaching in urban nightclubs, organizing a tract-dissemination network by hiring Africans as bicycle couriers, training African preachers through correspondence courses, and teaming up with an African evangelist. Some success followed, but he also ran into difficulty with the VM for his expansion beyond his original brief. Bonnke resigned from the VM in 1974, while retaining a partnership with them as he built up his own evangelism ministry, called Christ for all Nations (CfaN). Bonnke soon acquired fame as a mass evangelist, at first buying ever larger tents to host the crowds (including one that could seat 34,000 people) and finally resorting to

Figure 20: Reinhard Bonnke
Photo of Reinhard Bonnke, 11 March 2014.
Wikimedia Commons, CC BY-SA 4.0.

open fields with crowds in the hundreds of thousands. From 1986 onward, Bonnke ran the so-called annual leadership "Fire Conferences," a multiplier event focused on training African pastors to be evangelists.[44]

Bonnke's success was driven by the miracles of healing attributed to him and showcased on his "crusade" stages as well as in CfaN campaign material— from regular displays of restoration of sight for blind people and hearing for deaf individuals and the restoration of full mobility for disabled people to claims of people being raised from the dead. Medical verification was not sought for the reported miracles; hence, the evidence remained contested. In 1987, Bonnke moved his family from Johannesburg to Frankfurt, Germany, where he established the headquarters for CfaN, periodically travelling the world to conduct massive campaigns of healing evangelism. All in all, Bonnke's crusades attracted some of the largest crowds in the history of mass

---

44. H. V. Synan, "Reinhard Willi Gottfried Bonnke," in *NIDPCM*, ed. Stanley M. Burgess and Eduard M. van der Maas (Grand Rapids: Zondervan, 2002), 438–39.

evangelism. One crusade attracted as many as 250,000 to one service. His crusades in Soweto included Whites and Blacks together, despite the official government policy of apartheid. Everywhere he ministered, Bonnke refused to condone racial segregation.[45]

Heidi Baker (1959–) sensed a call to the mission field at age sixteen when she was living on a Native American reservation in Mississippi as an American Field Service student. Several months after she was led to Jesus by a Navajo evangelist, she was taken up in a vision for several hours and heard Jesus speak audibly to her and tell her to be a minister and a missionary to Asia, England, and Africa. When she returned home to Laguna Beach, California, she began ministering at every opportunity and leading short-term mission trips. She and her husband met at a small charismatic church in Dana Point and got married six months later after realizing they had the same radical desire to see revival among the poor and forgotten of the world.[46]

Baker founded Iris Global in 1980 with her husband Rolland, and they began ministering together in Asia. In 1995, they were called to the poorest country in the world at the time, Mozambique, and faced an extreme test of the Gospel. They began by pouring out their lives among abandoned street children, and, as the Holy Spirit moved miraculously in many ways, a revival movement spread to adults, pastors, churches and then throughout the bush all across Mozambique's ten provinces. Baker is now "Mama Heidi" to thousands of children and oversees a broad holistic ministry that includes Bible schools, medical clinics, church-based orphan care, well drilling, primary schools, evangelistic and healing outreaches in remote villages, and a network of thousands of churches. She has B.A., M.A., and Ph.D. degrees, has authored four books, and travels the world as a conference speaker.[47]

Formative Assessment

As Allan Anderson sees it, Cho and like-minded healing evangelists preach "a salvation that encompasses all of life's experiences and afflictions, and they offer an empowerment providing a sense of dignity and a coping mechanism for life." This message has played well in the Global South, so much so that Anderson states, "The main attraction of Pentecostalism in the Majority

---

45. Synan, "Reinhard Willi Gottfried Bonnke," *NIDPCM*, 438–39.

46. Gary B. McGee, "H. A. Baker," in *NIDPCM*, ed. Stanley M. Burgess and Eduard M. van der Maas (Grand Rapids: Zondervan, 2002), 352.

47. McGee, "H. A. Baker," *NIDPCM*, 352.

World[48] is still the emphasis on healing and deliverance from evil." Because it is a message that promises solutions for present felt needs, the full gospel of Pentecostal preachers has been readily and widely accepted.[49] However, despite its wide appeal in many sectors of the Spirit-empowered movement, the holistic dimension of the full gospel has come under a penetrating critique for its materialistic implications, as seen in prosperity theology. Critics assert that the full gospel preached by Cho and others focuses primarily on material possessions, physical well-being and success in this life, abundant financial resources, good health, clothes, housing, cars, promotion at work, and success in business as well as other material benefits. Further, critics take umbrage at the claims proffered by many healing evangelists, beginning with Oral Roberts and Cho, that believers have the right to the blessings of health and wealth and that they can obtain these blessings through positive confessions of faith and the "sowing of seeds" through the faithful payments of tithes and offerings.

Sang Yun Lee offers a balanced critique of prosperity theology intended as a corrective, noting that "Christian faith cannot be reduced to being equivalent with a secularized desire or a selfish wish for a prosperous present life since there is also the kingdom to come with the second advent of Christ."[50] He contends, "However, it is necessary to resist the idea that the kingdom of God can be reduced to prosperity theology and what humans need and want." Lee calls for balance between the kingdom here and now and the kingdom to come. To maintain this balance, he suggests that Korean Pentecostals ought to take to heart three theological affirmations: (1) The kingdom is not intended solely to fulfill personal desires for a prosperous life; (2) Suffering can be used by God to grow faith in his people; and (3) What is most important is to participate in the eternal now of the kingdom, not to claim the promises of health and prosperity in the present life.[51] While Sang Yun Lee's judicious critique is theologically astute, it may fall short of getting to the heart of the problem with prosperity theology.

---

48. The term "Majority World" designates areas in which most of the world's population, natural resources, and landmass are located, but are often economically poorer. These areas are also commonly referred to as the Global South, Developing Countries, or the Third World.

49. Anderson, *Introduction to Pentecostalism*, 234.

50. S. Y. Lee, "Kingdom of God in Korean Pentecostal Perspective," 153.

51. S. Y. Lee, "Kingdom of God," 157.

10

Pastorpreneur Paradigm

The pastor is the fourth leadership gift of Ephesians 4:11. The Pastorpreneur Paradigm of Spirit-empowered leadership represents an adaptation of the fourth ascension gift to a new situation. The "pastorpreneur" combines traditional functions of the pastoral office with entrepreneurial savvy and business acumen, an amalgam that resonates with today's global consumer society. The upsurge of megachurches in the 1970s necessitated a rethinking of the shape of pastoral leadership. Previously, the role of the pastor in Pentecostal circles focused on the pastoral care of constituents in a congregation of small to medium size.[1] The organizational complexity of the megachurch called for a shift in thinking about the role of the pastor. The Hartford Institute for Religion Research defines a megachurch as a Protestant church with regular attendance of 2,000 or more adults and children.[2] Pastors of megachurches came to recognize the pragmatic value of business models of leadership and the acquisition of entrepreneurial skills. Increasingly the success and notoriety of pastors of megachurches set the bar for the aspiration of most pastors to grow their churches.

This chapter begins by defining the term *pastorpreneur* and explicates the biblical patterns and principles of the ascension gift of pastor. The chapter then delineates the components of the Pastorpreneur Paradigm and presents two case studies of notable leaders in the Spirit-empowered movement who are pastorpreneurs. The chapter ends with a formative assessment of this paradigm.

---

1. H. V. Synan, "Role of the Pastor," in *Dictionary of Pentecostal and Charismatic Movements*, ed. Stanley M. Burgess and Gary B. McGee (Grand Rapids: Zondervan, 1988), 663.

2. Warren Bird and Scott Thumma, "Megachurch 2020: The Changing Reality in America's Largest Churches," *Hartford Institute for Religion Research*, (2020): 2, accessed November 18, 2023, http://www.hartfordinstitute.org/megachurch/2020_megachurch_report.pdf.

Definition of Pastorpreneur

The notion of a pastorpreneur is associated with the explosion of megachurches, which can be classified as growth churches.[3] Jennings reasons that this is not surprising, given that growth churches are typically led by powerful entrepreneurial figures. *Pastorpreneur*, a portmanteau of *pastor* and *entrepreneur*, is a neologism coined by John Jackson. Jackson holds a M.Div. from Fuller Theological Seminary and a Ph.D. in Public Administration with emphasis in organizational behavior and leadership from the University of California in Santa Barbara. He currently serves as the President of Jessup University in Rocklin, California. Jackson defines a pastorpreneur as "a pastoral innovator and creative dreamer who is willing to take great risks in ministry in the hope of great gain for Christ and his kingdom."[4] He states, "I believe a Spirit-led burst of entrepreneurial activity will lead the church into greater cultural impact than ever before. Even now, God is calling a church-transformation and church-planting movement into being across the country that demonstrates an entrepreneurial passion to reach the lost in our generation."[5] Miranda Klaver, Faculty of Religion and Theology Professor of Anthropology of Religion, Head Department Beliefs and Practices, Faculty Religion and Theology Vrije Universiteit Amsterdam, is a recognized expert on evangelical and Pentecostal Christianity. She posits that the kinds of churches that pastorpreneurs plant are often independent and do not take on the characteristics of a denominational church. Rather, as they depend heavily on the leadership of the pastorpreneur, such churches are "personalized and embodied" in that they become shaped in the image of their leaders.[6] Hence, the pastorpreneur, ready to risk all to follow the bold call of God, both models for their congregation the risky neoliberal individual and implicitly valorizes risk itself.[7] Although not acknowledged by most scholars who investigate the pastorpreneur phenomenon, Jackson's model is grounded in biblical principles of pastoral leadership.

---

3. Mark Alan Charles Jennings, "Great Risk for the Kingdom: Pentecostal-Charismatic Growth Churches, Pastorpreneurs, and Neoliberalism," in *Multiculturalism and the Convergence of Faith and Practical Wisdom in Modern Society*, ed. Ana Maria Pascal (Hershey, PA: IGI Global, 2017), 242.

4. J. Jackson, *Pastorpreneur: Creative Ideas*," 2; for Jackson's initial publication, see John Jackson, "Pastorpreneur: Tired of Playing It Safe, This Pastor Hears a Higher (and Harder) Calling," *Leadership Journal* 24, no. 4 (Fall 2003), accessed November 19, 2023, https://www.christianitytoday.com/le/2003/fall/7.59.html.

5. Jackson, *Pastorpreneur: Creative Ideas*, 7.

6. Miranda Klaver, "Pentecostal Pastorpreneurs and the Global Circulation of Authoritative Aesthetic Styles," *Culture and Religion: An Interdisciplinary Journal* 16, no. 2 (2015): 149.

7. Jennings, "Great Risk for the Kingdom," 242–43.

Biblical Patterns and Principles

The English word "pastor" is commonly used in front of a person's name as a title of someone in a leadership position within a church or religious organization, denoting an office. In the Bible, the term "pastor" is mainly associated with the function of a shepherd. The word "pastor" literally means a shepherd, one who tends a flock. In our English translations of the Bible, we have two words that mean the same thing and are translated from the same word in the original Greek language. Those words are "shepherd" and "pastor." They can be used interchangeably, and there is no difference in meaning since both words translate the same word in the Greek language used in the New Testament and the Septuagint, the Greek translation of the Hebrew Old Testament. That word is ποιμήν (Latin *pastor*). The term can refer to those who are occupied with tending livestock (Luke 2:8–15), or it can refer figuratively to rulers and leaders.[8]

In the Old Testament, the term "shepherd" was also frequently used to refer to political and religious leaders. The prophet Jeremiah prophesies against the idolatry and corruption of the leaders of his day, referring to them as shepherds (Jer. 25:34–36). The prophet Ezekiel employs the evil shepherd theme to illustrate selfish and irresponsible leadership and to rebuke kingship based on domination and oppression (Ezek. 34:2–4). In the Old Testament, God is also referred to as a shepherd. In Jacob's blessing of Joseph, he appeals to "the God who has been my shepherd all my life to this day" (Gen. 48:15b). God is pictured by the prophet Isaiah as one who "tends his flock like a shepherd: He gathers the lambs in his arms and carries them close to his heart; he gently leads those that have young" (Isa. 40:11), alluding to Israel's journey in the desert when God was their protector and guide.[9] In Psalm 23 David exclaims, "The LORD is my shepherd, I lack nothing. He makes me lie down in green pastures, he leads me beside quiet waters, he refreshes my soul. He guides me along the right paths for his name's sake" (Ps. 23:1–3).

In the New Testament, of the twelve times the word ποιμήν is used as a metaphor for "leader," only in Ephesians 4:11 is it translated as "pastor" instead of "shepherd."[10] This means that the term "pastor" in Ephesians 4:11 refers to a

---

8. B. H. Throckmorton, Jr., "Pastor," *The Interpreter's Dictionary of the Bible* (Nashville: Abingdon, 1962), 3: 668.

9. Jack W. Vancil, "Sheep, Shepherd," in *The Anchor Bible Dictionary*, ed. David Noel Freedman (New York: Doubleday, 1992), 5: 1189.

10. Walter A. Elwell, ed., "Pastor," *Baker Encyclopedia of the Bible* (Grand Rapids: Baker, 1988), 2: 1618.

leadership role in the New Testament church. "So Christ himself gave the apostles, the prophets, the evangelists, the pastors and teachers, to equip his people for works of service, so that the body of Christ may be built up…" (Eph. 4:11–12). Jesus is presented in the Synoptic Gospels as going to "sheep without a shepherd" (Mark 6:34; Matt. 9:35; Luke 19:10). The figure of the shepherd is applied to Jesus as the Good Shepherd, as articulated in the benediction of Hebrews 13:20 with the phrase, "our Lord Jesus, that great shepherd of the sheep."[11] The most developed shepherd and flock imagery of the New Testament appears in the gospel of John (John 19:1–18, 22–29). As a compassionate shepherd, Jesus lays down his life for his sheep. In his post-resurrection reinstatement of Peter, Jesus implores Peter to exercise a shepherding function, "feed my lambs," "take care of my sheep," and "feed my sheep" (John 21:15–17). Similarly, the apostle Peter uses the term "shepherd" metaphorically in exhorting the elders, "Be shepherds of God's flock that is under your care, watching over them—not because you must, but because you are willing, as God wants you to be" (1 Peter 5:2).[12]

In the New Testament concept of pastoral leadership, a pastor served a distinct function that complemented the roles of the apostle, prophet, evangelist, and teacher. The shepherding function applied to three offices of church leadership in the New Testament, namely, the bishop, elder, and deacon, all of which are directly linked to the work of shepherding or pastoring. Hence, the church was to be sustained by the responsible oversight of these pastoral leaders, who were the shepherds over God's flock.[13] It is the pastor's responsibility to build up the body of Christ by watching over the congregation and tending its members. Subsequently, this view has undergone significant alteration in the course of time, leading up to the present, especially since John Jackson introduced the term *pastorpreneur*.[14]

Components of the Pastorpreneur Paradigm

The pastorpreneur paradigm represents a new approach to pastoral leadership and authority. The pastorpreneur model is not exclusive to the Spirit-empowered movement; however, it is highly amenable to current developments in global Pentecostalism. In global contexts, we have seen

11. B. D. Napier, "Sheep," *The Interpreter's Dictionary of the Bible* (Nashville: Abingdon, 1962), 4: 316.

12. Vancil, "Sheep, Shepherd," 1190.

13. Vancil, "Sheep, Shepherd," 1190.

14. J. Jackson, "Pastorpreneur: Tired of Playing It Safe," 59–65.

the emergence of charismatic megachurches affiliated with apostolic networks that are different from denominations. These networks are usually constellations of independent churches, organized in loose national or transnational webs, linked not by denomination traditions but by personal affiliations of pastorpreneurs. Jackson uses the term "pastorpreneur" to describe megachurch pastors who are using marketing techniques and other entrepreneurial business skills to create networks of like-minded leaders and churches that challenge the top-down structures of denominationalism. In *Pastorpreneur*, Jackson employs business-like strategic planning and innovation skills to enhance congregational leadership. His practical strategies and visionary approach are designed to empower leaders to explore creative ideas and methods for maximum impact on their church and community.[15] Although not acknowledged by most scholars who investigate the pastorpreneur phenomenon, Jackson's model is the product of a well-established trend in pastoral leadership.

The pastorpreneur paradigm did not appear out of nowhere. It was an outgrowth of sustained attempts at redefining pastoral leadership, best exemplified by the megachurch pastors Rick Warren and Bill Hybels. David Fisher reviews a series of proposals for updating the traditional biblical-theological conception of pastoral leadership with secular, psychological, and sociological theories.[16] Over recent decades, the focus of publications on pastoral leadership has shifted from tending the flock by means of enabling and equipping leadership to visionary executive leadership as the primary responsibility of the effective, successful pastor. Pastors have turned to resources beyond an ecclesial context, gravitating toward leadership literature inspired by methods derived from the corporate business culture.

One of the initial proponents of visionary pastoral leadership is George Barna, pollster, founder of the Barna Research Group in 1984, and author of more than fifty books addressing cultural trends, pastoral leadership, and church dynamics. In *Today's Pastors*, Barna states,

> Having spent much of the last decade researching organizational behavior and ministry impact, I am convinced that there are just a handful of keys to successful ministry. One of the indispensable characteristics of a ministry that transforms lives is leadership. This may sound simplistic. Unfortunately, relatively few churches actually have a leader at the helm. In striving to understand why most churches in this country demonstrate

---

15. J. Jackson, *Pastorpreneur: Creative Ideas*, 7.

16. David Fisher, *The 21st Century Pastor: A Vision Based on the Ministry of Paul* (Grand Rapids: Zondervan, 1996), 1.

little positive impact on people's lives, I have concluded that it is largely due to the lack of leadership.[17]

To address the leadership gap in the pastorate, Bob Cooley, president of Gordon-Conwell Theological Seminary "recognizing the need for stronger, biblical leaders in the local church..." initiated a Lilly Endowment funded study to examine leadership involving sixty-two evangelical seminaries.[18] Cooley and other seminary educators were concerned that much of the literature on pastoral leadership draws to a limited extent upon biblical or theological sources. Instead, there is a heavy reliance upon models that are rooted in sociology, psychology or business, politics, and the military. This trend is indicative of a recalibration of pastoral leadership. As a case in point, Olan Hendrix, whom John Maxwell credits as the first person who taught him Christian management and leadership principles, assumes that leadership and pastoring are similar and describes leadership primarily in pragmatic and success-oriented terms, particularly in relation to the tasks it accomplishes. He speaks in terms of leadership skills, which are required for effectiveness in any context, be it "pastor, president, CEO, executive director, [or] vice-president."[19]

Another influential writer who spearheaded the shift in conceptions of pastoral leadership is C. Peter Wagner, whose views on the restoration of the leadership gift of apostle were discussed in a preceding chapter. As Professor of Church Growth at Fuller Theological Seminary, he examined factors that enable churches to grow. He came to the conclusion that the "the primary catalytic factor for growth in a local church is the pastor" whose "dynamic leadership has been used to catalyze the entire church into action for growth."[20] Wagner states, "the pastor in most demand is the one who provides strong leadership, makes things happen, is somewhat of an entrepreneur," while the candidate now being passed over is "the more passive person who waits for people to take the lead."[21] Carl F. George, leader of the Charles E. Fuller Institute, partnered with C. Peter Wagner, John Wimber, Rick Warren, Bill Hybels, John Maxwell, Bob Logan, and others in training a generation of leaders for the megachurch era. In *Prepare Your Church for the Future*, George developed a meta-church model based on David

---

17. George Barna, *Today's Pastors* (Ventura, CA: Regal Books, 1993), 117.

18. John Eric McDonald, "Teaching Pastors to Read," *Christianity Today* (February 5, 2001): 80.

19. Olan Hendrix, *Three Dimensions of Leadership* (St. Charles, IL: ChurchSmart Resources, 2000), 33.

20. C. Peter Wagner, *Your Church Can Grow: Seven Vital Signs of a Healthy Church* (Glendale, CA: Regal Books, 1976), 55, 57.

21. Wagner, *Your Church Can Grow*, 80.

Yonggi Cho's cell group structure, stating that the role of pastoral leadership and church staff "...is to effectively manage the leadership development structures."[22] George states that "in a large church the senior pastor's position is much like a CEO (chief executive officer) in a business organization. CEOs make only a small percentage of a corporation's decisions...[but] a CEO's major influence comes through vision casting."[23] In construing the role of the megachurch leader as a CEO, George commends a corporate business understanding of the senior pastor as a chief executive. According to Ernest White, the CEO model has become more prevalent, especially as "churches have taken on more of the corporation ethos as the megachurch has become the ideal."[24]

It is clear from the leadership literature in past decades that the role of pastor has been recast from shepherding and servanthood into a conception of leading and power wherein the pastor is depicted as the chief executive officer of a congregation. In documenting the prevailing corporate image of pastoral leadership, Shawchuck and Heuser summarize the results of interviews conducted by Leadership Network in over 1,000 congregations in six categories:

1. The church must live out of a vision, which originates with the senior pastor and leaders, and is announced and advocated by the senior pastor, that keeps the church focused on Christ and generates a pervasive attitude of enthusiasm and defines the uniqueness of that church.
2. Preaching that is biblically based, clear and practical; gives practical handles for everyday situations and motivates persons to put the concepts into practice in their daily lives.
3. Worship must be of superior quality, dynamic, with excellent music, appropriate to the age and sub-cultures of the people. It must be motivating and healing.
4. The senior pastor must give strong leadership and enable the staff and lay leaders to also give strong leadership, which gives a clear sense of purpose and direction in ministry and which puts strong emphasis on involving increasing numbers of laypersons in carrying out ministries of service. There must be effective and innovative programming to meet the needs of the congregation and the community.
5. A comprehensive assimilation process that puts major emphasis on an increasing number of small connecting groups, which develop strong interpersonal relationships and allows every person to feel known and wanted in a large congregation, and provides for continual spiritual growth.
6. The pastor must continually give himself or herself to the daily disciplines that keep him or her living out of a heart for God, releases the Spirit within him or her, and

---

22. Carl F. George, *Prepare Your Church for the Future* (Tarrytown, NY: Fleming H. Revell, 1991), 59–60.

23. George, *Prepare Your Church for the Future*, 185.

24. Ernest White, "The Crisis of Christian Leadership," *Review & Expositor* 83 (Fall 1986): 549.

enables him or her to keep a clear vision and sense of priorities for himself or herself and the church.[25]

It should be readily apparent that the above responses heavily favor a directive and hence pastorpreneurial style of pastoral leadership.

Analysis of the Pastorpreneur Paradigm

In bringing the notion of the pastorpreneur to the discussion on pastoral leadership, John Jackson has no qualms about dependence upon business acumen. He calls for risk-taking entrepreneurial leaders to develop innovative and effective strategies for reaching the culture, beginning with an unmistakable call from God and a bold vision that addresses the needs of those we hope to reach. Jackson states, "Entrepreneurs know they must do this to conduct a profitable business venture, and pastorpreneurs must likewise see the community around them in human terms."[26] He recalls a comment made by Bill Hybels of Willow Creek Community Church at a leadership conference: "It is a blight on the church that the average McDonald's owner knows more about his community than we do."[27] Jackson's point is that methods of ministry must be constantly adapted to be relevant. These methods must be fashioned in a way that is appealing and memorable. For instance, Jackson notes that the church he pastored in Nevada found Rick Warren's baseball diamond model to be helpful in articulating a strategy for faith development, from which Jackson came up with a three-base plan: Invite-Connect-Serve.[28] Hence, pastorpreneurs can lead the church to embrace entrepreneurial strategies to reach people without ever compromising the message.[29] Jackson delineates five basic strategies: (1) Grab the community's attention; (2) Build strategic partnerships; (3) Conduct big faith-building events; (4) Challenge people to find their niche; and (5) Multiply your impact.[30] Each of these strategies is explained in detail in Jackson's book, with practical examples and action plans that can be adapted to a local context.

---

25. Shawchuck and Heuser, 114.

26. Jackson, *Pastorpreneur: Creative Ideas*, 36.

27. Jackson, *Pastorpreneur: Creative Ideas*, 36.

28. Jackson, *Pastorpreneur: Creative Ideas*, 130. Warren's analogy pictures discipleship as akin to the bases in baseball game. First base is conversion. Second base is affiliating with a church or small group. Third base is growth in discipleship and discovery of spiritual gift(s). Home base is serving on a missions or evangelism team.

29. Jackson, *Pastorpreneur: Creative Ideas*, 44.

30. Jackson, *Pastorpreneur: Creative Ideas*, 52–55.

Case Study: Southeast Asia

Terence Chong[31] provides an overview of Spirit-empowered leaders in Southeast Asia in "The State of Pentecostalism in Southeast Asia: Ethnicity, Class and Leadership."[32] He posits the thesis that charismatic leaders in Pentecostal churches enjoy great deference and sway over large congregations. He identifies two main types of leaders of Pentecostal churches in Southeast Asia: the Joshua Generation Leader and the Redemption Story Leader. The first type describes those who are passing the torch from older to younger leaders, akin to Joshua succeeding Moses. The second type includes those with a dramatic redemptive life-story, involving a background of vice, immorality, serious illness, and/or socio-economic deprivation, who then find Christ and proceed to lead life anew. Chong claims that the leadership style of both are authoritarian, because "the charismatic leader is avowedly entrusted to articulate God's will and vision for the church."[33] Chong provides sketches of both types.

Kong Hee, a Joshua Generation Leader, founded City Harvest Church in Singapore in 1989, starting with twenty members. City Harvest Church (CHC) is a Pentecostal megachurch located within the Yunnan subzone of Jurong West planning area, Singapore. When Kong Hee returned to Singapore after completing a doctorate in theology in the United States, CHC began to grow rapidly. In 2009, it opened a megachurch facility that cost thirty-four million Singapore dollars. Kong Hee was well-connected in the upper echelon of a network of megachurch Spirit-empowered leadership, as a board member of David Yonggi Cho's Church Growth International (South Korea) and Luis Bush's Transform World (Indonesia). Kong Hee was a protégé, friend, and mentee of Phil Pringle, the founder and senior pastor of C3 Church Global (Australia) and advisory pastor to City Harvest Church. Sadly, Kong Hee was implicated in unscrupulous business practices that landed him in court.

According to a BBC report in 2015, Singaporean authorities launched an investigation into the church in 2010 after receiving complaints and arrested the leaders two years later following a review by the commissioner of charities that uncovered irregularities. During the trial, prosecutors outlined a convoluted

---

31. Terence Chong is Senior Fellow and Coordinator of the Regional Social and Cultural Studies Programme in Singapore.

32. Terence Chong, "The State of Pentecostalism in Southeast Asia: Ethnicity, Class and Leadership," *ISEAS Perspective* 53 (September 25, 2015): 1–8. This document draws from ongoing research at the ISEAS-Yusof Ishak Institute on Pentecostalism in Kuala Lumpur, Singapore, Surabaya, Jakarta and Manila.

33. Chong, "State of Pentecostalism in Southeast Asia," 7.

money trail in which six church leaders and accountants, including Kong, funneled twenty-four million Singapore dollars from a church building fund into sham bond investments. The defendants were later accused of using another twenty-six million Singapore dollars to cover up their tracks. The judge found no evidence of "wrongful gain" by the defendants but found them guilty of varying counts of criminal breach of trust and falsification of accounts. They are facing lengthy jail terms. The leaders remain adamant that they have done no wrong, insisting they only had honest intentions of doing the Lord's work, a stance that is supported by City Harvest Church, yet which—according to the BBC—has largely drawn scorn and criticism from Singaporeans.[34] Along with five accomplices, Kong was convicted and sentenced to prison. He was held at Changi Prison Complex from April 21, 2017, to August 22, 2019. Kong's story serves as a cautionary tale for emerging leaders of Pentecostal megachurches, who might be tempted to carelessly engage in unsavory business practices that may be common in the upwardly mobile middle class.[35]

Philip Mantofa, a Chinese Indonesian Canadian pastor, is an Indonesian redemption story leader. He endured a childhood of illness, suffered ethnic marginalization, and drifted into crime before he heard the voice of Jesus calling out to him at a church altar where he experienced evil spirits leaving his body. Mantofa earned a degree in theology from Columbia Bible College, British Columbia, Canada. Since 1998, he has served as lead pastor of Mawar Sharon Church, a growing assembly of 30,000 in Surabaya, Indonesia. Currently, he heads the Gereja Mawar Sharon network, which consists of seventy local churches. Since his youth, Mantofa has led more than 100,000 people to Christ. His passion is to ignite a fire within the younger generation to become pastors and spiritual leaders all around Asia.[36] According to En-Chieh Chao, Associate Professor of Sociology at National Sun Yat-sen University in Taiwan, Indonesia, has a Pentecostal community of an estimated six million, among which Mantofa's Mawar Sharon Church is one of the most dynamic and popular. Also known as "The Rose of Sharon" (GMS), this youth-centered ministry is particularly attractive to students in Indonesian college towns. While GMS has a strong ethnic Chinese constituency, particularly among the leadership strata, its congregations are made up of multiethnic, middle-class individuals oriented

---

34. BBC News, "Inside Singapore's City Harvest Scandal," October 15, 2015, accessed December 29, 2023, https://www.bbc.com/news/world-asia-34589932.

35. City Harvest Church, "The City Harvest Story," CHCSA, accessed December 3, 2023, https://www.chc.org.sg/the-city-harvest-story/.

36. Chong, "State of Pentecostalism in Southeast Asia," 4.

towards the global Spirit-empowered movement. GMS takes a market-driven approach to evangelism with mega-worship services that strongly echo an ethos of mass consumption that is well-suited to the metropolitan city of Surabaya where GMS was founded.[37]

According to Chong, the above biographies are powerful cultural models for congregations. They serve as crucial narratives for Pentecostal conversion among the Indonesian Christian youth where sin and sickness are replaced by salvation. Life stories of transformed Spirit-empowered leaders are thus attractive to young urban youths lost in the market economy and the cosmopolitan jungle. Whether a "Joshua Generation" or a "Redemption Story" leader, it seems that charismatic leaders in Southeast Asia tend to fit the pastorpreneur paradigm. Power and authority are attributed to the head or senior pastor who is entrusted to articulate God's will and vision for the Church. In this manner, the charismatic leader's legitimacy is beyond question because it lies with God who has chosen him (usually a male) to shepherd the flock over matters of theological direction, administrative organization, and even business decisions. The charismatic leader will thus not tolerate dissent or alternative views, which may undermine or reduce the ethical integrity of his leadership position.[38]

Formative Assessment

Miranda Klaver posits that the kinds of churches that pastorpreneurs plant depend heavily on the leadership of the pastorpreneur. Such churches are "personalized and embodied" in the sense that they become shaped in the image of their leaders.[39] Hence, the pastorpreneur, ready to risk all to follow the bold call of God, both models for their congregation the risky neoliberal individual and implicitly valorizes risk itself.[40] It is clear from the leadership literature in recent decades the role of pastor has been recast from shepherding and servanthood into a style of leading and power wherein the pastor is depicted as the chief executive officer of a congregation, network or movement. Shawchuck and Heuser state that "the metaphors for leadership most often used by Jesus—

---

37. En-Chieh Chao, "Counting Souls: Numbers and Mega-church Worship in the Global Christian Network of Indonesia," *International Network for Asian Studies* 75 (Autumn 2016), accessed December 3, 2023, https://www.iias.asia/the-newsletter/article/counting-souls-numbers-mega-worship-global-christian-network-indonesia.

38. Chong, "Pentecostalism in Southeast Asia," 7.

39. Klaver, "Pentecostal Pastorpreneurs," 149.

40. Jennings, "Great Risk for the Kingdom," 242–43.

Servant and Shepherd—seem not to fit well with current understandings and practice of church leadership."[41] They credit Peter F. Drucker, whom they regard as "… the master without peer in the fields of leadership and management" for his influence upon their thinking and writing.[42] Shawchuck and Heuser define leadership as "…seeing to it that the right things are done."[43] In attempting to shift the pastoral role from one of management to one of leadership, they quote Warren Bennis and Bert Nanus to describe how leadership differs from management: "By focusing the attention on a vision, the leader operates on the emotional and spiritual resources of the organization, on its values, commitment, and aspirations. The manager, by contrast, operates on the physical resources of the organization, on its capital, human skills, raw materials and technology."[44]

It is readily apparent that recent leadership studies document a tilt toward a personalized and directive style of pastoral leadership. This model of pastoral leadership has prevailed due to the wide influence of more pragmatic approaches to pastoral leadership, which privileged the importance of a take-charge leader and set the stage for the emergence of the pastorpreneur paradigm.

One might rightly ask if the pastorpreneur paradigm should be seen as a normative model for pastoral leadership in Spirit-empowered contexts. There are legitimate reasons why an entrepreneurial model should not be seen as prescriptive. Some pastors are more inclined to see their role in the original biblical sense that of a shepherd of the flock, in accordance with a servanthood model. Such pastors would probably flinch at the idea that all pastors should be entrepreneurial. Given the tendency, noted above, of take-charge charismatic leaders to squelch dissent or thwart alternative views, as Shawchuck and Heuser allege, it follows that pastorpreneurs gravitate toward a personalized and directive style of leadership. This critique is well taken and calls for strictures against leaders who abuse their authority through self-aggrandizing tactics. Yet we should be wary of ruling out the value of entrepreneurial skills in pastoral leadership.

An entrepreneur is one who pursues an opportunity despite limited resources. There are times when a pastoral leader must make do with limited resources by means of a skill set of initiative, creativity and teamwork. Having served as a local church pastor, the author's experience has shown him that making do

---

41. Shawchuck and Heuser, *Leading the Congregation*, 19.
42. Shawchuck and Heuser, *Leading the Congregation*, 13.
43. Shawchuck and Heuser, *Leading the Congregation*, 21.
44. Shawchuck and Heuser, *Leading the Congregation*, 22.

with limited resources is required of a pastoral leader when, for instance, there is a budget shortfall, requiring cutbacks in spending. One must find ways to maximize available resources. The point is that at times pastoral leaders must manage the problem of limited resources with entrepreneurial skills. We acknowledge that entrepreneurial skills are not specified in the lists of biblical qualifications for pastoral leadership. Yet this omission does not in itself rule out the pastorpreneur as a paradigm of Spirit-empowered leadership.

11

TEACHER-SCHOLAR PARADIGM

The Teacher-Scholar Paradigm is adapted from the fifth leadership gift of Ephesians 4:11—teachers. It is important to understand the two distinct approaches to this paradigm of leadership. On the one hand, there is the *pragmatic* Teacher-Scholar and on the other hand is the *academic* Teacher-Scholar. In early Pentecostalism most of the teacher-scholars were of the pragmatic sort, whereas today we are seeing an upsurge in the academic sort of teacher-scholars. The difference between the two relates to the level of formal education.

This chapter begins by expositing the components of the pragmatic teacher-scholar and discusses the challenges of anti-intellectualism in the discourse of early Pentecostalism, resulting from a distrust of formal academic education and critical scholarship. Then, the chapter shifts to the academic teacher-scholar, expositing its components and narrating the transition in the Spirit-empowered movement from rudimentary Bible institutes to accredited universities and seminaries, academic societies, journals, scholars, and publishers. The chapter concludes with an assessment of the success of academic teacher-scholars in cultivating a research culture in the Spirit-empowered movement.

Biblical Patterns and Principles

The leadership paradigm of the teacher-scholar (Eph. 4:11) is rooted in biblical practices of teaching and education. Jewish education during the biblical period consisted of acquisition of intimate knowledge of the Law, study of the history of the Jewish people, and proficiency in reading and recitation of the Hebrew Bible. Since the time of Moses, teaching has been one of the leadership functions of priests and Levites (Deut. 33:10; 2 Chron. 35:3). Parents were also tasked with teaching the Lord's commands to their children (Deut. 11:19). Before the exile, prophets also assumed a teaching function, imploring the people of Israel to keep the covenant and practice justice and righteousness. During the exile, the synagogue took on primary importance as the nexus of instruction in the Jewish faith. The rabbi (teacher) performed the function of recording and preserving ancient customs and maintaining the traditions of Israel. After the exile, the scribes took on greater importance in transcribing and teaching the Law. In the New Testament, the scribes are identified as doctors of the law (Luke 5:17), lawyers (Matt. 22:35), and rabbis (Matt. 23:8). Many of the scribes opposed Jesus due to his critique of the "traditions of the elders," a system of interpretation (oral law) that erected a fence around the Law, while, according to Jesus, obfuscating the heart of the Law.

Very little information is available on education in the early Christian era. We know that Jesus read and expounded the Scriptures, confounding the religious leaders of his day in theological debate. As a normal Jewish boy, he learned at home and received religious education at the synagogue in Nazareth. He memorized the Hebrew alphabet and copied and recopied passages from the written Law and was given a personal text beginning with the first letter of his name and ending with the last. As soon as he demonstrated ability to read, he received a scroll containing the *Shema*: "Hear, O Israel: The LORD our God, the LORD is one" (Deut. 6:4), which was recited morning and evening, along with passages from the *Hallel*, (Ps. 113–118), and parts of the Law from Leviticus. Prayer was an important feature of synagogue worship too. Based on Jesus's teaching on prayer in Matthew 6, it is apparent that he was not only schooled in prayer but also practiced a regular discipline of solitary prayer and meditation.[1]

A good deal is known about the role of the teacher in the New Testament. According to P. H. Menoud, the task of the teacher was to interpret the Christian message, to show its relation to the Old Testament, and to bring to light its theological richness.[2] In the Greek version of the Old Testament, known as the Septuagint, the Hebrew verb לָמַד (*lamad*), to teach, is translated with the Greek verb διδάσκω (*didaskō*). Both words mean "to teach" or "learn."[3] In the New Testament, the Greek word for a teacher is διδάσκαλος (*didaskalos*), a masculine noun derived from the verb διδάσκω (*didaskō*), meaning "to teach," "to hold discourse with others in order to instruct them," "deliver didactic discourses," "to be a teacher," "to discharge the office of a teacher," or "to conduct oneself as a

---

1. Hazel W. Perkin, "Education," in *Baker Encyclopedia of the Bible*, ed. Walter A. Elwell (Grand Rapids: Baker, 1988), 1: 658–59.

2. P. H. Menoud, "Life and Organization of the Church," in *The Interpreter's Dictionary of the Bible* (Nashville: Abingdon, 1962), 1: 624.

3. Karl Heinrich Rengstorf, "διδάσκω," in *Theological Dictionary of the New Testament*, ed. Gerhard Kittel (Grand Rapids: Eerdmans, 1964), 2: 136.

teacher imparting instruction or doctrine."[4] Of the sixty or so uses of διδάσκαλος in the New Testament, more than thirty refer to Jesus, mostly as an address. John 1:38 equates the terms "teacher" and "rabbi." Parker notes that it is likely that διδάσκαλος correlates with usage of the term "rabbi" in the underlying oral tradition and implies a teaching function rather than a formal position; instead, "…it indicates Jesus' status as leader of a group; and also, perhaps, that the authoritativeness of his teaching was publicly recognized (Matt. 7:29; Mark 1:22; Luke 4:32)."[5] The word for "teaching" in the New Testament is διδάσκειν (*didaskein*). Teaching was one of the most prominent functions of Jesus in his public ministry. His teaching often took the approach of interpreting key texts of the Old Testament (Luke 4:16–21), yet he also announced a new teaching that required "new wineskins" (Mark 2:21–22). Through a variety of modes of instruction (e.g., parables, beatitudes, woes, metaphors, and prophecies), Jesus advanced radical outcomes in his teaching. Perhaps the most radical outcome was that his followers were to love their enemies (Matt. 5:43–48).[6]

The title "teacher" is also given to leaders of the New Testament church, nearly always, according to Parker, "with some hint of official position (Acts 13:1; Eph. 4:11; 2 Tim. 1:11)."[7] The apostle Paul ranks teachers next below apostles and prophets, and above miracle-workers, healers, administrators, and those who speak in tongues, to all of which he affords special recognition (1 Cor. 12:28–30). Similarly, in naming important grace-gifts, Paul includes teaching (Rom. 12:7). At Antioch, prophets and teachers are identified among those who commissioned Barnabas and Saul for their first missionary journey (Acts 13:1–3). Unlike the Christian prophet, the teacher had a pre-existing model in the Jewish synagogue and the rabbinate. It seems likely that the office of teacher in the Early Church was adapted from the rabbi. The teacher was held in high honor as a herald of the gospel. The teacher's task was to instruct the community of faith, engaging in a pedagogical function including theological formation. Based on Paul's admonitions to Timothy to study to show himself approved and his insistence that the worker was worthy of his hire, one suspects that the teacher's work was a full-time occupation to the extent that the congregation was responsible for his livelihood.[8]

---

4. Pierson Parker, "Teacher," *The Interpreter's Dictionary of the Bible* (Nashville: Abingdon, 1962), 4: 522–23.

5. Parker, "Teacher," 523.

6. Rengstorf, "διδάσκω," *TDNT*, 2: 140.

7. Parker, "Teacher," 523.

8. Parker, "Teacher," 523.

Adolf Harnack presupposed that in the Early Church there were two distinct forms of organization. He states, "These forms were (1) the church as a missionary church, created by a missionary or apostle whose work it remained; and (2) the church as a local church, complete in itself, forming thus an image and expression of the church in heaven."[9] These forms of organization gave rise to two forms of leadership: (1) local leaders consisting of presbyter-bishops (elders and overseers) and the diaconate (deacons and deaconesses), and (2) translocal leaders consisting of apostles, prophets, and teachers. Harnack writes, "Thus in that early age there existed those who are now called bishops, but who were then called apostles, discharging the functions for a whole province [that] those who are nowadays ordained to the episcopate for a single city and a single district."[10] Parker counters that this formulation assumes a degree of systematization that was highly unlikely at so early a period.[11] A more feasible scenario would be more fluid forms of leadership. Nonetheless, Harnack is correct in asserting that the teacher was a highly reputed vocation in early Christianity. Yet, along with repute came a high standard of accountability. The apostle James warned, "Not many of you should become teachers, my fellow believers, because you know that we who teach will be judged more strictly" (James 3:1). The teaching of false doctrines is strictly reprimanded (1 Tim. 6:3) and the maintenance of integrity in one's teaching is strongly commended (Titus 2:7). Paul's charge to Timothy aptly captures the calling of teachers in the Spirit-empowered movement: "What you heard from me, keep as the pattern of sound teaching, with faith and love in Christ Jesus. Guard the good deposit that was entrusted to you—guard it with the help of the Holy Spirit who lives in us" (2 Tim. 1:13–14).

Components of the Pragmatic Teacher-Scholar

As stated above, there are two sorts of teacher-scholars in the Spirit-empowered movement, the pragmatic and the academic. Both sorts of leaders are highly gifted and capable, yet each brings different skill sets and assets to the table. By the close of this section, it is hoped that the reader will understand not only the value of the pragmatic teacher-scholar but also the need for its counterpart, the academic teacher-scholar.

---

9. Adolf von Harnack, *The Mission and Expansion of Christianity in the First Three Centuries*, ed. and trans. James Moffatt (Gloucester, MA: Peter Smith, 1972), 466.

10. Harnack, *Mission and Expansion of Christianity*, 445.

11. Parker, "Teacher," 523.

Early Pentecostalism was blessed by a preponderance of leaders who exemplified the pragmatic teacher-scholar paradigm. Early Pentecostal leaders may not have been academic scholars, yet many were scholars nonetheless in a practical sense, in that they were knowledgeable students of the Bible and engaged in creative theological reflection as they probed the meaning of the Pentecostal experience. According to Grant Wacker, "The plain truth is that the Pentecostal sky was studded with stars, luminaries of the flesh and blood variety, and their trajectories both illumined and ordered the world around them. Together they defined the movement's identity more than most imagined."[12] Wacker names several such leaders who were the founders and heads of Pentecostal denominations, including Eudorus N. Bell of the Assemblies of God, Florence Crawford of the Apostolic Faith, G. T. Haywood of the Pentecostal Assemblies of the World, Joseph H. King of the Pentecostal Holiness Church, Charles H. Mason of the Church of God in Christ, Aimee Semple McPherson of the International Church of the Foursquare Gospel, and A. J. Tomlinson of the Church of God (Cleveland, Tennessee).[13] These leaders were pragmatic teacher-scholars who published treatises laying out the formative doctrines of their confessional communities.

Our analysis of the pragmatic teacher-scholar focuses on a particular leader, David Wesley Myland (1858–1943), and the "Latter Rain Discourse" that he originated. Myland was a remarkable pragmatic teacher-scholar in early Pentecostalism, a leader of leaders, and a prolific speaker, educator, and author. He was a prominent leader in the Christian and Missionary Alliance (CMA). After hearing about the outpouring of the Holy Spirit at the Azusa Street Mission in November 1906, he sought and received baptism in the Spirit and immediately started preaching the Pentecostal message. In 1906, he wrote the first Pentecostal hymn, "The Latter Rain," and in 1910 composed *The Latter Rain Covenant*. Upon leaving the CMA in 1912, he founded several Pentecostal educational institutes, including the Gibeah Bible Institute in Plainfield, Indiana (1912), the Ebenezer Bible Institute in Chicago (1915), and Beulah Bible Institute in Atlanta (1918). Starting with the hermeneutical principle that Scripture can be interpreted on three levels—historical or literal, spiritual or typological, and dispensational or prophetical—Myland took as his main text Deuteronomy 11:13–15 and interpreted it as a biblical framework for the Pentecostal Revival. He held that *literally* the early and latter rains refer to spring

---

12. Wacker, *Heaven Below*, 144.
13. Wacker, *Heaven Below*, 145.

and autumn rains; *typologically* they refer to justification and Spirit baptism; and *prophetically* they point to the second coming of Christ.[14] In support of his interpretation, he presented evidence in the form of a precipitation chart from Palestine, courtesy of the American Colony, documenting increasing rainfall in Palestine between 1890 and 1900, from which he concluded that this increase was a sign of "God's last work for this dispensation, to bring about the unity of the body, the consummation of the age, and the catching away of the spiritual Israel, the Bride of Christ."[15]

Myland's message resonated with a group of fellow early Pentecostal pragmatic teacher-scholars, and they adopted his formative theological framework. Together, these early Pentecostal leaders compiled an impressive body of theological reflection, referred to here as the Latter Rain Discourse. This discourse was a grand scheme for organizing the interpretation of the Pentecostal movement and upholding Pentecostal identity. The Latter Rain Discourse also served as a hermeneutical lever with which Pentecostal leaders utilized the Bible as an ideological text to legitimize their movement. The Latter Rain Discourse can be credited with two achievements: (1) it communicated the vision of early Pentecostalism as a restoration of apostolic Christianity, and (2), it distilled a Pentecostal view of history. Early Pentecostals made the claim that their movement had fully restored the apostolic faith of the New Testament church. Specifically, they believed that the fullness of the Holy Spirit had been restored through the restoration of pneumatic manifestations that had been relatively dormant since the second century of church history. Now, asserted prominent early Pentecostals, this same power was once again fully manifested in the church. So says the British Pentecostal journal, *Confidence*: "No movement since the apostles has been so attended with Scriptural signs and wonders and miracles and salvation."[16]

Perhaps the most distinctively Pentecostal aspect of the Latter Rain Discourse was its linkage of pneumatology and eschatology. Aimee Semple McPherson alluded to this linkage when she stated, "Hundreds are being saved and baptized

---

14. E. W. Robinson, "David Wesley Myland," in *NIDPCM*, ed. Stanley M. Burgess and Eduard M. van der Maas (Grand Rapids: Zondervan, 2002), 920–21.

15. David Wesley Myland, *The Latter Rain Covenant: And Pentecostal Power*, ed. Donald W. Dayton, *Three Early Pentecostal Tracts* (New York: Garland Press, 1985), 95; see Eric N Newberg, *The Pentecostal Mission in Palestine: The Legacy of Pentecostal Zionism* (Eugene, OR: Pickwick, 2012), 161–62.

16. "The Pentecostal Movement," *Confidence* 2, no. 6 (June 1909): 8.

with the Holy Spirit .... The wedding garment is being put upon His people...."[17]
Pentecostals claimed that the restoration of the Holy Spirit was a sign that the
Second Coming of Christ was imminent. As J. Roswell Flower saw it, "Ever since
the day in which the Latter Rain was first poured out upon the waiting believers
in Los Angeles five years ago, the fact that Jesus Christ was soon coming for His
bride has been impressed upon our hearts with great force over and over again."[18]
Finis Dake aptly depicted the connection:

> Previous to 1906, Christians everywhere felt the need of a revival in their own lives
> and in the life of the Church as whole. Prayer meetings were held everywhere, until
> at last God began to pour out His Spirit as He did in apostolic days. People of all
> denominations were filled with the Holy Spirit and began to speak with other tongues
> as the Spirit gave them utterance, the sick were healed, the blind were made to see, the
> deaf to hear, the dumb [sic] to speak, and mighty signs and wonders were wrought,
> and are still being wrought in the Name of Jesus Christ. A deeper life and walk in the
> Spirit, a clearer vision of the whitened harvest fields, and a deeper realization of Christ's
> coming were the results of this outpouring of God's Spirit.[19]

In the last sentence, Dake pointed to "a clearer vision of the whitened harvest
fields." He was advancing a widely held view that the connection between
restorationism and eschatology provided the impetus for the global missionary
expansion of early Pentecostalism. However, I believe that there was another
key component motivating the missionary impulse. While pneumatological
restorationism and premillennial eschatology constituted the distinctive core of
the early Pentecostal metanarrative, we should not lose sight of a remarkable sense
of historical continuity, perhaps even a philosophy of history—rudimentary as it
may be—in the Latter Rain Discourse.

While we can credit the pragmatic teacher-scholars of early Pentecostalism for
their creativity in the literary task of constructing classical Pentecostal doctrine, we
also must acknowledge a problem that was endemic in the outlook of pragmatic
teacher-scholars toward academic scholarship. The founders of early Pentecostal
schools were so deeply affected by belief in the imminent return of Christ that
they focused on preparing students as quickly as possible for deployment in local
churches and mission fields. They saw no need for formal education and opted
for schools that offered basic practical training in Pentecostal beliefs and praxis

---

17. Aimee Semple McPherson, "Behold I Come Quickly," *Word and Work* 40, no. 29 (September 21, 1918): 4.

18. J. R. Flower, "The Bride of Christ," *The Pentecost* 2, nos. 11–12 (November-December 1910): 10.

19. Finis Dake, "The Second Coming of Christ," *The Elim Evangel and Foursquare Revivalist* 10, no. 20 (September 13, 1929): 318.

(experience). Often the only faculty member was the founder of the school, and the only textbook was the Bible. Hence, these schools were known as Bible institutes. The method of instruction was indoctrination rather than intellectual development. Courses were designed to encourage faith in the power of the Word as opposed to critical analysis.[20] The merits of early Pentecostal education must be weighed against an inherent limitation, namely, an attitude of anti-intellectualism. Its proponents ensconced this attitude within the mindset of early Pentecostal thought leaders, largely because of a distrust of academic scholarship. Had the pragmatic teacher-scholars acquired a more sanguine attitude toward academic studies and research, they might have been equipped to diagnose the root of the problem of anti-intellectualism and offer a corrective remedy.

Many scholars maintain that contemporary Pentecostalism still harbors traces of anti-intellectualism. In his seminal work on anti-intellectualism in the North American context, Richard Hofstadter offers a provisional definition of anti-intellectualism as "a resentment and suspicion of the life of the mind and of those who are considered to represent it, and a disposition constantly to minimize the value of that life."[21] From a Spirit-empowered perspective, Rick Nanez defines anti-intellectualism as "a prejudice against careful and deliberative use of one's intellect."[22] Theologian James K. A. Smith writes, "Pentecostal faith and practice is strongly opposed to any intellectualizing of the faith."[23] Roger Olson takes the view that the allegation of anti-intellectualism is difficult to shed.[24] Russell Spittler states, "Abiding anti-intellectualism is one of our flaws."[25] Veli-Matti Kärkkäinen argues that Pentecostalism is marked by a strong anti-intellectualism that persists to this day.[26] Wolfgang Vondey acknowledges, "Continual education and dedication

---

20. Lewis F. Wilson, "Bible Institutes, Colleges, Universities," in *NIDPCM*, ed. Stanley M. Burgess and Eduard M. van der Maas (Grand Rapids: Zondervan, 2002), 373–75.

21. Richard Hofstadter, *Anti-Intellectualism in American Life* (New York: Vintage, 1963), 7.

22. Rick M. Nanez, *Full Gospel, Fractured Minds? A Call to Use God's Gift of the Intellect.* (Grand Rapids: Zondervan, 2005): 29.

23. James K. A. Smith, "Scandalizing Theology: A Pentecostal Response to Noll's *Scandal*," *Pneuma: The Journal of the Society for Pentecostal Studies* 19, no. 2 (1997): 226.

24. Roger E. Olson, "Pentecostalism's Dark Side: Troublesome Teachings and Practices," *Christian Century* 123, no. 5 (2006): 27–30.

25. Madison Trammel and Rob Moll, "Grading the Movement: Three Leaders Talk Frankly about Pentecostalism: the Good, the Bad, and the Unpredictable." An interview with Derrick Hutchins, Lee Grady, and Russell Spittler. *Christianity Today* 50, no. 4 (2006): 38.

26. Veli-Matti Kärkkäinen, "Pentecostal Hermeneutics in the Making: On the Way from Fundamentalism to Postmodernism," *Journal of the European Pentecostal Theological Association* 18 (1998): 80.

to the life of the mind were simply not practical aspects of Pentecostal worldview and spirituality."[27] Lee Roy Martin finds this to still be the case, given that Pentecostal ministers are the least educated group within the Christian ministry. Hence, he proposes an approach to theological education that prizes the competencies of a Pentecostal worldview and provides a safe place to engage modern culture's philosophies and questions.[28]

Several Spirit-empowered scholars have advanced a revisionist perspective on the question of Pentecostal anti-intellectualism. Chris Thomas argued that Pentecostal anti-intellectualism is clearly a misnomer in view of the long history of Pentecostals establishing educational institutions.[29] Grant Wacker contends that early Pentecostals were not anti-intellectual but rather skeptical of the conventional norms of secular society and higher education.[30] Given their experience of supernatural empowerment of the Holy Spirit, Pentecostals opposed the naturalistic worldview that prevailed in Western higher education. Rather than being opposed to learning or the use of one's intellect, they were anti-naturalists. According to Doug Jacobsen in *Thinking in the Spirit*, the early Pentecostal movement had more than its fair share of intellectuals who articulated imaginative and creative Spirit-focused apologetics for Pentecostal spirituality.[31]

Lee Roy Martin contends that Pentecostalism's distrust of academic education was not without warrant. Pentecostals had good reasons to distrust higher education.[32] Their spirituality was in a sense counter-cultural, arising from a pre-critical worldview that privileges the affections over intellectual ability.[33] Wonsuk Ma argues that while earlier Pentecostalism is known for its anti-intellectualism, the academic community today needs to avoid the pitfall of Christian scholasticism.[34] Operating on the level of oral rather than written

27. Vondey, *Pentecostalism*, 135.

28. Lee Roy Martin, "'You Shall Love the Lord with All Your Mind': The Necessity of an Educated Pentecostal Clergy," *Pharos Journal of Theology* 97 (2016): 1, http//: www.pharosjot.com.

29. Jonathan Olson, "The Quest for Legitimacy: American Pentecostal Scholars and the Quandaries of Academic Pursuit," *Intermountain West Journal of Religious Studies* 4, no. 1 (2012): 106.

30. Wacker, *Heaven Below*, 31.

31. Douglas Jacobsen, *Thinking in the Spirit: Theologies of the Early Pentecostal Movement* (Bloomington: Indiana University Press, 2003), x–xi.

32. L. R. Martin, "You Shall Love the Lord with All Your Mind," 2.

33. Asamoah-Gyadu, *Contemporary Pentecostal Christianity*, 24.

34. Wonsuk Ma, "Theological Education in Pentecostal Churches in Asia," in *Handbook of Theological Education in World Christianity: Theological Perspectives—Regional Surveys—Ecumenical Trends*, ed. Dietrich Werner, David Esterline, Namsoon Kang, and Joshva Raja (Oxford: Regnum Books International, 2010), 729–35.

discourse, says Hollenweger, Pentecostals conveyed revelations of the Spirit by means of testimony, story, and song.[35]

Pentecostal anti-intellectualism abated to a certain extent with the development of Pentecostal scholarship in the 1970s and 1980s. The Society of Pentecostal Studies (SPS) was founded in 1970, coinciding with an increase in research by Pentecostal scholars on biblical studies, theology, and church history. Pentecostal scholars must navigate a course between succumbing to the rigorous claims of secular academics on one hand and regressing to the old ethos of Pentecostal anti-intellectualism on the other hand. The best way forward may be a concerted renewal of the Pentecostal distinctive of thinking in the Spirit,[36] which leads to our analysis of the academic teacher-scholar.

Components of the Academic Teacher-Scholar

The second sort of teacher-scholar in the Spirit-empowered movement is the academic. Above we hypothesized that the problem of anti-intellectualism in Pentecostalism could be remedied by means of critical scholarship. The aim of this section is to test that hypothesis against the outcome of the emergence of academic scholarship in Pentecostalism, beginning with acknowledgement of the first generation of academic scholar-teachers in the Spirit-empowered movement and recognizing the legacy these leaders left for subsequent teacher-scholars in the Pentecostal academy. Then we will consider newer global developments in the development of a research culture in the Spirit-empowered movement. The aim of this section is for the reader to appreciate the important role played by academic teacher-scholars as counterparts to pragmatic teacher-scholars.

From the 1970s on, there has been a significant increase in the emergence of Pentecostal teacher-scholars. The first generation of academic scholars in the Spirit-empowered movement published academic articles and books and were recognized as leaders who showed the way for others to follow. There are many who could be mentioned, yet the most notable include Walter Hollenweger (1927–2016), Vinson Synan (1934–2020), Kilian McDonnell (1921–2019), Gordon Fee (1934–2022), Stanley M. Burgess (1937–2025), Russell P. Spittler (1931–2023), and Cecil M. Robeck (1945–).

Walter Hollenweger (1927–2016) was the pioneer of Pentecostal academic teacher-scholars, and his life spanned the continuum from the pragmatic to

---

35. Walter J. Hollenweger, *Pentecostalism: Origins and Developments Worldwide* (Peabody, MA: Hendrickson, 1997), 196.

36. See Jacobsen, *Thinking in the Spirit*, Passim.

the academic teacher-scholar. Hollenweger grew up in a Pentecostal church in Zürich, Switzerland. He was ordained by the Swiss Pentecostal Mission and served as a Pentecostal lay preacher in Zürich until 1958 when conflict with the local church leadership and their acerbic accusations led to his abrupt resignation. Hollenweger joined the Swiss Reformed Church and studied theology at the University of Zürich, receiving his doctorate in theology in 1966 with a ten-volume dissertation on global Pentecostalism, titled *Handbook of the Pentecostal Movement*. Hollenweger published many scholarly articles and books, including *The Pentecostals* (1972) and *Pentecostalism: Origins and Developments Worldwide* (1976). In the latter work, he advanced a markedly non-sectarian theory of the origins of Pentecostalism, proposing five distinct roots: Black Oral, Catholic, Evangelical, Critical, and Ecumenical.[37]

Hollenweger was a committed ecumenist, serving as secretary of evangelism of the World Council of Churches (1965–71). He held the position of Professor of Mission at Birmingham University and Selly Oak Colleges from 1971 to 1989. Forty-seven students received doctorates under his supervision, and thirty-two master's degrees were directed by him.[38] Hollenweger's major accomplishment at Birmingham was gaining a hearing for the study of Pentecostalism as a credible academic theological discipline. His most prodigious protégé was Allan Anderson, a consummate historian who issued a post-colonial critique of Western Pentecostalism. Following retirement, Hollenweger served as guest professor at the Universities of Bern and Zürich and conducted religious services through German-speaking Europe, presenting original drama and music. After retirement, Hollenweger bequeathed his library to the Hollenweger Centre for Interdisciplinary Studies of Pentecostalism and Charismatic Movements, established in 2002, named in his honor, at the Vrije Universiteit (Free University) Amsterdam, the Netherlands.

Towards the end of his life, as he was suffering from dementia, the Swiss Pentecostal Mission met with his wife Erica and asked forgiveness for its misguided behavior towards them in the late 1950s. A part of his private book collection is now housed at the offices of the Swiss Pentecostal Mission.[39] According to his successor at Birmingham, Allan Anderson, "more than

---

37. Walter J. Hollenweger, *Pentecostalism: Origins and Developments Worldwide* (Peabody, MA: Henrickson, 1997), 2.

38. David D. Bundy, "Walter Jacob Hollenweger," in *NIDPCM*, ed. Stanley M. Burgess and Eduard M. van der Maas (Grand Rapids: Zondervan, 2002), 729.

39. Jean Daniel Plüss, "Walter J. Hollenweger," *BEGP*, ed. Michael Wilkinson, Connie Au, Jörg Haustein, and Todd M. Johnson (Leiden: Brill, 2021), 299–300.

any other person, Hollenweger is responsible for the gradual recognition in the western academic world of the importance of studies of Pentecostalism and the beginning of serious academic research undertaken by Pentecostals themselves."[40] I and many of my colleagues in the Society of Pentecostal Studies look to Hollenweger as the progenitor of our craft.

Vinson Synan (1934–2020) was the second pathfinding academic teacher-scholar. Synan was a leader in the International Pentecostal Holiness Church (IPHC) where he served as director of evangelism. Synan published or edited more than twenty-five books. His many titles include the classic *Holiness and Pentecostal Tradition* and *Century of the Holy Spirit.* In addition to being a noted author and professor, Synan was among the founders of the Society for Pentecostal Studies (SPS). He held the position of Director of the Holy Spirit Research Center and Scholar in Residence at Oral Roberts University (ORU).

I had the privilege of meeting Dr. Synan in 1975 at the Word of God Catholic Charismatic Community in Ann Arbor, Michigan. Years later I was one of the first graduates of the Ph.D. program in Renewal Studies at Regent University School of Divinity, a significant accomplishment of Synan during his tenure as Dean of Regent University School of Divinity (1994–2006). In more recent years, I worked closely with Synan in launching the Ph.D. program in Contextual Theology at ORU. In October 2018, the Virginia History Series inducted Synan into its Historical Hall of Fame.

When news of his death was publicized, tributes poured in, expressing deep respect and gratitude for Vinson Synan as a person and a scholar. Doug Beacham, general superintendent of the IPHC, in a statement posted on the IPHC website writes, "The IPHC is grateful for the life of Dr. Vinson Synan. No one in our movement has been more influential in global Christianity than him. He was a pillar in the mid-twentieth century move of the Holy Spirit that impacted Christians from nearly every faith family within Protestantism and Catholicism."[41] According to Regent University, "One of his [Dr. Synan's] greatest accomplishments was his dedication in joining with other Christian leaders in opening the door to dialogue, building understanding, and fostering honor and mutual respect among leaders and participants in the Pentecostal

---

40. Allan Anderson, *An Introduction to Pentecostalism*, 245.

41. IPHC Tribute, accessed March 24, 2024, https://iphc.org/gso/2020/03/16/celebrating-dr-vinson-synan/.

and Charismatic movements."[42] The founder of Regent University, the late Pat Robertson stated, "Synan was a leader in Pentecostal ecumenism and the Charismatic Renewal. Dr. Vinson Synan was a powerhouse minister who God used to bring His people together and grow His kingdom. He was also a world-class scholar who recorded God's mighty works and trained new generations of ministers as dean of the Regent University School of Divinity."[43]

Kilian McDonnell (1921–2019), a third leader of the first wave of Spirit-empowered academic theologians, was a Roman Catholic priest of the Benedictine order and leader of the Catholic Charismatic Renewal. He entered the Benedictine monastery at St. John's Abbey in Collegeville, Minnesota, in 1945. After completing graduate work in liturgy at the University of Notre Dame, he was ordained to the Roman Catholic priesthood in 1951. He earned the S.T.D. from the Theological Faculty of Trier, completing a major work, *John Calvin: The Church and the Eucharist*, in 1967. That year, he became the executive director of the Institute for Ecumenical and Cultural Research. He conducted specialized studies of the charismatic leaders Arnold Bittlinger, Larry Christenson, and J. Rodman Williams. For nearly fifteen years (1972–1992), he co-chaired the Roman Catholic/Pentecostal Dialogue with David du Plessis. Father McDonnell's research on Pentecostal and charismatic renewal movements produced several significant outcomes.

It was McDonnell who coined the term "classical Pentecostalism." With the encouragement of Cardinal Suenens, McDonnell authored two major documents articulating the theological foundations of the Catholic Charismatic Renewal: "Statement of the Theological Basis of the Catholic Charismatic Renewal" (1973) and "Theological and Pastoral Orientations on the Catholic Charismatic Renewal" (1974). From 1974 to 1985, McDonnell served as informal liaison to the Vatican. His other publications include *The Charismatic Renewal and the Churches* (1976), *Presence, Power, Praise* (1980), *Open the Windows: The Popes and Charismatic Renewal* (1989), and *Christian Initiation and Baptism in the Holy Spirit: Evidence from the First Eight Centuries* (1991). McDonnell attended the organizing meeting of the Society for Pentecostal Studies and addressed those present at its inaugural meeting in 1971, although as a Catholic he did not qualify for membership at

---

42. Regent University Tribute, accessed March 24, 2024, https://www.regent.edu/news/regent-mourns-the-loss-of-theologian-dr-vinson-synan/.

43. Robertson Tribute, https://www.regent.edu/news/regent-mourns-the-loss-of-theologian-dr-vinson-synan/, accessed March 24, 2024.

that time.[44] Mel Robeck credits McDonnell as the leading interpreter of the Roman Catholic Charismatic Renewal.[45]

Gordon Fee (1934–2022), the fourth leader of the initial wave of Pentecostal academic teacher-scholars, was an ordained Assemblies of God minister, New Testament scholar, and Professor Emeritus at Regent College in Vancouver, Canada. He received B.A. and M.A. degrees from Seattle Pacific University, was ordained in the Assemblies of God in 1959, and earned his doctorate from the University of Southern California in 1966. Fee is internationally known for his work on the New International Version translation committee and his numerous publications, including commentaries on *1 Corinthians* (1987), *1 and 2 Timothy, Titus* (1988), *Paul's Letter to the Philippians* (1995), and *The First and Second Letters to the Thessalonians* (2000), as well as his *New Testament Exegesis: A Handbook for Students and Pastors* (1993), and *How to Read the Bible for All Its Worth* (1993). Fee's opus is *God's Empowering Presence: The Holy Spirit in the Letters of Paul* (1994).

According to Patrick Alexander, "Fee's conviction about the truth of the Pentecostal experience coupled with his reputation as a scholar made this work perhaps the most substantial contribution to Pauline pneumatology in the twentieth century."[46] Nevertheless, Fee's critique of two fundamental Classical Pentecostal doctrines put him at odds with denominational leaders of the Assemblies of God. First, he challenged the Pentecostal hermeneutic underlying the belief that baptism in the Spirit necessarily occurs after conversion. Second, he raised questions about the doctrine that speaking in tongues constitutes the initial physical evidence of baptism in the Spirit. Alexander points out that within Pentecostal circles, Fee was both denounced and admired. He was denounced by those who saw him as a threat to central Pentecostal beliefs, and he was admired by those who regarded him as a constructive critic whose skills as a biblical interpreter merited due consideration.

In his final analysis, Alexander concludes Fee epitomizes the heretofore oxymoron, "a Pentecostal scholar."[47] Be that as it may, Fee's legacy was undeterred by opposition from insiders, who missed an opportunity to benefit from the

---

44. Glen W. Menzies, "The First Fifty Years of the Society for Pentecostal Studies: A Brief History," *Pneuma: The Journal of the Society for Pentecostal Studies* 42, nos. 3–4 (2020): 337, Note 7.

45. Cecil M. Robeck, Jr., "Kilian McDonnell," in *NIDPCM*, ed. Stanley M. Burgess and Eduard M. van der Maas (Grand Rapids: Zondervan, 2002), 853.

46. Patrick H. Alexander, "Gordon Donald Fee," in *NIDPCM*, ed. Stanley M. Burgess and Eduard M. van der Maas (Grand Rapids: Zondervan, 2002), 635.

47. Patrick H. Alexander, "Gordon Donald Fee," *NIDPCM*, 636.

wisdom of a master in the field of textual criticism, and Fee's scholarly works reached a wide audience beyond the Pentecostal-charismatic movements. There is a lesson to be learned here. We may feel uncomfortable when an academic scholar-teacher serves a prophetic function of speaking truth to power but let us not be defensive and miss out on a word that may be from the Holy Spirit.

Stanley M. Burgess (1937–2025). Many other representatives of the first generation of academic teacher/scholars in the Spirit-empowered movement deserve mention, yet only a few can be acknowledged due to limitations of space. Stanley M. Burgess, a charter member of the Society for Pentecostal Studies and an ORU trustee emeritus, blazed new paths in the study of historical pneumatology in his groundbreaking trilogy, tracing the golden thread of renewal in the Holy Spirit through three epochs of church history.[48] Burgess' contribution to the Pentecostal academy was an expanded view of the historical roots of Pentecostal spirituality, driven by his study of the mystical theology of Eastern Christianity. Burgess also collaborated with Gary McGee in the first edition of the *Dictionary of Pentecostal and Charismatic Movements* (1988) and was the driving force with Eduard van der Maas in producing the revised and expanded second edition, *The New International Dictionary of Pentecostal and Charismatic Movements* (2002), both of which represented a major boon to Renewal scholarship.

Russell P. Spittler (1931–2023) also attended the founding meeting of the SPS and served as president in 1973. He published the papers presented at that meeting as *Perspectives on the New Pentecostalism* (1976). Along with serving as professor of New Testament, specializing in the spirituality found in 1 Corinthians and Hebrews, Spittler held several important administrative positions at Fuller Theological Seminary, including director of the David J. du Plessis Center for Christian Spirituality, Provost, and Vice President of Academic Affairs. His supervision of dissertation projects made a profound effect on the development of American Pentecostal scholarship.[49]

Cecil M. "Mel" Robeck, Jr. (1945–) Assemblies of God minister, historian, and ecumenist, is a longstanding member of the Society for Pentecostal Studies. He edited *Pneuma: The Journal of the Society for Pentecostal Studies*

---

48. For a discussion of the findings of the Burgess trilogy, see Eric N. Newberg, "Stanley Milton Burgess and the Artifacts of Renewal," in *Children of the Calling: Essays in Honor of Stanley M. Burgess and Ruth V. Burgess*, ed. Eric Nelson Newberg and Lois E. Olena (Eugene, OR: Pickwick, 2014), 10–19.

49. Cecil M. Robeck, Jr., "Russell Paul Spittler, in *NIDPCM*, ed. Stanley M. Burgess and Eduard M. van der Maas (Grand Rapids: Zondervan, 2002), 1102–04.

for eight years (1984–92). Robeck is unequaled in productivity as an author of academic articles and the leading force of the Pentecostal ecumenical dialogues. He collaborated with Kilian McDonnell as co-chairman of the International Roman Catholic/Pentecostal Dialogue and served on the Faith and Order Commission of the World Council of Churches. Robeck has filled several leadership positions at Fuller Theological Seminary, including Assistant and Associate Dean of the School of Theology and Director of the David du Plessis Center for Christian Spirituality.[50] His major historical work is *The Azusa Street Mission and Revival: The Birth of the Global Pentecostal Movement.*

To summarize, the first wave of leading academic teacher-scholars in Pentecostalism laid the groundwork for the development of a research culture in the Spirit-empowered movement. Subsequent teacher-scholars in the Spirit-empowered movement have carried on the legacy of the first wave and built institutions that prize the value of a research culture.[51] A research culture encompasses the behaviors, values, expectations, attitudes and norms of a given academic community. It escalates the importance afforded to the production of research, accessibility to research tools and facilities, and the provision of opportunities to publish that research. It shapes researchers' career paths and determines the way that research is conducted and communicated. Dave Johnson writes, "The school's leadership must be committed to the vision of a research culture and be willing to provide the time and resources necessary to make that dream a reality... Creating a research culture can be costly."[52] The leadership of two educational institutions in the Spirit-empowered movement—Regent University and Oral Roberts University—demonstrated a requisite level of commitment to the development of a research culture by allocating significant resources for the initiation and accreditation of Ph.D. programs. The Regent program reconceptualized the study of the Pentecostal and charismatic movements as "renewal studies," launching in 2003 with tracks in theology and church history and subsequently adding biblical studies. The ORU Ph.D. focuses its program design on "contextual theology,"

---

50. Russell P. Spittler, "Cecil Melvin Robeck, Jr." in *NIDPCM*, ed. Stanley M. Burgess and Eduard M. van der Maas (Grand Rapids: Zondervan, 2002), 1023–24.

51. Menzies, "The First Fifty Years of the Society for Pentecostal Studies," 335–69.

52. Dave Johnson, "Creating and Expanding a Research Culture at Pentecostal and Charismatic Seminaries and Graduate Schools in the Majority World," in *Pentecostal Theological Education in the Majority World: The Graduate and Post-Graduate Level*, ed. Dave Johnson and Rick Wadholm, Jr. (Baguio City: Asia Pacific Theological Seminary Press, 2022), 76.

prioritizing Spirit-empowered theological initiatives in the Global South and launching in 2019 with a single track. Both Ph.D. programs are accredited by the Association of Theological Schools (ATS) for modular format with a combination of online instruction and short-term residencies.

The process of building a research culture is underway in many areas of the world other than the United States. Academic teacher-scholars are developing graduate programs in the UK, Africa, Europe, Latin America, and Asia. Notable examples include Dave Johnson in the Philippines, Kwabena Asamoah-Gyadu and Opoku Onyinah in Ghana, Peter White in South Africa, and William K. Kay, Allan Anderson and Wolfgang Vondey in England. The development of a research culture in Spirit-empowered circles is reflected in the appearance of academic journals, the first of which was the *EPTA Bulletin*, which originated in 1985 and was re-named as the *Journal of the European Pentecostal Theological Association* in 1996. Next came *Pneuma: The Journal of the Society for Pentecostal Studies*, established in 1979 with aim of publishing five types of articles, including exegetical, historical, theological, social sciences, and practical. Other journals appeared afterward, including the *Journal of Pentecostal Theology* in 1992, Pneuma Review in 1998, the *Asian Journal of Pentecostal Studies* in 1998, *Australasian Pentecostal Studies* in 1999, *PentecoStudies*, the journal of GloPent, the European Research Network on Global Pentecostalism, in 2002.[53] Asamoah-Gyadu observes, "PentecoStudies offers a distinctly interdisciplinary forum for the study of Pentecostal and Charismatic Christianity. Authors from the social sciences, the humanities, cultural studies, religious studies and theology are welcome to submit research on global expressions of Pentecostalism defined in its broadest sense."[54] Several digital platforms for dissemination of research on global Pentecostalism by non-Western scholars have appeared in the Global South. Wolfgang Vondey surmises from this that "Pentecostal scholarship seems poised to become a central player in the theological academy."[55] This is a significant development when one considers the former "persistent stance of anti-intellectualism, a rejection of higher education and learning, and criticism of the academic world."[56]

---

53. Menzies, "First Fifty Years of the Society for Pentecostal Studies," 349.

54. J. Kwabena Asamoah-Gyadu, "'I Will Not Leave You Orphaned': Select Impactful Contributions of Global Pentecostalism to World Christianity," *Pneuma: The Journal of the Society for Pentecostal Studies* 42 (2020): 383–84.

55. Vondey, *Pentecostalism*, 134.

56. Vondey, *Pentecostalism*, 139.

Formative Assessment

While we have credited the pragmatic teacher-scholars of Pentecostalism with significant positive accomplishments, these leaders were also responsible for at least one negative effect, namely, a strain of anti-intellectualism in attitudes toward higher education. As Daniel Topf has pointed out, Western Pentecostal missionaries brought these limitations with them when they established Bible colleges in the mission fields of Asia, Africa, and Latin America.[57] These limitations hindered the development of a research culture in both the United States and the Majority World. Nevertheless, some would agree with Asamoah-Gyadu that the "virtual rejection of intellectual approaches to life and hostility demonstrated toward theological education at the academic level by Pentecostals in the past have changed dramatically."[58] Yet more work remains to be done by today's teacher-scholars. It is incumbent on those of us who are engaged in educating the next generation of Spirit-empowered leaders to carry forward the work of building a research culture in the Spirit-empowered movement.

Summative Assessment

This study of Spirit-empowered leadership has employed two kinds of analyses—diachronic and synchronic. Part II employed diachronic analysis, following the historical development of Spirit-empowered leadership across four periods of time and finding that Spirit-baptism and charismatic gifting were constants despite changing historical circumstances. The diachronic approach helps us understand the evolution of Spirit-empowered leadership and the influences that shaped its growth and development. Part III employed synchronic analysis, constructing a typology of Spirit-empowered paradigms of leadership, adapted from the fivefold ministry gifts of Ephesians 4:11: apostle, prophet, evangelist, pastor, and teacher. The synchronic approach helps us to appreciate the distinctive components of each of the paradigms of leadership in the Spirit-empowered tradition. Now let's briefly discuss the internal coherence of our paradigms. So, where do we find continuity? To answer that question, we will turn to the context of Ephesians 4 and related references.

---

57. Daniel Topf, "Pentecostal Theological Education in the Majority World: A Century of Overcoming Obstacles and Gaining New Ground," in *Pentecostal Theological Education in the Majority World: The Graduate and Post-Graduate Level*, ed. Dave Johnson and Rick Wadholm Jr. (Baguio City: Asia Pacific Theological Seminary Press, 2022), 120–21.

58. Asamoah-Gyadu, "I Will Not Leave You Orphaned," 381.

In the verses that follow Ephesians 4:11, Paul clearly states the purpose of the ministry leadership gifts given by the resurrected Christ. These gifts share a common purpose, which is "to equip his [Christ's] people for works of service, so that the body of Christ may be built up until we all reach unity in the faith and in the knowledge of the Son of God and become mature, attaining to the whole measure of the fullness of Christ" (Eph. 4:12–13). In short, leaders were to train the people for service. This would entail the equipping and encouragement of the people to exercise their spiritual gifts so that the body of Christ can move toward maturity. The picture here is developmental. The intended outcome is attainment of the whole measure of Christ, involving a process of development from spiritual infancy (blown here and there by shaky doctrine) to maturity (speaking the truth in love). The growth toward maturity is collective, as it is achieved "as each part does its work" (Eph. 4:16). The imagery of Ephesians 11:15–16 recalls the image of the body in 1 Corinthians 12: 27ff: "Now you are the body of Christ, and each one of you is a part of it. And God has placed in the church first apostles, second prophets, third teachers, then miracles, then gifts of healing, of helping, of guidance, and of different kinds of tongues."

Here is the point of continuity: Each of the leadership gifts—in tandem with the spiritual gifts given to each member—shares a common purpose, which is the equipping of the members of the body with manifestations of the Spirit (1 Cor. 12:7), and a common goal, which is maturity by means of attaining the whole measure of the fullness of Christ. To put it simply, we see the continuity of the leadership gifts in the roles they play in the upbuilding of the Body of Christ toward maturity through empowerment of the Spirit. The role of apostles and prophets is foundational, in that the Church is "built on the foundation of the apostles and prophets" (Eph. 2:20). The role of evangelists is to "do the work of an evangelist," (2 Tim. 4:5), building on the foundation and helping the Church to grow. The role of pastors is to "be shepherds of God's flock that is under your care, watching over them—not because you must, but because you are willing... being examples to the flock" (1 Peter 5:2–3). The role of teachers is to communicate the truth of the gospel, passing on the "apostles' teaching" (Acts 2:42), "so that the body of Christ may be built up until we all reach unity in the faith and in the knowledge of the Son of God and become mature ..." (Eph. 4:12–13). Taken together, the grand outcome of the work of gifted leaders will be that the members "grow to become in every respect the mature body of him who is the head, that is, Christ" (Eph. 4:16). Herein lies the continuity of the gifts of the charismatic ministry.

Likewise, we find an internal coherence in the different paradigms of global Spirit-empowered leadership. The paradigms are linked by a point of continuity. While apostles, prophets, healing evangelists, pastorpreneurs, and teacher-scholars differ in their distinct giftings, they share the common purpose of equipping of the members of the body with manifestations of the Spirit (1 Cor. 12:7), and a common goal of developing the Body of Christ toward maturity through empowerment of the Spirit.

This brings us to a question of practical import: How shall we develop the next generation of Spirit-empowered leaders?

IMPLICATIONS FOR LEADERSHIP DEVELOPMENT

The field of leadership development is among the least investigated within the academic study of leadership.[1] The gap in research on leadership development is surprising, considering the scale of financial and organizational resources devoted to leadership development initiatives. Nevertheless, in the last decades scholars have made considerable theoretical progress in understanding leadership development, especially in the development of leadership expertise[2] and leader identity.[3] The same cannot be said concerning the study of Spirit-empowered leadership. Minimal attention has been given to a research-based analysis of leadership in Pentecostal-charismatic Christianity, and much less to leadership development. To some extent Truls Åkerlund, Byron Klaus, and Loren Triplett have addressed the need for critical reflection on leadership development. Åkerlund observes a "lack of empirical research on how leaders in the Pentecostal movement understand their leadership" and insists that "self-awareness is a critical element in leadership development."[4] Klaus and Triplett call for redirecting the focus on leadership development in Pentecostal mission. Taking up J. Robert Clinton's theory of leadership emergence, they write, "Pentecostals must redirect their concern for training national leaders to include an understanding of the patterns of leadership emergence and selection processes as they occur globally."[5] The final part of the book represents a modest attempt to fill this gap. Chapter 12 summarizes the major findings

1. Bruce J. Avolio, "Promoting More Integrative Strategies for Leadership Theory-Building." *American Psychologist* 62, no. 1 (2007): 25–33.

2. Robert G. Lord and Rosalie J. Hall, "Identity, Deep Structure and the Development of Leadership Skill." *Leadership Quarterly* 16 (2005): 591–615.

3. David V. Day and Michelle M. Harrison, "A Multilevel, Identity-Based Approach to Leadership Development." *Human Resource Management Review* 17 (2007): 360–73.

4. Åkerlund, *A Phenomenology of Pentecostal Leadership*, 45, 133; see Franklin Markow and Truls Åkerlund, "Pentecostal Leadership: Exploring a Global Phenomenon," *Journal of Management, Spirituality and Religion* 20, no. 5 (2023): 526–50; https://10.51327/JHKQ5569.

5. Byron D. Klaus and Loren O. Triplett, "National Leadership in Pentecostal Missions," *Called and Empowered: Global Mission in Pentecostal Perspective*, ed. Murray A. Dempster, Byron D. Klaus, and Douglas Peterson (Peabody, MA: Hendrickson, 1991), 236.

of our research and addresses the implications for leadership development that flow from the findings. The Epilogue proposes a plan for a course in leadership development in Spirit-empowered context.

12

BENCHMARKS FOR DEVELOPING SPIRIT-EMPOWERED LEADERS

Part I formulated an anatomy of Spirit-empowered leadership, discussing defining characteristics and gaps in the study of the topic. The first chapter laid the groundwork for our research by employing a methodology inspired by Max Weber's theory of charismatic leadership, starting from the assumption that Spirit-empowered leadership is amenable to analysis by means of Weber's theory. This is by no means an original venture. Many scholars have blazed this path, finding resonances between Weber's theory of charismatic authority and patterns of charismatic gifting and empowerment in Pentecostalism. The new contribution in our research pertains to the application of contemporary theories of charismatic leadership to an analysis of the historical development and paradigms of Spirit-empowered leadership.

We identified the prototype of Spirit-empowered leadership as replication of the Acts 2 experience of Spirit baptism and advanced the claim that Spirit baptism constitutes a formative experience in the development of a Spirit-empowered leader. Secondly, in Part I we made the claim that the prototype of Spirit empowerment represents a continuance of the biblical depiction of the charismatic gifting of leaders. Here we followed what has been the standard origin narrative of Pentecostal and charismatic movements. Through the outpouring of the Holy Spirit, the leaders of the new Pentecostal movement underwent a dramatic transformation. As they were baptized in the Spirit, they were equipped to mediate the prototypical experience of transformation in the Spirit. Pentecostals have, from the beginning, claimed that their movement has restored the apostolic faith, by which they mean baptism in the Spirit with signs following (Mark 16:17–18).

While there is much to commend in the domain of Spirit-empowered leadership, there is also room for honest appraisal. In our critique of Spirit-empowered leadership, we used information from modern researchers who formulated a theory of charismatic leadership and hypothesized two general approaches to charismatic leadership: personalized and socialized. We delineated the characteristics of each category, made applications of these two approaches to Spirit-empowered leadership, and discovered that some Spirit-empowered leaders have been susceptible to self-aggrandizing behaviors. To address the problem of authoritarian leadership, we provided recommendations for amelioration of abuses of power and brought to light three lacunas in the study of Spirit-empowered leadership: spiritual formation, moral integrity, and power distance. Part I provided a diagnosis of each lacuna, appraises the problem presented by these gaps, and offers recommendations for corrective measures.

Part II offered a diachronic analysis composed of historical sketches of notable Spirit-empowered leaders, organized in four epochs: Precursors, Early Pentecostal Leaders, Neo-Pentecostal Leaders, and Global South Charismatic Leaders. The sketches reveal the historical continuance of the prototypical experience of Spirit baptism as the normative point of entry in the process of leadership development. The sketches also reveal a pattern of increasing global diffusion of the ethos of Spirit-empowered leadership. We concluded that the global diffusion of the Pentecostal mission occurred through culturally relevant contextual engagement.

Part III presented a typological exposition of the paradigms of Spirit-empowered leadership. Following the grid of the ascension gifts of Ephesians 4:11, five paradigms or models of Spirit-empowered leadership were replicated, with some modification. The five leadership gifts in Ephesians were updated to fit how they are comprehended by contemporary Spirit-empowered leaders. The five paradigms—as we construe them—are the apostle, prophet, healing evangelist, pastorpreneur, and teacher-scholar. This study utilized a consistent structure in discussing each paradigm, consisting of biblical principles and patterns, components of the paradigm, examples of pertinent leaders, and formative assessments. This study also concluded with a summative assessment of the continuity of the paradigms, finding that the context of Ephesians 4 shows that each paradigm shares a common purpose and a common goal. Each of the paradigms shares the purpose of equipping the members of the body with manifestations of the Spirit (1 Cor. 12:7) with the goal of becoming mature by attaining the whole measure of the fullness of Christ. To put it simply, we see the continuity of the leadership gifts in the roles they play in moving the Body of Christ toward maturity through empowerment of the Spirit. So, in light of our findings, what are the implications for leadership development?

Definition of Leadership Development

At the outset, it's our responsibility to define the term "leadership development" and clarify our approach to it. David V. Day draws a distinction between leadership development and leader development, wherein leader development focuses on the development of individual leaders, and leadership development is concerned with the development of organizational structures and processes. The traditional approach of the former "is focused on building individual capabilities," whereas the latter is oriented toward "teambuilding and organizational development."[1] Our approach leans toward the side of leader development. In that vein, Aubrey Malphurs and Will Mancini define leadership development as "the intentional process of helping established and emerging leaders at every level of ministry to assess and develop their Christian character and to acquire, reinforce, and refine their ministry knowledge and skills."[2] What stands out in this definition is that leaders are emerging at "every level of ministry." Hence, leadership development is not confined to a certain level of ministry (e.g., entry, intermediate, or advanced); instead, the development of a leader is ongoing. Nor is leadership development limited to leaders who hold an official position at the head of or in various departments of an organization. Rather, leadership development encompasses leaders who are performing formal and informal roles, some of whom have formal titles and others who may not. If we understand leadership as the ability to influence others, we can suppose that there are different ways of influencing, and if that is the case, then leadership is not the exclusive domain of extroverts. Introverts can also influence and lead.[3]

To encompass the full scope of leadership development, this study opts for a comprehensive definition of leadership. J. Robert Clinton defines leadership as "a dynamic process in which a man or woman with God-given capacity influences a specific group of God's people toward His purposes for the group."[4] Clinton's conception of a leader includes institutional offices such as presidents of organizations, denominational superintendents, pastors,

---

1. David V. Day, "Leadership Development," in *The SAGE Handbook of Leadership*, ed. Alan Bryman, David Collinson, Keith Grint, Brad Jackson, and Mary Uhl-Bien (London: Sage Publications, 2011), 38.

2. Aubrey Malphurs and Will Mancini, *Building Leaders: Blueprints for Developing Leadership at Every Level of Your Church* (Grand Rapids: Baker, 2004), 23.

3. Erich Baumgartner, "Do We Need a New Approach to Leadership Development?" *Journal of Applied Christian Leadership* 11, no. 1 (2017): 22.

4. J. Robert Clinton, *The Making of a Leader: Recognizing the Lessons and Stages of Leadership Development*, 2nd edition (Colorado Springs: NavPress, 2012), 10.

directors of ministries, professors, and teachers. It also includes other less formal functions such as Sunday school teachers, small group leaders, mentors, evangelists, event planners, and community organizers. Clinton writes, "To be considered a leader, one does not require a professional position nor need to be a full-time Christian worker."[5]

Clinton delineates five types of Christian leaders, according to differences in the scope of their influence:

> **Type A**—local internal sphere of influence; workers in a local church, home group, or youth ministry.
>
> **Type B**—local external sphere of influence; bi-vocational pastor, part-time evangelist or pastor, pastor shared by two congregations, or church plant helper.
>
> **Type C**—local or regional sphere of influence; full-time paid pastor, youth worker, evangelist, or other staff worker in a larger local church.
>
> **Type D**—regional or national sphere of influence; heads of small mission organization in region or country, denominational workers with regional or national influence, national evangelists, teacher in seminaries or other training institutes, authors of works used across denominations and in seminaries or institutes, theologians of national influence.
>
> **Type E**—national or international sphere of influence; head of international organizations, Christian statesmen who travel internationally and influence several nations, prominent theologians, trainers of type D leaders, prominent authors of Christian literature who set trends or support global movements, charismatic leaders who begin movements and organizations that expand worldwide or across nations.[6]

Most of the patterns and processes of leadership development apply to professional and voluntary leaders. Leader development occurs in the context of daily life, not just through formal training. Leaders are shaped by both life experience and deliberate training. Leadership emergence includes both inherent traits and acquired skills. Leadership emergence refers to the overall process in which God is at work in selecting and shaping a leader. It is in the purview of a lifetime that a potential leader discovers and expands his or her capacity for influence and becomes the leader God wants him or her to be.[7]

Julianne R. Cenac notes that one of the most contested questions in the field of leadership is whether leaders are born or made. She entertains the possibility that both are true, following Stephen Zaccaro's comprehensive model, which holds that while inherited traits supply an emerging leader with a cognitive and social

---

5. Clinton, *The Making of a Leader*, 10.
6. Clinton, *Leadership Emergence Theory*, 46–48.
7. Clinton, *Leadership Emergence Theory*, 69.

repertoire, environmental factors shape the leader's evolution.[8] The implication is that under certain environmental contexts, leaders will emerge. Cenac asks questions that are germane to our topic: "How does leadership emerge?" "What is the context of emergence?" and "What are the characteristics that are present in leaders as they emergence? Cenac's view of leadership emergence differs from Clinton's leadership emergence theory. Whereas Clinton examines how Christian leaders develop throughout their lifetime, Cenac examines the emergence of leadership in a decisive event of biblical history. Her particular interest is with the event of the Christian Pentecost in Acts 2. We share her particular interest, but we also acknowledge that there is something to be learned from both approaches—decisive events and over a lifetime. The development of one's leadership occurs in moments of intense manifestation of the outpouring of the Spirit and through a development process that extends over the lifespan of a leader. We are open to both aspects of leadership emergence.

In her rhetorical analysis of the outpouring of the Holy Spirit in Acts 2, Cenac describes the effect of Peter's discourse in verses 14–42. She says that "the disciples underwent a significant transformation to fulfill the ministry of Jesus and by receiving the Holy Spirit, any previous deficiencies were mitigated as they prepared to continue Jesus' work."[9] The impact of the experience effected a dramatic turning point in the leadership emergence of Peter and the disciples. However, she does not stop there. Cenac draws out significant connections between the Acts 2 phenomenon and the experiences of the Holy Spirit by many leaders throughout biblical history. She finds consistent phenomena of leadership emergence in Bezalel, the seventy, Joshua, Samson, Saul, David, Isaiah, Jesus, and Peter.[10] In each case, the inner workings of the Holy Spirit intensified the process of leadership emergence. We accept Cenac's claim that these experiences represented decisive moments of infilling and equipping; however, these experiences of the Spirit were not isolated cases. In fact, they extended over a lengthy span of time, from the lifetime of Moses to that of Jesus and the apostles. Further, the impact was not limited to a narrow time frame. The working of the Spirit was ongoing and essential to the outworking of God's redemptive plan. As Cenac puts it, "persons of various statuses were called into their roles of leadership by virtue of God's Spirit

---

8. Cenac, "Leader Emergence and the Phenomenological Work of the Holy Spirit," 125.

9. Cenac, "Leader Emergence," 130.

10. Cenac, "Leader Emergence," 131.

filling them or enduing them with a special grace, power, or ability."[11] What we see here is a portrait of God's sovereign design for leadership as empowered by the Holy Spirit, the inner workings of which occur in moments of intense encounter as well as over the lifespan of a leader.

Leadership Emergence

Leaders are constantly emerging in a wide range of contexts. According to Clinton, leadership emergence is a process in which God intervenes throughout a lifetime in crucial ways to shape that leader towards His purposes for the leader. Leadership emergence does not start in a vacuum. According to Erich Baumgartner, leadership emergence "builds on a process that was already begun by God himself."[12] When viewed from a whole-life perspective, God's activity in shaping the development of a leader is intentional. God intends to develop the leader's capacity by guiding the leader to operate at realized potential in terms of giftedness—natural abilities, acquired skills, and spiritual gifts. However, this process is not fixed or pre-determined. In fact, the outcome hinges on the emerging leader's response. Leadership emergence can be thwarted or enhanced, depending on the emerging leader's response to God's initiative. Clinton's theory provides us with an overall picture of how a leader develops or fails to do so.[13]

Reasons for employing Clinton's theory here are research-based. Recent research data collected by Developmental Dimensions International indicates that leaders are increasingly dissatisfied with most programs for leadership development instituted by their organizations.[14] Despite huge investments in leadership development by companies, the results are viewed as disappointing. One reason for the disappointing results could be due to an erroneous assumption that the development of leaders occurs primarily through mandated programs. Leader development is defined as "the expansion of a person's capacity to be effective in leadership roles and processes."[15] This sort of development unfolds over time, is maximized by experiences that provide feedback, challenge, and support, and is contingent upon the individual's capacity to learn from

---

11 Cenac, "Leader Emergence," 132.

12 Baumgartner, "Do We Need a New Approach to Leadership Development?" 16.

13 Clinton, *Leadership Emergence Theory*, 7–8.

14 Day, "Leadership Development," 37.

15. Cynthia D. McCauley and Ellen Van Velsor, ed., *Handbook for Leadership Development* (San Francisco: Jossey-Bass, 2004), 2.

experience. As an emerging leader progresses from entry to intermediate levels of leadership development, progress is contingent upon factors that transcend a one-off training event.

The process of leader identity formation extends over time. Some theorists estimate that it takes approximately ten years for one to arrive at the level of an expert leader.[16] In a study of leader identity development with college students, Komives et al. observed a gradual shift from a heroic-centric view of leadership to one that sees leadership as a collaborative and relational process. Komives et al. compared statements about leadership at the early stages in the developmental process ("I am not a leader") to those later ("I can be *a* leader even when I am not *the* leader").[17] These findings illustrate that one's leadership identity development commences in late adolescence or earlier and continues through adulthood. Other researchers recommend a lifespan perspective on leadership development, which is what our plan endorses. We recognize that the needs of leadership development evolve as an emerging leader takes on greater leadership challenges and responsibilities. Leadership development is a lifelong journey that coincides with ongoing processes of adult development.[18]

All of this comes down to the value of taking a lifespan approach to shaping the development of successive generations of emerging leaders. Following is a delineation of the *benchmarks* we are proposing for developing emerging Spirit-empowered leaders.

Three Benchmarks of Spirit-Empowered Leadership Development

I am proposing that there are three benchmarks in the process of leadership development in the context of the Spirit-empowered movement. These benchmarks designate crucial junctures in the process of leadership development. The benchmarks can serve as a general backdrop for formulating a plan for the development of Spirit-empowered leaders.

---

16. Day, "Leadership Development," 39.

17. Susan R. Komives, Julie E. Owen, Susan D. Longerbeam, Felicia C. Mainella, and Laura Osteen, "Developing a Leadership Identity: A Grounded Theory," *Journal of College Student Development* 46, no. 6 (November/December 2005): 605, accessed November 18, 2023, https://doi.org/10.1353/csd.2005.0061.

18. David V. Day, Michelle M. Harrison, and Stanley M. Halpin, *An Integrative Approach to Leader Development: Connecting Adult Development, Identity and Expertise* (Milton Park, UK: Routledge/Taylor & Francis Group, 2009).

Benchmark # 1—Calling and Empowerment

The starting point in developing an emerging Spirit-empowered leader is a formative experience of the Holy Spirit. This experience consists of an immersive encounter with the Holy Spirit, known in Pentecostal parlance as "baptism in the Spirit." This is not to assume that this encounter necessarily entails the classical Pentecostal doctrine of initial evidence. It may or may not. The point is that this experience represents the prototypical initiation into the leadership development process. We have now zeroed in on the prototype of Spirit-empowered leadership, which is derived from the Pentecost event in Acts 2. In the Spirit-empowered tradition, it goes without saying that as the apostles were baptized in the Spirit, and they were being equipped for leadership in a global mission (Acts 1:8).

Pentecostals and charismatics believe that the same dynamic is in play today in the Spirit-empowered community. They look to Acts 2 to support their conviction that leaders who are filled and empowered with the Holy Spirit are equipped to mediate the transforming agency of the Holy Spirit to their followers. This conviction flows from the way the Bible is read and interpreted in many sectors of the Spirit-empowered movement. Allan Anderson elucidates the logic of the typical Pentecostal approach to the Bible. Led by the Spirit, with a minimum of theological education, Pentecostals view the Bible as an independent source of authority, with greater immediacy than in the Western theological tradition. They interpret the Bible in a very literal way, drawing the conclusion that if early Christians spoke in tongues, healed the sick, and cast out demons, they should emulate these practices. If Spirit-filled people in the New Testament did these things—miracles, healings, deliverance from evil spirits, prophecy and speaking in tongues—they should do them, and they did so with great effect. Many scholars of global Christianity, beginning with Philip Jenkins and Lamin Sanneh, have attributed the growth of the Spirit-empowered movement as a global phenomenon to a high view of the contemporary relevance of the Bible.[19]

Emerging Spirit-empowered leaders typically experience a call to leadership and empowerment to pursue their calling. According to Frank Markow, "Pentecostals believe that a calling is a special claim that God places on the life of the believer to be in ministry and that not everyone receives one. The theological

---

19. Allan Heaton Anderson, "Stretching Out Hands to God: Origins and Development of Pentecostalism in Africa," in *Pentecostalism in Africa: Presence and Impact of Pneumatic Christianity in Postcolonial Societies*, ed. Martin Lindhardt (Leiden: Brill, 2015), 61–63.

underpinning for a Pentecostal understanding of calling begins with the belief that the Spirit of God has transformed the believer and called them to live out what the Sprit has placed in them."[20] Claudia Währisch-Oblau explains that a call to Pentecostal-charismatic pastoral ministry is customarily received through a vision; an auditory impression; a dream; a supernatural enabling; or a sense of God speaking through Scripture, another person, or in an unmediated manner. Such a call is always specific and personal. A key factor in determining the authenticity of a call is if it can be recounted in a narrative. She writes, "If someone has a call, he or she will necessarily have a narrative."[21] A call narrative is much like a testimony. Both can be seen as legitimating narratives in that they establish authority or legitimacy and set a person's identity within group boundaries.[22]

Throughout the history of the Spirit-empowered movement, there are scores of examples of call narratives recounting the experiences of emerging leaders. Two examples are shared here. The first example is taken from my research on the Pentecostal mission in Palestine.[23] Lucy Leatherman shares a personal account of her experience of baptism in the Holy Spirit in 1906:

> While seeking for the Baptism of the Holy Spirit in Los Angeles, after Sister Ferrel [sic] laid hands on me, I praised God and saw my Savior in the heavens. And as I praised, I came closer and closer and I was so small. By and by I swept into the wound in His side, and He was not only in me but I in Him, and there I found that rest that passeth all understanding, and He said to me, you are in the bosom of the Father. He said I was clothed upon and in the secret place of the Most High. But I said, "Father, I want the gift of the Holy Ghost," and the heavens opened and went through me. He said, "Praise Me," and when I did, angels came and ministered unto me. I was passive in His hands working on my vocal cords, and I realized they were loosing [sic] me. I began to praise Him in an unknown language.[24]

Based on this experience, Leatherman traveled with two others as missionaries to Palestine. A report in the first issue of *The Apostolic Faith* reads, "A band of three missionaries, Bro Andrew Johnson and Sisters Louise Condit and Lucy M. Leatherman, who have been baptized in the Holy Ghost and received the gift of languages, have left for Jerusalem."[25]

---

20. Frank A. Markow, "Calling and Leader Identity: Utilizing Narrative Analysis to Construct a Stage Model of Calling Development" (Ph.D. diss., Regent University, 2007), 24.

21. Claudia Währisch-Oblau, *The Missionary Self-Perception of Pentecostal/Charismatic Church Leaders from the Global South and Europe* (Leiden: Brill, 2009), 85.

22. Währisch-Oblau, *Missionary Self-Perception of Pentecostal/Charismatic Church Leaders*, 86.

23. Newberg, *The Pentecostal Mission in Palestine*, 14, 24.

24. *The Apostolic Faith* 1, no. 3 (November 1906): 4.

25. *The Apostolic Faith* 1, no. 1 (September 1906): 4.

The second example is extracted from the research of Claudia Währisch-Oblau on the call narratives of African Pentecostal ministers in Germany. This is the testimony of a young man from Ghana, Africa, who recalled his decision to serve as a pastor.

> At the age of fifteen I was born again, and at the age of twenty-one I more or less began a full-time ministry. Right from the onset in Ghana, I basically had this desire to serve Christ when I got born again…. I ended up studying mechanical engineering—being a mechanical engineer. But afterwards I felt called to ministry, and so I had study in the Maranatha Bible College. And so, after my conversion, I had the zeal to serve the Lord….I joined Christ Apostolic Church where I started to go to their seminary school. A friend advised me, the first time we went to a prayer meeting. It was an all-night prayer meeting, and then at this prayer meeting, I knew that what I had [was] also clear, that the Lord really was calling my attention to serve him.[26]

In this case, the man noted that although his calling into the ministry occurred at the time of his conversion when he was a teenager, it did not come to fruition until later after he had pursued studies at a Bible college.

Leadership development does not start in a vacuum; it starts with calling and empowerment and then builds on a process already begun by God. Opportunities are presented for entry-level ministry through which the emerging leader's calling and empowerment are affirmed. Yet, before long the emerging leader recognizes a need for training in the craft of leadership. At this point, he or she is ready to proceed to the next benchmark of leadership development.

Benchmark #2—Ongoing Learning

At this juncture, a Spirit-empowered leader arrives at the realization that while calling and empowerment have laid an essential foundation, more is required for the maturing of his or her leadership. As with any foundation, to serve its purpose, a superstructure must be built upon it. At this point, the emerging leader has had sufficient experience in leadership to realize a need for further training and improvement. As a result, he or she decides to seek further learning in any number of venues, such as an informal mentoring relationship or a structured program of continuing education. As the emerging leader participates in training events, workshops, and conferences, he or she is exposed to new ideas, stories of successful leaders, and proven methods of leadership.

My denomination, the Evangelical Covenant Church, holds an annual midwinter conference for its ministers and for the purpose of ongoing learning.

---

26. Währisch-Oblau, *Missionary Self-Perception of Pentecostal/Charismatic Church Leaders*, 87.

The schedule features internationally known speakers who are leaders of highly effective ministries. It also includes a full slate of breakout sessions on topics of relevant concern. Most importantly, adequate time is afforded during breaks for informal fellowship, mentoring, and pastoral care. My first pastoral position after seminary was as an associate pastor in an interracial congregation in Minneapolis. My teaching gift became apparent based on feedback from congregants. I wanted to know more about spiritual gifts, so I attended a breakout session at the Midwinter Conference. The Spiritual Gifts Inventory confirmed that my primary spiritual gift is teaching. The leader of the session helped me to understand the concept of a gift mix[27] and determine that mine is teaching, wisdom, and knowledge. As I discovered how I was wired by the Holy Spirit, I learned the importance of setting boundaries to protect myself from burnout. Well-intentioned board members, who were accomplished leaders in the corporate world, urged me to acquire the leadership style of a CEO. I felt as if they were trying to recreate me in their image in a way that did not match how I was shaped by the Holy Spirit. Here is the takeaway: When we minister in our area of giftedness, we are energized. I confess that this is a lesson that I have had to learn repeatedly.

During another midwinter conference, the attendees were bused to Willow Creek Community Church to hear Bill Hybels speak on leadership and observe a demonstration of a seeker-friendly worship. The outcome of this event was deeply impactful, as our local church adopted a seeker-sensitive philosophy of ministry and leadership. I am not commending the seeker-sensitive approach to everyone. Rather, I am commending the vital importance of ongoing learning. I believe that the development of a Spirit-empowered leader follows a general pattern or progression. In the intermediate level of leadership emergence, ongoing learning serves the purpose of instilling principles and patterns that are essential for leadership development. Often these learnings are extricated from the stories told by successful and influential leaders.

I recall the first time I heard Rick Warren speak at the Willow Creek Leadership Summit. His presentation was simple, clear, and profound. He

---

27. The term "gift mix" refers to the mix of spiritual gifts that are given to a Christian. "Now to each one the manifestation of the Spirit is given for the common good .... All these are the work of one and the same Spirit, and he gives them to each one, just as he determines" (1 Cor. 12:7, 11). The Holy Spirit often gives more than one gift to a Christian. The combination of these gifts is what is called a "gift-mix." One's gift-mix is what equips one to engage effectively in particular functions of Christian ministry, including leadership. See Ministry Tools Research Center, "FAQ About Our Spiritual Gift Mix," accessed March 23, 2024, https://mintools.com/spiritual-gifts-mix.htm.

told the story of Saddleback Church and extracted from his narrative specific principles of purpose-driven leadership. Like Hybels, Warren stresses the importance of a vision of a preferred future as the key to leadership. Vision is a mental picture of a destination. It is the key to a strategic plan consisting of clearly defined goals, objectives, timetables, and assigned responsibilities. It defines an organization's purpose, strategies, and action plans. If fully implemented and regularly monitored, a vision can result in the success to which one aspires. It gives direction for a leader to chart a course for moving an organization toward long-term goals and outcomes that will make the destination a reality. As Warren shared the steps for aligning a church with a vision, I realized the importance of vision in my leadership of a local church. This realization proved to be a major asset in the development of my mastery of the craft of leadership.

Leadership competencies are the product of knowledge and skill acquired through ongoing learning. The craft of Spirit-empowered leadership did not "tumble from the skies like a sacred meteor," to use Grant Wacker's image.[28] It did not leap directly from the pages of the Bible into modern times. It evolved through stages in a learning process that extends beyond seminars and workshops. Structured programs are essential for instilling knowledge, but that knowledge must be applied in real-life situations. When knowledge is applied, it takes the form of skills. You can attend a seminar on time management and learn all sorts of principles on how to budget your time. It is only when the principles are put into practice that one will develop skills.

Let me share an example. A leader in a church in which I was serving as senior pastor, George Duff, President of the Seattle Chamber of Commerce, took me under his wing and had me make a chart of how my time was allocated in a normal week. I estimated the amount of time devoted to administrative duties, attending meetings, counseling, sermon preparation, and visitation. Then George instructed me to rate the importance of each category. I could see a problem right away in that I rated sermon preparation as a high priority, yet the time I devoted to it was less than indicative of its importance. This realization led to a major reallocation of my time. From that point on I protected a day for sermon preparation. The results were quite positive.

Much of what leaders learn is the product of reflection on experience. We learn not only by experience, but also from the accumulated knowledge

---

28. August Cerillo and Grant Wacker, "Historiography," in *NIDPCM*, ed. Stanley M. Burgess and Eduard M. van der Maas (Grand Rapids: Zondervan, 2002), 393.

of what experience teaches us. We do not learn from experience unless our behavior is transformed. Baumgartner borrowed a model from David Kolb, a cognitive psychologist who developed the experiential learning cycle, which shows how reflection on experience can lead to changes in behavior. Kolb postulates that true learning goes through an experiential learning cycle of (1) experience, (2) reflecting on experience, (3) thinking about it in models, and (4) experimenting in one's own context.[29] In my case, the model was time allocation. During three senior pastorates, I had struggled with managing the multiple demands of pastoral leadership. I was pulled in many good directions—building relationships with colleagues, leaders, and newcomers; commitment to social justice; service to my denomination on boards and commissions; passion for evangelism; and care for the lonely, the sick, and the bereaved. What was lacking, I finally realized, was concentrated time to leverage my spiritual gift mix (teaching-wisdom-knowledge). After setting aside a day for prayer and sermon preparation, along with clarifying my priorities, the struggle over time management abated.

There is a point at which a leader senses that he or she is ready to transition to the next benchmark. Sufficient ongoing learning prepares one for a season of fruitfulness. This often comes when a leader's identity is established, and a succession plan is put in place.

Benchmark #3—Leader Identity and Succession

The third benchmark is leader identity and succession. These attainments are outcomes of a long process of ongoing learning, which eventuates in a realization of one's purpose as a leader and a focus on sustainability. This realization constitutes a definitive upgrade in one's leadership development. Usually, the realization of leader identity is not the product of conscious effort, but rather a by-product of wrestling with mistakes, miscalculations, and dissatisfaction—compelling a leader to reflect on how he or she got to this place. As one works through the experiential learning cycle of (1) experience, (2) reflecting on experience, (3) thinking about it in models, and (4) experimenting in one's own context, that person is, as it were, led to take responsibility for a course correction that ensures sustainability of purpose.

Each person has arrived at his or her identity as a leader when that person can say, "This is who I am as a leader, and this is how I want to leverage my gifting from now on." A shift in one's current position may be required, but this

---

29. Baumgartner, "Do We Need a New Approach to Leadership Development?" 20.

is not necessarily so. What is required is that a leader is faithful to his or her identity, whatever that may mean. In some cases, this means staying where one is located; in others it means moving on and re-establishing a base of operations that will sustain one's purpose. For me the latter was the case. As I was thumbing through *Christianity Today* in the fall of 2003, I came across an ad for a new Ph.D. program in Renewal Studies at Regent University. Immediately I sensed a stirring in my spirit. I had started doctoral work years before at Graduate Theological Union in Berkeley, California, but stopped due to burnout. Perhaps this was an opportunity to resume my doctoral work. I applied, was accepted, and moved from Seattle to Virginia Beach. Things started to fall in place, especially due to the mentoring I received from Stan and Ruth Burgess. Stan served as my advisor and model of a consummate church historian. Ruth taught me the craft of research-based pedagogy. Before long, I realized that my leader identity was as a scholar and Professor of Church History. After completing the Ph.D. at Regent, I was hired by a Pentecostal college in Australia affiliated with Hillsong Church. From there, with the recommendation of Dr. Burgess, I was hired at Oral Roberts University, where I now serve as Senior Professor of Theological and Historical Studies.

Presently, I am living out my succession plan. Succession can be defined as planning for the future sustainability of one's leadership. Some leaders do this by selecting a successor. I do it in my role as a college professor by preparing the next generation of leaders in the Spirit-empowered movement. I often say to my students at both undergraduate and graduate levels, "You are the leaders of the next generation of the Church of Jesus Christ. I am here to prepare you for your calling and purpose in the Kingdom of God." How do I do it? I am intentional about strategic priorities in my teaching by assigning creative learning activities that simulate real life situations in ministry leadership, designing collaborate learning models for simulating team leadership, and coaching students who demonstrate potential for leadership.

Let me hasten to say that I do not see myself as the ideal exemplar of Spirit-empowered leadership. I share my narrative simply to provide the reader with a concrete example of the principles I have derived from lifelong learning. Spirit-empowered leaders are not monochrome reproductions of a single template of leadership. It is important that we prize the differences in gifting and style. Spirit-empowered leaders share a common purpose—to build up the body of Christ to maturity (Eph. 4:12–13). Yet, as we have shown in Part III of the book, there are different leadership paradigms. The diversity of models is a positive feature.

Every leader has his or her model, gifts, or gift mix. This is the beauty of the Body of Christ. We all belong to Christ, yet we have our unique endowments for ministry. One of the most prominent characteristics of the global Spirit-empowered movement is its cultural diversity.

Where do we go from here? Guided by the benchmarks of the process of leadership development and appreciation of cultural diversity as a defining characteristic of Spirit-empowered leadership, we will put our findings to work. The need for leadership development in the Spirit-empowered movement has become more apparent with the explosive growth of Pentecostal-charismatic Christianity in the Global South. There is wide recognition that a growing movement requires well-trained leaders to guide and strengthen young, vibrant, and growing churches, missions, compassion ministries, and educational institutions. Yet, the training methods must not be dominated by Western leadership development models. Rather, they must adapt to the diverse cultural contexts of the global Spirit-empowered movement.

John Easter proposes four parameters for effective leadership training in Africa. He writes, "First, Pentecostal leadership training must be contextual; second, it should utilize experiential learning methods patterned after traditional ways of instruction and biblical principles; third, it must understand its missional *raison d'être*; and last, it should foster a culture of the Spirit leading to transformational outcomes."[30] Easter's parameters for Africa are largely congruent with how I think of leadership development in the Spirit-empowered movement as a whole. A growing segment of the classes I teach at Oral Roberts University are populated by international students whose cultural contexts and social customs are not Western. The educational backgrounds of students in my classes are varied. Roughly half of the students were educated in Western systems, the other half in Majority World systems. This presents a challenge for the educator. It cannot be assumed that students from the Global South will thrive if we expect them to conform to Western systems of education. Research shows that Western methods are less effective with Majority World students and Majority World methods are less effective with Western students.[31] So then, what is a teacher to do? For the sake of the achievement of transformational learning outcomes, a blend of the two would be in order.

---

30. John L. Easter, "Under the Mango Tree: Pentecostal Leadership Training in Africa," *Pneuma Africa Journal* 1, no. 1 (2013): 3.

31. Easter, "Under the Mango Tree," 5.

In designing leadership development that is contextually relevant to the Spirit-empowered movement, we should be sensitive to a diverse cultural palette. John Easter stresses the responsibility of Pentecostal trainers to understand the learning styles of their learners. He cites the findings of Murriell McCulley, who delineates eight characteristics of African learning styles:

1. They are sensitive to what others think.
2. They value interpersonal relationships.
3. They are socially oriented collectivists rather than individualists.
4. They seek social reinforcement.
5. They have a high regard for authority.
6. Gender and age roles are often rigid and culturally determined.
7. They are not analytical in their problem solving.
8. They value social acceptance over autonomy.[32]

McCulley offers this challenge: It now becomes the responsibility of teaching institutions across Africa to create a safe learning environment that incorporates the holistic, interconnectedness of the African learning styles. Classes must allow space for the learner to see him or herself embedded in the learning process and not separate from it. Classes need to move away from teaching that promotes acquisition of knowledge without living out what is learned.[33]

It's wise to accept McCulley's challenge, which can be accomplished in four phases: (1) afford space for emerging leaders from the West and Global South to see their learning styles as mutually included in the learning process; (2) strike a balance between the acquisition of knowledge and practical application; (3) incorporate multiple perceptions of what good leadership looks like and how it functions in different sociocultural settings; and (4) implement an interactive process through learning groups that are designed to encourage emerging leaders to think reflectively.[34]

Pedagogy of Leadership Emergence

Simply put, pedagogy is the study of the process of teaching and learning. The terms "pedagogy" and "pedagogue" come from the Greek words *paidos* "boy, child" and *agogos* "leader." The literal meaning of pedagogy is "the process by which a child is led to learning." Pedagogy can be defined as the science or

---

32. Murriell G. McCulley, *Beyond the Classroom: Teach for Life* (Springfield, MO: Life Publishers International, 2008), 53.

33. McCulley, *Beyond the Classroom*, 54.

34. Easter, "Under the Mango Tree," 8.

understanding of how learning takes place and the philosophy and practice that supports that understanding of learning. Leadership is often defined as the act of influencing or guiding individuals or groups. A Spirit-empowered pedagogy of leadership development will guide emerging leaders in a process that is superintended by the Holy Spirit. We start from the premise that the Spirit has been and will continually develop an emerging leader over a lifetime, to conform him or her to the image of Christ by means of the maturing of his or her leadership.

As we postulate a pedagogy of Spirit-empowered leadership emergence, our general approach is to concentrate on experiences of the leading of the Holy Spirit over the lifespan of a leader. The details of the process will differ from individual to individual. Although all emerging leaders will go through the phases, they will not do so similarly. As observed above, there are differences in teaching models and learning styles related to cultural background. Cross-cultural leadership development is complex because emerging leaders and trainers carry within themselves values and beliefs formed through life experience. These values and beliefs are sometimes referred to as "the hidden curriculum." They are hidden because they are caught rather than taught. At first glance, most of us are not aware of our cultural values and social biases. Everyone needs to be brought to conscious awareness of cultural orientations to comprehend how one's context affects one's intercultural relations and approach to leadership.

The path to transcending the limitations of cultural bias leads to development of a transcultural perspective. Ruth Burgess has produced a program of transcultural enrichment, *Shantistan*, with an addendum resource, the *Shantistan Tablet*. The *Tablet* is composed of thirteen themes: civility, devotion to beliefs, doing good, faith and forgiveness, harmony, human dignity, human kindness, integrity, love, protection of life, reconciliation, sacrifice, and tolerance. These themes are based on a theory and methods of constructing transcultural understanding that expedites peace. The program is designed to bring together people with various cultural mindsets—whether they are religious, familial, or political—and engage them in conversations about the above themes. Participants share brief narratives of experiences, values, wisdom principles, and cultural traditions. Through cross-cultural sharing, they are enabled to extract transcultural principles and applications, leading to an affirmation of what Ruth Burgess calls "a co-cultural perspective." Instead of conceiving one's culture as primary and others' cultures as secondary, one sees diverse cultures as different yet equal in value.[35] Emerging leaders in a movement as culturally diverse as Pentecostal-charismatic Christianity would be well-served by cultivating a co-cultural perspective. Having addressed the complexity of intercultural relations in constructing a pedagogy of leadership emergence, the following epilogue proposes a plan for a course in global, Spirit-empowered leadership development.

---

35. Ruth Vassar Burgess and Stanley M. Burgess, *Shantistan Tablet: Enabling a Land of Peace* (Strafford, MO: n.p., 2021), i.

Epilogue

Course Plan for Spirit-Empowered Leadership Development

The course plan presented below is designed to addresses the need for leadership development in the Spirit-empowered movement. The plan can bridge theoretical and practical aspects of leadership emergence and is adaptable to diverse global contexts. The need for leadership development in the Spirit-empowered movement has become more apparent with the explosive growth of Pentecostal-charismatic Christianity in the Global South. There is wide recognition that a growing global movement requires well-trained leaders to guide and strengthen young, vibrant, and growing churches, missions, compassion ministries, and educational institutions. Yet the methods of training must not be dominated by Western models of leadership development. Rather, they must be adaptable to the diverse cultural contexts that comprise the global, Spirit-empowered movement. This plan allows space for emerging leaders from the West and Global South to see their learning styles as mutually included in the learning process. This is accomplished by finding a balance between the acquisition of knowledge and practical application. Further, this plan encourages incorporation of multiple perceptions of what good leadership looks like and how it functions in different sociocultural settings. This plan also implements an interactive process through learning groups that are designed to encourage emerging leaders to think reflectively.[1]

Structure of a Plan for Developing Spirit-Empowered Leaders

The structure of this proposed plan is based on the work of J. Robert Clinton, formerly Senior Professor of Leadership at the School of Intercultural Studies at Fuller Theological Seminary. Clinton's "Leadership Emergence Theory" presupposes that leadership emergence is a lifelong process consisting of developmental stages. The general stages can be illustrated with a timeline

---

1. Easter, "Under the Mango Tree," 8.

displaying six phases of leadership development: foundations, training, maturing, fruitfulness, convergence, and afterglow.

Diagram of the Timeline

The diagram of the six phases in leadership emergence, utilized below, is adapted from J. Robert Clinton's *The Making of a Leader*.[2] The timeline is a sounding board for helping emerging leaders to calibrate the phase that fits where they are in the process of leadership emergence. The aim is to evoke insights as an emerging leader compiles data for the emerging leader's timeline. As an emerging leader reflects on his or her location on the timeline, each leader comes to self-awareness of where he or she is in the process of leadership emergence. This awareness comes as the person recalls and reflects on one's experiences of negotiating the phases of the process of leadership development. In short, the timeline is a pedagogical tool for leadership development.

Phase I—Foundations

In Phase I, an emerging leader senses interest in leadership. Circumstances unfold in which the person senses a desire for experiences to instill confidence and develop an awareness of an inner stirring that could be indicative of the sovereign work of the Holy Spirt. This stirring in one's spirit often eventuates in an outright conversion experience and commitment to spend one's life in embracing a call to leadership.

Phase II—Inner Growth

In Phase II, the emerging leader seeks to know God in more personal and intimate ways. Often this comes about as the leader discovers the joy of prayer, worship, and hearing God. As the leader grows in faith and discernment, taking first steps in ministry, he or she is put to the test. Clinton states, "These early tests are crucial experiences that God uses to prepare the leader for the next phase of leadership."[3] Leadership potential is affirmed, and character is developed in this phase.

Phase III—Training

In Phase III, the emerging leader seeks growth by reaching out to others for fellowship and guidance, sensing a need for mutual encouragement. He or

---

2. Clinton, *The Making of a Leader*, 37–40.
3. Clinton, *The Making of a Leader*, 38.

she is becoming more aware of his or her spiritual gifts, albeit without mature leadership development yet. Ministry is the focus of the leader at this stage as opportunities for service are increasing. Feedback from congregants and peers helps the emerging leader to see the need for training to be more effective. God is developing the leader by confirming areas of giftedness and skill and revealing inadequacies in his or her personal life.

Phase IV—Maturing

In Phase IV, a shift occurs as God moves beyond working in the leader to working through the leader. God is quietly evaluating leadership potential and teaching the person to minister out of his or her grace-gifts. By this time the emerging leader is moving into fruitfulness. The leader is adept at moving in his or her spiritual gifts and, as Clinton puts it, "understanding that learning what not to do is as important as learning what to do. A mature fruitfulness is the result."[4] The leader arrives at a realization that communion with God is more important than success. The key to development in this phase is "a positive response to the experiences God ordains."[5]

Phase V—Convergence

In Phase V, the leader moves into convergence as his or her role matches his or her gift-mix and experience in ministry. The leader is freed from ministry for which he or she is not gifted or suited. Many leaders do not achieve convergence because they are hindered by their own lack of personal development or because the organization that employs them stifles the achievement of convergence. It is incumbent upon a leader to seek the Lord's guidance in deciding whether to stay the course or make a change. This decision is providential in either case.

Phase VI—Afterglow

Phase VI is a season of afterglow, consisting of deepening lessons learned as a leader processes experiences of adversity, mainly conflict and crises. In this phase, God is working to develop the character of a leader and open the door for ongoing recognition of the leader's expanded influence. During this phase the maturing leader seeks out successful and seasoned leaders for their storehouse of wisdom. There is still recognizable development in this phase along with honor

---

4. Clinton, *The Making of a Leader*, 39.
5. Clinton, *The Making of a Leader*, 39.

and recognition received for faithfulness over a lifetime of leadership. Many leaders do not arrive at this phase for several reasons, one of which is noted below.

Dynamics of Leadership Emergence

Clinton argues that progress in the above phases is catalyzed by three categorical dynamics of leadership emergence: process items, boundary events, and spheres of influence. Since this terminology is used in our plan, these terms deserve some explanation.

Process Items

Process items are lessons about leadership that take different forms. One of these forms relates to recognition and appropriation of the power of the Holy Spirit. This study of the lives of Spirit-empowered leaders in Part II identified process items that shaped their development. During their early development, emerging leaders experience the power of the Holy Spirit taking different forms such as conversion, Spirit baptism, healing, and a divine calling to ministry. In the middle stages of development, leaders learn lessons about skills in ministry in a variety of settings, including the mission field, local church, and itinerant evangelism. Spirit-empowered leaders are particularly concerned with the acquisition and meditation of God's power for preaching, healing, and exorcism. In the later stages of development, Spirit-empowered leaders launch into institution building and formal education. These process items prove to be crucial for the advancement of a Spirit-empowered leader's progress in leadership development.

Boundary Events

Boundary events are points of significant growth in development of a leader. These events are instrumental in bringing about the shift from one phase to the next. According to Clinton, they include such factors as crises, promotions, a new ministry, learning a major new concept, unusual experiences, life-changing encounters with a person, an experience of divine guidance, or a geographic move.[6] They mark the end of one stage and the beginning of another. Boundary events of Spirit-empowered leaders could include transitions from leading a local church to coordinating a network of leaders or launching an international ministry.

---

6. Clinton, *The Making of a Leader*, 41–42.

Spheres of Influence

Influence is integral to the nature of leadership. Clinton states, "God endows leaders with the capacity to influence."[7] Spheres of influence pertain to a level or type of influence. They can be spatial or temporal fields, zones, or areas in which an individual leader or organization has power to affect people, events, and movements. According to Clinton, a change in sphere of influence, either an increase or decrease, usually signals a shift in a leader's development.[8]

When I was in seminary, a conference superintendent, Ed Larson, presented a talk that hit home with me. He declared that God rewards faithfulness in ministry leadership with greater responsibility, (i.e., an expanded sphere of influence). I have found the "little-big principle" to hold true. If one is faithful in little, one may be given greater responsibility. In Spirit-empowered leadership, our view of spheres of influence begins with the premise that God endows leaders with capacity for influence. Usually this is a matter of the exercise of spiritual gifts at a given level of influence. As Clinton puts it, "A leader will exercise his [or her] gifts most effectively at a given level of influence."[9] The Holy Spirit uses various means to release the potential of a leader at a given level of influence. One example could be the case of a pastor with administrative gifts who is selected to serve in a denominational or non-denominational leadership role.

Components of the Plan

The plan is based on the structure of Robert Clinton's theory of leadership emergence, which was developed during his thirty years of service at Fuller School of World Mission, now the School of Intercultural Studies. Clinton worked with students to compose numerous case studies of specific leaders, most of whom were contemporary leaders, including a number from non-Western cultures. He holds that these case studies can be seen as "validating the notion that leadership emergence theory as seen in his book does apply to leaders of other cultures."[10] Although Clinton's claim of cross-cultural validity is open for debate, I am proceeding with tentative acceptance of his theory as a foundational framework for a plan of intercultural leadership development.

---

7. Clinton, *The Making of a Leader*, 44.

8. Clinton, *The Making of a Leader*, 44.

9. Clinton, *The Making of a Leader*, 44.

10. Clinton, The Making of a Leader, 217.

The plan describes a program to which participants are invited to attend over a given span of time. It could be a workshop, a continuing education module, or a class offered by a church, a ministry, or an educational institution. The title of the program is "On Becoming a Spirit-Empowered Leader." The pedagogy for this program takes a lifespan approach. Its premise is that leaders emerge over a lifetime of development and formation. The learning outcomes for the program are as follows:

After completing this course successfully, students will be able to the following:

A. **Share** a personal account of their leadership emergence, recounting a timeline of points in their lives when they sensed that the Holy Spirit was calling, nurturing, and empowering their development as Spirit-empowered leaders.

B. **Recall** the stories of at least three notable Spirit-empowered leaders in the Bible (Old and New Testaments) and explain lessons learned from each of them concerning leadership.

C. **Select** two Spirit-empowered leaders in church history, identify the positive traits and attributes of their leadership, and share how each one serves as a model of integrity for emerging leaders.

D. **Summarize** the five paradigms of global Spirit-empowered leadership and explain which paradigm resonates with his or her leadership style.

E. **Identify** the characteristics of the prototype of charismatic leadership and indicate how one can determine if a particular leader exhibits these characteristics.

F. **Identify** the two kinds of charismatic leadership (personalized and socialized) and indicate how one can discern evidence of one or the other in a particular leader.

The above outcomes serve as a reference point for planning and assessment of the sessions in the program. The facilitator communicates the outcomes to the learners at the outset of the program and refers to them as a roadmap during the program.

Lesson Sessions

What follows is an overview of eight sessions in which the topics, format, and concepts are adapted from Clinton's earlier work, *Leadership Emergence Theory* and the 2012 edition of *The Making of a Leader*. Chapters of the latter work by Clinton (2012 edition), along with selections from my book, *Paradigms of Global Spirit-Empowered Leadership*, will be incorporated as assigned readings. Some of the discussion questions at the back of each chapter of *The Making of a Leader* will be incorporated into the sessions. To run this program, a site must be secured with a room for plenary sessions and breakout rooms. A facilitator and group leaders will need to be recruited and trained. The venue should have adequate facilities for restrooms and preparation of refreshments. The plan is conveyed in the form of lesson plans for eight sessions with learning outcomes and instructions for step-by-step implementation. The length of each session should be approximately 1.5 hours.

SESSION #1—LEADERSHIP EXPERIENCE

Assigned Readings

- Clinton, The Making of a Leader, Ch. 2, pp. 33–47.
- Newberg, *Paradigms of Spirit-Empowered Leadership*, selections from Ch. 1, "Defining Characteristics," pp. 13–39.

Outcome

By the end of the session, learners will be able to calibrate where they see themselves in the continuum of phases of leadership development—foundation, inner growth, training, maturing, convergence, and afterglow.

Plenary Meeting

The **first session** should begin with a welcome, introductions, brief devotional, and prayer by the facilitator, and the devotional should relate to a foundational leadership experience. The introduction of my book includes a few of my foundational experiences in spiritual formation and leadership development. A facilitator can reiterate my telling of these experiences or interject an account of his or her own.

In the first session participants are seated around tables. The facilitator engages participants in a practical exercise for locating where they are in the phases of leadership development. To do this, we will employ a simple tool, a timeline. The leader then shares an overview of each of the six phases, briefly explaining the growth that occurs in each phase, as delineated by Clinton.[11]

Diagram of Timeline

Phase I	Phase II	Phase III	Phase IV	Phase V	Phase VI
Foundations	Inner Growth	Training	Maturing	Convergence	Afterglow

Each participant receives a timeline (see diagram above) and writing implements, with which they locate where they see themselves in the continuum of phases: foundation, inner growth, training, maturing, convergence, and afterglow. Participants will be asked to mark their timelines with notes,

---

11. Clinton, *The Making of a Leader*, 37–40.

denoting formative experiences in the process of leadership emergence, such as a call, confirmation of the call, empowerment in the Holy Spirit, open doors to ministry, opportunities for leadership, development of leadership skills, breakthroughs, setbacks, failures, resistance from critics, demonic attacks, deepening of commitment, and second chances, etc.

When it appears that participants have completed their timelines, the facilitator invites participants to share a foundational experience in their leadership development with those at their table and recall how the foundational experience anticipated what was to come later.

At the opportune time, the facilitator dismisses the session, encouraging participants to read chapter 3 in Clinton's book, *The Making of a Leader*, and reflect on the discussion questions on pages 46–47, to reinforce what they learned in the first meeting. If the program is offered as a college class, the discussion questions should be assigned as homework.

SESSION #2—INNER GROWTH

Assigned Reading

- Clinton, *The Making of a Leader*, Ch. 3, pp. 49–64.
- Newberg, *Paradigms of Spirit-Empowered Leadership*, selections from Ch. 2, "Lacunas of Spirit-Empowered Leadership," pp. 41–62.

Outcome

By the end of the session, learners will share an experience in which their character was tested as they were in the process of taking on a ministry task.

Plenary Meeting

The **second session** should commence with a prayer and brief devotional thoughts related to Jesus' method of leadership development, shared by the facilitator. At the outset, participants will be assigned to a learning group; most leadership development programs utilize learning groups and peer coaching. Jesus, himself, assembled a learning group when he called together his twelve disciples. According to Baumgartner, one can learn in a bigger group, but an inner circle is more conducive to challenging old habits, bringing about lasting change, and coaching new ways of doing things. There needs to be a certain intensity of focus and attention, and that happens best in a small community. Neuro-scientific studies have found that with peer coaching, eighty-five percent of the participants were able to transfer their learning into their own context and sustain it. Without peer coaching, only fifteen percent were able to do that.[12]

Learning Groups

After the devotional, participants should break out into learning groups, and the group leaders function as peer coaches. The peer coaches give an overview of the processes that Jesus used to develop the inner growth of his emerging leaders—the disciples. Typically, as emerging leaders take on early ministry tasks, they encounter checks that test their character. Clinton identifies these checks as integrity checks, obedience checks, and word checks. Summaries of these processes are found in pages 50–62 in Clinton's book, *The Making of a*

---

12. Baumgartner, "Do We Need a New Approach to Leadership Development?" 21.

Leader. Group leaders then describe each check separately and ask participants if anyone wishes to share an experience before moving on to the next check.

Integrity Check

An integrity check refers to a special kind of process test that God uses to evaluate heart intent. God uses such tests as foundations from which to expand the leader's capacity to influence and/or expand one's actual sphere of influence. There are three parts to an integrity check: the challenge to consistency with inner convictions, the response to the challenge, and, if passed successfully, the resulting expansion.[13] Sometimes evidence of the resulting expansion may be delayed or take place over time, but it can be seen to stem from the integrity check. There are various uses for integrity checks:

1. To see follow-through on a promise or vow.
2. To ensure burden for a ministry or vision.
3. To allow confirmation of inner-character strength.
4. To build faith.
5. To establish inner values is very important in leadership development.
6. To teach submission.
7. To warn others of the seriousness of obeying God.[14]

Obedience Check

Emerging leaders early on in their informal training are often given small tasks by mentors, masters, supervisors, pastors, or other leaders who are associated with them. The tasks can be small and informal or formal. These tasks are often indicators of loyalty, submission, use of gifts, initiative, and further usefulness. God honors the principle of Luke 16:10: "He that is faithful in that which is least is faithful also in much; and he that is unjust in little is unjust in much." An important thing to keep in mind about ministry tasks is that the ultimate assignment is from God whether the ministry task is self-initiated or assigned by another. Ultimate accountability is to God. One of the signs of maturity in an emerging leader is the recognition of this fact and the desire to please the Lord in a ministry task.[15] A ministry task is an assignment from God that primarily tests a person's faithfulness and obedience but also often allows use of ministry gifts

---

13. Clinton, *The Making of a Leader*, 50.
14. Clinton, *The Making of a Leader*, 52.
15. Clinton, *The Making of a Leader*, 137.

in the context of a task that has closure, accountability, and evaluation. Clinton concludes, "Leaders will be responsible for influencing specific groups of people to obey God. They will not achieve this unless they themselves know how to obey God."[16]

Word Check

A word check is a process item that tests a leader's ability to understand or receive a word from God personally and see it worked out in life with a view toward enhancing the authority of God's truth and a desire to know it.[17] Following are examples from two biblical characters.

1. Barnabas was sent to Antioch (Acts 11) to ascertain genuineness of the experience there. He had just been exposed to truth concerning God's acceptance of Cornelius. The test—Can he use this truth in a life situation?
2. Peter was told by the Holy Spirit (Acts 10) to go with the three Gentiles to Cornelius' home. This happened concurrently with the thrice repeated vision concerning the clean and unclean. He immediately perceived new truth—the Gentiles were not unclean. He was then ready for God's expansion of that truth in Cornelius' home. Peter was tested on two truths: God accepts Gentiles, and Jesus will baptize them in the Holy Spirit.

A successful pass of a word check should increase an emerging leader's ability to discern God's voice and to respond with obedience. This, then, leads to internalization and authoritative use of truth (word gift).[18] Leaders usually have more than a single word gift (apostleship, evangelism, prophecy, teaching, pastoring, exhortation, faith, word of knowledge, word of wisdom) as part of their gift mix (the set of primary spiritual gifts). The word check processing is usually a springboard leading to perception of one of these gifts and its use. Word checks usually lead to public sharing of a testimony concerning the check, a first step in experiencing use of a word gift.[19]

Leaders greatly used of God have evidenced a love for truth. They study the written word to feed their own souls as well as to help those to whom they minister. They are quick to discern God's truth in everyday life. They learn to hear the voice of God through the ministry of other people. So then, one

---

16. Clinton, *The Making of a Leader*, 56.
17. Clinton, *The Making of a Leader*, 133.
18. Clinton, *The Making of a Leader*, 133.
19. Clinton, *The Making of a Leader*, 136.

would expect God to develop a leader in his or her ability to appreciate truth and to cultivate habits of intake.[20]

Group leaders then wrap up the sharing and dismiss the participants to reconvene with the larger group for a short wrap-up prior to dismissal. As the facilitator dismisses the session, he or she should encourage participants to reflect on the discussion questions on pages 83–84 in Clinton's book and ponder what they experienced in the initial meeting with their learning group. If this program is offered as a college class, the discussion questions should be assigned as homework.

20. Clinton, *The Making of a Leader*, 136.

SESSION #3—TRAINING

Assigned Reading

- Clinton, *The Making of a Leader*, Ch. 4, pp. 65–84
- Newberg, *Paradigms of Spirit-Empowered Leadership*, selections from Ch. 3, "Precursors" & Ch. 4, "Early Pentecostal Leaders," pp. 63–102.

Outcome

By the end of the session learners will reflect on where they are in the process of training in terms of these phases—entry, training, fruitfulness, and harvest.

Plenary Session

In the **third session**, the facilitator should open with prayer and share a brief devotional on a ministry task in the Bible, such as organization of the growing newborn Church in Acts 2:42–46. The apostles organized the large influx of new believers into home groups where they devoted themselves to the core practices of communal life in the Spirit. This was an impressive ministry task.

The facilitator then presents a brief overview of Clinton's ideas on training. Clinton says, "The ministry task provides a transition from the Inner Growth phase to the Ministry Maturing phase."[21] He sees two sub-phases in ministry maturing: the first having to do with God's work in the leader and the second with the leader's work for God. We are opting to designate the first part as training. The focus of the training phase is on the acquisition of leadership skills. Leaders who sense a need for upgrading their skills generally opt for some kind of formal training. The training experience affords an opportunity for a leader to pick up skills through instruction, coaching, and feedback. It provides a leader with new ideas and self-confidence, encouraging him or her to expand his or her influence and impact.

The facilitator should stress that formal training comes in different forms. It can be a continuing education event, such as a conference, workshop or seminar, a more personalized approach with a consultant who comes on site to coach a leader, or a one-on-one mentoring relationship. My entry into formal training started with a seminar led by an expert in small group ministry, Dale Galloway.

---

21. Clinton, *The Making of a Leader*, 75.

The premise of the seminar was that small groups were the key to church growth by means of multiplication. When a group reaches a certain number of attendees, it multiplies itself by forming two groups, and so on. At this seminar I first learned of David Yonggi Cho's system of cell groups at the Yoido Full Gospel Church in Seoul, South Korea. I bought into the model and attempted to integrate it into the church in San Francisco where I was serving as senior pastor. We selected a leader of small groups, recruited and trained group leaders, and launched a system of home groups.

Learning Groups

The facilitator then dismisses the participants into their learning groups. The group leader invites participants to share their experiences with formal and informal training. He or she could pose these questions: What is the most important leadership skill that you acquired from a training event or coaching relationship? How did God build that skill into your life? How far along in the training process are you? Clinton sees the discovery of spiritual gifts as important in the training stage of leadership development. He writes, "A spiritual gift is a unique capacity for channeling the Holy Spirit's power into a ministry."[22] The group leader could refer participants to Clinton discussion of spiritual gifts, gift-mix, and gift-cluster on pages 78–81.

As a strategic moment, the group leader should make connections with the phases delineated above. These connections should be made in the form of questions, such as "At the time of that training experience, where would you place yourself in terms of the phases—entry, training, fruitfulness, and harvest? And where would you place yourself after the training? What made the difference?

A group leader could refer participants to the case studies of early Pentecostal leader in chapter 4 of the Newberg text and engage the group in discussion of the training methods of such leaders.

Group leaders wrap up the sharing and dismiss the participants to reconvene with the larger group. As the facilitator dismisses the session, he or she should encourage participants to reflect on the discussion questions on pages 83–84 in Clinton's book and ponder them. If the program is offered as a college class, the discussion questions should be assigned as homework.

---

22. Clinton, *The Making of a Leader*, 78.

Session #4—Maturing

Assigned Reading

- Clinton, *The Making of a Leader*, Ch. 5, pp. 85–107
- Newberg, *Paradigms of Spirit-Empowered Leadership*, selections from Ch. 5, "Neo-Pentecostal Leaders" & Ch. 6, "Global Charismatic Leaders," pp. 103–144.

Outcome

By the end of the session learners will be able to determine which of the stages in the Maturing Phase God is taking them through at this time and what insights they have gained from being mentored or mentoring emerging leaders in their ministry.

Plenary Session

The facilitator should open the **fourth session** and offer a brief devotional based on a biblical passage that addresses an authority lesson. Examples could include the following:

- Miriam and Aaron (Num. 12:1–16)
- The centurion (Luke:1–10)
- James and John (Matt. 20:20–28)
- Healing of the paralytic (Luke 5:1–17)

The facilitator should give an illustration of an authority lesson from his or her own life, describing the incident. The facilitator should then ask the participants to identify which of Clinton's five primary authority lessons apply to the illustration shared by the facilitator: (1) negative lessons of authority, (2) search for and understanding legitimate authority, (3) a desire to model legitimate authority, (4) insights about spiritual authority, and (5) increasing use of spiritual authority as a source of power.[23] If a participant recalls a painful experience, the facilitator should pause the discussion for a time of prayer for healing.

The facilitator then states that the leadership lessons in the maturing phase tend to be complex. Clinton describes four such lessons. He says that they fall in the categories of relational learning and discernment. The authority lesson belongs to the category of relational learning and the other three—spiritual

---

23. Clinton, *The Making of a Leader*, 88.

warfare, the plateau barrier, and ministry philosophy—belong to the category of discernment lessons. The facilitator should then direct participants to Clinton's discussion of discernment lessons in pages 85–104. The facilitator points out that normally there are two outcomes in the maturing phase: stalemated development and progress to the convergence phase.

Learning Groups

The facilitator dismisses the participants to their learning groups, signaling that the discussion of leadership lessons in the maturing phase will continue. Group leaders should be sensitive to raw feelings that may have surfaced when the facilitator remarked that there are two outcomes in the maturing phase—stalemated development and progress to the next phase. The group leader can refer group members to pages 104–105 in Clinton's book for his sober remarks on emerging leaders whose development is arrested. He says that they fall into two categories: (1) those who plateau at some level of ministry competency and then show relatively little ongoing growth, and (2) those who are disciplined or for one reason or another set aside or step outside of leadership position.

This is even more reason for an emerging leader in the maturing phase to be intentional about their ongoing development. At this point the group leader should point out that there are four major stages in the maturing phase:

1. Entry stage
2. Training stage
3. Relational learning stage
4. Discernment state

The group leader may refer participants to the case studies of neo-Pentecostal leaders in chapter 5 of the Newberg text and engage the group in discussion of the stages of the maturing process of these leaders (Hagin, Roberts, Cho, and Prince). Then the group leader should raise these questions for reflection and discussion:

1. Which of these stages do you think God is taking you through currently?
2. Is God giving insights for you personally or for you to use with emerging leaders in your ministry?
3. Which stage is most crucial for you now, and which is most useful for you in helping emerging leaders in your ministry?

Group leaders need to allow time for reflection on these questions and then lead a brief discussion before offering a closing prayer and dismissing the group. As the group leaders dismisses the session, they should encourage participants to reflect on the discussion questions on pages 106–107 in Clinton and ponder what they experienced in the initial meeting with their learning group. If this program is offered as a college class, the discussion questions should be assigned as homework.

Session #5—Convergence

Assigned Reading

- Clinton, *The Making of a Leader*, Ch. 6, pp. 109–131
- Newberg, *Paradigms of Spirit-Empowered Leadership*, selections from Ch. 7, "Apostle Paradigm," & Ch. 8, "Prophet Paradigm," pp. 147–169.

Outcome

By the end of this session, learners will assess the extent to which their current role is congruent with their gift mix and what guidance they might seek to confirm that congruence or incongruence.

Plenary Session

The facilitator should open the **fifth session** with an opening prayer. Then he or she welcomes the participants and tasks for feedback on the program. How are we doing so far? What has been helpful? Where do we need to improve? The facilitator needs to display the six learning outcomes of the program (listed below) and ask participants to offer verbal feedback, evaluating the extent to which we have addressed each outcome in terms of what they have learned.

A. **Share** a personal account of their leadership emergence, recounting a timeline of points in their lives when they sensed that the Holy Spirit was calling, nurturing, and empowering their development as Spirit-empowered leaders.

B. **Recall** the stories of at least three notable Spirit-empowered leaders in the Bible (Old and New Testaments) and explain lessons learned from each of them concerning leadership.

C. **Select** two Spirit-empowered leaders in church history, identify the positive traits and attributes of their leadership, and share how each one serves as a model of integrity for emerging leaders.

D. **Summarize** the five paradigms of global Spirit-empowered leadership and explain which paradigm resonates with their leadership style.

E. **Identify** the characteristics of the prototype of charismatic leadership and indicate how one can determine if a particular leader exhibits these characteristics.

F. *Identify* the two kinds of charismatic leadership (personalized and socialized) and indicate how one can discern evidence of one or the other in a particular leader.

The facilitator should record the comments of the participants in writing and thank the participants for their feedback.

This is the Convergence Phase. The facilitator should provide an overview of the task of guidance in this phase of leadership development. In this phase God moves the leader into a role that matches his or her gift mix and experience, maximizing his or her leadership influence. The leader has by now acquired the wisdom to step away from a leadership role for which he or she is not gifted. Many leaders do not experience convergence because the current position is not well suited for maximum effectiveness. However, when and if convergence occurs, the leader's potential is maximized.

The major developmental task in Phase V Convergence is guidance. According to Clinton, guidance is "one of the crucial elements of leadership." Guidance is implied in Clinton's definition of a leader as "a person with God-given capacity and God-given responsibility who influences a group of followers toward God's purposes for the group."[24] An emerging leader first learns about guidance in his or her own life. Clinton writes, "guidance comes through one's ongoing, obedient, daily walk with God as a leader meets with God in his or her devotional time and personal study of the Word."[25] Clinton delineates six ways that are used by God to provide guidance to leaders: divine contacts, mentors, double confirmation, negative preparation, flesh acts, and divine affirmation. Each of these is discussed in pages 111–122.

Learning Groups

Having summarized Clinton's conception of guidance, the facilitator dismisses the participants to their learning groups. The group leader should either share a story of divine guidance or invite group members to share.

Clinton notes that, based on biblical examples of divine guidance, God sometimes uses conflict—whether personal or ministry related—to develop a leader's dependence upon God and to trust in his leading. The prophet Jeremiah's life was filled with conflict, as was the apostle Paul's, not to mention Jesus. The group leader should ask, according to James 1:2–4, what the major thing is that God wants to do in a leader through crisis. Allow for group members to offer responses. Paul suggests in 2 Corinthians 1:3–4 and 2 Timothy 3:10–11 how God uses crises as guidance in a leader's life. What principles concerning crises do you see in these passages? Again, allow for group members to offer responses, and then summarize the sharing.

A leader who is moving in convergence will see God's hand working during

---

24. Clinton, *The Making of a Leader*, 110.
25. Clinton, *The Making of a Leader*, 111.

difficult times, orchestrating the leader's development. A leader must be patient in these situations, refraining from making major decisions intended to escape the ordeal of conflict. Clinton states, "Leaders tend to move ahead in major decisions before receiving a certainty word of guidance."[26] Waiting on the Lord is difficult. Yet Clinton stipulates the following principle of guidance and two patterns worth heeding. The principle: "A leader must learn to get guidance from God if he or she is to lead groups toward God's purpose." From this, two patterns follow. The first is that a leader learns from guidance to experience God's direction for his or her personal life that in turn builds confidence to discern guidance for groups that he or she leads. The second is that God will confirm significant truth upon which a leader acts from more than source to give credibility to his or her leadership.[27] This is what Clinton calls double confirmation.

Clinton observes that there are many incidents of double confirmation in the Bible and insists that the concept of double confirmation should be heeded by leaders with certain spiritual gifts. This axiom is particularly relevant to leaders in the Spirit-empowered movement. He writes, "Some spiritual gifts need the cautions that come by using double confirmation. Apostleship, words of knowledge, words of wisdom, discerning of spirits, tongues, and words of prophecy serve as sources through which truth comes. To be credible, there needs to be outside or multiple confirmation when the gift is revealing truth from God that will affect others' lives. This axiom is frequently abused by strong leaders having these gifts."[28]

The group leader will ask participants for feedback on Clinton's discussion of guidance. In closing, group leaders will suggest that participants look closely at the questions Clinton gives in pages 130–131 for processing the exercise of their leadership. If the program is offered as a college class, Clinton's suggestions should be assigned as homework. Then the learning group will be dismissed.

---

26. Clinton, *The Making of a Leader*, 127.
27. Clinton, *The Making of a Leader*, 128.
28. Clinton, *The Making of a Leader*, 129.

SESSION #6—AFTERGLOW/DEEPENING LESSONS

Assigned Reading

- Clinton, *The Making of a Leader*, Ch. 7, pp. 133–151
- Newberg, *Paradigms of Spirit-Empowered Leadership*, selections from Ch. 9, "Healing Evangelist Paradigm," Ch. 10, "Pastorpreneur Paradigm," & Ch. 11, "Teacher-Scholar Paradigm," pp. 171–224.

Outcome

By the end of the session learners will have reflected on how God has used the crises to develop their character.

Plenary Session

The facilitator will open the **sixth session** with a prayer and then state that the focus of this lesson will be on the deepening lessons of leadership that come with maturing of a leader. The facilitator will read two passages in which the apostle Paul reflects on deepening lessons he learned from adversity: 2 Corinthians 1:8–11 and 2 Corinthians 4:7–12.

Then the facilitator will share the following thoughts from chapter 7 in *The Making of a Leader* (pp. 134–137). Throughout a leader's lifespan, God works to deepen character as well as to develop ministry skills. God continues to form character throughout the life of a leader. This development consists of the deepening of qualities of love, compassion, empathy and discernment. God uses a leader's experiences to develop character, the most common of which are conflict and crises. Leaders face unexpected situations involving sickness, loss, and resistance. At the time few leaders see these experiences as necessary for the deepening of their leadership development. Perhaps you are facing some such experience in your leadership.

How do you perceive what is happening to you? Clinton would have you understand that such experiences are used by God to deepen character.

We all know that leaders are busy people. They are so preoccupied with the many demands of leadership that they may not notice that they are growing, particularly in spiritual formation. God often breaks into a leader's life at this point. Clinton identifies a syndrome that he calls the reflective evaluation pattern, comprised of five stages:

1. God initiates intense processing to gain the attention of the leader.
2. The leader is forced to do serious reflection about ministry, life, and ultimate reality.
3. The leader does an evaluation that results in formative thinking and commitment to growth measures learned in the processing.
4. The leader experiences a renewed determination to know God more deeply.
5. God blesses the commitment and renewed determination by deepening the relationship between him and the leader.[29]

If a leader refuses to see the hand of God during "intense processing," but instead blames God or people, or rationalizes away the processing, then the reflective evaluation pattern may be cut short.

Learning Groups

On this note, the facilitator dismisses participants to their *learning groups*. Group leaders will invite the participants to reflect on their experiences of adversity and see the hand of God in them. He will invite group members to recall an experience of crisis or conflict. Perhaps you previously saw this experience as a rough patch to get over and didn't realize that God was in it, working to develop you. Without retelling the ordeal, would anyone care to describe the lessons that you learned about yourself or leadership (deepening of faith, dependence on God, insights about character development, empathy, compassion, and so on).

Paul clearly believes that God uses crises to deepen one's character and leadership. Read 1 Corinthians 1:3–4; 2 Timothy 3:10–11. Group leaders will ask, "What principles concerning crisis do you see in these passages and how do they apply to you?"

The group leader should be sensitive to allow space for the expression of tender feelings and prayer ministry, as needed. Following the time of sharing, the group leader will dismiss participants, reminding them that there are two more sessions coming up. He or she will encourage participants to reflect on the discussion questions on pp. 130–131 in Clinton and ponder what they experienced in the meeting with their learning group. If the program is offered as a college class, the discussion questions should be assigned as homework.

---

29. Clinton, *The Making of a Leader*, 135.

SESSION #7—MINISTRY PHILOSOPHY

Assigned Reading

- Clinton, *The Making of a Leader*, Ch. 8, pp. 153–176
- Newberg, *Paradigms of Spirit-Empowered Leadership*, selections from Ch. 12, "Benchmarks for Developing Spirit-Empowered Leaders," pp. 227–244.

Outcome

By the end of the session learners will have coalesced formative aspects of a leadership philosophy—biblical leadership values, changes in culture and society, and unique gifts and personal development.

Plenary Session

At this juncture, the **seventh session**, participants will be adequately equipped to construct their ministry philosophy. The facilitator will open the session with words of affirmation and encouragement. He or she will offer a prayer that celebrates God's grace in developing the leadership capacities of the participants.

The facilitator will then explain Clinton's concept of a ministry philosophy. Clinton is convinced that all leaders operate from a ministry philosophy. Ministry philosophy is the result of leadership emergence—the ideas, values, and principles, whether implicit or explicit, that a leader uses as guidelines for decision-making, exercising influence, and evaluating his or her ministry. A growing awareness of one's ministry philosophy leads to more effective leadership.

Clinton states his premise "Leaders must develop a ministry philosophy that simultaneously honors biblical leadership values, embraces the challenges of the times in which they live, and fits their unique gifts and personal development if they expect to be productive over a lifetime."[30] There are three sections of a ministry philosophy:

1. **Biblical Leadership Values**
   A Christian leader bases his or her values, methodology, motivation and goals on Scripture. The Bible is the source of our leadership values. In the introduction we made the claim that the Bible is book about leadership. We can see from stories about Moses, prophets, and kings in the Old Testament that leaders are

---

30. Clinton, *The Making of a Leader*, 158.

commissioned and empowered by the Holy Spirit. In the New Testament Jesus sets the tone for Christian leadership with his teaching on servant leadership. The apostle Paul introduced teaching on spiritual gifts. But the Bible does not speak to all specific issues of leadership. It often gives general ideas or specific examples from which a leader must be led by the Holy Spirit to applications.

2. **Embracing the Challenges of the Times**
   A Christian leader is faced with the challenge of understanding the times and adapting to changes in society and culture. The leaders of the Early Church carried the Gospel across Mediterranean world on the wings of the Pax Romana and the system of Roman roads. The spread of the Reformation was propelled by the invention of the printing press and the global reach of the modern missionary movement followed on the coattails of European colonialism and international exploration. More recently the explosive growth of Pentecostal-charismatic Christianity has been jettisoned by digital modes of telecommunication and progressive approaches to Christian ministry and social engagement. The challenge of the times forces a ministry philosophy to be a dynamic changing entity and not a static, perfect guideline for all times.

3. **Leader's Unique Gifts and Personal Development**
   A ministry philosophy must be geared to the unique gifts of a particular leader. Giftedness consists of natural endowments, acquired skills, and spiritual gifts. Clinton refers to each leader's gifting as a gift-cluster, involving natural abilities and spiritual gifts. There is great value of knowing and moving in one's gift cluster, in that such self-knowledge helps a leader to maximize his or her ministry effectiveness.

A ministry philosophy acts as a GPS, a directional device that is based on biblical values, responsiveness to the times, and a leader's gifting, thereby directing a leader in a path that will lead to success. As Clinton sees it, a leader develops a ministry philosophy by reflecting on the lessons of life and compiling them in a ministry philosophy.

Learning Groups

Having presented an overview of the ministry philosophy and fielded questions, the facilitator will dismiss participants into their *learning groups.*

The group leader should ask participants to reflect on three categories of ministry philosophy, first writing down their ideas and secondly sharing if they wish. Ideally, the participants will direct the course of the discussion in the learning groups, as they discuss the following questions:

1. What are biblical leadership values that you would include in your ministry philosophy?

2. What are the challenges of the times that you would include in your ministry philosophy?
3. What are your unique gifts and personal character strengths?

In summarizing the key points of the sharing, the facilitator should be sensitive to the need for prayer. Perhaps it may be appropriate to have the participants intercede with each other. In closing the session, group leaders should encourage participants to continue working on their ministry philosophies on their own time, consulting chapter 8 in Clinton's book for further clarification. The leader will encourage participants to reflect on the discussion questions on p. 176 in Clinton and ponder what they experienced in their learning group. If the program is offered as a college class, the discussion questions should be assigned as homework. The group leader should encourage the participants to return for the final session next week.

SESSION #8—SUMMATIVE ASSESSMENT

Assigned Reading

- Clinton, *The Making of a Leader*, Ch. 9, pp. 177–187
- Newberg, *Paradigms of Spirit-Empowered Leadership*, selections from "Epilogue," & "Conclusion," pp. 273–276.

Outcome

By the end of the session learners will calibrate where they are on the timeline now as compared to the first session and share the most apparent leadership challenges they face as they continue to develop as a leader.

Plenary Session

The facilitator should open the *final session* with prayer and ask for feedback on the preceding sessions.

1. What were the most helpful sessions?
2. Where do we need to improve?

Then the leader thanks the participants for their input and record the suggestion so that the participants can see that their ideas matter. To transition to the agenda for the final session, the facilitator should say, "Let's return to the timeline with which we started."

Diagram of Timeline

Phase I	Phase II	Phase III	Phase IV	Phase V	Phase VI
Foundations	Inner Growth	Training	Maturing	Convergence	Afterglow

The leader will then ask the participants to ponder where they would locate themselves on the timeline, now as compared to our first session.

There certainly are challenges that remain for each of us to negotiate in the ongoing development of our leadership. So, let's talk about that. What are the most apparent leadership challenges for you as you continue to develop as a leader?

The facilitator will record each challenge as it is identified, offering words of confirmation and thanking the participants for their feedback. Then he or she will say, "Today we will continue our discussion of leadership challenges in our groups and then gather together for a debrief and final farewell." Participants will then be dismissed to their learning groups.

Learning Groups

The group leaders will begin by asking participants to identify what they have found to be the most difficult leadership challenges in their career or ministry. Group leaders will guide the sharing, introducing one challenge at time, allowing about five to ten minutes for each. The leader should endeavor to keep the sharing on track so that it remains constructive and does not drift into the realm of therapy, but focuses on describing, understanding and validating the reality of each challenge.

As the opportune time, the group leader will offer a prayer, thanking God for the wisdom imparted by group members, and dismiss them to the larger group.

Plenary Session Reconvened

Wrap-up: summary of findings and farewell.
The facilitator will hand out an *evaluation form* and ask the participants to fill out the form.

EVALUATION FORM

Having completed the course, students will rate their achievement of the learning outcomes, by rating the level of their achievement and offering a comment as to their evaluation of the program:

1. As I shared a personal account of my leadership emergence with a small group, I recalled points in my life when I sensed that the Holy Spirit was calling, nurturing, and empowering my development as a Spirit-empowered leader.
    4 = High _______ 3 = Medium _______ 2 = Low _______ 1 = None _______
    Comment:

2. I can recall the stories of at least three notable Spirit-empowered leaders in the Bible (Old and New Testaments) and explain lessons learned from each of them concerning leadership.
    4 = High _______ 3 = Medium _______ 2 = Low _______ 1 = No _______
    Comment:

3. I selected two Spirit-empowered leaders in church history, identified the positive traits and attributes of their leadership, and shared how each one serves as a model of integrity for my emerging leadership.
    4 = High _______ 3 = Medium _______ 2 = Low _______ 1 = No _______
    Comment:

4. I can summarize the five paradigms of global Spirit-empowered leadership and explain which paradigm resonates most with my leadership style.
    4 = High _______ 3 = Medium _______ 2 = Low _______ 1 = No _______
    Comment:

5. I can describe the characteristics of charismatic leadership and indicate how one can determine if a particular leader exhibits these characteristics.
   4 = High _____ 3 = Medium _____ 2 = Low _____ 1 = No _____
   Comment:

6. I can identify the two kinds of charismatic leadership (personalized and socialized) and indicate how one can discern evidence of one or the other in a particular leader.
   4 = High _____ 3 = Medium _____ 2 = Low _____ 1 = No _____
   Comment:

Note:

The model outlined above is designed to be offered as a course at Oral Roberts University. The model could be easily adapted to the format of a local church class, home group, or seminar series.

Let me close the book by reaffirming the invitation I extended to the reader at the outset. It is my privilege to have been your guide in this amazing journey, as we traversed places near and far where the Holy Spirit has called and empowered leaders. You have seen how the Holy Spirit has raised leaders and equipped them as servants of the Kingdom. The story of Spirit-empowered leadership began in the Bible, carried on throughout church history, and continues today in every corner of the globe. Ministry leaders are emerging everywhere. You may or may not think of yourself as a leader. The way I define leadership is by drawing a circle in such a way that there is a place for you. Leadership is influence. You don't have to oversee something to be a leader. At the close of the book, I invite you to see yourself as following in the footsteps of a long line of Spirit-empowered leaders who have gone before us.

Let me suggest a few takeaways from our study of Spirit-empowered leadership. Cultivate the spiritual disciplines of prayer and meditation on the Word of God. Aim for the image of Christ as the aim of your spiritual formation. Pursue moral integrity at all costs. Seek accountability partners who will provide honest feedback. Devote yourself to building up those who are in your circle of influence and span of care. Surround yourself with people who are without guile, hidden agendas, and duplicity. Separate the impurities from the metal. Evaluate your leadership according to the touchstones of the Holy Spirit and the Bible. Let the Holy Spirit unmask your fleshly desires and give you a new heart and mind in Christ. Love the people you serve with grace and mercy. Speak the truth in love. Love Jesus and show your love by following his commandments (John 14:21).

The leaders we studied in the historical sketches can serve as models for the emergence of your leadership. You can follow these precursors by seeking an immersive encounter with the Holy Spirit, known then and now as baptism of the Holy Spirit. Along with the early Pentecostal leaders, you can verify with evidence of ecstatic speech that the power promised by Jesus in Acts 1:8 is as operative today as it was on the day of the Christian Pentecost. With the Neo-Pentecostal pacesetters, you can enter a deeper dimension of faith focused not only on the spiritual realm, but also on the good things in life, such as health and wealth, flourishing and growth. As with the global charismatic trailblazers, you can embrace the worldwide expansion of indigenous and multicultural Spirit-filled communities of faith that are producing contextual theologies, engagement with social issues, and ecumenical partnerships. Many of us are at the forefront of these developments, where we find innovative, charismatic leaders not bound by the restrictions of past forms. I pray that you will join this procession.

BIBLIOGRAPHY

Aguilar, Malou L. "Miracles Are His Business." *Asian Journal* (January 4, 2008): 1–2.

Åkerlund, Truls. *A Phenomenology of Pentecostal Leadership.* Eugene, OR: Wipf & Stock, 2018.

Akin-David, Morack. *The Leadership Secrets of David O. Oyedepo: The Secrets of Men Are in Their Stories.* Lagos: Book Addict Publications, 2015.

Alexander, Estrelda. "G. T. Haywood and the Emergence of Oneness Pentecostalism." *From Aldersgate to Azusa Street: Wesleyan, Holiness, and Pentecostal Visions of the New Creation.* Eugene, OR: Pickwick, 2010.

Alexander, Patrick H. "Gordon Donald Fee." In *New International Dictionary of Pentecostal and Charismatic Movements,* edited by Stanley M. Burgess and Eduard M. van der Maas, 635. Grand Rapids: Zondervan, 2002.

Alt, Albrecht. "The Formation of the Israelite State in Palestine." In *Essays on Old Testament History and Religion,* 171–237. Sheffield: JSOT Press, 1989.

Amano, David T. "The African Background of the Prosperity Gospel." *Theologia Viatorum* 45, no. 1 (2021): 1–10.

Amoako, Henry Kwadwa. "Biography of Faith Emmanuel Idahosa." *African Research Consult.* https://african-research.com/research/biography/the-marvelous-son-of-the-late-archbishop-benson-idahosa-bishop-feb/.

Anderson, Allan. "Pentecostal Approaches to Faith and Healing." *International Review of Missionary Research* 91, no. 363 (2003): 525.

———. *Introduction to Pentecostalism: Global Charismatic Christianity.* Cambridge: Cambridge University Press, 2004.

———. "Pandita Ramabai, the Mukti Revival and Global Pentecostalism." *Transformation* 23, no. 1 (2006): 47.

———. *Spreading Fires: The Missionary Nature of Early Pentecostalism.* London: SCM Press, 2007.

———. *To the Ends of the Earth: Pentecostalism and the Transformation of World Christianity.* Oxford: Oxford University Press, 2013.

———. "Stretching Out Hands to God: Origins and Development of Pentecostalism in Africa." In *Pentecostalism in Africa: Presence and Impact of Pneumatic Christianity in Postcolonial Societies,* edited by Martin Lindhardt. Leiden: Brill, 2015.

Anim, Peter. *The History of How the Full Gospel Church Was Founded in Ghana.* Accra: Christ Apostolic Church, n.d.

"Anthony Norris Groves: The First Brethren Missionary to India." Borivali Assembly. https://borivaliassembly.net/ministry-corner/anthony-norris-groves/.

The Apostolic Faith 1, no. 1 (September 1906): 4.

The Apostolic Faith 1, no. 3 (November 1906): 4.

The Apostolic Faith 1, no. 2. "The Pentecostal Baptism Restored" (October 1906): 1.

Arthur, Michael B. "The Motivational Effects of Charismatic Leadership: A Self-Concept Based Theory." *Organizational Science* 4, no. 4 (1993): 577–594.

Aryeh, Daniel Nii Aboagye. "Academic versus Spiritual: Theological Education and the Anointing of the Holy Spirit in Contemporary Prophetic Ministries in Ghana." *Journal of Contemporary Ministry* 4 (2018): 61–77.

Asamoah-Gyadu, J. Kwabena. *African Charismatics: Current Developments within Independent Indigenous Pentecostalism in Ghana.* Leiden: Brill, 2005.

———. *Contemporary Pentecostal Christianity: Interpretations from an African Context.* Oxford: Regnum Books International, 2013.

———. "Pentecostalism and the Transformation of the African Christian Landscape." In *Pentecostalism in Africa: Presence and Impact of Pneumatic Christianity in Postcolonial Societies,* edited by Martin Lindhardt, 100–114. Leiden: Brill, 2015.

———. "'Your Miracle is on the Way': Oral Roberts and Mediated Pentecostalism in Africa." *Spiritus: ORU Journal of Theology* 3, no. 1 (2018): 5–26.

———. "'I Will Not Leave You Orphaned': Select Impactful Contributions of Global Pentecostalism to World Christianity." *Pneuma: The Journal of the Society for Pentecostal Studies* 42, no. 3–4 (2020): 383–384.

Associated Press. "Disgraced Pastor Faces More Gay Sex Allegations." January 24, 2009.

Atansuyi, H. O. "Gospel and Culture in the Perspective of African Instituted Churches." *Cyberjournal for Pentecostal Charismatic Research,* n.p. http://pctii.org/ccyerj/cyber3/aic.html.

Au, Connie. "Elitism and Poverty: Early Pentecostalism in Hong Kong (1907–1945)." *Global Chinese Pentecostal and Charismatic Christianity.* Leiden: Brill, 2017.

———. "Mok Lai Chi," In *Brill's Encyclopedia of Global Pentecostalism,* edited by Michael Wilkinson, Connie Au, Jörg Haustein, and Todd M. Johnson, 432. Leiden: Brill, 2021.

———, trans. *Pentecostal Truths* 2, no. 8 (October 1909): 1. https://pentecostalarchives.org/?a=cl&cl=CL2.1909.10&sp=PTHK&e=-------en-20--1--img-txIN-----------.

Avolio, Bruce J. "Promoting More Integrative Strategies for Leadership Theory-Building." *American Psychologist* 62, no. 1 (2007): 25–33.

Bae, Hyeon Sung. "Full Gospel Theology and a Korean Pentecostal Identity." In *Asian and Pentecostal; The Charismatic Face of Christianity in Asia,* edited by Allan Andersson and Edmond Tang, 432–433. Eugene: Wipf & Stock, 2011.

Ball, Henry C. "Mexican Work." *Weekly Evangel* (June 12, 1920): 10–11.

Banks, Robert, and Bernice M. Ledbetter. *Reviewing Leadership: A Christian Evaluation of Current Approaches.* Grand Rapids: Baker Academic, 2004.

Barna, George. *Today's Pastors.* Ventura, CA: Regal Books, 1993.

———. *Leaders on Leadership: Wisdom, Advice and Encouragement on the Art of Leading God's People.* Ventura, CA: Regal, 1997.

Baron, Beth. "Mama Trasher and the Assiout Orphanage." Paper presented at the conference "Competing Kingdoms: Women, Mission, Nation, and American Empire, 1812–1930." Rothmere American Institute, University of Oxford, (April 2006).

Baron, Beth. "Nile Mother: Lillian Trasher and the Orphans of Egypt." *Competing Kingdoms: Women, Mission, Nation, and the American Protestant Empire, 1812–1960*. Durham: Duke University Press, 2010.

Bass, Bernard M. *Leadership and Performance beyond Expectations*. New York: Free Press, 1985.

Baumgartner, Erich. "Do We Need a New Approach to Leadership Development?" *Journal of Applied Christian Leadership* 11, no. 1 (2017): 16–25.

BBC News. "Inside Singapore's City Harvest Scandal." October 15, 2015. https://www.bbc.com/news/world-asia-34589932.

Beatty, Jerome. "Nile Mother." *The American Magazine* (June 1939): 55–56, 180.

———. *Nile Mother: The Story of Lillian Trasher*. Springfield, MO: General Council of the Assemblies of God, n.d.

Bekker, J. Corné. "Toward a Theoretical Model of Christian Leadership." *Journal of Biblical Perspectives in Leadership* 2, no. 2 (2009): 142–152.

Bennis, Warren, and Burt Nanus. *Leaders: Strategies for Taking Charge*. 2nd ed. New York: Harper Business, 1997.

Betz, Hans Dieter. "Apostle." In *The Anchor Bible Dictionary*, edited by David Noel Freedman. Vol. 1. New York: Doubleday, 1992.

"Biography of Bishop David Oyedepo." *Believers Portal*, September 8, 2016. http://believersportal.com/biography-bishop-david-oyedepo/.

Bird, Warren, and Scott Thumma. "Megachurch 2020: The Changing Reality in America's Largest Churches," 1–41. *Hartford Institute for Religion Research*, 2020. http://www.hartfordinstitute.org/megachurch/2020_megachurch_report.pdf.

Blackaby, Henry T., and Richard Blackaby. *Spiritual Leadership: The Interactive Study*. Nashville: Broadman & Holman, 2006.

Blumhofer, Edith. "John Alexander Dowie." In *New International Dictionary of Pentecostal and Charismatic Movements*, edited by Stanley M. Burgess and Eduard M. van der Maas, 586. Grand Rapids: Zondervan, 2002.

———. "Consuming Fire: Pandita Ramabai and the Global Pentecostal Impulse." In *Interpreting Contemporary Christianity: Global Processes and Local Identities*, edited by Ogbu U. Kalu, 220–221. Grand Rapids: Eerdmans, 2008.

Blumhofer, Edith Waldvogel. *Aimee Semple McPherson: Everybody's Sister*. Grand Rapids, Eerdmans, 1997.

Boaheng, Isaac, Clement Amoako, and Samuel Boahen, "A Critique of Prosperity Theology in the Context of Ghanaian Christianity," *Noyam: E-Journal of Humanities, Arts and Social Sciences* 4, no. 11 (November 2023): 1356–1367. https://doi.org/10.38159/ehass.20234114.

Boddy, Alexander A. "The Welsh Revivalists Visited," *Confidence: A Pentecostal Paper for Great Britain*. Monkwearmouth, Sunderland, England, (March 1913): 47–49.

Bonk, Jonathan. "The Dictionary of African Christian Biography: A Proposal for Revising Ecclesiastical Maps," *Missiology: An International Review* 27, no. 1 (January 1999): 71–83.

Boring, M. Eugene. "Early Christian Prophecy." In *The Anchor Bible Dictionary*, edited by David Noel Freedman. Vol. 5. New York: Doubleday, 1992.

Brown, Candy Gunther. "Introduction: Pentecostalism and the Globalization of Illness and Healing." In *Global Pentecostal and Charismatic Healing*, edited by Candy Gunther Brown. Oxford: Oxford University Press, 2011.

Brown, Michael. "Are There Modern-Day Apostles?" *Ask Dr. Brown Podcast*, May 24, 2016. https://askdrbrown.org/library/are-there-modern-day-apostles.

Bundy, David D. "Edir Macedo." In *New International Dictionary of Pentecostal and Charismatic Movements*, edited by Stanley M. Burgess and Eduard M. van der Maas, 854. Grand Rapids: Zondervan, 2002.

———. "G. T. Haywood: Religion for Urban Realties." In *Portraits of a Generation: Early Pentecostal Leaders*, edited by James R. Goff and Grant Wacker. Fayetteville: University of Arkansas Press, 2002.

———. "Gordon and Freda Theresa Lindsay." In *New International Dictionary of Pentecostal and Charismatic Movements*, edited by Stanley M. Burgess and Eduard M. van der Maas, 842. Grand Rapids: Zondervan, 2002.

———. "Léon Joseph Suenens." In *New International Dictionary of Pentecostal and Charismatic Movements*, edited by Stanley M. Burgess and Eduard M. van der Maas, 1108–1109. Grand Rapids: Zondervan, 2002.

———. "Walter Jacob Hollenweger." In *New International Dictionary of Pentecostal and Charismatic Movements*, edited by Stanley M. Burgess and Eduard M. van der Maas, 729. Grand Rapids: Zondervan, 2002.

Burchard, Mary Jo. "Toward Deeper Synthesis of Biblical Perspectives in Organizational Leadership: A Literature Review of the Journal of Biblical Perspective in Leadership." *Journal of Biblical Perspectives in Leadership* 4, no. 1 (2012): 171-179.

Burge, Gary M. *The Anointed Commentary: The Holy Spirit in the Johannine Tradition*. Grand Rapids: Eerdmans, 1987.

Burgess, Ruth Vassar, and Stanley M. Burgess, *Shantistan Tablet: Enabling a Land of Peace*. Strafford, MO: n.p., 2021.

Burgess, Stanley M., and Gary B. McGee. "Trunelveli and Travancore (1860–1880)." In *New International Dictionary of Pentecostal and Charismatic Movements*, edited by Stanley M. Burgess and Eduard M. van der Maas, 118–119. Grand Rapids: Zondervan, 2002.

Campos, Roberta Bivar. "Sharing Charisma as a Mode of Pentecostal Expansion." *Social Compass* 61, no. 3 (2014): 277–289.

Cannistraci, David. *The Gift of Apostle: A Biblical Look at Apostleship and How God Is Using It to Bless His Church Today*. Ventura, CA: Regal Books, 1996.

Carter, Jeffrey D. "Celestial Church of Christ." In *New International Dictionary of Pentecostal and Charismatic Movements*, edited by Stanley M. Burgess and Eduard M. van der Maas, 467. Grand Rapids: Zondervan, 2002.

Cartledge, David. *The Apostolic Revolution: The Restoration of Apostles and Prophets in the Assemblies of God in Australia*. Chester Hill, Sydney, NSW: Paraclete Institute, 2000.

Cartledge, Mark J. "Charismatic Prophecy: A Definition and Description," *Journal of Pentecostal Theology* 2, no. 5 (1994): 79–120.

———. *Practical Theology: Charismatic and Empirical Perspectives*. Eugene, OR: Wipf & Stock, 2018.

Cartwright, D. W. "George Jeffreys." In *New International Dictionary of Pentecostal and Charismatic Movements*, edited by Stanley M. Burgess and Eduard M. van der Maas, 807. Grand Rapids: Zondervan, 2002.

Cenac, Julianne R. "Leader Emergence and the Phenomenological Work of the Holy Spirit in Acts 2." *Journal of Biblical Perspectives in Leadership* 3, no. 1 (2011): 123–135.

Cerillo, August, and Grant Wacker. "Bibliography and Historiography of Pentecostalism in the United States." In *New International Dictionary of Pentecostal and Charismatic Movements*, edited by Stanley M. Burgess and Eduard M. van der Maas, 382–405. Grand Rapids: Zondervan, 2002.

Chakravarti, Uma. *Rewriting History: Life and Times of Pandita Ramabai*. New Delhi: Zubaan, 2013.

Chandler, Diane J. "The Perfect Storm of Leaders' Unethical Behavior: A Conceptual Framework." *International Journal of Leadership Studies* 5, no. 1 (2009): 69–93.

Chao, En-Chieh. "Counting Souls: Numbers and Mega-church Worship in the Global Christian Network of Indonesia." *International Network for Asian Studies* 75 (Autumn 2016). https://www.iias.asia/the-newsletter/article/counting-souls-numbers-mega-worship-global-christian-network-indonesia.

Chappell, Paul G. "Granville Oral Roberts." In *New International Dictionary of Pentecostal and Charismatic Movements*, edited by Stanley M. Burgess and Eduard M. van der Maas, 1024. Grand Rapids: Zondervan, 2002.

Chetty, Irving G. "Origin and Development of the 'New Apostolic Reformation' in South Africa: A Neo-Pentecostal Movement or a Post-Pentecostal Phenomenon?" *Alternation Special Edition* 11 (2013): 190–206.

Cho, David Yonggi. *Salvation, Health and Prosperity*. Altamonte Springs, FL: Creation House, 1987.

———. *The Story of Fivefold Gospel for Modern People*. Seoul: Logos, 1997.

———. "Church Ministry Taking Steps with the Holy Spirit: Interview with the Rev. Cho." In *Charis and Charisma: David Yonggi Cho and the Growth of Yoido Full Gospel Church*, edited by Sung-hoon Myung and Young-gi Hong. Oxford: Regnum Books, 2003.

Chong, Terence. "The State of Pentecostalism in Southeast Asia: Ethnicity, Class and Leadership." *ISEAS Perspective* 53 (September 25, 2015): 1–8.

Chong, Terence, and Daniel P. S. Goh. "Asian Pentecostalism: Revivals, Mega-churches, and Social Engagement." In *Handbook of Religions in Asia*, edited by Bryan S. Turner and Oscar Salemink, 402–417. London: Routledge, 2014.

Christel, Virginia A. "The Pentecostal Pastor." In *Religious Leadership: A Reference Handbook*, Vol 1, edited by Sharon Henderson Callahan, 119–26. Thousand Oaks, CA: Sage Publications, 2013.

Christian Diet. "Biography of Bishop David Oyedepo," July 27, 2021. https://christiandiet.com.ng/bishop-david-oyedepo-biography-ministry-lessons-from-his-life/.

Church Gist. "Abacha I Did Not Come to Pay Homage, I Have Come to Advise You. You Cannot Stay Here without My Prayer: An Interview with Archbishop Joseph Imariabe Ojo." Https://churchgist.org/abacha-i-did-not-come-to-pay-homage-i-have-come-to-advise-you-you-cannot-stay-here-without-my-prayer-archbishop-benson-idahosa/.

City Harvest Church. "The City Harvest Story." CHCSA. https://www.chc.org.sg/the-city-harvest-story/.

Clark, Matthew. "Contemporary Pentecostal Leadership: The Apostolic Faith Mission of South Africa as Case Study." *Cyberjournal for Pentecostal Charismatic Research* 16 (January 2007): n.p.

Clemmons, Ithiel. "Charles Harrison Mason." In *New International Dictionary of Pentecostal and Charismatic Movements*, edited by Stanley M. Burgess and Eduard M. van der Maas, 865–866. Grand Rapids: Zondervan, 2002.

Clifton, Shane. *Pentecostal Churches in Transition: Analyzing the Developing Ecclesiology of the Assemblies of God of Australia*. Leiden: Brill, 2009.

Clinton, J. Robert. *Leadership Emergence Theory: A Self-Study Manual for Analyzing the Development of a Christian Leader*. Altadena, CA: Barnabas Resources, 1989.

———. *The Making of a Leader: Recognizing the Lessons and Stages of Leadership Development*. 2nd ed. Colorado Springs: NavPress, 2012.

Coleman, Simon. "The Faith Movement: A Global Religious Culture." *Culture and Religion* 3, no. 1 (2002): 3–19.

Collins, James M. *Exorcism and Deliverance Ministry in the Twentieth Century: An Analysis of the Practice and Theology of Exorcism in Modern Western Christianity*. Eugene, OR: Wipf & Stock, 2009.

Collins, Kenneth J. *John Wesley: A Theological Journey*. Nashville: Abingdon, 2003.

Conger, Jay A., and Rabindra N. Kanungo, ed. *Charismatic Leadership: The Elusive Factor in Organizational Effectiveness*. San Francisco: Jossey-Bass, 1988.

Conger, Jay A. "The Dark Side of Leadership." *Organizational Dynamics* 19, no. 2 (1990): 44–55. https://doi.org/10.1016/0090-2616(90)90070-6.

Coulter, Dale M. "The Whole Gospel of the Whole Person: Ontology, Affectivity, and Sacramentality." *Pneuma: The Journal of the Society for Pentecostal Studies* 35, no. 2 (2013): 157–161.

Creech, Joe. "Visions of Glory: The Place of the Azusa Street Revival in Pentecostal History." *Church History* 65 (Spring 1996): 405–424.

Crowther, Steven S. "Integral Biblical Leadership." *Journal of Biblical Perspectives in Leadership* 3, no. 2 (2011): 60–76.

Czövek, Tamás. *Three Seasons of Charismatic Leadership: A Literary-Critical and Theological Interpretation of the Narrative of Saul, David and Solomon*. Milton Keynes, UK: Paternoster, 2006.

da Silva, Vagner Gonçalves. "Neo-Pentecostalism and Afro-Brazilian Religions: Explaining the Attacks on Symbols of the African Religious Heritage in Contemporary Brazil," translated by David Allan Rodgers. *Mana* 3 (2007): n.p. http://socialsciences.scielo.org/pdf/s_mana/v3nse/scs_a03.pdf.

Dake, Finis. "The Second Coming of Christ." *The Elim Evangel and Foursquare Revivalist* 10, 20 (September 13, 1929): 318.

Dallimore, Arnold. *The Life of Edward Irving: The Forerunner of the Charismatic Movement*. Edinburgh: Banner of Truth, 1983.

Daniels, David D. "Charles Harrison Mason: The Interracial Impulse in Early Pentecostalism." In *Portraits of a Generation: Early Pentecostal Leaders*, edited by James R. Goff and Grant Wacker, 256. Fayetteville: University of Arkansas Press, 2002.

Daniels, Michael A., and Gary J. Greguras. "Exploring the Nature of Power Distance." *Journal of Management* 40, no. 5 (2014): 1202–1229.

Dawes, Charles T. D. "The Jesus Prayer for Pentecostals: A Fresh Proposal for Spiritual Formation in the Pentecostal Church." D.Min. diss., George Fox Evangelical Seminary, 2013.

Day, David V. "Leadership Development." In *The SAGE Handbook of Leadership*, edited by Alan Bryman, David Collinson, Keith Grint, Brad Jackson, and Mary Uhl-Bien, 39–50. London: Sage Publications, 2011.

Day, David V., and Michelle M. Harrison. "A Multilevel, Identity-Based Approach to Leadership Development." *Human Resource Management Review* 17 (2007): 360–373.

Day, David V., Michelle M. Harrison, and Stanley M. Halpin. *An Integrative Approach to Leader Development: Connecting Adult Development, Identity and Expertise*. Milton Park, UK: Routledge/Taylor & Francis Group, 2009.

Dempster, Murray A., Byron D. Klaus, and Douglas Peterson, ed. *Called and Empowered: Global Mission in Pentecostal Perspective*. Peabody, MA: Hendrickson, 1991.

DeVries, Brian A. "Divine Empowerment: The Holy Spirit and Church Revitalization." *In die Skriflig/In the Writing* 47, no. 1 (2015): 1–8.

Dieter, Melvin E. *The Holiness Revival of the Nineteenth Century*. Metuchen, NJ: The Scarecrow Press, 1980.

Dodd, Brian J. *Empowered Church Leadership: Ministry in the Spirit According to Paul*. Downers Grove: InterVarsity Press, 2003.

Dodson, Michael. "Pentecostals, Politics and Public Space in Latin America." In *Power, Politics and Pentecostals in Latin America*, edited by Edward L. Cleary and Hanna W. Stewart-Gambino. Boulder, CO: Westview Press, 1997.

Drucker, Peter F. *The Practice of Management*. London: Heinemann, 1955.

Easter, John L. "Under the Mango Tree: Pentecostal Leadership Training in Africa." *Pneuma Africa Journal* 1, no. 1 (2013): 1–22.

Elwell, Walter A., ed. "Pastor." *Baker Encyclopedia of the Bible*. Vol. 2. Grand Rapids: Baker, 1988.

"Empowered21 Global Council." https://empowered21.com/about/global-leaders/.

Engh, Michael E. "'A Multiplicity and Diversity of Faiths': Religion's Impact on Los Angeles and the Urban West, 1890–1940." *The Western Historical Quarterly* 28, no. 4 (1997): 480.

Eskelin, Neil. *The New ORU: Empowered for the 21st Century*. Tulsa: ORU Press, 2018.

Espinosa, Gaston. "Francisco Olazábal: Charisma, Power, and Faith Healing in the Borderlands." In *Portraits of a Generation: Early Pentecostal Leaders*, edited by James R. Goff and Grant Wacker, 179. Fayetteville: University of Arkansas Press, 2002.

———. "Latino Pentecostal Healing in the North American Borderlands." In *Global Pentecostal and Charismatic Healing*, edited by Candy Gunther Brown, 135. Oxford: Oxford University Press, 2011.

Faupel, D. William. "Theological Influences on the Teachings and Practices of John Alexander Dowie." *Pneuma: The Journal of the Society for Pentecostal Studies* 29 (2007): 227.

Feller, Jeremy Amos. "Spirit-Filled Discipleship: Spiritual Formation for Pentecostal Leadership." D.Theo. diss., University of South Africa, 2015.

Feller, Jeremy, and Christo Lombaard. "Spiritual Formation Towards Pentecostal Leadership as Discipleship." *KOERS: Bulletin for Christian Scholarship* 83, no. 1 (2018): 1–12.

Firth, David G. "The Spirit and Leadership: Testimony, Empowerment and Purpose." In *Presence, Power and Promise: The Role of the Spirit of God in the Old Testament*, edited by David G. Firth and Paul D. Wegner. Downers Grove: IVP Academic, 2011.

Fisher, David. *The 21st Century Pastor: A Vision Based on the Ministry of Paul*. Grand Rapids: Zondervan, 1996.

Flower, J. R. "The Bride of Christ." *The Pentecost 2*, nos. 11–12 (November–December 1910): 10.

Fogarty, Stephen G. "The Dark Side of Charismatic Leadership." *Australian Pentecostal Studies* 13 (2010): 7–20.

Fortunado-Sanchez, Esmeralda, and Thomas M. Landy. "El Shaddai and the Charismatic Transformation of Philippine Catholicism." Catholic & Cultures, S.J. Center for Religion, Ethics and Culture, College of the Holy Cross, n.p.. https://www.catholicsandcultures. org/philippines-el-shaddai-serves-largest-population-charismatic-followers.

Foster, Richard. *Celebration of Discipline: The Path to Spiritual Growth*. San Francisco: Harper, 1978.

Fountain, A. K. "An Investigation into Successful Leadership Transitions in the Old Testament." *Asian Journal of Pentecostal Studies* 7, no. 2 (2004): 187–204.

Francis (Pope), quoting Cardinal Suenens. In "Address of His Holiness Pope Francis to the Renewal in the Holy Spirit Movement." *The Holy See*, July 3, 2015. https://www.vatican. va/content/francesco/it/speeches/2015/july/documents/papa-francesco_20150703_ movimento-rinnovamento-spirito.html.

French, John R. P., Jr., and Bertram Raven. "The Bases of Social Power." In *Studies in Social Power*, edited by Dorwin P. Cartwright, 150–167. Ann Arbor: University of Michigan, 1959.

French, Talmadge Leon. "Early Oneness Pentecostalism, Garfield Thomas Haywood, and the Interracial Pentecostal Assemblies of the World." Ph.D. diss., University of Birmingham, 2011.

Freston, Paul, ed. *Evangelical Christianity and Democracy in Latin America: Evangelical Christianity and Democracy in the Global South*. New York: Oxford University Press, 2008.

Garlock, Ruthanne. *Fire in His Bones: The Story of Benson Idahosa*. Tulsa: Praise Books, 1998.

Garrard, David J. "Ezekiel H. Guti." In *New International Dictionary of Pentecostal and Charismatic Movements*, edited by Stanley M. Burgess and Eduard M. van der Maas, 683. Grand Rapids: Zondervan, 2002.

————. "Leadership Versus the Congregation in the Pentecostal-Charismatic Movement," *Journal of the European Pentecostal Theological Association* 29 (2009), 90–103.

Garrard, Virginia. "Hidden in Plain Sight: Dominion Theology, Spiritual Warfare, and Violence in Latin America." *Religions* 11, no. 648 (2020). doi:10.3390/rel11120648.

Garrard-Burnett, Virginia. "Stop Suffering?: *The Iglesia Universal del Reino de Dios* in the United States" In *Conversion of a Continent: Contemporary Religious Change in Latin America*, edited by Timothy Steigenga and Edward L. Cleary, 218–238. Ithaca, NY: Rutgers University Press, 2007. https://doi.org/10.36019/9780813544021-012.

———. "Neo-Pentecostalism and Prosperity Theology in Latin America: A Religion for Late Capitalist Society." *Iberoamericana: Nordic Journal of Latin American and Caribbean Studies* 42, nos. 1–2 (2012): 21–34.

Gary, Jay. "Spirit Empowered Leadership: Exploring Three Dimensions." *Spiritus: ORU Journal of Theology* 5, no. 2 (2020): 235–251.

Gee, Donald. *The Pentecostal Movement*, 117–118. Quoted in Keith Warrington, Pentecostal Theology: *A Theology of Encounter*. London: T&T Clark, 2008.

Geivett, R. Douglas, and Holly Pivec. *A New Apostolic Reformation? A Biblical Response to a Worldwide Movement*. Wooster: Weaver Book Company, 2014.

Genischen, Hans-Werner. "Rhenius, Carl Theophilus Ewald," *Biographical Dictionary of Christian Missions*, edited by Gerald H. Anderson, 565. New York: Macmillan Reference USA, 1998.

Geoffrion, Timothy C. *The Spirit-Led Leader: Nine Leadership Practices and Soul Principles*. Herndon, VA: The Alban Institute, 2005.

George, Carl F. *Prepare Your Church for the Future*. Tarrytown, NY: Fleming H. Revell, 1991.

Gifford, Paul. *African Christianity: Its Publica Role*. Bloomington: Indiana University Press, 1989.

———. *Ghana's New Christianity: Pentecostalism in a Globalizing African Economy*. Bloomington: Indiana University Press, 2004.

———. "Healing in African Pentecostalism: The 'Victorious Living' of David Oyedepo." In *Global Pentecostal, and Charismatic Healing*, edited by Candy Gunther Brown, 253. New York: Oxford University Press, 2011.

Goff, James R., Jr. "Charles F. Parham and His Role in the Development of the Pentecostal Movement: A Reevaluation." *Kansas History* 7 (Autumn 1984): 232.

———. *Fields White unto Harvest: Charles F. Parham and the Missionary Origins of Pentecostalism*. Fayetteville: University of Arkansas Press, 1988.

Gohr, Glenn W. "Benedictus 'Benny' Hinn." In *New International Dictionary of Pentecostal and Charismatic Movements*, edited by Stanley M. Burgess and Eduard M. van der Maas, 714. Grand Rapids: Zondervan, 2002.

———. "Lillian Trasher: Serving the Widows and Orphans of Egypt," AG News. December 23, 2021. n.p. https://news.ag.org/en/articles/news/2021/12/this%20week%20in%20ag%20history%20dec%2021%201935.

Golder, Morris E. *The Life and Works of Bishop Garfield Thomas Haywood, 1880–1931*. Indianapolis: Indiana University, 1977.

Gordon, Raymond D. "Conceptualizing leadership with respect to its historical–contextual antecedents to power," *The Leadership Quarterly* 13, no. 2 (April 2002): 151–167.

Habib, Usman I. "A New Paradigm of Leadership Development: Church of God Mission International." Ph.D. diss., University of Manchester, 2014.

Hamm, M. Dennis. "Gifts of Healing." In *The Anchor Bible Dictionary*, edited by David Noel Freedman. Vol. 3. New York: Doubleday, 1992.

Hammond, Frank, and Ida Mae Hammond. *Pigs in the Parlor: A Practical Guide to Deliverance.* Kirkwood, MO: Impact Christian Books, 1990.

Hamon, Bill. *Apostles, Prophets and the Coming Moves of God: God's End-Time Plans for His Church and Planet Earth.* Shippensburg, PA: Destiny Image, 1997.

Harnack, Adolf von. *The Mission and Expansion of Christianity in the First Three Centuries,* edited and translated by James Moffatt. Gloucester, MA: Peter Smith, 1972.

Harrell, David Edwin, Jr. *All Things Are Possible: The Healing and Charismatic Revivals in Modern America.* Bloomington, IN: Indiana University Press, 1979.

————. *Oral Roberts: An American Life.* Bloomington, IN: Indiana University Press, 1985.

Harrison, R. K. "Healing." *Interpreter's Dictionary of the Bible: An Illustrated Encyclopedia.* Vol. 2. Nashville: Abingdon, 1962.

Hendrix, Olan. *Three Dimensions of Leadership.* St. Charles, IL: ChurchSmart Resources, 2000.

Heuser, Andreas. "Megachurches, Dominion Theology and Development." In *Does Religion Make a Difference? Religious NGO's in International Development Collaboration,* 243–262. Baden-Baden: Nomos, 2020. https://edoc.unibas.ch/76720/.

Heuser, Roger, and Byron Klaus. "Charismatic Leadership Theory: A Shadow Side Confessed." *Pneuma: The Journal of the Society for Pentecostal Studies* 20, no. 2 (1998): 161–174.

Hewett, J. A. "Office of Apostle." In *New International Dictionary of Pentecostal and Charismatic Movements,* edited by Stanley M. Burgess and Eduard M. van der Maas, 319. Grand Rapids: Zondervan, 2002.

"Hillsong Leader Brian Houston Breaks Silence on Pedophile Father." *The Daily Telegraph,* October 13, 2014. https://www.dailytelegraph.com.au/news/nsw/hillsong-leader-brian-houston-breaks-silence-on-paedophile-father-it-was-wrong-not-to-report-him/news-story/ 6530b4352962bc835e8fb2f906d657cf;

"Hillsong's Brian Houston Resigns from Megachurch." *The Guardian,* March 23, 2022. https://www.theguardian.com/world/2022/mar/23/hillsongs-brian-houston-resigns-from-megachurch.

Hofstadter, Richard. *Anti-Intellectualism in American Life.* New York: Vintage, 1963.

Hofstede, G. H. "National Culture." 2013. http://geert-hofstede.com/national-culture.html.

Hofstede, Geert H. *Culture's Consequences: Comparing Values, Behaviors, Institutions and Organizations across Nations.* Thousand Oaks, CA: Sage, 2001.

Hofstede, Geert, Jan Hofstede, and Michael Minkov. *Cultures and Organizations: Software of the Mind.* 3rd ed. New York: McGraw-Hill, 2010.

Hollenweger, Walter J. *Pentecostalism: Origins and Developments Worldwide.* Peabody, MA: Hendrickson, 1997.

Hoppe, Leslie. *Joshua, Judges, With an Excursus on Charismatic Leadership in Israel (Old Testament Message).* Wilmington, DE: Michael Glazier, 1982.

House, R. J., M. Javidan, P. Hanges, P. Dorfman, and V. Gupta, ed. *Culture, Leadership and Organizations: The GLOBE Study of 62 Societies.* Thousand Oaks, CA: Sage, 2004.

House, Robert J. "A 1976 Theory of Charismatic Leadership." In *Leadership: The Cutting Edge*, edited by J. G. Hunt and L. L. Larson. Carbondale, IL: Southern Illinois University, 1977.

House, Robert J., and Jane M. Howell. "Personality and Charismatic Leadership." *Leadership Quarterly* 3, no. 2 (1992): 81–108.

Howard, Linda. "A New Beginning." *Charisma* (April 1984): 38–43.

Huizing, Russell. "Bringing Christ to the Table of Leadership: Moving Towards a Theology of Leadership." *Journal of Applied Christian Leadership* 5, no. 2 (2011): 58–75.

Hunt, Stephen, ed. *Christian Millenarianism: From the Early Church to Waco*. New York: New York University Press, 2001.

Hunter, Harold D. "Pentecostal Social Engagement: Excerpts from Around the World." In *Engaging the World: Christian Communities in Contemporary Global Societies*, edited by Afe Adogame, Janice McLean, and Anderson Jeremiah. Regnum Edinburgh Centenary Series. Vol. 21. Minneapolis: Fortress Press, 2014.

Idahosa, B. A. *4 Facts You Need to Know*. Benin City: Gift-Prints Associates, 1995.

"Integrity." In *Cambridge English Dictionary*. https://dictionary.cambridge.org/us/dictionary/english/integrity.

International Pentecostal Holiness Church. "Tribute to Vinson Synan." https://iphc.org/gso/2020/03/16/celebrating-dr-vinson-synan/.

Irons, Kendra Weddle. "Phoebe Palmer: Chosen, Tried, Triumphant: An Examination of Her Calling in Light of Current Research." *Methodist History* 37, no. 1 (October 1998): 28–36.

Irvin, Dale T. "Pentecostal Historiography and Global Christianity: Rethinking the Question of Origins." *Pneuma: The Journal of the Society for Pentecostal Studies* 27, 1 (Spring 2005): 40–41.

Isgrigg, Daniel D. "Oral Roberts: A Man of the Spirit." *Spiritus: ORU Journal of Theology* 3, no. 2 (2018): 325–350.

———. "Toward Spirit-Empowered Leadership Distinctives: A Literature Review." *Spiritus: ORU Journal of Theology* 5, no. 2 (2020): 199–216.

Isichei, Elizabeth. *A History of Christianity in Africa from Antiquity to the Present*. London: SPCK, 1995.

Iyawe, V. I. *Archbishop Benson Idahosa: Achievements and Legacies of a Colossus*. Benin City: Gift-Prints Associates, 1999.

Jackson, Bill. *The Quest for the Radical Middle: A History of the Vineyard*. Cape Town: Vineyard International Publishing, 1999.

Jackson, John. "Pastorpreneur: Tired of Playing It Safe, This Pastor Hears a Higher (and Harder) Calling." *Leadership Journal* 24, no. 4 (Fall 2003): 59–65. https://www.christianitytoday.com/pastors/2003/fall/7.59.html.

———. *Pastorpreneur: Pastors and Entrepreneurs Answer the Call*. Friendswood, TX: Baxter Press, 2003.

———. *Pastorpreneur: Creative Ideas for Birthing Spiritual Life in Your Community*. Colorado Springs: Biblica Publishing, 2011.

———. *The Prevailing Church: Confronting the Five Giants of Culture*. Rocklin, CA: Jessup University Press, 2021.

Jackson, Thomas. *Works of John Wesley, Letters*. Vol. 12, Letter 416. Cited in Mark K. Olson. "John Wesley's Doctrine of Baptism with the Holy Spirit: An Exegetical Study." Wesleyscholar.com. https://wesleyscholar.com/john-wesley's-doctrine-of-the-baptism-with-the-holy-spirit-an-exegetical-study-part-two_ftn17.

Jacobs, Cindy. *The Voice of God*. Ventura, CA: Regal Books, 1995.

Jacobsen, Douglas. *Thinking in the Spirit: Theologies of the Early Pentecostal Movement*. Bloomington: Indiana University Press, 2003.

Jenkins, Philip. *The New Faces of Christianity: Believing the Bible in the Global South*. Oxford: Oxford University Press, 2006.

———. *The Next Christendom: The Coming of Global Christianity*. New York: Oxford Academic Press, 2011.

———. "South African Zionists, Notes from the Global South." *Christian Century* (June 14, 2011): 45.

Jennings, Mark Alan Charles. "Great Risk for the Kingdom: Pentecostal-Charismatic Growth Churches, Pastorpreneurs, and Neoliberalism." In *Multiculturalism and the Convergence of Faith and Practical Wisdom in Modern Society*, edited by Ana Maria Pascal, 236–248. Hershey, PA: IGI Global, 2017.

Johnson, Bob L., and Rickie D. Moore. "Soul Care for One and All: Pentecostal Theology and the Search for a More Expansive View of Spiritual Formation." *Journal of Pentecostal Theology* 26 (2017): 125–152.

Johnson, Dave. "Creating and Expanding a Research Culture at Pentecostal and Charismatic Seminaries and Graduate Schools in the Majority World." In *Pentecostal Theological Education in the Majority World: The Graduate and Post-Graduate Level*, edited by Dave Johnson and Rick Wadholm, Jr. Baguio City: Asia Pacific Theological Seminary Press, 2022.

Johnson, Todd M., and Ken R. Ross, ed. *Atlas of Global Christianity*. Edinburgh: Edinburgh University Press, 2009.

Joose, Paul. "Max Weber's Disciples: Theorizing the Charismatic Aristocracy." *Sociological Theory* 35, no. 4 (2017): 334–358.

Kalu, Ogbu. African *Pentecostalism: An Introduction*. New York: Oxford University Press, 2008.

Kanjamala, Augustine. *The Future of Christian Mission in India: Toward a New Paradigm for the Third Millennium*. Eugene, OR: Pickwick Publications, 2014.

Kärkkäinen, Veli-Matti. "Pentecostal Hermeneutics in the Making: On the Way from Fundamentalism to Postmodernism." *Journal of the European Pentecostal Theological Association* 18 (1998): 80.

———. "Church as Charismatic Fellowship: Ecclesiological Reflection from the Pentecostal-Roman Catholic Dialogue." *Journal of Pentecostal Theology* 18 (2001): 100–121.

Katola, Michael T., and Bernard Gechiko Nyabwari. "The Leadership Style of Jesus Christ in the New Testament and its Relevance for Africa." *International Journal of Political Science, Law and International Relations* 3, no. 2 (2013): 1–8.

Kessler, Volker. "Pitfalls in 'Biblical' Leadership." *Verbum et Ecclesia* 34, no. 1 (2013): 1–7.

Klaus, Byron D., and Loren O. Triplett. "National Leadership in Pentecostal Missions." In *Called and Empowered: Global Mission in Pentecostal Perspective*, edited by Murray A. Dempster, Byron D. Klaus, and Douglas Peterson, 236. Peabody, MA: Hendrickson, 1991.

Klaver, Miranda. "Pentecostal Pastorpreneurs and the Global Circulation of Authoritative Aesthetic Styles." *Culture and Religion: An Interdisciplinary Journal* 16, no. 2 (2015): 145–159.

Klein, Katherine J., and Robert J. House. "On Fire: Charismatic Leadership and Levels of Analysis." *Leadership Quarterly* 6, no. 2 (1995): 183–198.

King, Johnny. "G. T. Haywood." In *Brill's Encyclopedia of Global Pentecostalism*, edited by Michael Wilkinson, Connie Au, Jörg Haustein, and Todd M. Johnson, 277–278. Leiden: Brill, 2021.

Kingsley, Thomas. "The Televangelist Who Claimed to Heal Aids and Counted Premier League Stars among His Followers." *Independent*, February 13, 2023. https://www.independent.co.uk/news/uk/home-news/constance-marten-tb-joshua-mark-gordon-b2279954.html.

Knight, Henry. *From Aldersgate to Azusa Street: Wesleyan, Holiness, and Pentecostal Visions of the New Creation*. Eugene, OR: Pickwick, 2010.

Komives, Susan R., Julie E. Owen, Susan D. Longerbeam, Felicia C. Mainella, and Laura Osteen. "Developing a Leadership Identity: A Grounded Theory." *Journal of College Student Development* 46, no. 6 (November/December 2005): 593–611. https://doi.org/10.1353/csd.2005.0061.

Kommers, J. Hans. "Attaining the Correct Balance: Exploring the Challenges and Spirituality of Single Women Missionaries in the Victorian Era." *In die Skriflig* 54, no. 1 (2020): 1–9. https://www.scielo.org.za/pdf/ids/v54n1/37.pdf.

Kung, Hans. *Theology for the Third Millennium: An Ecumenical View*. New York: Doubleday, 1988.

Laguerre, Joshua C. "Can Leadership Be Developed by Applying Leadership Theories? An Examination of Three Theory-based Approaches to Leadership Development." Honors project, Rhode Island College, 2010.

Larbi, E. Kingsley. *Pentecostalism: The Eddies of Ghanian Christianity*. Accra: Centre for Pentecostal and Charismatic Studies. 2001.

———. "Peter Newman Anim." In *Dictionary of African Christian Biography*. N.d. https://dacb.org/stories/ghana/anim-peter/.

Larbi, Emmanuel Kingsley Kwabena. "The Development of Ghanaian Pentecostalism: A Study in the Appropriation of the Christian Gospel in Twentieth Century Ghana Setting with Special Reference to the Christ Apostolic Church, the Church of Pentecost, and the International Central Gospel Church." Ph.D. diss., University of Edinburgh, 1996.

Lee, Sang Yun. "The Kingdom of God in Korean Pentecostal Perspective." In *Global Renewal Christianity: Spirit-Empowered Movements, Past, Present and Future*. Vol. 1, Asia and Oceania, edited by Vinson Synan and Amos Yong. Lake Mary, FL: Charisma House, 2016.

———. "Yonggi Cho." In *Brill's Encyclopedia of Global Pentecostalism*, edited by Michael Wilkinson, Connie Au, Jörg Haustein, and Todd M. Johnson, 127. Leiden: Brill, 2021.

Lee, Young-hoon. "The Life and Ministry of Yonggi Cho and the Yoido Full Gospel Church." *Asian Journal of Pentecostal Studies* 7, no. 1 (2004): 3–20.

Levada, William J. "Origins." CNS Documentary Service 26, no. 5 (June 20, 1996): The Charism of Cardinal Suenens.

Levada, William J. "Pentecostal Catholics––A History of the Catholic Charismatic Renewal." Archdiocese of San Francisco, Catholic Charismatic Renewal. https://www.sfspirit.com/renewal-history.html.

LFS News. "Meet Eight Spiritual Sons of Oyedepo." August 22, 2020. https://lightfeatherstoriesw.home.blog/2020/08/22/men-of-god-mentored-by-bishop-david-oyedepo/.

Lindhardt, Martin. "Pentecostalism and Politics in Neoliberal Chile." *Iberoamericana. Nordic Journal of Latin American and Caribbean Studies* 42, nos. 1–2 (2012): 59–83.

———, ed. *Pentecostalism in Africa: Presence and Impact of Pneumatic Christianity in Postcolonial Societies*. Leiden: Brill, 2015.

Longenecker, Richard N. *New Testament Social Ethics for Today*. Grand Rapids: Eerdmans, 1984.

Lord, Robert G., and Rosalie J. Hall. "Identity, Deep Structure and the Development of Leadership Skill." *Leadership Quarterly* 16 (2005): 591–615.

Lukose, Wessly. *Contextual Missiology of the Spirit: Pentecostalism in Rajasthan, India*. Oxford, UK: Regnum Books International, 2013.

Lunenburg, Fred C. "Power and Leadership: An Influence Process." *International Journal of Management, Business, and Administration* 15, no. 1 (2012): 1–9.

Ma, Wonsuk. "When the Poor Are Fired-Up." *Transformation* 24, no. 1 (January 2007): 28–34.

———. "Theological Education in Pentecostal Churches in Asia." In *Handbook of Theological Education in World Christianity: Theological Perspectives—Regional Surveys—Ecumenical Trends*, edited by Dietrich Werner, David Esterline, Namsoon Kang, and Joshva Raja, 729–735. Oxford: Regnum Books International, 2010.

———. "The Tragedy of Spirit-Empowered Heroes: A Close Look at Samson and Saul." *Spiritus: ORU Journal of Theology* 2, no. 2 (2017): 23–38.

———. "The Future Growth of Global Christianity and Yoido Full Gospel Church: Its Potential Role in the New Context." *Great Commission Research Journal* 10, no. 1 (Fall 2018): 10–31.

———. "The Prophetic Servant: The Ideology of Spirit-Empowered Leaders." *Spiritus: ORU Journal of Theology* 5, no. 2 (2020): 217–234.

Macchia, Frank D. *Baptized in the Spirit: A Global Pentecostal Theology*. Grand Rapids: Zondervan, 2006.

———. "Spirit Baptism and Spiritual Formation: A Pentecostal Proposal." *Journal of Spiritual Formation and Soul Care* 13, no. 1 (2020): 44–61.

Malamat, Abraham. "Charismatic Leadership in the Book of Judges." In *Magnalia Dei, The Mighty Acts of God: Essays on the Bible and Archaeology in Memory of G. Ernest Wright*, edited by Frank Moore Cross, Werner E. Lemke, and Patrick D. Miller, Jr., 152–168. Garden City, NY: Doubleday, 1976.

Malcolm, Teresa. "March on Behalf of Macedo," *National Catholic Reporter* 32, no. 13 (January 26, 1996): 7.

Malphurs, Aubrey, and Will Mancini. *Building Leaders: Blueprints for Developing Leadership at Every Level of Your Church*. Grand Rapids: Baker, 2004.

Mansfield, Stephen, *Derek Prince: A Biography, Father, Statesman, Teacher and Leader*. Lake Mary, FL: Charisma House, 2005.

Markow, Frank A. "Calling and Leader Identity: Utilizing Narrative Analysis to Construct a Stage Model of Calling Development." Ph.D. diss., Regent University, 2007.

Markow, Franklin, and Truls Åkerlund. "Pentecostal Leadership: Exploring a Global Phenomenon." *Journal of Management, Spirituality and Religion* 20, no. 5 (2023): 526–50. https://10.51327/JHKQ5569.

Martin, David. *Tongues of Fire: The Explosion of Pentecostalism in Latin America*. Oxford: Blackwell, 1990.

———. *Pentecostalism: The World Their Parish*. Malden, MA: Blackwell, 2002.

Martin, Francis. "Gift of Healing." In *New International Dictionary of Pentecostal and Charismatic Movements*, edited by Stanley M. Burgess and Eduard M. van der Maas, 697. Grand Rapids: Zondervan, 2002.

Martin, Lee Roy. "Towards a Biblical Model of Pentecostal Prophetic Preaching." *Verbum et Ecclesia* 37, no. 1 (2015): 1–9.

———. "'You Shall Love the Lord with All Your Mind': The Necessity of an Educated Pentecostal Clergy." *Pharos Journal of Theology* 97 (2016): 2. https://www.pharosjot.com/uploads/7/1/6/3/7163688/pharos_article_15_vol_97_2016.pdf

Mattos, Paulo Ayres. "Edir Macedo." In *Brill's Encyclopedia of Global Pentecostalism*, edited by Michael Wilkinson, Connie Au, Jörg Haustein, and Todd M. Johnson, 401. Leiden: Brill, 2021.

Maxwell, David. *African Gifts of the Spirit: Pentecostalism and the Rise of a Zimbabwean Transnational Religious Movement*. Oxford: Oxford University Press, 2006.

Maxwell, John C. *The Irrefutable Laws of Leadership Workbook*. Nashville: Thomas Nelson, 1998.

Mayfield, Alex. "The Question of Power in African Pentecostalism." *Spiritus: ORU Journal of Theology* 3, no. 1 (2018): 87–107.

Mbefo, Luke N. *The True African: Impulses for Self-Affirmation*. Onitsha, Nigeria: Spiritan Publications, 2001. https://archive.org/stream/trueafricanimpul00mbef/trueafricanimpul00mbef_djvu.txt.

McCauley, Cynthia D., and Ellen Van Velsor, ed. *Handbook for Leadership Development*. San Francisco: Jossey-Bass, 2004.

McCauley, John F. "Africa's New Big Man Rule? Pentecostalism and Patronage in Ghana." *African Affairs* 112, no. 446 (2012): 1–21.

———. "Pentecostalism as an Informal Political Institution: Experimental Evidence from Ghana," *Politics and Religion* 7 (2014): 765–770.

McClelland, David C. *Power: The Inner Experience*. New York: Irvington, 1975.

McClung, L. Grant, Jr., ed. *Azusa Street and Beyond: Pentecostal Missions and Church Growth in the Twentieth Century*. South Plainfield, NJ: Bridge Publishing, 1986.

McClung, L. Grant. "Evangelism." In *New International Dictionary of Pentecostal and Charismatic Movements*, edited by Stanley M. Burgess and Eduard M. van der Maas, 617. Grand Rapids: Zondervan, 2002.

McClymond, Michael. "Granville Oral Roberts." In *Brill's Encyclopedia of Global Pentecostalism*, edited by Michael Wilkinson, Connie Au, Jörg Haustein, and Todd M. Johnson, 553-554. Leiden: Brill, 2021.

————. "Kenneth Hagin." In *Brill's Encyclopedia of Global Pentecostalism*, edited by Michael Wilkinson, Connie Au, Jörg Haustein, and Todd M. Johnson, 270. Leiden: Brill, 2021.

McCulley, Murriell G. *Beyond the Classroom: Teach for Life*. Springfield, MO: Life Publishers International, 2008.

McDonald, Eric. "Teaching Pastors to Read." *Christianity Today* (February 5, 2001): 80.

McGee, Gary B. *"This Gospel...Shall Be Preached": A History and Theology of Assemblies of God Foreign Missions to 1959*. Springfield, MO: Gospel Publishing House, 1986.

————. "Pentecostal Mission Strategies: A Historical Review." *Missionalia* 20, no. 1 (1992): 22.

McGee, Gary B. "H. A. Baker." In *New International Dictionary of Pentecostal and Charismatic Movements*, edited by Stanley M. Burgess and Eduard M. van der Maas, 352. Grand Rapids: Zondervan, 2002.

————.'The Lord's Pentecostal Missionary Movement': The Restorationism Impulse of a Modern Mission Movement." *Asian Journal of Pentecostal Studies* 8, no. 1 (2005): 57–58.

McLoughlin, William G. *Modern Revivalism: Charles Grandison Finney to Billy Graham*. New York: Ronald Press, 1959.

McPherson, Aimee Semple. "Topics of the Day." *Bridal Call Foursquare* (May 1918): 7.

————. "Behold I Come Quickly." *Word and Work* 40, no. 29 (September 21, 1918): 4.

————. "The Commissary." *Bridal Call Foursquare* 24 (June 1929): 6.

Menoud, P. H. "Life and Organization of the Church," *The Interpreter's Dictionary of the Bible*. Vol. 1. Nashville: Abingdon, 1962.

Menzies, Glen W. "The First Fifty Years of the Society for Pentecostal Studies: A Brief History." *Pneuma: The Journal of the Society for Pentecostal Studies* 42, nos. 3–4 (2020): 335–369.

Miller, Donald E., and Tetsunao Yamamori. *Global Pentecostalism: The New Face of Christian Social Engagement*. Berkeley: University of California Press, 2007.

Milosevic, Ivana, and A. Erin Bass. "Revisiting Weber's Charismatic Leadership: Learning from the Past and Looking to the Future." *Journal of Management History* 20, no. 2 (2014): 224–240.

Ministry Tools Research Center. "FAQ About Our Spiritual Gift Mix." https://mintools. com/spiritual-gifts-mix.htm.

Mohammed, Bakheeta Abd El-Aziz, Yasser Mohamed Badereldin, and Amera Ezzat Abd El-Naser. "Psychological Aspects Among Children and Adolescents of Orphanages at Assiut City." *Assiut Scientific Nursing Journal* 6, no. 14 (August 2018): 88–98.

Mohr, Adam. "Out of Zion into Philadelphia and West Africa: Faith Tabernacle Congregation, 1897–1925." *Pneuma: The Journal of the Society for Pentecostal Studies* 32, no. 1 (2010): 56–79.

Mohr, Adam. "Zionism and Aladura's Shared Genealogy in John Alexander Dowie." *Religion* 45, no. 2 (2015): 239–251. https://www.tandfonline.com/doi/abs/10.1080/004872 1X.2014.992105.

Moore, S. David. "Shepherding Movement." In *New International Dictionary of Pentecostal and Charismatic Movements*, edited by Stanley M. Burgess and Eduard van der Maas, 1060–1062. Grand Rapids: Zondervan, 2002.

Morse, Mary Kate. "Evangelism, Discipleship, and Spiritual Formation." Missio Alliance. https://www.missioalliance.org/evangelism-discipleship-and-spiritual-formation-which-is-what/.

Moskala, Jiří. "The Holy Spirit in the Hebrew Scriptures." *Journal of the Adventist Theological Society* 24, no. 2 (2013): 18–58.

Muindi, Samuel W. "The Nature and Significance of Prophecy in Pentecostal-Charismatic Experience: An Empirical-Biblical Study." Ph.D. diss., University of Birmingham, 2012.

Munroe, Myles. *Becoming a Leader: Everyone Can Do It*. Landham, MD: Pneuma Life Publishing, 1993.

Mwenje, Judith. "An Investigation of the Leadership Styles of Pentecostal Church Leaders in Zimbabwe." *African Journal of Business Management* 10, no. 3 (2016): 55–74.

Myland, David Wesley. *The Latter Rain Covenant: And Pentecostal Power* 1910 reprint, ed. Donald W. Dayton, *Three Early Pentecostal Tracts*. New York: Garland Press, 1985.

Nanez, Rick M. *Full Gospel, Fractured Minds? A Call to Use God's Gift of the Intellect*. Grand Rapids: Zondervan, 2005.

Napier, B. D. "Sheep." *The Interpreter's Dictionary of the Bible*. Vol. 4. Nashville: Abingdon, 1962.

Newberg, Eric N. *The Pentecostal Mission in Palestine: The Legacy of Pentecostal Zionism*. Eugene, OR: Pickwick, 2012.

Newberg, Eric N. "Stanley Milton Burgess and the Artifacts of Renewal." In *Children of the Calling: Essays in Honor of Stanley M. Burgess and Ruth V. Burgess*, edited by Eric Nelson Newberg and Lois E. Olena, 10–19. Eugene, OR: Pickwick, 2014.

———. *Charles G. Finney and the Civil War: How Evangelical Religion Affects American Politics*. Lewiston, NY: Edwin Mellen Press, 2017.

Noronha, Konrad. "Jesus' Charismatic Leadership." Center for Pastoral Management, De Nobili College, Pune, India. (2019): 1–8.

Nwaigo, Ferdinand. "Authority and Charisma in the Bible." *Biblical Studies Journal* 1, no. 1 (2019): 1–12.

Obadan, P. *The Legend: Archbishop Prof. Benson Idahosa, 11th September 1938–12th March 1998*. Benin City: Glopet Limited, 2006.

Oden, Thomas C., ed. *Phoebe Palmer: Selected Writings*. New York: Paulist Press, 1988.

Ofereau, Julien M. "Paul's Leadership Ethos in 2 Corinthians 10–13: A Critique of 21st Century Pentecostal Leadership." *Australasian Pentecostal Studies* 13 (2010): 21–40.

Ojo, M. A. *The End-Time Army: Charismatic Movements in Modern Nigeria*. Trenton: Africa World Press, 2006.

Okoranta, Grace Ogechukwu. "The Impact of Leadership Styles in the Pentecostal Churches on the Growth of the Gospel in Kaduna State." Master's thesis, Ahmadu Bello University, Zaria, Nigeria, 2015.

Okpara, Daniel. *15 Success Habits of Bishop David Oyedepo*. St. Peters, MD: Better Life Media, 2016.

Oliphant, Margaret. *The Life of Edward Irving*. 5th ed. London: Hurst and Blackett, 1862.

Olson, Jonathan. "The Quest for Legitimacy: American Pentecostal Scholars and the Quandaries of Academic Pursuit." *Intermountain West Journal of Religious Studies* 4, no. 1 (2012): 93–115.

Olson, Roger E. "Pentecostalism's Dark Side: Troublesome Teachings and Practices." *Christian Century* 123, no. 5 (2006): 27–30.

Onyinah, Opoku. *Apostles and Prophets: The Ministry of Apostles and Prophets throughout the Generations*. Eugene, OR: Wipf & Stock, 2022.

———. *Pentecostal Exorcism: Witchcraft and Demonology in Ghana*. Leiden: Brill, 2012.

Openshaw, Kathleen. "Universal Church of the Kingdom of God." In *Brill's Encyclopedia of Global Pentecostalism*, edited by Michael Wilkinson, Connie Au, Jörg Haustein, and Todd M. Johnson, 645. Leiden: Brill, 2021.

O'Reggio, Trevor. "The Rise of the New Apostolic Reformation and Its Implications for Adventist Eschatology." *Journal of the Adventist Theological Society* 23, no. 2 (2012): 131–160.

"Oral Roberts University Gives Its Law School to CBN University." *Christianity Today*, February 7, 1986. https://www.christianitytoday.com/ct/1986/february-7/oral-roberts-university-gives-its-law-school-to-cbn.html.

"Oral Roberts University O. W. Coburn Law School | Tulsa." Lawyer.com. https://www.lawyer.com/lawschool/lawschool.php?lid=LAW259.

Orgu, Cletus C. "The Holy Spirit and Power in Luke-Acts and their Significance for Christian Service." *Kampala International University Journal of Humanities* 5, no. 2 (2020): 355–359.

"ORU Vision." Oral Roberts University. https://oru.edu/news/oru-general-info-media-kit.php#:~:text=God%20gave%20the%20following%20commission,uttermost%20bounds%20of%20the%20earth.

Osborne, Ryan. "'We Are Deeply Sorry': Gateway Church Cancels Major Conference in Wake of Robert Morris Resignation." WFFA Dallas, August 15, 2024. https://www.wfaa.com/article/news/local/gateway-church-robert-morris-allegations-gateway-conference-canceled-investigation-tony-evans/287-07160d0d-3d05-4058-b4c4-c3df32cb0d5a.

"Our History." *Global Servants*. https://globalservants.org/our-history.

Oyedepo, David. *Exploring the Secrets of Success*. Lagos, Nigeria: Dominion Publishing House, 1998.

———. *Exploits in Ministry*. Lagos, Nigeria: Dominion Publishing House. 2006.

Ozman, Agnes. "The First One to Speak in Tongues." *Latter Rain Evangel* (January 1909): 2.

Pace, Enzo. "The Catholic Charismatic Movement in Global Pentecostalism." *Religions* 11, no. 351 (July 2020): 1–19.

Parham, Sarah. *The Life of Charles F. Parham*. Baxter Springs, KS: Apostolic Faith Bible College, 1930.

Park, Myung Soo. "David Yonggi Cho and International Pentecostal/Charismatic Movements." *Journal Pentecostal Theology* 12, no. 1 (2003): 107–128.

Parker, Pierson. "Teacher." In *The Interpreter's Dictionary of the Bible*. Vol. 4. Nashville: Abingdon, 1962.

Parsons, Talcott. "Introduction." In Max Weber, *The Theory of Social and Economic Organization*, edited by Talcott Parsons, translated by A. M. Henderson and Talcott Parsons. New York: The Free Press, 1947.

Patterson, Stan. "A Synthesis of Leadership Principles Emerging from the New Testament." *Faculty Publications*. Andrews University, Center for Adventist Research. Paper 12 (2010): 1–23.

Payne, Leanne. *Heaven's Calling: A Memoir of One Soul's Steep Ascent*. Grand Rapids: Baker, 2000.

"The Pentecostal Movement." *Confidence* 2, no. 6 (June 1909): 8.

Perkin, Hazel W. "Education." In *Baker Encyclopedia of the Bible*, edited by Walter A. Elwell. Vol. 1. Grand Rapids: Baker, 1988.

Petersen, Douglas. "The Azusa Street Mission and Latin American Pentecostalism." *International Bulletin of Missionary Research* 39, no. 2 (2006): 66–67.

Pew Research Center. "Spirit and Power: 10 Country Survey of Pentecostals." October 5, 2006. https://www.pewforum.org/2006/10/05/spirit-and-power/.

Piaget, Jean. *The Moral Judgment of the Child*. New York: Free Press, 1932.

Pik, Lim Siew. "Toxicity in Clergy Leadership: An Emerging Phenomenon of Leaders' Personal Power in the Pentecostal Charismatic Church." *Journal of Religious Leadership* 15, no. 1 (2016): 31–54.

Piper, Otto A. "Gospel (Message)." *Interpreter's Dictionary of the Bible: An Illustrated Encyclopedia*. Vol. 2. Nashville: Abingdon, 1962.

Pizzolitto, Ella, Ida Verna and Michellina Venditti. "Authoritarian Leadership Styles and Performance: A Systematic Literature Review and Research Agenda." *Management Review Quarterly* 73 (2023): 841–871; https://doi.org/10.1007/s11301-022-00263-y.

Plüss, Jean Daniel. "Walter J. Hollenweger." In *Brill's Encyclopedia of Global Pentecostalism Online*, edited by Michael Wilkinson, Connie Au, Jörg Haustein, and Todd M. Johnson. http://dx.doi.org.oralroberts.idm.oclc.org/10.1163/2589-3807_EGPO_COM_043822 2021.

Poloma, Margaret. "The Millenarianism of the Pentecostal Movement." In *Christian Millenariansim from the Early Church to Waco*, edited by Stephen Hunt, 169. Bloomington: Indiana University Press, 2001.

Porterfield, Amanda. *Healing in the History of Christianity*. Oxford: Oxford University Press, 2005.

Price, Terry L. *Understanding Ethical Failures in Leadership*. Cambridge: Cambridge University Press, 2006.

Prince, Derek. *Life's Bitter Pool*. Harpenden, 1984.

Prince, Derek. "Home to Jerusalem, Part 9, Derek Prince's Life Story." Filmed 2001 in Jerusalem. https://www.youtube.com/watch?v=AEOtOkEPBII.

———. *Jubilee 1995 Celebration: 50th Year in Ministry*, 1–23.

———. *Blessing or Curse: You Can Choose*. 3rd ed. Baldock: Derek Prince Ministries-UK, 2007.

Quayesi-Amakye, Joseph. "Prophetic Practices in Contemporary Pentecostalism in Ghana." *Canadian Journal of Pentecostal Charismatic Christianity* 6 (January 2015): 43–69.

Rabey, Steve. "Editor Decries Pentecostal Shrugs over Moral Failures." *Christian Century* (June 15, 2010): 117–118.

Regent University. "Tribute to Vinson Synan." https://www.regent.edu/news/regent-mourns-the-loss-of-theologian-dr-vinson-synan/.

Rengstorf, Karl Heinrich. "διδάσκω." In *Theological Dictionary of the New Testament*, edited by Gerhard Kittel. Vol. 2. Grand Rapids: Eerdmans, 1964.

Rigaud, Oliver. "A Christian Servant Leadership Model and Training for the Adventist Church in France." D.Min. thesis, Andrews University, 2012.

Riss, R. M. "Kenneth E. Hagin." In *New International Dictionary of Pentecostal and Charismatic Movements*, edited by Stanley M. Burgess and Eduard M. van der Maas, 687. Grand Rapids: Zondervan, 2002.

Rivera, Joan Benek. "Visionary Versus Crisis-Induced Charismatic Leadership: An Experimental Test." Ph.D. diss., Texas Tech University, 1994.

Robeck, Cecil M., Jr. "Aimee Semple McPherson." In *New International Dictionary of Pentecostal and Charismatic Movements*, edited by Stanley M. Burgess and Eduard M. van der Maas, 856–59. Grand Rapids: Zondervan, 2002.

———. "Azusa Street Revival." In *New International Dictionary of Pentecostal and Charismatic Movements*, edited by Stanley M. Burgess and Eduard M. van der Maas, 344–350. Grand Rapids: Zondervan, 2002.

———. "Gift of Prophecy." In *New International Dictionary of Pentecostal and Charismatic Movements*, edited by Stanley M. Burgess and Eduard M. van der Maas, 999–1012. Grand Rapids: Zondervan, 2002.

———. "Kilian McDonnell." In *New International Dictionary of Pentecostal and Charismatic Movements*, edited by Stanley M. Burgess and Eduard M. van der Maas, 853. Grand Rapids: Zondervan, 2002.

———. "Russell Paul Spittler." In *New International Dictionary of Pentecostal and Charismatic Movements*, edited by Stanley M. Burgess and Eduard M. van der Maas, 1102–1104. Grand Rapids: Zondervan, 2002.

———. *The Azusa Street Mission and Revival: The Birth of the Global Pentecostal Movement*. Nashville: Thomas Nelson, 2006.

Roberts, Oral. "We Are Returning to Television." *Abundant Life* (February 1969): 2–7.

———. *The Miracle of Seed-Faith*. Tulsa: Oral Roberts Evangelistic Association, 1970.

———. *Expect a Miracle*, Korean edition. Seoul: Word of Seoul, 1998.

Robinson, James. *Divine Healing: The Years of Expansion, 1906–1930*. Eugene, OR: Wipf & Stock, 2014.

Sande, Normatter. "Faith and Equality: Rethinking Women in Leadership Positions in Pentecostalism." *Journal of Gender and Religion in Africa* 22, no. 2 (2016): 50–62.

Sanders, J. Oswald. *Spiritual Leadership: Principles of Excellence for Every Believer.* Chicago: Moody Press, 1967.

Sanneh, Lamin. "Global Christianity and the Re-education of the West." *Religion Online.* https://www.religion-online.org/article/global-christianity-and-the-re-education-of-the-west/.

Sapp, Gary L. *Handbook of Moral Development.* Birmingham, AL: Religious Education Press, 1986.

Schmitt, John J. "Preexilic Hebrew Prophecy." In *The Anchor Bible Dictionary*, edited by David Noel Freedman. Vol. 5. New York: Doubleday, 1992.

SCOAN International. "Prophet T. B. Joshua." https://www.scoan.org/about/prophet-tb-joshua/.

Serbin, Ken. "Brazilian Church Builds an International Empire." *Christian Century* 113, no. 12 (April 10, 1996), 401.

Serrano, Carlo. "It Seemed Good to the Holy Spirit and to Us: A Biblical Example of the Organizational Decision-Making Process." *Journal of Applied Christian Leadership* 12, no. 1 (2018): 10–15.

Shamsundar, M. Adhav. *Pandita Ramabai.* Madras: Christian Literature Society, 1979.

Sharpe, Eric J. "Ramabai Dongre Medhavi (Pandita Ramabai Sarasvati)." In *Biographical Dictionary of Christian Missions*, edited by Gerald H. Anderson, 557. Grand Rapids: William B. Eerdmans Publishing Company, 1999.

Shawchuck, Norman, and Roger Heuser. *Leading the Congregation: Caring for Yourself While Serving the People.* Nashville: Abingdon Press, 1993.

Shemeth, Scott. "Lillian Hunt Trasher." In *New International Dictionary of Pentecostal and Charismatic Movements*, edited by Stanley M. Burgess and Eduard van der Maas, 1153. Grand Rapids: Zondervan, 2002.

Shepherd, M. H. "Apostle." *The Interpreters Bible Dictionary.* Vol. 1. Nashville: Abingdon, 1962.

Singer, Dorothy G., and Tracey A. Revenson. *The Essential Piaget: How a Child Thinks.* New York: Penguin Books, 1997.

Smith, Gregory A. "The Holy Spirit in the New Testament." *Scholar's Crossing*, Faculty Publications and Presentations, Liberty University 68 (2000): 1.

Smith, James K. A. "Scandalizing Theology: A Pentecostal Response to Noll's Scandal." *Pneuma: The Journal of the Society for Pentecostal Studies* 19, no. 2 (1997): 226.

Smith, John P. "Acts 2: Spirit-Empowered Leadership." *Emerging Leadership Journeys* 1, no. 1 (2008): 25–38. https://www.regent.edu/acad/global/publications/elj/issue1/elj_v1is1.pdf.

Smith, Timothy L. "The Doctrine of the Sanctifying Spirit: Charles G. Finney's Synthesis of Wesleyan and Covenant Theology." *Wesleyan Theological Journal* 13, no. 1 (Spring 1978): 92–113.

"Spirit-Empowered Christianity: An Interview with Todd M. Johnson and Gina A. Zurlo." *Pneuma Review: Journal of Ministry Resources and Theology for Pentecostal and Charismatic*

Ministries & Leaders (January 6, 2021). http://pneumareview.com/spirit-empowered-christianity/.

Spittler, Russell P. "Cecil Melvin Robeck, Jr." In *New International Dictionary of Pentecostal and Charismatic Movements*, edited by Stanley M. Burgess and Eduard M. van der Maas, 1023–1024. Grand Rapids: Zondervan, 2002.

Stanley, Brian. "From Plato to Pentecostalism: Sickness and Deliverance in the Theology of Derek Prince. *Studies in Church History* 58 (2022): 394–414. https://doi.org/10.1017/stc.2022.19.

Stronstad, Roger. *The Prophethood of All Believers: A Study in Luke's Charismatic Theology*. Sheffield: Sheffield Academic Press, 1999.

Sutton, Matthew. *Aimee Semple McPherson and the Resurrection of Christian America*. Cambridge: Harvard University Press, 2007.

Symons, Emma-Kate. "Preacher Power." *Wall Street Journal* (May 14, 2010): n.p.

Synan, H. Vinson. "Role of the Pastor." In *Dictionary of Pentecostal and Charismatic Movements*, edited by Stanley M. Burgess and Gary B. McGee, 662–663. Grand Rapids: Zondervan, 1988.

————. *The Holiness-Pentecostal Tradition: Charismatic Movements in the Twentieth Century*. Grand Rapids: Eerdmans, 1997.

————. "Reinhard Willi Gottfried Bonnke." In *New International Dictionary of Pentecostal and Charismatic Movements*, edited by Stanley M. Burgess and Eduard M. van der Maas, 438–439. Grand Rapids: Zondervan, 2002.

Tasker, David. "Ruach Elohim: The Holy Spirit in the Old Testament." *Ministry: International Journal for Pastors* 85, no. 1 (January 2013): 16–19. https://www.ministrymagazine.org/archive/2013/01/ruach-elohim:-the-holy-spirit-in-the-old-testament.

Telford, John, ed. *The Letters of the Rev. John Wesley*, A.M. Vol. 5. London: Epworth Press, 1931.

Thompson, Marjorie. *Soul Feast: An Invitation to the Christian Spiritual Life*. Louisville: Westminster John Knox, 1995.

Throckmorton, B. H., Jr. "Pastor." *The Interpreter's Dictionary of the Bible*. Vol. 3. Nashville: Abingdon, 1962.

Thurston, L. F. "C. H. Mason: Sanctified Reformer." In *From Aldersgate to Azusa Street: Wesleyan, Holiness, and Pentecostal Visions of the New Creation*. Eugene, OR: Pickwick, 2010.

Topf, Daniel. "Pentecostal Theological Education in the Majority World: A Century of Overcoming Obstacles and Gaining New Ground." In *Pentecostal Theological Education in the Majority World: The Graduate and Post-Graduate Level*, 120–121, edited by Dave Johnson and Rick Wadholm Jr. Baguio City: Asia Pacific Theological Seminary Press, 2022.

Torres, Renee Ann. "Emissaries for the Lord: American Protestant Women Writers and Missionaries 1930s." Master's thesis, Washington State University, 2017.

Tracy, Diane. *The Power Pyramid: How to Get Power by Giving It Away*. New York: William Morrow & Co., 1990.

Trammel, Madison, and Rob Moll. "Grading the Movement: Three Leaders Talk Frankly about Pentecostalism: The Good, the Bad, and the Unpredictable." An interview with Derrick Hutchins, Lee Grady, and Russell Spittler. *Christianity Today* 50, no. 4 (2006): 38.

Trasher, Lillian. "Assiout Orphanage: A Testimony to God's Faithfulness." *Pentecostal Evangel* (December 21, 1935): 11.

————. *Letters from Lillian.* Springfield, MO: Assemblies of God Division of Foreign Missions, 1983.

Tushima, Cephas. "Leadership Succession Patterns in the Apostolic Church as a Template for Critique of Contemporary Charismatic Leadership Succession Patterns." *HTS Theological Studies* 72, no. 1 (2016): 1–8.

Vancil, Jack W. "Sheep, Shepherd." *The Anchor Bible Dictionary*, edited by David Noel Freedman. Vol. 5. New York: Doubleday, 1992.

Vanguard Media. "Despite Covid, We Planted 10,000 Churches without Raising an Offering—Bishop Oyedepo." December 12, 2020. https://www.vanguardngr.com/2020/12/despite-covid-we-planted-10000-churches-without-raising-an-offering-%E2%80%95-bishop-oyedepo/.

————. "Winners Chapel to Commence 100,000 Capacity Ark Auditorium Project Soon." January 24, 2021. https://www.vanguardngr.com/2021/01/winners-chapel-100000-ark-auditorium/.

————. "Why I Have a Fleet of Private Jets, Bishop Oyedepo Reveals." September 2, 2023. https://www.vanguardngr.com/2023/09/why-i-have-a-fleet-of-private-jets-bishop-oyedepo-reveals/.

Volf, Miroslav. *After Our Likeness: The Church as the Image of the Trinity.* Grand Rapids: Eerdmans, 1998.

Vondey, Wolfgang. *Pentecostalism: A Guide for the Perplexed.* London: Bloomsbury, 2013.

Wacker, Grant. *Heaven Below: Early Pentecostals and American Culture.* Cambridge: Harvard University Press, 2001.

Wacker, Grant, Chris R. Armstrong, and Jay S. F. Blossom. "John Alexander Dowie: Harbinger of Pentecostal Power." In *Portraits of a Generation: Early Pentecostal Leaders*, edited by James R. Goff and Grant Wacker, 4. Fayetteville: University of Arkansas Press, 2002.

Wagner, C. Peter. *Your Church Can Grow: Seven Vital Signs of a Healthy Church.* Glendale, CA: Regal Books, 1976.

————. *The New Apostolic Churches.* Ventura, CA: Regal Books, 1998.

————. *Churchquake! How the New Apostolic Reformation Is Shaking Up the Church as We Know It.* Ventura, CA: Regal, 1999.

————. *The Church in the Workplace: How God's People Can Transform Society.* Ventura, CA: Regal Books, 2006.

————. *Dominion: How Kingdom Action Can Change the World.* Grand Rapids: Chosen Books, 2008.

————. "Year in Review: The New Apostolic Reformation Is Not a Cult." *Charisma News*, August 24, 2011. https://www.charismanews.com/opinion/31851-the-new-apostolic-reformation-is-not-a-cult.

Währisch-Oblau, Claudia. *The Missionary Self-Perception of Pentecostal/Charismatic Church Leaders from the Global South and Europe.* Leiden: Brill, 2009.

Wälchli, Walo. "Touching Precious Metals." *Gold Bull* 14, no. 4 (1981): 154–158. https://link.springer.com/content/pdf/10.1007/BF03216559.pdf.

Walls, Andrew. "Structural Problems in Mission Studies." *International Bulletin of Missionary Research* 14, no. 4 (October 1991): 146–155.

Walsh, Arlene. "Henry Ball, Francisco Olazábal, Alice Luce, and the Assemblies of God Borderlands Mission." *From Aldersgate to Azusa Street: Wesleyan, Holiness, and Pentecostal Visions of the New Creation.* Eugene, OR: Pickwick, 2010.

Walton, John H. "The Ancient Near Eastern Background of the Spirit of the Lord in the Old Testament." In *Presence, Power and Promise: The Role of the Spirit of God in the Old Testament*, edited by David G. Firth and Paul D. Wegner, 48. Downers Grove: IVP Academic, 2011.

Wan, Yee Tham. "Bridging the Gap Between Pentecostal Holiness and Morality." *Asian Journal of Pentecostal Studies* 4, no. 2 (2001): 153–180.

Warner, Wayne E. *Kathryn Kuhlman: The Woman behind the Miracles.* Ann Arbor: Servant, 1993.

———. "Maria Woodworth-Etter." In *New International Dictionary of Pentecostal and Charismatic Movements*, edited by Stanley M. Burgess and Eduard M. van der Maas, 1213. Grand Rapids: Zondervan, 2002.

———. "Smith Wigglesworth." In *New International Dictionary of Pentecostal and Charismatic Movements*, edited by Stanley M. Burgess and Eduard M. van der Maas, 1195. Grand Rapids: Zondervan, 2002.

Warrington, Keith. "Healing and Kenneth Hagin." *Asian Journal of Pentecostal Studies* 3, no. 1 (2000): 119–138.

———. *Pentecostal Theology: A Theology of Encounter.* London: T&T Clark, 2008.

Weber, Max. *The Theory of Social and Economic Organization*, edited by Talcott Parsons, translated by A. M. Henderson and Talcott Parsons. New York: The Free Press, 1947.

———. *On Charisma and Institution Building: Selected Papers*, edited with an Introduction by S. N. Eisenstadt. Chicago: University of Chicago Press, 1968.

White, Ernest. "The Crisis of Christian Leadership." *Review & Expositor* 83 (Fall 1986): 545–557.

White, Jerry E. "Leading with Integrity." *Christian Leadership Challenge.* https://ym.christianleadershipalliance.org/page/leadingwithintegrity.

White, Peter. "A Missional Study of Ghanaian Pentecostal Churches' Leadership and Leadership Formation." *HTS Theological Studies* 71, no. 3 (2015): 1–8.

———. "Centenary of Pentecostalism in Ghana (1917–2017): A Case Study of Christ Apostolic Church International." *HTS Theological Studies* 75, no. 4 (2019): 1–8.

Wiegele, Katharine L. *Investing in Miracles: El Shaddai and the Transformation of Popular Catholicism in the Philippines.* Honolulu: University of Washington Press, 2005.

———. "Catholics Rich in Spirit: El Shaddai's Modern Engagements." *Philippine Studies* 54, no. 4 (2006): 495–520.

Willard, Dallas. *The Great Omission: Reclaiming Jesus' Essential Teachings on Discipleship.* Oxford, UK: Monarch Books, 2006.

Wills, Garry. *Certain Trumpets: The Call of Leaders.* New York: Simon & Schuster, 1994.

Wilson, Dwight J. "Paul Yonggi Cho." In *Dictionary of Pentecostal and Charismatic Movements,* edited by Stanley Burgess, Gary McGee, and Patrick Alexander, 161–162. Grand Rapids: Zondervan, 1988.

———. "Kathryn Kuhlman." In *New International Dictionary of Pentecostal and Charismatic Movements,* edited by Stanley M. Burgess and Eduard M. van der Maas, 826. Grand Rapids: Zondervan, 2002.

Wilson, Everett. "Francisco Olazábal." In *New International Dictionary of Pentecostal and Charismatic Movements,* edited by Stanley M. Burgess and Eduard M. van der Maas, 936. Grand Rapids: Zondervan, 2002.

Wilson, Lewis F. "Bible Institutes, Colleges, Universities." In *New International Dictionary of Pentecostal and Charismatic Movements,* edited by Stanley M. Burgess and Eduard M. van der Maas, 373–375. Grand Rapids: Zondervan, 2002.

Wimber, John. "Power Evangelism: Definitions and Directions." In *Wrestling with Dark Angels: Towards a Deeper Understanding of the Supernatural Forces in Spiritual Warfare,* edited by C. Peter Wagner and F. Douglas Pennoyer, 15–29. Ventura, CA: Regal Books, 1990.

———. "Power Evangelism." *Renewal Journal* 22 (July 2011). https://renewaljournal.com/2011/07/22/power-evangelism-byjohn-wimber/.

Winter, David G. *The Power Motive.* New York: Free Press, 1973.

Witherington, Ben, III. *The Acts of the Apostles: A Socio-Rhetorical Commentary.* Grand Rapids: Eerdmans, 1997.

Wright, Christopher J. H. *Knowing the Holy Spirit through the Old Testament.* Downers Grove: InterVarsity Press Academic, 2006.

Yee, Tham Wan. "Bridging the Gap Between Pentecostal Holiness and Morality." *Asian Journal of Pentecostal Studies* 4, no. 2 (2001).

Yong, Amos. *Spirit Poured Out on All Flesh: Pentecostalism and the Possibility of Global Theology.* Grand Rapids: Baker Academic, 2005.

Yukl, Gary. "An Evaluation of Conceptual Weakness in Transformational and Charismatic Leadership Theories." *Leadership Quarterly* 10, no. 2 (1999): 285¬–305.

———. *Leadership in Organizations.* 8th ed. Boston: Pearson, 2013.

Zeigler, J. R. "John Graham Lake." In *New International Dictionary of Pentecostal and Charismatic Movements,* edited by Stanley M. Burgess and Eduard M. van der Maas, 828. Grand Rapids: Zondervan, 2002.

Zell, Jennifer, and Shawn Grimsley. "What Is Power Distance?" https://study.com/learn/lesson/what-is-power-distance.html.

X-Z

Scripture Index